For Lust of Knowing

ARCHIE ROOSEVELT

For Lust of Knowing

Memoirs of an Intelligence Officer

LITTLE, BROWN AND COMPANY

BOSTON   TORONTO

FIRST EDITION

The author is grateful to Cambridge University Press for permission
to quote from "Third Ode of Hafiz," as it appeared in *Literary History
of Persia* by Edward G. Browne (1920), and to A. P. Watt Ltd. and
James Sherwood for permission to quote from *Hassan: A Play in Five
Acts* by James Elroy Flecker (1922).

Map *The Islamic World* by George W. Ward.

Map of southern Iraq by K. C. Jordan. By permission of Wilfred
Thesiger.

Book design by Robert G. Lowe.

The first chapter of this book originally appeared in *American Heritage*.

Library of Congress Cataloging-in-Publication Data

Roosevelt, Archibald, 1918–
    For lust of knowing: memoirs of an intelligence officer
Archibald Roosevelt, Jr.—1st ed.
        p. cm.
    Includes index.
    ISBN 0-316-75600-8
    1. Roosevelt, Archibald, 1918–   . 2. Intelligence officers—
—United States—Biography.   3. United States. Central Intelligence
Agency—Biography.   4. Islamic countries—Description and travel.
I. Title.
UB271.U52R66 1988
327.1'2'0924—dc19
[B]   87-24930
                                                                              CIP
10 9 8 7 6 5 4 3

                                        FG

*Published simultaneously in Canada
by Little, Brown & Company (Canada) Limited*

PRINTED IN THE UNITED STATES OF AMERICA

To Lucky

Whose warm and glowing nature,
joyful spirit, and loving heart
have made life's journey a delight.

We travel not for trafficking alone;
By hotter winds our fiery hearts are fanned:
For lust of knowing what should not be known,
We take the Golden Road to Samarkand.

— James Elroy Flecker, *Hassan:*
A Play in Five Acts

Contents

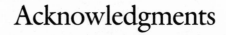

Acknowledgments

THIS IS NOT the story of my life, but of my experiences as an intelligence officer in the Islamic world and its fringes. It does tell of my beginnings and how I got pointed in that direction, but once launched on this course, I confine the narrative mostly to what I witnessed myself in that part of the world. Also, requirements of space necessitated my sticking to a single story line, and I hope my relatives, friends, and colleagues won't be disappointed when I fail to name them as I plunge headlong on my way.

I have so many persons to thank for helping me in my career that I could not possibly mention them all. First there were my parents. Then my teachers, at home, at school, and in college. Truman Smith, Edwin Wright, and Paul Converse were among the many army officers who guided my youthful steps. And ambassadors, particularly Loy Henderson, George Allen, George Wadsworth, John Davis Lodge, and David Bruce, all, alas, no longer able to read these pages, and one, George McGhee, who I hope will do so. At least two of my three favorite directors of the Central Intelligence Agency can still read my words of appreciation. To my colleagues in the Agency and the Foreign Service with whom I passed those adventurous years, apologies for naming so few of you. You deserve better of me.

I also wish to pay tribute to friends and colleagues in the dozen or so years I've passed at the Chase Manhattan Bank. Some of my favorite trips to the countries described in this book were made with our successive chairmen, David Rockefeller and Bill Butcher, in the "company plane."

I must make special mention of the wonderful secretaries, too many to name but all remembered, who have helped me throughout my career — and who sometimes saved me from disaster. More than once, having written a cable full of wrath before lunch, I hurried back afterward to try to alter it, only to find a wise secretary had delayed it for me to consider from a calmer perspective. The Agency secretaries, like its officers, are an elite corps. I also had a first-rate secretary at the Chase Manhattan Bank, Liz Callaghan, who, alas, died before she could read this tribute.

This book is based almost entirely on my own recollections, so there are no sources to cite, and only a couple of times did I call on others to help me remember a few details. So for special contributions to the raw material of this book I shall mention only my former wife, Katharine Tweed, who returned to me the letters I wrote her during the war; David Grinwis, for lending me his diary of his horrifying experiences as vice-consul in Stanleyville; Barbara Rossow, widow of Bob Rossow, who likewise lent me his memoirs of his adventures as consul in Tabriz; John Waller, who enlivened our trip together in East Africa with stories of his own life as an embassy officer in Africa; Joseph "Cy" Cybulski, who provided me with forgotten details I've referred to in my chapter on Spain; and Anne Fischer for her help in certain "gray areas."

I have with me, of course, a living source on all the latter part of the book, my wife, Lucky, who is an editor by training. She is at the same time an encouraging but exacting reviewer and editor of this book, which I am really writing because of her. Even though there are many pages in which I do not mention her, she is always subliminally present, my companion on the Road to Samarkand, the road she has brightened with her gaiety of spirit, her courage, and her love.

While she is my home editor, Little, Brown and Company provided me an official one, who turned out to be a real jewel. Christina Ward has guided my footsteps through the windy wastes of my early drafts. Thanks also to Deborah Jacobs, a painstaking and understanding copyeditor.

Of course I must thank George Weidenfeld, my friend of

more than twenty years, who persuaded me to write this book; Leona Schecter, my literary agent; and you who read it — my heartfelt gratitude to you all.

In the true tradition of an intelligence officer, I have confined my narrative to what I saw and let you form your own opinions, rarely giving any of my own. I have viewed my role as one of telling the facts for others to study and use to make policy decisions. I make observations and try, not always successfully, not to say what action, if any, should be taken based on my findings. I've always been a reporter, not an editorialist.

One note, to avoid carping about minutiae: I do not follow any rules for the spelling of Arabic names. T. E. Lawrence, in his preface to *The Seven Pillars of Wisdom,* insists on his right to transliterate Arab names as they sounded to him as he traveled in Arabia. In the whole breadth of the Moslem world, pronunciation varies far more than in the Arabian peninsula, the scene of most of his actions. I spell the name and word often not in its official transliteration, but according to the pronunciation of the country I am visiting. Thus, the word for son can be *ben, ibn,* or *bin,* for father, *Bou* or *Abu* or *Abi;* the traditional headdress a *kufiyya* in literary style, or a *chefiyya* in Iraq. The letter *q* can be pronounced in the classical manner like a *k* deep in the throat, or a *g* in most of the Arab world, a *j* in Iraq, or a glottal stop in Lower Egypt and the Levant — and in Persian it becomes *gh.* Thus, the classical name Qasim becomes Gasim, Jasim, 'Asim, or Ghasim depending on where the man lives. The classical spelling of the name of Tunisia's president, Habib Bourguiba, is Abu Ruqaibah! On top of all this, there are the Persian and Kurdish versions of the many Arabic names and words they have adopted. So reviewers, scholars, readers — spare this diversity. It's part of the Middle East!

And this suggests a final tribute, one to friends and acquaintances in all parts of the world visited in my story, for their patient teaching, their warm reception of me, and their qualities as human beings — Arabs, Iranians, Jews, Kurds, Turks, Africans, Armenians, and others of all races, colors, and religions — and still others not so much part of that world, but not quite as alien as I was at first myself, a few French, many British, Spaniards, and even a Russian here and there! Let us hope that all these peoples among whom I lived will, in the wisdom of time, find a way to bury ancient hatreds, settle their feuds, and enjoy the goodness of our lovely oasis in the desert of space together in peace and happiness.

Perhaps if we can all learn the truth about each other, the truth shall make us free.

List of Maps

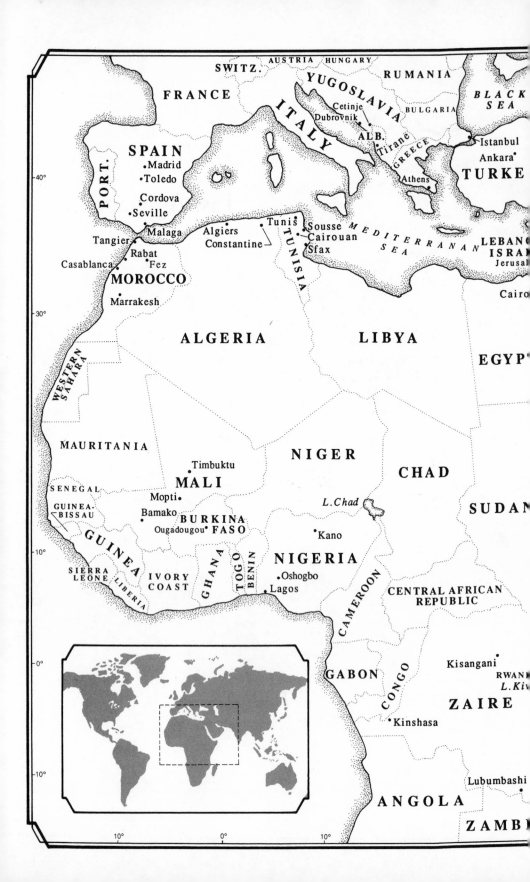

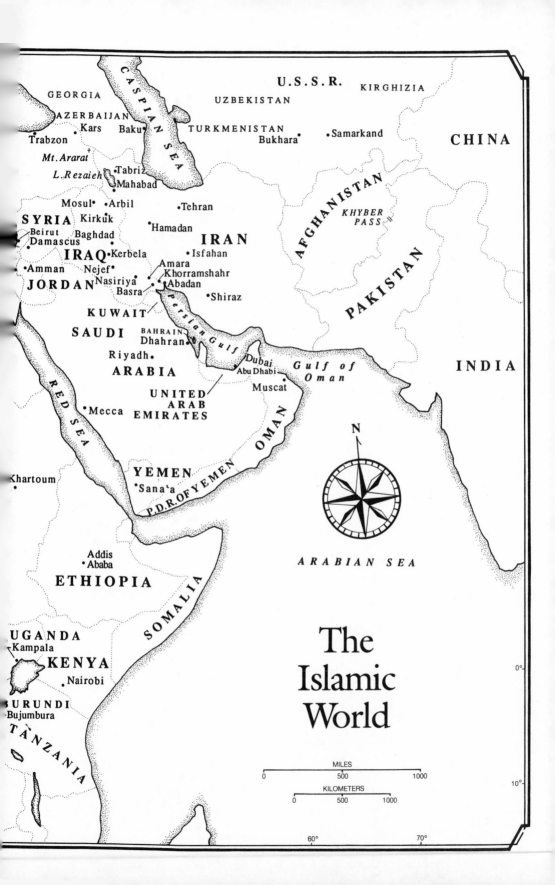

The
Islamic
World

PART ONE

The Talents

The Ghost of Sagamore Hill

THERE USED TO BE a chain in front of the driveway at Sagamore Hill. My grandmother put it there to stop the hordes of curiosity seekers who came to Sagamore, thinking perhaps that no one lived there anymore. So, grumbling, my father would stop the car to let us in, and I could, for a moment, observe from a distance the old gray house brooding in its nest of stately elms. I felt, with that peculiar instinct of a child, that this large Victorian structure had some kind of life of its own. And as we drove under the *porte cochère* my sense of adventure quickened, for I always anticipated these visits with an excitement the late master of the house would have appreciated. I was lucky as a small boy to spend many weeks of my summer and winter vacations at Sagamore Hill, and adventure was always there.

We were a large family he left behind. Besides my immediate family — my parents and three sisters — there were my boisterous uncles Ted and Kermit, with their wives, the brilliant and elegant Auntie Eleanor and the glamorous Auntie Belle; my fairy godmother, Auntie Ethel (Derby), and her kindly doctor-husband Uncle Dick; and the mysterious and romantic figure of "Auntie Sister" (Alice Roosevelt Longworth), who lived far away in Washington and made a brief, queenly appearance from time to time. (We never quite understood as children how an aunt could be "Sister" as well, but eventually found out that she had always been called Sister by our parents' generation. Her real name, Alice, was never used in the family.)

And with all these came masses of cousins — a dozen or so — quite a few close to my age.

Grandmother was an awesome chatelaine. She ruled the house and its unruly visitors in her soft and precise voice, an iron hand scarcely hidden in the velvet glove. Only when we were older did we realize she was small and frail. To us she seemed eight feet tall, and although she never raised that quiet voice, it could take on an icy tone that made even the largest and strongest tremble.

Even so, she was not the absolute ruler of Sagamore Hill. My grandfather was — though he had died many years before, when I was less than a year old. The house had been left exactly as it was the day he died, and his spirit permeated every corner of it, as well as the grounds outside. Now I realize the house was truly haunted, but we children would never have called it that, because our ghost was a kindly one who kept a jolly and benevolent eye on all of us, balancing Grandmother's familiar figure. He was our hero and our playmate. All the activities of the house followed the patterns he had set during his lifetime: the food, the games, the celebrations, the stories, and even the phrases and words he had made so much his own. He just had too much vitality to die and leave all those grandchildren deprived of his companionship.

I felt his presence strongly the minute I came through the door into a hall cluttered with his possessions — an elephant's foot stuffed with his canes, the walls festooned with majestic heads of African beasts. His study was on the right, and I always liked to sit at his desk a minute and look out the large window at the elms. I was half-afraid I might be trespassing, because he was there, all right. The room was crammed with books and pictures and memorabilia, but the lion rugs on the floor were the objects of our special affection. It was fun to lie on them and pretend they were alive. Grandmother used to read to us, generally from Howard Pyle's *Robin Hood* or something else by him, because Pyle was one of Grandfather's favorite authors, especially for reading to the children.

On the left was Grandmother's parlor, where we children were not permitted. She secluded herself there to read and did not like to be disturbed. It was a "withdrawing" room in the true sense of the word. She had an endless curiosity, and when, in her seventies, she did leave Sagamore, it was to go on long voyages all over the world. However, we children really did not mind being excluded from her drawing room, since it contained only one item of interest to us — a luxurious polar bear skin that we sneaked onto now and then.

Farther down the hall, on the right, was the dining room, its door flanked by a large gong used to summon us to meals. It was always rung by Clara, the waitress, Grandmother's downstairs lieutenant. Clara was a distinguished-looking light-skinned black woman of a commanding authority who kept us in our place within her domain.

Grandfather definitely was with us at table. As in his lifetime, we consumed mounds of good food, running to rich, homemade soups and succulent roasts and always a delicious dessert. This last course was particularly exciting because of the importance of who got which doily under the finger bowl. There were only two that mattered — the red dragon was the best, but the green dragon was good, too. We often ate off dessert plates with holes around the sides and heard how our nearsighted grandfather used to pour the cream until it flowed through the holes and then look up guiltily to see if Grandmother had noticed. To us it was natural to suppose that he was a bit in awe of her himself.

The best times were at Christmas holidays, when all the family gathered to eat the great Christmas dinner, with its turkey and suckling pig that fathers and uncles vied to carve. After lunch we would go through the pantry, admiring its archaic wooden icebox, to the huge kitchen to congratulate Bridget, the cook, a merry miniature of a woman with a lovely, lilting brogue.

Following this heavy meal we were sent upstairs to nap. The stairs themselves were in Stygian blackness, and we had to feel our way along. This caused much talk among our parents of the dangers of falling, but we children got a certain thrill from these dark, mysterious stairs. The second-floor hall surrounding the stairwell, which gave onto the bedrooms, was equally dark and hung with pictures of vaguely threatening ancestors. It took a bit of courage to cross this hall to the bathroom during the night, especially when I looked at an ancestress known as the Lady with Eyes. Her eyes followed me malevolently as I crept along, guided only by a tallow light flickering on a table. (This had been placed there years ago for Uncle Quentin — the other ghost in the house — who as a small boy had been afraid of the dark. He was later killed in World War I.) Occasionally I had a nightmare in which that light slowly flickered out, leaving me in the dark hall alone! There are ten bedrooms on that floor, counting Grandfather's dressing room, and as a child I slept in every one except, of course, the master bedroom. Each had a distinct character and history, as did the big bathroom that for a long time had been the only one in the house. Its huge antique tub stood magnificently on a pedestal, and the old-fashioned washbowls still sat in various spots, unused since Grandfather's day.

The ancient facilities of the house, commonplace to our parents, were a constant source of fascination. We discovered the speaking tubes, stuffed up with paper and no longer in use. We soon corrected that and for a day or two amused ourselves by exchanging messages from distant parts of the house, until the tubes were stopped up again by a grandmotherly ukase. Then we found the dumbwaiter, used primarily to transport wood to the fireplaces on the upper floors. For us it turned out to be a delightful mode of transportation up and down, but then we got a bad fright when Cousin Quentin lost control of the pulleys and crashed to the cellar, shaking the whole house and thereby producing another ukase.

And best of all, at the end of a dark hall on the third floor, was the gun room. Here, amid shelves of books about exploration and big game and a large collection of guns, Grandfather came on strongest of all, especially at his desk, where he once looked out the window over a broad panorama of Long Island Sound. It was very much his room. Grandmother — and even our parents — almost never went up there, and our ghost very kindly did not object to our playing with his weapons. The prize one for us was a wonderful rusting six-shooter, and we played the sort of games that nowadays would not meet with general approval. I once came to grief acting out the part of a Chinese general. My prop was an old sword — possibly the one Grandfather used as a Rough Rider. Its scabbard had rotted, and when I drew it to charge, I nearly cut off my fingers.

We did not mind which bedroom was assigned to us, but our parents did. They complained of the hardness of the mattresses, especially that of one bed, which for its stoniness was known as Pharaoh's Heart. But we could not tell the difference.

I felt Grandfather particularly haunted two of the rooms. One was the bedroom in the southwest corner, where he died, which had a bedspread in the design of an American flag. So strongly did I sense his presence there that once in that room I asked him to help me be worthy of him. He never answered, but I thought he might be listening. The other room was his small dressing room on the north side, where the wind, whistling eerily in the winter night, made it easy for spirits to return.

Oddly enough, I never felt his presence in the master bedroom. This was so much Grandmother's domain, with Irish Mary, the upstairs maid, hovering in the background. We would go in there only occasionally for a brief levee, when she would receive us after breakfast, sitting up in the massive double bed.

The largest room in the house, the North Room, was closed off and absolutely forbidden to us except on holidays. Grandfather had built this room to hold his game trophies and various presents from potentates all over the world, and to serve as a family feast room. We made the most of the rare occasions when we were allowed in. It was the most fascinating room of all, with its skins of lions and other beasts, two great bison heads over the fireplaces, and a pair of huge, splendid elephant tusks given him by the emperor of Ethiopia. The ceiling was twenty feet high, and I remember the room as very cold, so that much of the time we huddled in front of a roaring fire in its wide fireplace. Once a year a tall Christmas tree was brought in, and after Christmas lunch the whole family would gather to collect their spoils. To me the most evocative thing in the room today is the Rough Rider's hat, thrown casually over the horns of an elk.

I haven't said anything about nostalgia or the sadness of his loss, but of course we all felt that. I always missed the grandfather I was too young to know, though perhaps, hidden by the mists of infancy, I still kept some memory of the warmth of his vast store of affection. He first saw me at the end of March 1918, when I was six weeks old, and he wrote my father in France, "At last, Mother and I have seen darling Gracie and the blessed wee son." I have another letter from him to my mother dated July 14: "Darling Gracie — the picture of darling wee bunny Archikins made me so dreadfully homesick for him. I long for him, and shall croon every kind of aboriginal nursery

song to the blessed wee person, from Trippa Troppa* to
Hampton Race Track."

There is also a picture of him taken during a visit of Mother's
to Sagamore, beaming down on me as he held his latest
grandchild in his arms, but I was still too young to know he was
about to leave me. I used to feel saddest about this on the porch
in the evening, looking down over the broad fields toward the
woods, listening to the katydids. For his presence was almost as
strong outside the house as in it. Outside the North Room we
played on the cannon from the Spanish-American War, then
tramped through the autumn leaves to the garage. This was the
domain of Grandfather's genial black coachman, Charlie Lee.
He was Clara's husband, and he now drove Grandmother's
limousine for her trips to church and her other infrequent
sallies away from Sagamore Hill.

I shall never forget the delights of Grandfather's farm, with
its fruits and chickens and cows, to say nothing of the wonderful
old barn where, burrowing through the hay, he used to play
hide-and-go-seek with his children, just as our fathers did with
us.

The fields were perfect for playing, and my father and uncles
led us in the same strenuous games Grandfather had played
with them. To work off a big meal, there was "shinny" —
ground hockey, well named for the many blows borne by the
shins. I remember a sort of blindman's buff we called "Still
Pond No More Moving." One field was reserved for rifle
practice, and all of us male children were taken there by our
fathers to learn to shoot, just as their father had taught them.

Farther afield were other holiday pastimes of Grandfather's — the point-to-point walk, the paper chase, and the
run to the seashore down Cooper's Bluff. We were left in
freedom in the lovely woods surrounding Sagamore, just made
for children. Grandmother never ventured far, preferring the
rose arbor, where she cut a Victorian figure, dressed in white
chiffon, basket in hand, and accompanied by her aged, nasty-
tempered little dog, Shady.

And then there was the beach. We walked down an over-
grown path, passing through an orchard gone to seed — the

* A corruption of a nursery rhyme preserved in the family from Dutch ancestors:
    Trippel trippel toontjes
    Kippen in de boontjes...

Fairy Apple Orchard — where we could still see little gardens laid out by our parents when they were our age. Before we got to the beach, we passed a long, somewhat smelly saltwater creek, where we used to roll in the mud and chase fiddler crabs. We could also dig clams on the beach, or, more exciting, seine for shiners, flounder, and eels. And we knew the joys of an old-fashioned picnic just as Grandfather had loved it — a nice bonfire, steak, and potatoes roasting in the coals, with plenty of sandwiches thrown in and a little sand in everything. At nighttime Grandfather used to tell ghost stories. My father inherited the talent, building up suspense by the tone of his voice, which grew lower and more ominous as the story reached its climax, until we all shivered in excitement and not a little fear. On those nights a susceptible younger sister would have nightmares, and Father would be reprimanded by Mother, as his father must have been before him — with just as little effect.

So, though I passed a youth without grandfathers (my other grandfather died at almost the same time), this was in the physical sense only. Actually my Sagamore Hill grandfather was with us all the time and enlivened our young lives with his gay spirit even after death. We knew him only as a ghost — but what a merry, vital, and energetic ghost he was. And how much encouragement and strength he left behind to help us play the role Fate has assigned us for the rest of the century.

Later in my childhood, I did get to sneak into my grandfather's library in the North Room, and there, and at home, I indulged my taste in reading about distant lands and people. Of course, *The Arabian Nights* held a particular fascination, and I had a picture of Sindbad on one of his voyages over my bed. I think perhaps I had some premonition of things to come, and one event in my life has made me a strong believer in premonitions.

It was at the age of eight when I was playing in my room alone in our apartment in New York. I had only just become truly aware of the phenomenon of death, and it was naturally distressing. I had never thought about it before, and it seemed a horrible idea that not only my life would have to end someday but that of everyone I knew. I began to wonder — and talk with God a little bit — about this phenomenon. If death were to come to anyone, who among all those close to me, my relatives, could I spare to be removed from me by this fearful novelty?

The name of Cousin Gladys popped into my mind — she was a rather glamorous lady married to a second cousin of my father, and I just didn't know her well enough to really care about her one way or another. So if Death had to take anyone, it might as well be she. At that very moment, my mother burst into the room, saying, "Archie, the most dreadful thing has just happened! Cousin Gladys had a fall from her horse and is dead."

I never mentioned this to my mother, perhaps because there was no way I could prove it, but I have believed in premonition ever since. Premonition implies a belief in fate — that things to come are somehow programmed, perhaps because the past has already been lived in other dimensions and incarnations. I felt that fate, or God, had decreed that I be born in an extraordinary conjunction of place and time and circumstance, and expected me to make the most of it.

I was born in February 1918, in Boston, where my mother was staying with her parents while Father was at the front. My father, for whom I was named, was tall, and spare as a young man, with aquiline features and piercing gray eyes. He worshipped my grandfather and tried to live by his precepts. He went straight from college into infantry training and had commanded a company in the Regular Army First Division in World War I. With an arm and a knee shattered by wounds, he returned late in 1918 to have his first glimpse of me — and his last of his father, who died in January 1919. Father loved the army, and the infantry, to which he returned in World War II, and his spiritual time clock stopped at the same point as my grandfather's.

Most of his career was spent on Wall Street, but he went home to a different world — his guns, his boat, and his library crammed with books of history and poetry. The poetry he loved was that of the last few centuries, not of the present, and he had the remarkable ability inherited from my grandfather of being able to memorize a poem after two or three readings. I often heard him half chanting poetry to himself. The fascination with history I shared, but not his memory for poetry, though I loved to listen to him recite — especially Kipling's ballads, such as "East Is East and West Is West" and "Four Things Greater Than All Things Are, Women and Power and Horses and War."

My father was a great believer in reading aloud to his

children, and what he read to us made an impression for life —
again, especially Kipling (*Puck of Pook's Hill* and *Kim*) — and it
was perhaps Kipling who gave me my first glimpse of the Road
to Samarkand. But there was much else besides. Perhaps the
best of all was the Old Testament, which Father, an avowed
agnostic but occasional churchgoer, read as literature.

Despite these interests in common, when I ceased to be a little
boy, our ways began to part, and a communications gap grew
between us. But I remained close to my mother, who understood me better and was cozy and fun. She was a thin, birdlike
woman with sharp features softened by a mass of prematurely
white curly hair. She gave a first impression of frivolous
femininity, swiftly belied by a quick and curious mind. She was
Boston-born and a Unitarian, believing Jesus only had more of
the spirit of God that is in all of us; she saw into my own curious
mind and did what she could to help me develop it. Unlike my
father, a thoroughgoing American patriot who thought that
most virtues were embodied in the United States, she was an
internationalist. She had spent a year in school in Florence and
spoke French and Italian. She thought that every civilized
person should speak French. Throughout my childhood she
had a French ladies' maid, and we had a Swiss governess — now
an obsolete species. We were forced not only to learn French
but speak it at meals, and I have had reason to bless my mother
for this all my life.

My earliest days were passed in New York, but we summered
on Long Island, and in 1923, when I was four, my parents
bought an old frame house in Cold Spring Harbor, Long
Island, a few miles from Sagamore Hill, in Oyster Bay. At the
time, it was not part of suburbia as it is today, but still an old
whaling town, friendly and picturesque. We lived about a mile
away from the center of town in a house that predated the
Revolution. Near it was a pool fed by a spring, shaded by an
ancient hollow sycamore tree; George Washington spent one of
his famous nights in our house and mentions the sycamore tree,
old even then, in his diary.

When we first moved into the house, it was completely
surrounded by forests full of dogwood, cherry trees, apple
trees gone wild from old orchards, and cedars choked with
fragrant honeysuckle. It stood at the base of a hill with many
adventurous places for children — an old well, a dead chestnut

tree perfect for tree houses, killed by the blight that extinguished almost all American chestnuts in the early 1900s, and
a large field at the top of the hill. My mother gradually
converted most of the surroundings of the house into gardens:
rock gardens overflowing with white and purple blossoms,
ferns around the pool and a tiny brook that sprung out of a
nearby hill, then plots and terraces that stayed in bloom all
summer. Father tried hard to match Mother's miraculously
green thumb in his vegetable garden up on the field, pouring so
much fertilizer on the stony soil that Mother said they were the
most expensive vegetables on the island. A tennis court and
swimming pool completed our little paradise.

My father loved to shoot quail, which still nested in neighboring fields, and always kept a pair of English setters that
accompanied me on walks in the woods and meadows. Father
was a boat enthusiast and had a small sloop in the harbor on
which he took us on picnics on Sundays. We had a glorious time
digging clams or exploring the reeds in the large saltwater
swamp off Lloyds Neck, and when I got older, I would go
seining with my father, each of us holding one end of a long net
as we brought our catch in from the water, mostly whitebait, but
sometimes more exotic creatures such as eels, which my father
cooked to perfection.

Every season in Cold Spring Harbor seemed designed especially for the joys of our childhood — the spring with its natural
wonders of the flowering forest and Mother's ever-increasing
profusion of flowers, summer with long stretches with Father
spent in fields and on the water, and fall, which turned the
maple trees in our drive to red and gold, especially lovely when
you looked at them from a high limb of the Norway spruces
that overshadowed the house. In winter we played in the heavy
snows of those days, skated on the ice of the ponds, and
snuggled around the roaring flames of the fireplaces, adorned
with blackened pots and andirons, listening to Father reading
or telling stories.

Alas, this idyll lasted only five years; my parents once more
took an apartment in the city, and the delights of Cold Spring
Harbor were curtailed to summer and the weekends. I had to
leave my nice country school and prepare for the rigors of St.
Bernard's, in New York, whose English headmaster believed
everyone should learn Latin from the age of eight — and I was

already nine. My mother had to tutor me in the language all summer to get me in. I took to Latin easily and to everything else at St. Bernard's, academically tops in the city. My world began to expand. While I had not yet traveled away from home, during my childhood my parents once passed a holiday in Germany, returning laden with toys, and my father even made a business trip that took him to Turkey, Iran, and the Caucasus, and for a time I kept one of his letters containing a drawing of a man wearing a fez.

Ever since childhood I have been mystified by the Parable of the Talents in the Gospel of Saint Matthew. A man sets out on a journey, leaving his servants to handle his wealth during his absence, consisting of a number of talents — a talent in the old sense of a large measure of gold, though now it has come to mean something else.

In the parable, one servant is given five talents. He uses them to make five more talents and gets congratulated by his lord on his return — "Well done, thou good and faithful servant." He is handsomely rewarded. The next servant received two talents and succeeded in getting two more talents, and he is rewarded in his turn. However, the third servant was given only one talent, which he buried in the ground and now happily gives back to his master, who castigates him for his inaction as "thou wicked and slothful servant." His lord then takes the talent away from him and gives it to the other man with ten talents. Then comes the mysterious verse: "For unto every one that hath shall be given, and he shall have abundance: but from him that hath not shall be taken away even that which he hath." And on top of it all, he was cast "into outer darkness."

This was very mysterious to me as a child — the poor fellow with one talent, whose only sin was overcautiousness, is forced to give up the only talent he has. This seems unfair enough, but then the story goes on, "but from him that hath not shall be taken away even that which he hath." How can one take away something from somebody who has nothing? I'm still waiting for an explanation.

I have often felt like the servant with five talents, because of where, when, and to what I was born — on this beautiful planet, in America, in the nick of time so that, with the help of modern medicine, I could live to enjoy it, and to a great family heritage. It's almost as if I had been allowed to choose.

The story of the talents makes me feel a little guilty some-times, especially now when I visit the East Wing of the White House, as I do once a month attending state dinners with my wife, who is the United States chief of protocol. Staring down at me from high on the wall in the corner of the room is the portrait of my grandfather, who is looking right at me and seems to be saying, "I worked hard to get here, and what have you done with the talents you were born with? You're here all right, but only as a guest."

I like to think, however, that I am not as bad as the slothful servant who buried his single talent in the earth, but perhaps I have produced a talent or so out of what I was given and thus will not be cast to outer darkness, but be let off a bit more easily. If it is a question of what *my* next reincarnation will be — as the Hindus believe — perhaps at least I won't be confined to the animal kingdom next time but will enjoy a human status, maybe not at the bottom of the heap or in some distant tribal homeland but somewhere near the middle.

Among the talents I was also born with — "talent" in the sense of gifts of God, whether material or otherwise — was a strong sense of curiosity. All children have a lot of this, but I never grew out of it. I have always had a fascination with the unfamiliar, the "Other," somewhere beyond my own surround-ings. Gazing at a map of Fairyland over the sofa in our New York living room I first felt the allure of far horizons, later enhanced by the pages of Father's historical atlas. My eyes often lingered on the maps of the eastern countries, changing colors and shapes through the ages.

And then the East came right to our Cold Spring Harbor home, with the arrival of a mysterious guest, who unwittingly played a key role in starting me on my journey to Samarkand. This was Prince Muhiddin, the son of Sharif Ali Haidar, of Mecca, who was backed by the Turks, and went into exile after the Arab revolt in World War I. Ali Haidar had been a friend of my grandfather's, and so his son looked up my father when he came to the States.

We all loved "Prince Mooi," as we called him, who looked like a gentler version of Richelieu with a small, pointed beard. He knew no English, but this seemed to make little difference, and my father made him feel at home, taking him out in his sailboat and singing "Abdullah Bul-Bul Ameer," one of the ditties in the

Groton School songbook dating back to the time of the Russo-Turkish wars of the late nineteenth century. He eventually managed to learn some English but didn't use it very much, as most of his time he spent playing the *oud,* the Middle Eastern lute, which he hoped to popularize in the United States. I could hear him play mysterious oriental tunes in the evening in the guest room, and sometimes we would sit on the porch together and talk, after a fashion, about his homeland. My father managed to get him a show in Carnegie Hall, but unfortunately, in that day before microphones, the oud just didn't make enough noise and Prince Muhiddin eventually went home to Baghdad, where we were to meet many years later.

In 1934, a few years after Prince Mooi's visit, my family took my oldest sister, Theodora, and me on a trip to the Mediterranean, where I got my first taste of what was then called the Near East — which included everything from the Balkans to India; in those days Greece and the southern Balkans still had more in common with the Islamic East than with Europe. Now they have moved west, and the rest of the old "Near East" is lumped with the Middle East.

It was a magic voyage for a boy like myself, a rather brash little fellow just entering his teens, and my mother wrote it up in a book published the following year, *We Owed It to the Children.* I naturally figure in it, but I don't even remember the first story she tells about me, during our trip on the Italian liner *Saturnia*:

> During dinner my maternal eye wandered to my offspring, whose experience as diners-out was very limited, and I was pleased to see that they were holding their own in fine style and doing credit to the quantities of delicious and unusual food being served to us. In fact all went well until Mussolini's name was mentioned, when a sudden lull came over the table, broken by Archie Jr.'s asking the Captain if he had heard the story about Mussolini at the movies. I waited breathlessly, all conversation stopped, the Italian and Yugoslav waiters clustered around. The Captain replied he had never heard any story about Mussolini ever, and Archie Jr. began: It seems Mussolini's car broke down in a city where no one expected him to be. While it was being mended, Mussolini entered a nearby movie. To his embarrassment, no sooner had he taken his seat than a movie of

himself making a speech was flashed on the screen. Everyone rose to his feet except Mussolini, who, rather uncertain what he ought to do, remained seated. At this, a little old lady leaned over and much to his surprise whispered in his ear, "Good for you, we all feel that way but haven't the courage to show it!"

As Archie terminated this story the waiters made a rush for the door while several of the guests gave nervous giggles. Everyone else looked rather apprehensively at the Captain, but he was quite equal to the situation. Rising to his feet he toasted me for my courage, my children for their beauty, and Archie Sr. for his endurance.

One of the *Saturnia*'s stops was Algiers, where a walk down the hill through the Casbah was my introduction to the Arab world. My mother was repelled by the filth and poverty, but I was fascinated by the Moorish scene, like something out of the "romances," the ballads of old Spain. The men all wore burnooses, and I found the women, despite their heavy robes, alluring in their coquettish little veils, often semitransparent, which revealed their huge eyes, darkened with kohl; these same large dark eyes were the most attractive feature of the little ragged children following us all the way. The houses were plastered in white, dazzling in the sun, but on either side of the narrow street leading down the hill to the harbor were dark alleys promising mystery and adventure. I was in the land of *Beau Geste,* and wished I could linger.

But we hurried back to the *Saturnia,* staying on it for more forays to Naples and Pompeii, Palermo, and then Patras, on the Peloponnesus, where we unloaded ourselves and our large open touring car — a Franklin, unique then with its air-cooled engine — and took a boat through the Corinth Canal to Athens.

Primed by Greek studies at school, I passed golden days in Athens, the temple at Sunion, the haunted gorge at Delphi. Father drove the great Franklin north through the unpaved roads, and we passed the nights in tents, in an olive grove near Thebes, in a field on the Thessalian plain, and in a Macedonian meadow with shepherds herding their sheep all around us. As my mother wrote:

In Greece there are only two kinds of meat: lamb and sheep. I don't know why I suddenly felt I had to have a chicken. None of the family spoke Greek, but we boldly entered a butcher shop. The excited populace crowded the doorways, while we stood somewhere in the centre of the mob trying to make ourselves understood. No luck. An impasse, until Archie Jr. taking a leaf out of his father's book started cackling and the streets of Larissa resounded with an excellent imitation of a hen.

Bursts of applause from surrounding Greeks showed that they had seized the point immediately. We were firmly grasped by many brown and rather dirty hands and, with the mob, surged down the street. We were brought to a shop where, alas, we found we had been misunderstood! It was an egg and cheese shop. Archie Jr. was discouraged, the mob was disappointed and puzzled, but the younger generation may be down — it is never out. Spreading his chest, he flapped his two arms like wings and jumped on the shop counter. I became embarrassed and thought he might be arrested for insanity, but a roar of applause went up and once more the mob pushed us forward. We found the chickens — but alas, chickens in Greece are only sold on the hoof!

After this, we crossed the border to Albania, to the Balkans evoked by the stories of Saki I'd just finished reading. The Albanians then were still people of the East, in baggy pants, cummerbunds, and red fezzes. We stayed with the American minister in Tirana, and I met my first prime minister at dinner, whom Mother claims I attacked with a barrage of questions about his troubled country, where King Zog sat on an uneasy throne.

"Were there many bandits? Had Italy or Yugoslavia the inside track? Was the King in constant danger? What was he like anyway?"

The Prime Minister withstood the onslaught nobly, but we were all rather relieved when Archie Jr. took himself off to bed.

We drove on through the Albanian mountains to the Montenegrin capital of Cetinje, in the midst of tall, fine-looking people whose sharp features reflected the toils of mountain life and pride in their noble past, when they stood alone against a sea of Turks.

Father had been personally decorated by the prince-bishop of Montenegro during World War I, and here he ran into an old acquaintance, the prince's former aide, an ancient general who had fought with the Russian general Mikhail Dmitrievich Skobelev in the 1870s. We had just visited the citadel high above the city, and the general pointed to it and said, "I remember, in my youth, that tower piled high with the ears of the Turks by our young men returned from battle!"

The trip continued with its wonders; we stopped briefly in Dubrovnik before steaming up the Dalmatian coast to Venice, then on via Milan and Switzerland to memorable weeks in Paris, but it was this taste of the East that stayed with me through the years.

This trip was my only adventure across the Atlantic before the war; the rest of my youth was completely American, and my education, conventional preppy Eastern Seaboard, with one exception. I did very well at St. Bernard's School and ended up taking preparatory exams for Groton School a year ahead of my age group. I was a very little boy — through most of my school years I was the smallest boy in the class — and my parents considered me too small and immature to go on to Groton. Instead, following the theory of both my grandfather and father that no one could really understand the United States unless they experienced our great West, they sent me out for a year at the Arizona Desert School, near Tucson.

They were so right. On the train trip west I began to experience that "America, the Beautiful" we sang about in school, with its "amber waves of grain" slipping by the window as we crossed the endless plains. The last morning I pulled up the shades on ocher-colored mountains that seemed close enough to touch — only to realize they were miles away in the clear air across the flat sands, so unlike the green mountains of Vermont, so remote in the misty air of New England. Fences of skinny paloverde sticks and prickly pear lined our road from the train to the school. Beyond, a forest of mesquite and sharp-fanged cholla cactus was sparsely scattered in the sand, topped here and there by tall green branches of saguaro. Our car, passing through the parched flora of the desert, with horizons bounded only to the north and east by those strange mountains, was transformed into a modern covered wagon.

The school was built on the Spanish pattern around a patio not far from a "wash," or empty streambed, like the *wadis* I would later find in the Arab East. The surrounding desert was a paradise for us boys from city homes, with lizards and horned toads scampering over the ground and an occasional jackrabbit jumping up almost between one's toes. Now and then we would come across a Gila monster dragging along its scaly body, or hear the sinister warning rustle of a rattlesnake. Nearby we could climb the stony foothills of the Santa Catalina Range, and on the eastern horizon the green peaks of the Rincon Mountains crowned with snow. In the evening you could look west across the great cactus space, sometimes clear, sometimes murky with dust, which made magnificent sunsets.

During that year I acquired a love for the desert and a nostalgia for it through the rest of my youth, until at last I attained the deserts on the other side of the world. My father came out to take me camping, on a mountain-lion hunt in the ranges just north of the Mexican border, and on a later expedition I actually shot a couple of them — a very exciting feat for an eleven-year-old. I enjoyed all the animal life of Arizona: the deer, the bighorn sheep, the chorus of coyotes, as well as little scuttling things like gophers and jumping mice.

Father adored his own father and shared most of his interests. He naturally expected me to follow in the ancestral footsteps; our camping trips, our hunting expeditions, and my western experience were part of my conditioning for this path. But, except for the very early years, when most boys worship their fathers, he was not my role model. I did share some of Father's interests, largely Grandfather's also, such as history, but others I could not. Grandfather used to say that he might have become an ornithologist. On the wall in Cold Spring Harbor hung a colored chart of the birds, and Father pointed them out to me while we were sitting at breakfast or tea on the porch. But birds never really got to me.

Animals, however, were something else, both wild and domestic. I devoured books such as those of Ernest Thompson Seton and Jack London's *Call of the Wild*. Animals included man, and physical anthropology. Henry Fairfield Osborn's *Men of the Old Stone Age* was a bible, like other books on paleontology. I caught and dissected frogs and small mammals, and put together a nice little skull collection. It was only on the publication of Sylvia Morris's wonderful *Edith Kermit Roosevelt* in 1980 that I learned that Grandfather, as a boy, had a "Roosevelt Museum of Natural History" with similar specimens, so it must have been in the genes.

Encouraging this interest, Father brought me several times to visit the Rockefeller Institute in New York, where I was shown the laboratory by his friend Dr. James B. Murphy; I was fascinated by the white mice and rats used for experiments, mostly on cancer. Then I made the connection with the great laboratory of Cold Spring Harbor, where they were carrying on similar experiments.

My parents had once given my sister and me a present of two tame house mice, named Doug and Mary after the famous Fairbanks movie couple. Now I was able to coax some mice out of the Cold Spring Harbor laboratory, first white mice, but gradually expanding my collection to include a number of varieties — I was especially attached to a spotted breed. I kept them in a large wooden box with screen sides, and took them everywhere with me. One time a school friend invited me to stay at his family's pastoral estate in Litchfield, Connecticut. When I insisted on bringing my mice, his father, concerned that they would get loose in his beloved stables, agreed on condition of a solemn promise that I keep them strictly confined. Unfortunately, spotted mice carry a dominant gene, and spotted mice were spotted in the stables soon after my visit.

I carried them to Arizona with me — one got loose in the train on the way. And even to Groton, where I often attended chapel with a mouse in my sleeve, who would occasionally pop out and wander about my person during services, to the entertainment of my fellow worshippers. But eventually, numbering almost a hundred, they began to interfere too much with other pursuits, and one day, near Cooper's Bluff, off Sagamore Hill, I gave them their freedom.

While the main purpose of the Arizona exercise was to toughen me up for Groton, and it was understood that I would not have to do much studying, a Frenchman who taught at the school took a special interest in me, the first of several teachers to help me find something extra outside routine classes. I had learned to speak a rather ungrammatical French at home, but it was he who led me through the subtleties of the language. We also read together Voltaire's *Zadig* — with its oriental setting providing still another nudge eastward.

After the freedom of a year of life in the western desert, it was not easy to enter the forbidding brick walls of a small New England church school, which were to hold me in semi-imprisonment for six long years.

The Realm of the Rector —
A Caravanserai

DR. ENDICOTT PEABODY, Rector of Groton School, was one of the great schoolmasters of the old tradition, rooted in the English public school. He was a large man with a squarish face, a high forehead, and sharp, austere features, anachronistic, like someone from a Victorian painting or an old daguerreotype. He left his mark on several generations of boys as they passed into adulthood, generally worthy, often distinguished, with a few sinking into failure along the way, in spite of it all.

He founded Groton in 1884 for the purpose of producing an American elite of Christian manhood with strong bodies, high moral standards, and a good classical education. They would be directed on the straight and narrow path by a puritan regimen on almost military lines. We lived in a collective rather than an individual society. The boys slept in cubicles, and the only rule of privacy was that you could not invade another boy's cubicle without permission. The windows of the cubicles were always kept open at night, even when it snowed and the temperature fell close to zero, as it sometimes did in the harsh eastern Massachusetts winters.

One's daily schedule was regulated by the sound of bells, beginning with the one that routed you out of your cubicle at seven o'clock in the morning, after which there was the required cold shower and washup in an individual tin washbasin. In half an hour the bell rang for breakfast, and at eight-ten exactly, "Outside" — the big bell in the schoolhouse tower —

rang for chapel. At eight-thirty classes started, interrupted by electric bells every hour right up to lunchtime, when all of us had to gather at our places in the cavernous study hall of Hundred House, the largest of the three colonial brick buildings surrounding the campus, for Assembly. At that time, or in another Assembly in the evening, announcements were made, including the monthly ranking of students, class by class.

The afternoons were reserved for a prescribed ninety minutes of exercise, and what time was left for individual study and private pursuits was soon cut short by the bell for Assembly and early supper. Afterward the lower forms spent a couple of hours in the study hall, envying seniors their tiny individual studies, before lining up to say good-night to the Rector and proceeding to the dormitory. The half hour before bedtime might be taken up by a reading from the master in charge. The lights went out promptly at ten o'clock.

One visit a week was allowed on Saturday afternoon to the small nearby town, where there wasn't much to do except go to the drugstore. There was the "Parents' House" near the campus, where relatives could visit and invite you over for breakfast and other meals; now and then a relative might treat you to a dinner in the town's only hostel. Sundays were free except for morning and evening chapel, but one had to wear a navy blue suit and stiff collar all day.

Chapel played a constant role in our lives, with the only good part, as far as I was concerned, being the choir, organized by our devoted music teacher, Twyning Lynes. I sang in successive years as soprano, alto, and tenor. The Rector's sermons were repetitious exhortations to clean living, with an occasional reference to the bad example of "the foulest man I ever knew." This unfortunate individual — a subject of some comment among us boys — had aroused the disgust of the Rector in his missionary year in Tombstone, Arizona, around 1880. (We often speculated about the Rector's life among the Bad Men, whose guns he must have silenced with a glance of those terrifying blue eyes.)

The Rector's sermons alternated with those of his lifelong deputy, Sherrard Billings, which had similar themes, delivered in less somber tones. Billings was a little man whose features were decorated with a walrus moustache that gave him, like the Rector, a Victorian look, and he shared the Rector's views of pronunciation of the English language. He said, for instance, that words like "good" should be pronounced as spelled, in this case to rhyme with "brood" — and that was how the Rector said it, too. But there the resemblance stopped. Mr. Billings was a gentle soul, and while we feared the Rector, we all, without exception, felt affection for Billings.

My father had not been certain Groton was right for me and thought of sending me to Andover, his alma mater, which he had preferred. He had first attended Groton himself, where he hated the rule of the bells. When he was temporarily reprieved for a year in Arizona to recover from diphtheria, he sent a classmate a postcard asking, "How is the old Christ Factory?" The Rector, no believer in the rights of boys to privacy, read the postcard and immediately asked my grandfather, then president of the United States, to refrain from sending Father back to Groton. He happily went to Andover.

The Rector really approved only of boys who conformed to Groton norms of muscular Christianity, a standard I did not meet. Immediately after our arrival in school, we were assigned to one of the two teams, the Monadnocks and the Wachusetts, named after Indian tribes, with navy or red sweatshirts. I hardly ever wore my red Wachusetts shirt. Organized sports were not for me, still the smallest in my class and usually the last to be chosen for a team.

Worse, in matters of religion, I was the only holdout in my class in refusing to be confirmed in the Episcopal faith. On several occasions as we passed by the Rector to say our ritual good-nights, he said to me those dreaded words, "I'd like to see you afterwards in my study." Twice we discussed my failure to seek confirmation in the faith. I was really an agnostic, but to admit that would have been unthinkable. So I took the easier way out by stating my loyalty to my mother's Unitarianism. Although he tried to persuade me that this would be no barrier to confirmation, I stood my ground.

On another occasion, though, I almost failed to survive. In this session he told me that I didn't "conform." Several boys who had been guilty of this in the past had been withdrawn from the school after their parents were told, "He is just not the type of boy we like to have here." I think the Rector thought about this possibility for me but really did not have sufficient excuse for it. While I was guilty of many minor misdemeanors and spent many of my weekends working off the various black marks I had received during the week — for such offenses as not wearing my overcoat when the temperature was below 60 degrees, or for not taking the requisite cold shower in the morning even when the temperature was near zero — I was not really bad enough to deserve the ultimate punishment. And I had a good academic record.

But if Groton was a prison, it was at least a minimum security one. The countryside was beautiful, especially during the New England fall, and was crossed by a river not far away on which we were permitted to canoe on weekends. A few other boys in my class did not fit the mold and shared one or more of my interests. These became my companions in one undertaking or another, and friends from then on. I invited some of them to the mixed house parties Father and Mother organized once or twice a year during vacations, along with my eldest sister and daughters of my parents' friends.

There were no girls to be seen on campus, and care was exerted to ensure that the maids and waitresses were of a type not to arouse the lust of growing boys. I remember one, however, whom we called the Water Nymph, who poured water at the tables — a lady of a certain age, but tall with a full figure. One or two of the younger masters also had wives who attracted a certain amount of adolescent attention, and the Rector had one granddaughter, a tall, haughty, blonde beauty, Marietta, with whom a great many of the older boys fell in love. (Marietta Tree, still a blonde beauty today, continues to have legions of admirers.) And once a year we could each invite a girl to spend a very carefully chaperoned weekend for the annual school dance. The Rector himself often acted as chaperon, going around turning on lights in darkened study halls.

Also, those six years were not wasted. Groton's classical education introduced me to many worlds beyond its walls. I loved the history classes, and, of course, already knowing French and Latin, I had a head start in languages. I grew tired of Latin as the Roman authors — with a few exceptions, such as Horace and Catullus — lost their appeal, and I never even liked Virgil, but since I was a good student I was forced to keep on in advanced courses willy-nilly. However, in my second year I was introduced to Greek and fell in love with all the shining facets of the "glory that was Greece." I devoured Homer, Plato, Herodotus, drama, the Lyric poets. My Greek teacher, Mr. Cushing, took a kindly interest in me and gave me private tutoring in those brief afternoon free periods.

He was only one of the many good teachers to help us expand the horizons of the mind within our geographic confinement. Our history and English classes were of a high quality, and the mathematics was so well taught that I excelled in a subject that had no charm for me. Science was pedestrian until the last two years, when we got a new biology teacher. Sacred studies taught by the Rector and Mr. Billings were a bit too much like their sermons, though my father had taught me to enjoy the Old Testament. Also, in my last two years we got an unconventional English clergyman, whose irreverent teachings of the Acts and the Journeys of Saint Paul were among the many pleasures of my Groton training.

In all this study of history and the classics, strangely, the losers of history always had an emotional appeal for me. In Homer I always sympathized with Hector and the Trojans. I really took a dislike to Caesar in my admiration of the Gauls, and the Celts in general, bravely going down in defeat through the centuries. In the same way I favored Carthage against Rome, the Moors of Spain against Castile, and the Byzantines against everybody.

The copious school library was my great refuge, and there I indulged my taste for the East. This included the Russians, especially Dostoyevski, and it was then I began looking into the Near and Middle East, including the Arabs — with Lawrence of Arabia as a starting point.

I remember one time reading on the front page of the *New York Times* a story about a man whose name I had never heard, King Ibn Saud, and his defeat of Imam Yahya of Yemen. Attached to the story was a picture of King Saud, magnificent in his *kufiyya*, the Arab headdress I had seen in the Lawrence of Arabia photographs, and I kept this yellowing clipping with me for many years.

Although I was a pretty good student, I followed my own paths and thus won few awards for excellence. But one I did win two years in a row was for public reading. The first year I read the speech from *Richard II* — one of history's losers:

For God's sake, let us sit upon the ground
And tell sad stories of the death of kings. . .

The other winning reading was James Elroy Flecker's *Hassan: A Play in Five Acts.*

Away, for we are ready to a man!
Our camels sniff the evening and are glad.
Lead on, O Master of the Caravan,
Lead on the Merchant-Princes of Bagdad.

. . . .

We are the Pilgrims, master; we shall go
Always a little further: it may be
Beyond that last blue mountain barred with snow
Across that angry or that glimmering sea.

White on a throne or guarded in a cave
There lives a prophet who can understand
Why men were born: but surely we are brave,
Who take the Golden Road to Samarkand.

. . . .

Sweet to ride forth at evening from the wells,
When shadows pass gigantic on the sand,
And softly through the silence beat the bells
Along the Golden Road to Samarkand.

We travel not for trafficking alone;
By hotter winds our fiery hearts are fanned:
For lust of knowing what should not be known,
We take the Golden Road to Samarkand.

"Open the gate, O watchman of the night!"

"Ho, travellers, I open. For what land
Leave you the dim-moon city of delight?"

"We take the Golden Road to Samarkand!"

As I memorized and then read these lines before the school assembly, I sensed that I was myself one of that caravan. It was perhaps at that moment that I first set off on my own life's journey on the Road to Samarkand.

3

Beyond the Walls of the Caravanserai

SCHOOL, OF COURSE, didn't last all the year, and for a few days, weeks, and months I was free to explore the rest of the United States. In addition to the Christmas and Easter holidays, and the months of summer, there was a welcome break, at Thanksgiving, just as the long wintry weather began to take hold. Every year my parents took me to pass the holiday with an eccentric relative who lived in Ipswich, Massachusetts, a couple of hours' drive from the school. His name was Francis Colby, and he was said to be extremely rich. He didn't seem to have any visible business, but spent a lot of his time on expeditions to Africa. The first floor of his house was a one-room natural history museum. Heads of antlered antelope or snarling lions or leopards stared down from the wall, while their furry skins littered the sofas and floors. Pots of clubs and arrows, with assegais and shields of hide, crowded every nook and corner. The mantelpiece of the giant fireplace was crowned with ivory and ebony carvings of animals, gods, and chieftains, and its sides were bedecked with swords, horsehair fly whisks, and magic staffs. After a sumptuous Thanksgiving dinner, Cousin Frannie would lead us down to the cellar, where he showed movies of charging tribesmen or big game on a lead screen, and we would take pistols and guns and shoot at them with explosive bullets. I still remember one film of an expedition among the Hadendoa tribesmen of eastern Sudan, the "Fuzzy-Wuzzies." After this, we would proceed upstairs, where

Cousin Frannie would reminisce about his experiences in the wilds of Africa. I was enthralled.

However, this was not the reaction of my parents and my Uncle Dunbar Lockwood, Mother's brother, and his wife. Not only did they find these affairs extremely boring, but they thoroughly disapproved of Cousin Frannie's life-style, including the fact that he preferred to remain a bachelor and produced a different girlfriend every year. My mother and my aunt invariably disliked each successive girlfriend and would make this rather clear in the course of the evening.

Later, toward the end of his life, Cousin Frannie appeared at my parents' house in Hobe Sound, Florida, with his latest girlfriend, a nurse, and was extremely miffed when my mother refused to introduce them as man and wife in that very proper society. Cousin Frannie apparently immediately changed his will. He left his collection of Africana to the Boston Museum of Science and a bequest of, I think, $700,000 — a lot of money in those days — with the proviso that the museum reconstruct his grand hall, complete with animal skins. My uncle's children received an annuity for life, but my three sisters and I, thanks to Mother's attack of puritanism, received nothing — which seems a little unfair, as I was probably the one who appreciated him most.

The summer vacations I usually spent in my family's house in Cold Spring Harbor, sometimes varied by a stretch in Sagamore. My parents used to call Cold Spring Harbor "Hot Summer Harbor," and in August we usually made an expedition north — including some kind of adventure when Father broke out of Wall Street for his vacation.

Often we went to Maine — a favorite summer resort for Bostonians in the old days; we would stay with Mother in Northeast Harbor until Father was free, and then go sailing on the coast or canoeing in the interior. Other times we cruised from Cold Spring Harbor up the coast to Maine or even to the Bay of Fundy, in Nova Scotia.

My father's pride in my scholastic achievements was mixed with a feeling that I was turning into more of a scholar than the outdoorsman he had hoped to have for a son. He did his best to develop the genes of the "strenuous life" he felt sure his son must have inherited.

Starting when I was very young, Father tried to turn me into

a mighty hunter he could be proud of, and gave me a
.410-gauge shotgun and a .22 rifle. He often took me to the old
firing range at Sagamore Hill where Grandfather had practiced, and in between times made sure I practiced by aiming at
spots on my bedroom wall. Finally, at the age of fourteen I was
graduated to a 20-gauge shotgun and a lovely little Mannlicher-
Shoener rifle from my grandfather's collection — I was still too
small to handle anything bigger. But now I was proudly ready
for big game, and he took me to the North Woods to try out my
new weapons.

Father drove me up to Quebec, and after a night in the
Château Frontenac we headed north to a large private game
preserve. There we were joined by four French-Canadian
guides, headed by one incongruously named Bébé, part Indian,
with fierce moustaches decorating the craggy face of a true
coureur de bois. It took me a couple of days to catch on to their
strange French, and then we became great friends. We met
only one or two other campers in all our two weeks of tramping
through the great forest, the remains of what all the eastern
part of North America must have been like before the white
man. The only sign of civilization was the occasional vacant log
cabin that gave us shelter during the silent nights, disturbed
only by the weird cry of the loon. I felt like a visitor to the scenes
of those evocative books of Francis Parkman, the historian of
French Canada and the old northwestern wilderness, which I
had read from cover to cover at Groton.

Every day we set out early in the morning, usually by canoe,
piercing the mirror surface of a lake, with fog slowly rising into
the dawn. Sometimes we fished for the abundant trout; twice I
caught two on a line. Sometimes we tramped in the forests,
from time to time shooting a partridge, so tame one was
ashamed to knock it off a limb — or squirrels, which we ate
happily for supper one day toward the end of our expedition.

One morning we saw an immense bull moose at the other end
of the lake, 250 yards away. I don't know who was the more
excited, my father or myself, and the guide seemed as anxious
as Father that I show off my skill. We stopped paddling, and I
took careful aim as the huge beast half turned in our direction.
For once in my life I did not let my father down — following his
careful instruction, I shot the moose right behind the shoulder,
and he dropped dead in the water. We could carry only the filet

cut, which we enjoyed the rest of the trip, as the main load was the great head of horn. It was a true moment of triumph when my father drove me past the walls of Groton, where the fall term had already begun, and my schoolmates could see the giant horns perched on the car.

As it turned out, this was to be the high point of my career as a big-game hunter. A couple of years later, in my last summer vacation as a Groton schoolboy, when I had at last grown into adolescence, Father arranged a fossil-collecting trip to Fairbanks, Alaska, for me sponsored by the American Museum of Natural History. My classmate Walter "Sully" Sullivan, now the noted *New York Times* science writer, was to accompany me. In making ready for our expedition, we boned up on mammology and improvised exercises in recognition of animal bones, collecting bits of old cow skeletons from the surrounding fields and examining them in a school attic. As experience proved, it was time well spent.

Alaska in 1935 had much of the old frontier about it, and Sully and I as teenagers stepped back a century in American history. We visited the half-Indian villages on the Inland Passage to Alaska and made our way to Fairbanks in a three-day journey on the old Alaska railroad, stopping at intervals to let the caribou across the tracks. In Fairbanks there were still people who gave no second names, in the old western tradition of a murky past. I remember Stone Age Bill, so named because he had been found chipping rocks to start a fire after he had run out of matches in the woods.

In Fairbanks we lived in the scattered buildings of the University of Alaska, still in its infancy, and spent most of our days along streams walled with hundred-foot-high cliffs of primeval muck, frozen into permafrost tens of thousands of years ago. Men hired by a gold company spent their days hosing down the muck to bare the gold-bearing gravel beneath, and we spent ours wandering up and down the streambed, picking up the bones that fell from the muck. These were not fossilized, but came from animals frozen in several successive years of intense glaciation. We found bits of skeletons of caribou, bison, bears, lions, and occasionally mastodon, and whole skeletons of small animals, sometimes with bits of skin and decayed gristle attached. We then took them back to our working shack, and classified and marked them.

We varied this routine by digging into mounds covering ancient Indian villages, throwing the dirt onto screens to find flints and artifacts, trying to keep in the smoke of a fire to fend off the no-see-ums who punished us in the heat of the Alaskan summer. To find these villages we dug deep trenches, and collected the bodies of jumping mice and shrews that fell into them. We sent their skins to the museum — and skinning a shrew is no mean feat. They included several previously unknown subspecies, and one was named after me!

At the end of our Fairbanks stint, Father appeared and took us hunting for mountain sheep in a range a railway ride south of Fairbanks, where we lived a few days in a log cabin on a creek. I set out for a long day's hunt up into the mountains with my museum boss, Jack Dorsch, and after stalking herds all day, I got some shots in at a troop of mountain sheep leaping up the slope. They ranged in size from the largest, leading the troop, to the young rams, bringing up the rear. I got off a few shots, missed the big ones, and finally brought down the two smallest in the rear. Jack could not hide his disappointment in me.

By the time we skinned and loaded them it was late in the day, and then the ordeal began. Over peak after peak of slippery shale we started home, but soon realized we didn't really know where we were. As we climbed and descended over the sliding rock, my strength began to give out, especially taxed by the chafing of ill-fitting boots. I was a tottering, walking automaton by nightfall, when I fell and sprained my leg. We built a fire, and Jack left to continue the search for our cabin and my father. With bear and wolf tracks all around, he didn't need to warn me to keep the fire going all night.

It was cold, and I was wet from crossing streams, and curled around the fire to keep one side warm. The wind rustled the willows surrounding my little island of light, sometimes sounding suspiciously like the stirrings of a wolf, but twice I fell asleep from exhaustion for a few minutes and woke to find the fire almost gone. At the first welcome sign of dawn, I struggled to my feet and staggered on in Jack's footsteps, keeping going by singing and talking to myself. Once I said, "I'm a man now. I can take almost anything after this." After a couple of hours I met my wonderful father carrying a pack filled with hot food and coffee. His joy at seeing me would have been much greater had he known that he had succeeded, that I had become a man and had found a strength that has never deserted me in time of testing.

In the long run, as I got older and went to college, I lost interest in these outings; in fact, I came to feel distaste for killing animals and birds. I never told my father this, but my failing interest in outdoor life was a great disappointment to him. He never knew that his efforts to train me had been successful in important ways. I grew up into a "real American," not just an Eastern Seaboarder, who felt in his bones the meaning of "America, the Beautiful." And he never knew, either, that I became a man in those mountains deep in Alaska.

My outings outside the walls of Groton were mostly in fields and streams and forests, but twice my parents took me to our country's capital, Father's childhood home, which was one day to become my own. In those days it was quite an expedition by road, along Route 1, interrupted by a ferry ride over Chesapeake Bay. Yet when we got there it was great fun. The first time, when I was still a Grotonian, Father had taken me to lunch at the British embassy with Ambassador Sir Esmé Howard. The second trip was more memorable and portentous.

Before I went to Groton, I had only been dimly aware that there was another branch of our family, the Franklin Roosevelts, of Hyde Park. We never heard much about them around Sagamore Hill — except that they were Democrats, not quite our kind of Roosevelt. It was only in the Rector's realm that I met them; two of FDR's sons, Franklin and John, were upperclassmen and treated me kindly in true cousinly fashion. I met Cousin Eleanor for the first time when she came up to visit them; she was very nice to me and asked me to join them a couple of times for meals at Parents' House.

I finally saw Cousin Franklin himself in 1933 when Father took me down to Washington to attend his inauguration. Although later publicly opposed to FDR, Father voted for him in 1932. His vote was canceled by that of my inflexibly Republican mother, and although he never voted for him again, family relations were maintained — at a distance. I was just under fifteen when I sat to hear Cousin Franklin say from the grandstand facing us from the Capitol that we had nothing to fear but fear itself, but I knew I was witnessing a momentous piece of history.

These Washington expeditions were only brief interludes in my generally rustic Groton years. One couldn't have asked for a better way to pass one's vacations in childhood and early adolescence, but past that age I began to yearn for the outside world I had already tasted. Local social life was limited to cousins and the children of my parents' friends, and I had already glimpsed more. The days grew longer, especially the last summer before college in 1936. I filled increasing stretches of time with books, indulging my taste for things far away.

Spurred perhaps by my interest in Dostoyevski, I decided to learn Russian and, by now having had some experience with languages, taught myself the grammar. Our gardener, known as Laddie (for Vladislav), came from the eastern part of Poland and spoke Russian. My parents used to give me many tasks — mowing the lawn, scything the fields, chopping wood — and a lot of these I accomplished as Laddie's assistant. Soon I was talking Russian with him, and I can still remember phrases we used, such as *kosit' kosoy, rubit' dyerevo:* "scything" and "woodcutting." Thus when I got to Harvard, I was able right off to take a course in Pushkin in Russian, a great experience, studying under one of Pushkin's well-known biographers, Professor Ernest Simmons.

4

Loading the Camels

HARVARD turned out to be almost the complete opposite of Groton — a free country. The Harvard administration had abolished nearly all rules for mandatory courses for those who had acquitted themselves well on the entrance examinations; thus, I did not even have to go through freshman English, mathematics, and history. I was completely free to choose my own courses within the limitations of fields of concentration.

I chose the field called Literature, comprising the twin subjects of ancient literature combined with either medieval or modern literature, and had a field day indulging myself with courses that may have added a great deal to my knowledge of linguistics and history but did not prepare me for much in the world — but now we have come to the realization that education is not just a preparation for employment.

I made Greek my ancient language and was extremely fortunate in having as my professor Maurice Bowra, who was spending a year at Harvard on exchange from Oxford, where he headed Wadham College. His greatest interest was in Homer and in Lyric poetry, and I took a course on the *Odyssey* from him and one on Pindar. He was one of the few really inspirational professors I had at Harvard.

I also improved my French with a course in French literature, and took another in elementary Italian, but that was my only bow to modern times. I sank into the Middle Ages with Anglo-Saxon, Old French, Middle High German, Old Norse —

and I indulged an attraction the Celts had for me by also learning Old Irish and Old Welsh.

Not through any foresight of mine, one of my exotic courses turned out to be most practical in my future career — in fact, the key to it. In my freshman year I got a special dispensation to take a course in Arabic, usually reserved for graduate students. My professor was a Scot who taught us Arabic with a Scottish accent and had experienced only one brief stay in the Middle East, during which he had been sick with dysentery the entire time and left vowing never to return. However, he was an excellent teacher. His main emphasis was on the complete mastery of the extremely complicated verbal system of Arabic, and after so many years I can still recite all the verbs today. Also, he wanted to give us a taste of modern spoken Arabic and brought in one of his graduate students to do the job, a Palestinian called Awni Dejany. Awni became a friend who began my education in the Middle East, and in the year following I arranged to have him tutor me on the Koran.

All the time I was immersed in matters far away and long ago, I could hardly ignore momentous developments in the great world outside. Hitler had come to power in Germany when I was still at Groton, and before I got to Harvard, Spain had exploded into civil war. In my last year at Groton, I began reading newspapers and following current events as well as ancient ones, and hence could not fail to be distracted from my scholarly life by the battle of ideas among my fellow students. At the time the rise of Fascism was naturally the international phenomenon getting the most attention, postponing the world ideological struggle between Soviet Communism and western democracy in which I was to be a participant all the later part of my life.

I never was a college radical, nor involved in the Marxist causes so popular on campus at the time. The appeal of Communism was much greater then than it is today, and the Young Communist League counted about one hundred members at Harvard, plus three times that in the affiliated American Youth Congress.

While still at Groton, I had happened on some copies of the *Daily Worker* in the library and found its message of class hatred a calumny on the ideals of America, in which I felt myself to be a proud participant. Now that I encountered my first Communists, I was repelled by them, despite, or perhaps partly because of, my Russophilia. Communism had destroyed the Russia I had come to love through books, the Russia described in *The Land of the Firebird*, Suzanne Massie's more recent masterpiece. I could not empathize with the heroes of its principal cause of the time, Republican Spain, although Franco's side also lacked appeal except to a few of the Catholics among us.

Although Fascism and Nazism had no support at Harvard, the Communists clearly did, and I thought the danger they represented could not be shrugged off with the indifference of most of my classmates. Along with some other like-minded students, I helped form a democratic group called The Independents, which never amounted to much except for a small forum for occasional discussions on current political topics.

Besides this bare minimum of political involvement squeezed in between my studies, I took some time off for a very pleasant social life in Boston, especially after my freshman year of adjustment to freedom. My mother was a Bostonian and so I was well received in Boston society of the day. I found "Society" in Boston far more congenial than the sterile materialism of its New York equivalent — almost its opposite. Intellectual pursuits were prized and material ones considered unworthy of discussion; these Bostonians were the true heirs of a culture dating from colonial times.

My maternal uncle, Dunbar Lockwood, had a fine old house with an octagonal projection over the Charles River, and every Sunday I used to walk there, often in the company of student friends, for a dinner and bridge afterward. His wife, my auntie Carrie, was and still is a lively lady from Charleston, and what's more, a Democrat, a good antidote to most of my family. My grandmother, who had produced both my uncle and my mother in her forties, was a delightful little old lady, rotund, cheerful, and deaf as a post. She called me her favorite grandson — not much of a compliment, as I was the only one she ever had among seven grandchildren. But I was her favorite in any case. I always sat next to her on Sunday nights, and thus my voice developed the carrying power it still has today.

Uncle Dunny was a big, gray-haired, gray-eyed man with prominent cheekbones that earned him the epithet of "the Eskimo" in his youth. In him I had what every young man on earth should have — a benevolent uncle who kept an eye on his errant nephew. He lent me his car, took me out to dinner at the Somerset Club, and gave me all sorts of advice I didn't take.

My social life also included a number of girls. Several became friends — more platonic than emotional — but there was one particular girl for whom I was beginning increasingly to feel greater affection, and I even began to think that she would make a wonderful wife.

Then came that fateful summer cruise. In the summer between my sophomore and junior years, Father ran our boat over some rocks and had to stop in Nantucket for repairs, and we found ourselves sitting in the Nantucket boatyard. Not far away, staying with her mother, was a cousin of my college roommate Graham Blaine, now a distinguished psychologist. Her name was Katharine Winthrop Tweed, known as K.W.

She was a tall, coltish girl with a shock of blond hair over her forehead. I had already got to know her through my roommate and found her interesting, especially since she was somewhat exotic. Her father was a well-known Wall Street lawyer, a craggy, rather bleak Yankee, but her mother was of a different breed. Born of a German family in Newport, Rhode Island, she was witty, sharp-tongued, considered a bit eccentric by her more conventional peers. While K.W. was still a young girl, her mother found the summers in Long Island, where they had a large Victorian house at Montauk Point, unbearable. She suffered from hay fever and could not endure the dull social life, most of it passed alone while her husband toiled on Wall Street. She began taking her summers abroad, and ended up by divorcing Mr. Tweed and becoming the fifth wife of a down-at-the-heels Hungarian count, Paoli Palffy, who brought her, K.W., and her sister to live in a cold and drafty castle near Bratislava, in Slovakia.

Palffy was able to refurnish the castle at Mr. Tweed's expense, and the girls for some time enjoyed an upbringing very different from that of other American girls. French was the common language of the count and countess, and became, in fact, K.W.'s first language. They were also able to chatter in Viennese German.

While I had seen a bit of K.W. in Boston in the company of Graham Blaine, our relationship was still that of casual acquaintance. Now, thrown together, along with a few others, in

Nantucket, we became friends, and I was invited later to take a cruise on her father's much grander boat, a schooner, with these same friends. In the course of time, I became increasingly intrigued and fascinated by her, and in my final year at Harvard we became engaged. My new fiancée wanted to finish one more college year before marriage, so off she went to Sarah Lawrence.

I was in the class of 1940 but completed my studies in three years, graduating that spring of 1939, Phi Beta Kappa and magna cum laude. I think I would have been summa if I hadn't missed an examination through absentmindedness. I was also elected a Rhodes scholar. I would have hurried myself off to Oxford, but unfortunately the program was postponed because of the war, and I soon disqualified myself by getting married.

However, all this was academic — and I was in an academic dilemma. I really wanted to go on to graduate school, as I was becoming interested in the life of academe. But my father had long since made clear his opposition to people "sitting around college collecting degrees," and I was faced with having to go out in the world: after hurrying through college in three years, I now didn't know which way to head.

I sought the advice of another kindly uncle, Uncle Ted Roosevelt, who thought that a newspaper would be a good place to start. I followed his advice and with parental help got myself a job as copyboy on the old *New York Herald Tribune* at a salary of fifteen dollars per week. While naturally I could not live on my paycheck in New York, it was not as tiny as it seems now, considering that a subway ride then cost exactly one nickel. I got to know the New York subway system very well.

The job was not particularly interesting, but the people I worked with were, in an atmosphere very much like the romanticized picture of newsrooms in the movies. I found myself often on the night shift, which was not too congenial, as I was born a morning man and normally got up about the time I was now coming home from work after the late shift.

Meanwhile, the war had started but had settled down into the "Phony War" of watchful waiting on either side of the Maginot Line. Few people in the United States realized how soon the whole world, including ourselves, would be involved. Pressure from the left for "collective security" ceased with the stunning news of the Hitler-Stalin pact, horrifying many who had

previously supported the Soviet Union. The Soviet invasion of
Finland created much sympathy for the Finns in England,
France, and neutral Scandinavia, as well as the United States.
The Communist party abruptly changed its position from
hostility to Germany to neutralism in what it termed an
imperialist war, attempting to exploit antiwar sentiment in the
United States.

One day I got a call from Murray Plavner, who had been
referred to me by a friend of my father's active in the
Republican party. He had been involved in youth organizations
and had participated in the early days of the American Youth
Congress, fighting a hopeless battle to turn it into something
other than a Communist-front organization. He had broken
with the congress at its convention in July, and he was planning
to go to Washington to expose the AYC as a Communist front
at its four-day Citizenship Institute meeting planned for early
January 1940. Since he would not be able to attend the AYC
meeting himself after publicly breaking with the organization,
he wanted me to attend and join a couple of others in an action.

Although since leaving college I had taken little interest in
politics, at the *Herald Tribune* I had become concerned about
the blatant Communist domination of the Newspaper Guild.
While the Communist party had lost much influence in the
United States since the Hitler-Stalin pact, it was still strong in
New York, where Representative Vito Marcantonio, although
not a Communist party member, was most active in Communist-
front activity. Thus I felt I could not refuse Murray's request,
though it certainly did not fit in with my normal pattern.

At the meeting of the American Youth Congress, some
twelve hundred members were seated in the auditorium of the
Labor Department Building on Constitution Avenue. Our little
trio of dissidents was carefully chosen: an Irish-American, F.
Stephen MacArthur, who headed a Young Democratic Club in
New Jersey; an Italian-American, Peter Tropea, another New
Jersey Democratic Club leader; and myself, a WASP with
dubious credentials as representative of the entirely fictitious
"Advocates of Decent Advertising." Murray, a Jew, masterminded the show from outside. We entered the hall and saw
Cousin Eleanor sitting in the second row. She played godmother to the congress, putting up no fewer than fifteen
members at the White House, inducing Cabinet wives to shelter

others and arranging for hotels to house three hundred more at one dollar a night. I ran into my fellow former Grotonian Franklin, Jr., and expressed my surprise at Cousin Eleanor's involvement with such a group. Without being disloyal he indicated that he wasn't too happy about it either.

We waited until the session was well under way, in the middle of an uninspiring speech by the organization's national chairman, and then Steve arose, crying, "Point of order — I want to make a resolution — we must clear ourselves of the charge of Communistic." He was brandishing one of the two resolutions we had prepared, demanding the expulsion of Communist-front organizations. "You're out of order," interrupted the chairman, and Steve was hustled out of the hall. Meanwhile Peter Tropea was on his feet, shouting, "He's not out of order," waving a parliamentary rule book in his hand. He was also given the bum's rush, but not before breaking loose — he was a powerful young man — and throwing his book at an AYC officer.

Then it was my turn. I rose, saying, "Point of order — I want to present a resolution condemning Russia for its invasion of Finland." Someone grabbed me by the sleeve as the hall burst into uproar. I managed to break away ("a slight young man in horn-rimmed glasses," as the press described me) and left the hall. Someone later identified me and asked Cousin Eleanor if it was I. She confirmed the fact — "I know Archie" — and later mildly commented that our interruption was out of order, as it was not on the agenda.

The next day, led by a young girl on horseback dressed as Joan of Arc, some four thousand AYC delegates trooped to the south lawn of the White House, somewhat dispirited in the pouring rain. Their spirits were dampened still further when FDR denounced the Soviet Union as "a dictatorship as absolute as any dictatorship in the world," said that 98 percent of the American people supported Finland, and termed the AYC's opposition to loans to Finland, on the basis that this would force America into the "imperialist" war, "absolute twaddle." They greeted this "spanking," to quote the press, mostly with silence, but there were a few timid boos and hisses.

Not surprisingly, they weren't receptive when I passed out copies of my resolution to them on the steps of the Labor Building that evening; however, I did get it presented to

Cousin Eleanor at the meeting, and she showed courage in answering it by stating that "our sympathies as a free people should be with Finland." But she followed this with another statement, "I don't think you should adopt resolutions on anything you don't believe," and the next day invited 150 AYC members to the White House for tea. She was a great lady filled with sympathy for those less fortunate, but her naiveté about the Youth Congress and Communists in general endured. Among the impressions she passed on to the press after the sessions, as reported by my own *Herald Tribune,* were that "some members of the American Youth Congress view the Soviet experiment in Communism as having made headway in solving the problems of Russia's millions of underprivileged" but that "to the bulk of the Congress membership, concerned with their own disheartening personal problems, the issue of Communism is utterly immaterial."

I returned to my humdrum copyboy world after this somewhat heady experience, hardly imagining that my next confrontation with Communists would be in the Azerbaijan Soviet Socialist Republic.

After K.W. and I got married in June, we headed west in accordance with my father's view that I should be an all-points American; he had gotten me a job as a reporter on the *Spokane Spokesman Review,* at a princely salary of twenty dollars per week!

A couple of Spokane's leading families, the Davenports, who owned the only first-class hotel, and the Cowleses, who owned both of the town's newspapers, were friends of my family's, and, of course, gave me the job. The Cowleses from time to time invited us for dinner, as well as Sunday lunch, at their summer home on Lake Coeur d'Alene. My colleagues on the paper, however, were not so friendly, and for a time in my innocence I couldn't quite understand why. One of them finally told me, "You know, some of the boys are suspicious of you because you're friends of the publishers." I think he was disarmed by my pained and surprised reaction, and the near-hostility in the newsroom gave way to camaraderie. I must have inherited a smidgen of ancestral ability to relate to every sort and condition of men, and this applied to Middle America as well as remote tribesmen.

Yet after the first few months of married life K.W. and I began to find Spokane a bit monotonous, though there were compensations. We skied at a nearby mountain, and the lakes and forests of the northern tip of Idaho provided a weekend escape from the dry flatland of the city. The work was quite boring — coverage of local events, conventions, fraternal orders, the National Guard, the produce market, etcetera — relieved only by the excitement of the 1940 election, in the course of which we had a visit from both Republican candidate Wendell Willkie and Socialist candidate Norman Thomas. Thus, I was not too sorry when my year's course in life in the heartland was completed and my father managed to get me a job in a much more exciting town, San Francisco.

We lived on a hill in Berkeley with a magnificent view of the whole Bay Area, and saw the gate and the city gradually veiled by fog every evening, like an enchanted castle across the bay. I felt I could breathe deeply once more after the closed-in homeliness of Spokane. It appealed to my "Other" yearnings, looking outward toward the Pacific with its strong scents of the Far East. Along with its large oriental population, San Francisco had a sizable Russian colony, and one of its members brushed up my Russian at the Berlitz School. The nearby campus of the University of California provided another asset — a missionary's wife who helped me improve my spoken Arabic.

The San Francisco Bay Area is also special to me for a very personal reason — it was here that my son and only child was born. We decided to call him Tweed, with no middle initial, for a number of reasons that seemed good to us. First, it was his mother's maiden name. Second, she didn't really like my own name; she thought it was "pretentious" — later I came to the conclusion, perhaps unjust, that it was me and not my name that she didn't really like! In any case, I had *not* liked being a Junior — especially when I grew old enough to have girlfriends and a private life of my own, and Father opened all my mail.

My father had been named for Archibald Bulloch, the Revolutionary governor of Georgia who was an ancestor of T.R.'s mother, Martha Bulloch. I have an old print of Martha and T.R. Senior in a coach after their wedding, leaving her ancestral home, Bulloch Hall, in Roswell, in Bulloch County, Georgia. I might say I have always been proud of my name and my Bulloch connections, and perhaps owe something to my Bulloch genes in my life's vocation. Martha Bulloch's brother, James D., was representative of the Confederate secret service in England. He was responsible for the clandestine construction and launching of the *Alabama* and other Confederate warships in Liverpool that did so much damage to Union shipping in the Civil War. His book, *The Secret Service of the Confederate States in Europe,* is a classic, and "Uncle Jimmie" provided the inspiration for T.R. in composing his own classic, *The Naval War of 1812.*

My mother, coming out from New York to attend my son's birth (late for the event, as Tweed was born two weeks early), carried the Bulloch family silver with her to present to us in honor of the child who she quite rightly thought would be named Archibald Bulloch Roosevelt III. In horror, she bundled up the silver and brought it all back to New York; it was eventually presented to Sagamore Hill.

Father was upset for more than one reason. It was galling to him not to have a grandson named after him, as did his brothers Ted and Kermit. But also, he assumed that Tweed was named after my wife's father, Harrison Tweed — and, as he later said when venting his displeasure, "I *hate* Tweed!"

Harrison Tweed himself had said something about sending a gift when Tweed was born — and we had hoped it would be a monetary one. My salary of thirty-five dollars a week, plus an almost equal monthly contribution from my wife's trust and Harrison Tweed himself, did not cover our expenses, especially with a newborn child. We began selling some of our wedding presents, waiting for the Tweed check. But Harrison Tweed, too, was unhappy with our son's name; he said "it didn't scan" the way it would have as Harrison Tweed Roosevelt, for instance! So instead of the check, we got a huge gardenia tree, already infected with a fatal fungus. My wife was feeling poorly at the time of its arrival, but instead of going into a decline, she laughed all afternoon at the absurdity of it all and felt much better.

I worked successively on the *San Francisco Chronicle* and the *San Francisco Examiner,* entirely in the city news departments. I found friends among my colleagues, a couple of whom remained so through the years. But local news, to which I was assigned like most beginners, I found boring, and I never got the knack of making it interesting. I simply didn't catch fire and perhaps didn't want to. I realized that news reporting to a city desk was not for me.

Instead, I took refuge again in my exotic studies, bringing

large books to the office and even writing an article on the life of Saint Patrick — unpublished! — based on Celtic sources. The only dramatic memory I have of my reporting days is a sad one, when I was sent out the day after Pearl Harbor to interview the families of sailors killed by Japanese bombs. I will never forget my interview with an old German couple who had lost their only son, nor their quiet dignity as they explained to me that they represented the old-fashioned kind of German who had gone out of style in their home country.

Meanwhile, I had been classified 3A for the draft, which meant that I would be called for military service after the pool of unmarried men, and now fathers of families, ran out. My father was a strong believer in the military tradition begun in my family so conspicuously by my grandfather. He had sent me to civilian military training camp during my first summer vacation in college and induced me to follow this up by joining the Massachusetts National Guard, from which I resigned after graduation, since I was leaving the state for good. Had I been able to keep this up, I would have been qualified as an army officer at the time of Pearl Harbor, and now I sought some way to qualify, thinking that this training, plus my language abilities, would be sufficient. I soon found out that at the time no one was accepted for officer training in any of the services without 20/20 vision — and alas, I had inherited my grandfather's nearsightedness instead of my parents' perfect vision.

Yet it was clearly time for me to get into the war. We said good-bye to San Francisco in the spring of 1942, a couple of months after Tweed's birth, and returned to Cold Spring Harbor, where my father was eager to help.

PART TWO

Barbary

The Journey Begins

THROUGH A FRIEND OF FATHER'S I met Colonel Truman Smith, who had distinguished himself in his service as military attaché in Berlin and was now a major figure in army intelligence, or G2. Colonel Smith told my father that there was a new program to bring into the army people with special abilities, such as mine in the language field, which bypassed the stiffer requirements of the army's physical examination. Only a few days later, after a routine examination in an army camp on Long Island, I received orders to report to Washington to join the Army Specialist Corps, a civilian organization to be partially integrated into the army for special assignments.

My orders appointed me a Grade 7 civilian, with a salary of $2,600 a year and a "relative rank" of second lieutenant. While I was to wear a uniform with plastic — not metal — insignia and was "subject to military law," the orders stated: "This appointment does not confer any military status, and you will at no time exercise command outside the Army Specialist Corps." The orders concluded with the words "Appointments made for duties involving light physical exertion."

At the old Munitions Building in central Washington, now demolished, which housed the War Department, I was brought through an enormous room to Colonel Smith, a tall, distinguished-looking, white-haired man who received me benevolently. First he brought me briefly into the office of the G2 (intelligence chief) of the army, General Hayes Kroner. Next, I was taken to Colonel Smith's deputy, Colonel Percy

Black, and then to a desk marked Prisoner of War Interrogation.

There I was introduced to two officers I had met before in the company of my parents, Major Bernard "Bunny" Carter, former director of Morgan Bank in Paris — I had visited his country house on that European trip — and Major Charles Codman, from Mother's Boston. I knew they were former residents of France, and this in itself might have given me a clue as to what was afoot, but no clues were needed. The walls above their desks were plastered with maps of Morocco with red marks under coastal towns such as Casablanca, Mazagan, Agadir, and Mogador. Fortunately, I was not a German spy, for no one seeing these maps could have failed to realize that these men were planning something in North Africa.

On September 1, 1942, I was bundled off to the newly created intelligence school at Camp Ritchie, Maryland, and crammed into a khaki uniform. I was assigned to Company B, First Training Battalion, and led to a row of tents reverberating with multilingual sounds, for the army had assembled here, through whatever system it had in that pre-computer age, a number of extraordinary individuals with varied backgrounds. Among my tentmates were two army privates who were Ph.D.'s. One, a German-Jewish refugee, was a musician and orchestra conductor, and another had been in my Greek class with Professor Bowra and was teaching Greek at Harvard.

We were divided up according to specialty, some of them technical, such as photo interpretation and reconnaissance. I was assigned to a French prisoner of war interrogation unit. A similar contingent had been organized for some of the German-speakers, who formed the majority of the camp's population, while others were assigned to a special battalion trained to act like a German army unit, uniforms and all, to play the role of the enemy in field exercises.

Also in the camp was a small group of Arab-Americans. A couple of them were officers, but most were enlisted men drawn from all sorts of backgrounds. Of course, I was immediately drawn to them and was sorry to find out that my Arabic was of little use, as they were almost all Syrian or Lebanese Christians who did not know the classical language. The only exception was a single Moslem, a certain Mohammed Siblini, with whom I established an immediate rapport.

Shortly after my arrival, I was called in to see the deputy commander of the camp, Lieutenant Colonel Walter A. Buck. In grave tones he informed me that he knew what I was there for, as did two others at the post. He instructed me mysteriously not to breathe a word about anything I might know. Presumably, he realized that I had seen too much in my visit to G2. A few days later the G2 himself, General Kroner, appeared and gave us a thundering speech about killing godless Huns and filthy Japs!

All day long we were given intensive instruction, largely about the German army and air force. This included their ranks, insignia, and general organization, and we were given some training in aircraft profiles as well. Other training was in technical matters such as radio, telephones, and various additional communication equipment. We also had a few sessions of close combat training — the only part that sticks with me was the instruction and demonstration of how to kick an opponent in the "family jewels."

We had a number of night field exercises in which we were divided into two-man teams. My teammate was usually Vernon "Dick" Walters, a newly minted second lieutenant, later General Walters, deputy chief of the CIA, ambassador at large, and the United States ambassador to the United Nations. At the time, however, his rank was the same as mine, though he had at least the experience of officer candidate training, which made him an invaluable companion. Although we worked hard, it was actually fun to be with like-minded people during that beautiful autumn in the foothills of the Blue Ridge.

This idyll, however, was to end abruptly. Although the course was supposed to last until the end of October, one evening at the beginning of the month we were summoned and told to pack for sudden departure, leaving our footlockers behind. The camp was sealed and all phones disconnected. Late in the night we were assembled and loaded into trucks, not before some of us had at least enjoyed a few last-minute drinks at the officers' club. We then started off to an unknown destination. I can remember only that one of my truckmates was Lieutenant Walters and we enjoyed ourselves singing as many songs as we could in assorted languages.

After a few hours' ride we were dumped in the gymnasium of a military installation, which, we learned in the morning, was

Fort Meyer, just outside Washington, where we were issued field uniforms, complete with steel helmets, and organized into interrogation teams. I headed a team of six, of whom one turned out to be Mohammed Siblini — this, although my Specialist Corps appointment stated that I was not to exercise command over army personnel! None of my team — in fact, nobody in Camp Ritchie — belonged to the Army Specialist Corps or had ever heard of it.

After a couple of days our interrogation teams were trucked off to Camp Pickett, somewhere in the middle of Virginia. On arrival, we found ourselves injected into the Third Infantry Division, which has a long and honorable history. Our disparate, militarily unprofessional group was clearly not welcome, as was made apparent to us by the deputy commanding general of the division, who called us into his presence.

"Well," he said, "you boys may be specialists, but now you'll have to be field soldiers; we are a field outfit. I don't know about this prisoner of war interrogation business — we aren't going to be much on taking prisoners — I guess you'll have to go out and take them yourselves!"

We had a miserable time during our ten days' assignment at Camp Pickett. It rained off and on every day, and we spent much of our time slogging through the mud. My team members lived in tents, getting wet all the time, and did lots of KP. At least I lived in an army barracks.

Each team was assigned to a regiment, and the G2 of mine, the Thirtieth Infantry, had no orders on our disposal, so he broke up our team and assigned us each to a different battalion. After a few days all the officers of our regiment were summoned to a hall where an officer, standing in front of a blackboard, pointed out the principal features of the unidentified coast on which we were destined to land. His pointer resting on a promontory on the coast, he said, "Here's the fort, which is our main target. Note the little river just below — and then this line of beach. Our three battalions will land here, along the beach, with a detachment landing on the north side of the fort, here, to take the target from the rear."

There was some speculation afterward about the mission of that detachment, and at a subsequent briefing we were unconvincingly told that we should not call it a suicide squad — as, of course, we did.

A couple of members of my team were slated to land in the first wave with the assault battalions. I was in the fourth wave, along with the G2, which was to land exactly four minutes after the first wave, assigned to clear our landing space.

Here was I, still a civilian appointed only for duties involving "light physical exertion," about to participate in the first few minutes of an assault landing. I realized that I was hardly prepared for this, as I had neglected to take the one essential bit of training available. Climbing up and down rope ladders had seemed rather pointless to me at the time.

Toward the end of our stay the whole camp was assembled in a stadium to hear a rousing speech by the man who was to lead our task force, General George Patton, in his cavalry officer uniform. It was meant to prepare us for participation in the opening campaign of a great crusade, but the weather was gloomy and I think most of us were feeling less inspired than impelled by a gigantic force to an unknown destiny. On October 22, we found ourselves on a train headed for Baltimore, and then loaded on an army transport in the harbor.

I was assigned to a room in the hold fitted with bunks soon to be filled by half a dozen previously unknown second lieutenants, who became fast friends during the next couple of weeks. I was especially popular as I had brought along a bottle of whiskey and rationed out "short snorts" to several of them as long as it lasted.

By evening we were at sea, pushing our way through Baltimore Harbor, and the next morning, when we climbed on deck, we were startled by the unforgettable panorama in the ocean surrounding us. We were in the midst of a convoy of some thirty-odd transports, with at least as many more destroyers encircling us. Beyond them were three cruisers and, looming on the horizon, three huge battleships — a great gray fleet in the middle of the ocean. It reminded me of a painting that used to hang over my father's desk, of the Great White Fleet my grandfather sent around the world.

We were clearly headed east, and I felt no confidence that the enemy would fail to figure out our destination. As it turned out, we initially began pointing in the direction of Dakar for deception purposes, and apparently the enemy was indeed deceived.

We could only assume that we were under observation by

enemy submarines, and no fewer than seven alerts were called during our two-and-a-half-week voyage when we would rush onto the deck and stand in our life jackets. I was not much worried about the submarines, in view of the strength and depth of our fleet, especially since the autumn sea was very rough and I thought that this would make it more difficult for the submarines to attack us. I was not encouraged, though, when a Canadian in our group told me, "High seas don't bother submarines — in my last trip a few weeks ago they torpedoed half the ships on my convoy way north of here, where the weather's much worse. And the last convoy from the States before this one really caught it from long-range bombers."

Apart from this, the voyage was relatively pleasant, at least for us officers, in our not uncomfortable cabins. The enlisted men, however, were miserably stashed in the lower reaches of the ship, and many were seasick in rough weather.

I spent much of the day on deck studying Arabic and getting to know some of my future comrades. I was particularly glad to find Bunny Carter again, especially since he turned out to be a fellow member of the Army Specialist Corps, the only other one, apparently, in the task force. In the middle of the voyage we read in the daily news bulletin that the Army Specialist Corps had been abolished. We both assumed — correctly, as it proved — that we would be absorbed into the U.S. Army, although we were not officially so informed for many weeks.

Despite our long confinement on the ship, the morale of both officers and men appeared to be high. Everyone was confident that our troops were going to clean up the enemy in nothing flat. The men spent a lot of time cleaning their guns and sharpening their bayonets. Only a few more imaginative souls worried about the possibility of death or dismemberment; most seemed eager to fight and felt if they did things right, they would *be* all right. I often heard the phrase "A good soldier is not one who dies for his country but who makes the enemy die for his."

A few days after our departure we learned that we were a part of Operation Torch, and various speculations on our landing place were dispelled by an announcement on the loudspeaker on November 3 in the name of task force commander General Patton: "We are on our way to . . . northwest Africa . . . to capture a beachhead . . . Casablanca. We may be opposed by a limited number of Germans. It is not known whether the French army will contest our landing. . . . The eyes of the world are watching us."

We were now briefed on Morocco, and my new friend and team member Mohammed Siblini turned out to be a real asset. After I had told my commanding officer about his background, he was asked to give a number of lectures, both in the Command Room to exalted staff officers and to the enlisted men in the hold, about Arabs, Moslems, and their ways. I also spent a lot of time with him practicing my written and spoken Arabic.

On November 7, we were told that we were approaching the coast of Morocco, and our convoy slowed down and took its position off the coast. To this day I don't understand how we could have escaped enemy attention. We were told that we would be disembarking shortly after midnight, and like all the others, I was filled with apprehension about what lay ahead. I felt I was in no shape to meet my fate, as I had a terrible cold (which was completely wiped out by events in the next twenty-four hours).

We were given a fine steak dinner, which naturally reminded us of the last meal of a person about to be executed. We all wrote letters to our wives and families, and many carried such letters on them to be found in case they were killed. One of my roommates said to me, "If you survive this landing, you have got a good chance of getting through the whole war." He also tried to get me to come to the church services being held that evening, but I refused in spite of a strong inclination, thinking that the hymns and prayers would only make me more depressed. "You better come, Archie," he said, "you may get it tonight."

I was sitting brooding about this when Siblini came into my cabin with good news. They had originally assigned him to go ashore with the so-called suicide battalion that had the difficult mission of attempting to take the fort from behind. The danger of its position was increased by the fact that if the fort's searchlights were turned on, the navy guns were to start shelling the battery and American troops might be hit along with the rest. Siblini's job was to advance ahead of our troops, calling on the battery to surrender in his best Arabic. The fact that the battery was composed exclusively of Frenchmen provided me with the rationale for trying, without any luck, to get him out of this assignment.

Now Siblini, with a broad grin on his face, said, "I am going with *you*, Lieutenant." I could not understand the reason for this sudden shift of assignment, having importuned every high-ranking officer in the last few days to no avail. It turned out that the major in our assault boat could find nobody to carry his dispatch case, and Siblini was strong!

We assembled on the upper deck and were divided into ten waves. Each of us was very heavily loaded, in accordance with the wishes of General Patton. In addition to large knapsacks full of equipment, and our weapons — in my case a tommy gun — we each had a gas mask, a canteen, three days' C rations, and two hundred rounds of .45-caliber ammunition, with which we staggered around the deck for an hour or two in the dark, looking like parodies of Christmas trees. With many shouts, much creaking and banging, the landing craft were lowered from the decks, oblong iron masses with ramps on the back, each armed with a machine gun.

Wave by wave the men began to climb down the mesh ropes hanging from the sides of the deck, and now I realized the importance of that training on climbing ropes I had skipped, as I saw my comrades clambering over the rail and down the net into the waiting boats. The only light was a thin beam from a lighthouse in the distance marking the site of the enemy fort. Finally, it came time for our wave to descend. Somehow I groped my way down the net with that huge load on my back. I heard later that several soldiers dropped into the sea and sank like stones to the bottom.

Once on the boat, we collapsed in various corners of it, lying like sardines close together or even on top of each other. On top of me was a man with a walkie-talkie. It was a bright night with many stars, and it was hard to believe that nobody saw us. We soon became very wet with spray and then very cold. We had to stuff the muzzles of our guns with paper to keep them dry while we waited. As we were circling around beside the ship, each wave was supposed to form a separate circle, and there was much yelling and cursing as the various boats tried to find their waves.

We never did find the rest of our wave or even our battalion commander. After several false starts, we heard a commanding voice shouting, "All right, let's go, men!" Our boat, along with some others, turned from circling and sped toward the invisible shore. We gritted our teeth and gripped our guns. Now we were allowed to raise our heads from the bottom of the boat and look over the side. Many of us took advantage of this to get seasick in the heavy swell — although they had given us nausea pills, we did not take them for fear we would not be sufficiently alert when we landed.

We were headed for what we supposed was our beach — we could now see a few red lights dimly blinking, placed by an advance reconnaissance team. We were not sure where our beach was, but we sped toward the red blinkers. "Get ready to land," someone shouted through a loudspeaker.

We heard the bottom of our boat scrape as we hit the rocks. Suddenly a huge searchlight went on and seemed to settle on me personally. Our boats fired on it with machine guns, and the French opened up with theirs, followed by their cannon, which could, of course, have blown us right out of the water, but we were so close they could not point them down at us.

Then our navy opened up on the fort with its big guns — a display of fireworks we were too frightened to appreciate. With each boat following its own orders, we wandered up and down the shore, but as it grew light, we decided to land at the first beach we came to. Loaded down as I was, I think I made pretty good time wading to land and rushing to cover in the brush that lined the shore.

Large dunes loomed in front of us. A sergeant looked for the nearest man and found me (I had no insignia) and ordered, "Hey, you, go over that hill and do a reconnaissance!" I did not argue the point. "Don't make a silhouette," he shouted.

From the top of the dune I could see nothing but wrecked barges and GIs running about; the French shore battery was still fighting it out with our navy with not much ammunition to spare for us. I kept going inland, after reporting seeing nothing, no human beings in front. A group of our medics was forming toward the fort on the left when a shell landed among them. All around me officers and men were running, shouting, "Where's the front?"

I found myself on a red dusty road along with Mohammed Siblini. Next to us a recently landed mortar was pumping shells into the French coastal battery. At the far end of the wall was a sort of wigwam made of reeds, near which we could make out some figures walking about with long robes blowing in the wind. We approached to ask them about the main road, where we were scheduled to place our battalion headquarters. There were three of them, all very dark, and wrapped in what looked like old and ragged sheets that may have once been white. As we came near, they flashed us smiles full of white teeth, and one held out his hand and said "Chewing gum." Clearly our boys had already passed this way.

Siblini took a piece of gum out of his pocket and handed it to him, saying, *"Es-salaam aleikum."* Three brown chins dropped and three pairs of black eyes stared at him as he gave the traditional Moslem greeting. A few seconds passed before one recovered enough presence of mind to give the polite answer, *"Wa-aleikum es-salaam!"* Then broke loose a torrent of questions in colloquial Moroccan Arabic: "Are you a Moslem and American too?" "Are there Arabs in America?" "Have you any more chewing gum?" I left him in the fast-growing crowd of admirers to find battalion headquarters.

I moved toward an intersection with another road leading to the interior and found the battalion intelligence chief, who said, "Lieutenant, we will set up our battalion headquarters here. You stay to interrogate any prisoners."

"But Captain," I protested, "this is a crossroads and we were told never to put our headquarters there because of the possibility of bombing."

He replied sarcastically, "Lieutenant, when I want your opinion, I'll ask for it."

Meanwhile, our forward echelons had stopped a train crossing the horizon to the east of us and were leading a number of French and Moroccan soldiers in colorful uniforms toward the road. Soon I was surrounded by some seventy French and Moroccan troops and proceeded to interrogate them. They were mostly very cooperative and glad to see us, though some of the officers maintained a correct standoffish manner. I took down the officers' names and the data they provided in my notebook; I did not take the names of the Moroccan troops but only their numbers, following the example of the French officers, who did not bother to learn their names.

In the middle of this, we were interrupted by the sound of approaching planes — I had been right about the crossroads after all — and we all headed for the ditch as they strafed us, ineffectively. As we picked ourselves up from the ditch, I felt a tap on my shoulder. I turned around to face a Moroccan soldier who said politely, *"Voilà vôtre fusil, mon lieutenant,"* and handed me my tommy gun. Of course, he could have wiped us all out!

Finally, the regimental commander came, and established a headquarters in roughly the same area. The fort had been taken — apparently by two of our rare French-speakers, a photographer and a doctor — although there were a number of American casualties. All the waves had landed by the middle of the day, and the boats began to be unloaded in an orderly fashion.

We bivouacked amid the stubble of a wheat field, turning to mud in the drizzle, and were ordered to dig slit trenches. Motivated by the strafing, I got mine dug in about thirty seconds, even though there weren't enough shovels to go around and I had to use my helmet. Then we settled down to eat our C rations — crackers, canned meat or fish, chocolate or dried fruit, three cigarettes, one stick of gum, and sometimes some dextrose tablets — and lay down in our red-mud slit trenches to get what sleep we could.

The following morning we spent nervously hopping in and out of our holes. French planes made a number of attacks, although now our own planes were beginning to appear overhead, and the attacks soon ceased. Our orders were to stay put.

Around noon, however, about thirty hours after our landing, I was told to report to division headquarters in the town of Fedhala, south of us, where they needed a French interrogator-interpreter. Our regular army, drawn largely from the south, had literally no French-speakers. According to the Articles of War, high-ranking officers had to be interrogated by officers of equal rank, and they were beginning to fall into our hands. I had to bum a ride from a Moroccan with a hay wagon to Fedhala, and there made my way to the Miramar — the luxury seaside hotel that had become task force headquarters.

There, to my astonishment, I ran into some of the people I had met in G2: Colonel Black, Charlie Codman, and Bunny Carter, who gave me a warm welcome. They were sitting, somewhat incongruously, having an aperitif at a round table on the hotel terrace. After a brief chat during which they showed

little interest in my interrogation reports, they sent me to the
forward command post on the way to Casablanca to act as
interpreter with the French brass. I was introduced to Colonel
Walter Lauer, the division chief of staff, and the commanding
general of the Third Division, General J. W. Anderson, and
went on with them to a beautiful French colonial house
surrounded by olive groves.

I spent the next night in the house — on the floor, of course,
as I was now the lowest-ranking member of the group. However,
by now we were living in greater style, and grabbed ourselves a
couple of bottles of wine and champagne from the house cellar
before being ordered to desist. This, and oranges and tangerines
from the garden, took away the taste of C rations.

In the course of the next day, November 10, a few French
senior officers were brought in to be interrogated, with my role
being that of interpreter to one of our own senior officers. One
of the French officers was the commander of the local air force,
which had tried to kill me.

In the afternoon General Patton himself appeared and
talked with one or two of the French officers. He was reputed
to speak French, but had to rely on me to interpret for him.

"I used to speak French in the First World War, but it's rusty
now," he said. "You're Archie's son, aren't you? I knew your
father in the last war. How is he?"

He chatted with me for a while and I was surprised to find
him so affable, hardly the crusty tyrant of his reputation. From
the vantage point of my twenty-four years I thought him a nice
old man.

I overheard enough conversation to learn that an attack on
Casablanca was being planned for dawn the next day, but
negotiations for an armistice were already under way. The
French had never been wholehearted in opposing us; the navy
was the most hard-nosed, bitter about its losses when the British
sank the bulk of the fleet in Mers-el-Kebir after the fall of
France. Its new battleship, the *Jean Bart,* had escaped destruction and now sat in Casablanca Harbor. Earlier in the day I
heard it shelling us, followed by the thump of our artillery
silencing it. But the army wanted to call it off. French officers
later told me that they knew the location of our headquarters
but decided not to shell us, for the sake of future good
relations.

During a night of frantic comings and goings, a cease-fire was finally agreed on, with the navy caving in at the last minute. General Patton and the French commander, General Auguste Paul Noguès, resident general of Morocco, met at the Miramar, attended by their respective force commanders, and agreed on peace. I might remark that General Noguès was visibly surprised by the generosity of the terms of the armistice, in view of his actions and those of some of his subordinates at the time of our landing. He was largely responsible for the French military opposition, which had cost hundreds of American and French casualties. On the night of November 8 Resistance leaders, headed by the commanding general of the Casablanca forces, had informed Noguès that an American landing was imminent. He checked with Admiral François Michelier, who told him there was no sign of an American fleet. Then at 4:00 A.M. Fort Blondin called him to report signs of a naval force, and half an hour later reported that their searchlight was being fired on by machine guns (one of them from my boat — and the searchlight had been directed at me!). Noguès promptly arrested the Resistance leaders, and ordered the French military to oppose our landing.

The morning after the cease-fire I was assigned to ride in the jeep with General Patton, as his interpreter, through the streets of Casablanca, crowded with cheering Frenchmen. He was in his traditional finery, complete with white helmet, cavalry riding breeches, and boots, while I wore fatigues still stained with red mud.

Then I sat in as interpreter of negotiations with the French commander of Casablanca, General Raymond Desre; fleet commander Admiral Michelier; and air force chief navy captain Jean de Gail, whom I had interrogated the day before. This was heady stuff for a twenty-four-year-old semi–second lieutenant. I then accompanied the headquarters contingent to the Hotel Anfa, near one of Casablanca's promontories. The best hotel in town, it had been occupied by the German Armistice Commission, which had hastily departed the night of our landing. I found myself in a luxurious room, obviously evacuated in a hurry by its previous occupant, as he left a number of pictures and books behind.

In those days even the most deluxe rooms did not have private bathrooms and the only piece of bathroom equipment in most of them were bidets. Clearly, our American boys did not know the purpose of these objects and made improper use of them. The following day I saw a number of GIs reading a three-page notice on the bulletin board and stood behind to see what it was about. It was written in typical army bureaucratese: The first paragraph stated that there were certain toilet installations in the rooms, the second paragraph, with some circumlocution, said what they were for, and the third paragraph contained a prohibition against using them as toilets. The GIs were expressing their interest and astonishment at this news, and one remarked, "You can say what you like about them Frogs, but they sure do care for their womenfolk!"

Soon my situation was regularized. I became the senior interpreter for the Third Division, working directly with General J. W. Anderson, the division commander; Colonel Lauer, his chief of staff; and any of the other senior officers who needed me. Besides Siblini, I had the services of one or two others fluent in French, and soon we were putting out a daily news bulletin. I also began taking trips around the town and its vicinity with the general, and once he took me to supper with the task force naval commander, Admiral H. K. Hewitt, in the bowels of his flagship, the cruiser *Augusta*. Our meal was abruptly ended by a submarine alert; German subs had attacked and sunk three of our transports off Fedhala a couple of days before.

Our headquarters was in a villa near the Anfa that had also been used by the German military mission. In the beginning its walls were hung with all sorts of German proverbs, including one saying, "What would the Führer say about this?" However, after a couple of days it was decided that headquarters should be moved to Morocco's capital, Rabat. I was dispatched, along with a couple of senior officers, to make the arrangements.

First, we examined the town hall, which was to be our headquarters. On its steps stood a few other structures occupied by vendors and, in particular, a large newsstand whose proprietor was a venerable French lady. The division G3, or operations chief, said to me, "Tell that old bag to get her stall off the steps right away!"

I turned to the lady and explained the necessity for this in very polite French: *"Madame, veuillez-vous bien . . . ,"* etcetera.

The colonel was annoyed. "What's all that you're saying?

Why does it take you so long to tell her a few simple words in French?" — one of his frequent complaints.

Then we went to the mayor to look for a suitable house for General Anderson. The mayor pointed out various locations to us on a wall map of the town. The colonel, examining it, pointed to one location that seemed particularly desirable. The mayor objected, *"Mais la maison est tout petite, tout petite, tout petite."*

The colonel slapped his thigh and said, "That's rich, Lieutenant, make him say that again!"

A third and very important mission was an inspection of the local houses of prostitution, where under the direction of the colonel, I interrogated the madams and inspected the facilities to make sure they came up to GI standards. One house was finally selected, and every afternoon and evening there were long lines of American soldiers waiting outside — the locals referred to it as "chez les Americains"!

Headquarters was then transferred to Rabat, and I found myself comfortably ensconced in Rabat's best hotel, the Balima.

6

The Veiled Medina

I IMMEDIATELY FELL IN LOVE with Rabat, located on a cliff high above a river, the Bou Regreg, flowing around the city into the sea. On the plain across the river lay the white Moorish houses of Rabat's sister city, Salé, once a nest of Andalusian pirates.

The Balima Hotel was on the main avenue, surrounded by pleasant colonial homes leading east from the Arab walled city, called, as everywhere in Morocco, the Medina. This and other Medinas had been declared out-of-bounds, especially since there had been unpleasant consequences when small parties of soldiers had gone on "veil-lifting" expeditions.

Even with the Medina barred to me, there was much to explore in Rabat. Heading west from the Balima, toward the banks of the Bou Regreg, I found the Tour Hassan, a ruined rose-colored minaret standing alone in a field of bricks, all that was left of a twelfth-century mosque. Farther on at the northwest corner of the wall of the old city, overlooking the mouth of the river, were the gardens of the Casbah of the Oudaias, perfumed with jasmine and orange blossoms.

East of the hotel, the boulevard led past the Mechouar, the royal palace, with the Black Guards standing sentry. A mile or so outside the city lay the Chellah, site of the tombs of past sultans, and the then only partly excavated ruins of the Roman town of Sala (which gave its name to Salé).

It was a virgin ruin, unlike the exposed and somewhat stripped Pompeii I had visited on my parents' Mediterranean cruise, and strangely haunted. There were no personal traces of these nameless and forgotten Roman frontiersmen among the fallen stones, rank with weeds, almost deserted — the Moors of today are indifferent to those ancient colonists, preoccupied as they are by their modern successors.

Many of Rabat's people still have Andalusian features. They then all wore native dress, the Moslems in their white woolen burnooses, the traditional Berber cloak with its hood drawn in cold or rain over their red fezzes, the Jews in black fezzes and often black garments as well. They walked on yellow leather *baboushes,* heelless slippers. The city women were completely covered, although the country women went barefaced, exposing their tattooed cheeks and chins.

In the beginning, I had very little contact with the local Arab population, but soon met some of the French, glad to make the acquaintance of those few army officers who knew that language. While many of the local French, both military and civilian, leaned toward the Vichy government and were not particularly friendly, others were extremely glad to see us and most hospitable.

My first brush with Arab society came thanks to my mother's friend from Boston, Major Charles Codman, who through French friends had been invited to an Arab home. First impressions are often the most vivid, and here are mine of the gastronomic delights of Morocco, from notes I made at the time:

> It was a magnificent place, walls and ceilings with mosaic and tiles covered with gold, beautiful carpets and rugs, exquisite filigree woodwork of the usual Moorish style.
>
> We sat around little circular tables, propped up on cushions. Our host, a wealthy merchant, did nothing but supervise our entertainment. He did not join us at the table, or in the conversation after dinner except incidentally. I was worried that he wasn't enjoying himself much — but the French officer told me he was gratifying his sense of hospitality, as well as enjoying hearing what we were saying — Arabs are great onlookers.
>
> As for the dinner — whew! With towels on our laps, and armed with nothing but our fingers, we went to it. First the soup — we did have spoons for that — in huge cups of thin china. Then an immense pie, approximately two feet across, with a plate of sugar in the middle. Under the pastry — light

and full of spicy flavor — was lots of pigeon meat and eggs. It's called "bastela," originally a Spanish Moslem dish, "pastilla." Thinking that this was probably the piece de resistance, I dug right in. But no, after this was taken away, a lamb roasted whole appeared. My mouth waters when I think of it. We tore that to pieces, leaving minimum room for dessert, only to face a huge turkey. I think I did away with my share of that — but when three chickens smothered in dates came along, I couldn't do justice to it. And THEN came the couscous — a complicated dish with steamed cracked wheat as a base, topped with succulent lamb and vegetables. You're supposed to roll it up in a ball and pop it in your mouth — using only the right hand of course, but this takes lots of practice, and because we were Europeans they let us have some spoons. I hardly touched mine, needless to say — and when the huge dish of tangerines and oranges appeared, I only got down two tangerines.

After dinner came the great rite of tea making and drinking — which our host, who had an excellent sense of the dramatic, performed in beautiful style. About five huge silver and brass containers were brought out. The tea leaves were green, looking fresh off the bush. They were placed in a pot, and then our host plumped in several large lumps of sugar, followed by mint and amber. We drank it in tall glasses edged with gold. It was really a drink of the gods — like none I have ever tasted.

However, I owed my real introduction to Moroccan society to Mohammed Siblini. Soon after his arrival with me in Rabat, he got permission to enter the Medina to say his prayers in the mosque. When he arrived at the house of worship in his U.S. Army uniform, he found a motley crowd of Arabs in front of the entrance, barring his way. "No! No!" they cried, plucking at his sleeve. "Moslem house! No go in!"

Siblini shouldered his way through and entered the mosque before the astonished followers of the True Religion could stop him. The crowd was about to surge in and drag him out by force, when they saw him take off his shoes, perform his ablutions, and start to pray like a good Moslem.

Half the city was waiting when Siblini came out. They watched him with wide eyes, silent except for an occasional expression of amazement, such as *"Ma sha'Allah!"* and *"Shei ajib!"* They followed him, pointing him out to others on the street, to the gate of the native quarters. There he was met by a magnificent turbaned figure, one of the principal men of the town, who greeted him warmly and kissed him on both cheeks, saying that he had been a guest of the Siblinis during his pilgrimage to Mecca, many years before (Mohammed himself had been on the pilgrimage with his family at the age of sixteen, and so was able to use and exploit the title of Hajj in Morocco). He asked Mohammed to meet the leaders of the Moslem community at a banquet in his home.

After that Friday, Hajj Mohammed Siblini became a familiar figure at Arab gatherings, and no feast was considered a success unless he was among the guests. As a result, Siblini began taking me to the homes of some of his Arab friends in the Medina, to which I now had a military pass.

A frequent host of ours was a genial local carpet manufacturer, Bou Helal. It was at his house that I met many of the Moroccans who were later to become friends. Most of these were of the younger generation, but one of Bou Helal's own vintage was a sort of holy man, Sherif el Guennouni, a tall figure with a great black beard and turban right out of a Persian miniature. He originally came from the Islands of Kerkenna, off the coast of Tunisia.

Once we were invited to a sort of Moslem salon, known as the *Raudha,* or garden, where we met a number of notables of the old school, with grave bearded faces. After lunch one of them entertained the company with two very long stories, heard in silence — with no laughter, for old-fashioned Moslems followed the Prophet in disapproving of it. In only one house where we were entertained was wine served, which was much criticized by other Moslems of our acquaintance. The house of one Arab we met was never visited by his friends because he had married a French woman, at the time not acceptable.

At the Bou Helal house I made a number of younger friends, most of them from well-known local families such as Bargash, of the family of the local Pasha (the name is derived from the Portuguese Vargas), and the Hadji family of Salé. My most important contact, however, turned out to be a young man from a relatively obscure family, Mehdi Ben Barka, a brilliant conversationalist who despite his youth seemed often to be the dominant figure at these gatherings. One day, after a dinner with Bou Helal, he took me aside and said that with the agreement of some "friends," he wished to tell me a bit about Moroccan nationalism. He was a member of the Istiqlal (Independence) party, then the principal nationalist party, banned by the French authorities. He spent considerable time with me at various places, such as the gardens of the Oudaias, educating me about French colonialism in Morocco. He knew of my fascination with the old ways of the Arab world, still followed by most of the Moroccans I met. But he was impatient with them. He believed that Moroccans should move into the twentieth century and leave behind these stifling ancient customs. He condemned many of the older generation for their subservience to the French — they were termed by the nationalists *Beni Oui Oui*.

Our dinners were always followed by lively conversations, which provided an excellent elementary education on Moslem North Africa. Two evenings stand out in my memory. Once a man from Fez with classical features and a white turban gave a beautiful recital of one of the great chapters of the Koran (Surat al-Rahman); I can still remember snatches of it. Another time a professional wit, hired for the after-dinner entertainment, appeared — a white-bearded oldster with a disorderly turban and skin the color of old wood. He had a large repertoire of jokes. The guests, obviously well acquainted with him, played a game, asking him for a proverb starting with various letters of the alphabet. He would immediately reply with one, generally off-color, followed by gales of laughter. He improvised songs and imitated accents of different sectors of the population, sometimes pretending to talk on the telephone — and even did a takeoff of chanting of the Holy Koran.

Meanwhile, my status with the U.S. military began to change for the better, which was especially welcome, as I was finding my job as interpreter excruciatingly boring — mostly dealing with minor housekeeping matters. I used my abundant free time to continue my education in classical Arabic and also began to write reports on the political situation of the Moslem population.

Colonel Lauer, the chief of staff, took a personal interest in my reports, and when he was promoted to brigadier general and transferred to Washington to take over as deputy commander of the Ninety-third Division, the famous "Colored

Division," he said he would take them with him to show to "higher authority." Still, I felt I had talents that were not being used. I wanted to get into counterintelligence or some type of G2 work — but hadn't been able to find an opening.

My fortunes began to improve on December 20, when I got a phone call from Charlie Codman, calling from Colonel Lauer's office. "Archie, we've got a new job for you. We're hereby assigning you to take over the censorship of the Arabic broadcasts on Radio Maroc — by force if necessary!" He added the last in a joking tone, and I later found out that the previous evening Colonel Black got a call from Allied Force Headquarters saying that General Patton was ordered to take over the radio station "by force if necessary." Someone had heard anti-Allied statements made on Radio Maroc's French broadcasts.

I went a few blocks up the boulevard, past the train station, to the large Post and Telegraph Building near the royal palace, and reported to Lieutenant Fernand Auberjonois. His had been the golden voice broadcasting to Morocco from shipboard at the time of the landing. He was a fair-haired Swiss-American a few years older than I with a slight accent and a European formality of manner who was to be an understanding mentor of mine for the next month or so.

He had a couple of French-speaking Office of War Information (OWI) officers to assist him monitoring the French broadcasts, while I was the sole Arabic speaker. For six weeks I made my way to the radio station early every morning and sat there intermittently until late at night, listening to the periodic Arab news broadcasts.

Though my new assignment was better than interpreting at headquarters, the novelty of it soon palled. However, I did enjoy the occasional recital of the Koran and an Andalusian orchestra with ten instruments, including my old friend Prince Muhiddin's oud, to the beat of drums, tambourines, hand clapping, and the clanking of little brass discs attached to the fingers. The music is traditional, never written, and dates from twelfth-century Moslem Spain.

Since I only had to monitor scheduled news broadcasts, I was able to devote some time to other activities — cultivating the local Arab community, spending the lunch and dinner hours with them, and distilling the information gleaned from these contacts into reports.

Initially these dealt almost entirely with the effects of Axis propaganda. Radio broadcasts in Arabic by the Germans were extensively listened to and believed. The Arab population had originally hoped for a German victory, although they had been discouraged by the fact that the Germans had left them in the hands of the Vichy French. Hitler himself was admired and the Arabs referred to him as *Ammi el-Hajj* — "my uncle, the Hajj"! They knew that he was backing the Arabs against the Jews in Palestine, and they still had hopes that he might win the war. Siblini and I worked among our circle of friends to counter this propaganda.

However, more and more my reports began to take into account the views expressed to me by the nationalists, their aspirations to throw off French rule, and their complaints that the French were taking advantage of the American presence to reinforce their position. They naturally referred a good deal to declarations by the American president and others about the "Fight for Freedom." These contacts did not pass unnoticed by the French authorities with whom I had established liaison on propaganda matters.

Under the resident general, General Noguès, the authority for "native affairs" was the Direction des Affaires Politiques, known by its initials, DAP. My Moroccan friends disparagingly called it *Diab* — jackals! After calling on the DAP chief, Colonel Augustin Guillaume, a rather forbidding, not overfriendly career army officer who had spent most of his life in Morocco, I was passed on to more junior officers.

I confined my discussions with them to questions of German propaganda aimed at the Arabs, listening with a display of proper attention to their comments on native affairs in general. I probably deluded myself in thinking that the French looked on me as they looked on most of our troops, as *des grands enfants* — amiable and naive children — and were not overly concerned about me.

My reports were read with interest not only by my U.S. military seniors (even by General Eisenhower, I was told) but also by the OWI officials with whom I was working. A few days after I was assigned to the radio station there appeared in Rabat the chief of a new psychological warfare division being established in Morocco, the well-known former war correspondent Jay Allen. In the course of his career as a correspondent, Allen had been twice captured by the Germans and on one of these occasions had the nerve to request an interview with Rommel. (I don't think it was granted.) He was a large genial man with a round face decorated with double chins, set in motion by rapid-fire conversation. He apparently took to me, because he asked my division to transfer me to his command and for bureaucratic reasons was promptly turned down. Nonetheless, I felt Jay Allen was somebody I would really like to work for, and he also appeared to be sympathetic to my contacts with the local Moslem population.

Just at this moment, Colonel Lauer told me that General Anderson was about to propose that I become his aide. General Anderson was destined for a larger command, and the colonel told me that this would be an interesting assignment that would put me in the middle of great military events. However, he was fair enough to point out the disadvantages of this kind of position — at that time military aides were known as "dog rubbers." I could not see myself tied to one individual as his personal retainer. I was at a loss as to how to turn this down, but the issue was forced on me when I was ordered to accompany the general on a trip to Fez.

We made the trip together by car, a journey I have enjoyed many times since. At that time the road was not as attractive as it now is, with orchards of fruit trees breaking the monotony of the countryside. It was then completely what a French writer termed the *morne bled* — the mournful, arid countryside relieved only here and there by a cluster of characteristic conical straw wigwams. Fez itself was unspoiled by the throngs of tourists who infest it today, an Andalusian city then clothed in the fog of winter. We stayed at the fabled Palais Jamai, the former home of a grand vizier, which is still one of Fez's top hotels.

When the time was ripe, I broached all my problems with General Anderson, a kind and understanding man, who granted all of my requests — not to be his aide, to transfer to Jay Allen's psychological warfare division, and to bring Siblini with me. He even undertook to make Siblini an officer.

My friend Hajj Mohammed Siblini had been cutting quite a swathe among Rabat's Moslem population, and his fame reached the ears of the sultan of Morocco himself, Sidi Mohammed ben Yusuf, acknowledged as Commander of the Faithful by seven million Moslem subjects.

The sultan had heard that Siblini, an American Moslem, had had an excellent religious education and was expert in the difficult and complicated art of chanting the Koran. The sultan's greatest joy was listening to the chanting of the sacred book, and he would sit up most of the night listening to broadcasts of the Koran from all parts of the world. The best readers come from the Middle East, and whenever the sultan heard of a man particularly gifted in the art, he would write and invite him to live at his court. But so far, in spite of the tempting rewards offered by the Commander of the Faithful, none had accepted the invitation. Morocco was too far from home.

So Siblini was a windfall. The sultan hastily dispatched an emissary to the American headquarters inviting Siblini to read in the royal mosque the following Friday.

The sultan's weekly procession to the mosque was a pageant from another age, still essentially observed today. Preceded by his famous Black Guards in their brilliant scarlet uniforms, and followed by white-robed notables mounted on spirited steeds, the sultan rode in a red carriage with gilt mountings, drawn by six white horses. As the band played, the people prostrated themselves on the ground, crying in unison, "Allah make our lord victorious!"

But on the appointed day Siblini was too nervous to enjoy the show. His knees were shaking as he entered the mosque behind the Commander of the Faithful. After the sultan had settled back in his screened stall and the murmur of voices was hushed, Siblini mounted the pulpit, cleared his throat, and started to read. He had chosen the chapter that tells of Joseph and his brethren — a favorite since the days of Mohammed. He read in a deep, resonant voice, with great depth of feeling.

The congregation was enthralled. They seemed almost to be hearing the voice of the Prophet himself, as he first recited the majestic words to the wild pagan tribesmen of Arabia, bringing them the enlightenment of the religion of the One God. Some of the listeners even burst into tears from an excess of emotion.

Even such a connoisseur as the sultan was impressed. He usually rapped with his cane as a stop signal after ten minutes or so, but he let Siblini go on for three quarters of an hour.

News travels fast in Morocco. That night everyone in Rabat knew of Siblini's success, and by the following evening all

Morocco had heard the story. Soon Moslems from all over the country were writing the authorities asking that Siblini be allowed to read the Koran regularly over the radio. Their request was willingly granted, and it wasn't long before Siblini's Sunday night Koran broadcasts were listened to by every Moslem who could get near a radio.

As a result of this, I did not hold on to Siblini more than a couple of months. Allied Force Headquarters in Algiers also heard about him. The very effective Axis Arabic-language broadcasts had twice referred to Siblini in disparaging terms, drawing attention to his usefulness to our side. Allied Force Headquarters transferred Siblini to Algiers, so he could be used by the AFHQ radio directly.

Shortly after my return from Fez, now sworn in as a second lieutenant in the Army of the United States, I was ordered back to Casablanca to work directly for Jay Allen's tiny office there.

Psyching the Moors

IT TOOK ABOUT A MONTH for me to transfer from Rabat to the psychological warfare shop in Casablanca, as I was tied to my job as a radio censor. I made good use of the time solidifying relationships with the local Arabs in Rabat, for I knew that in Casablanca the Arab community was then of little significance. One evening my acquaintance Mehdi Ben Barka took me to witness a historic event: the return of the Istiqlal party leader Hadj Ahmed Balafrege from years of exile. As we approached his house on the outskirts of Rabat, we could hear the women of his household celebrating with their traditional *yu-yu* chanting.

In addition to my political friends I got to know a couple of Moroccans my own age who were not married and faced the difficulties of finding a bride. The problem was twofold; first, one could not see the prospective bride in person. Negotiations were started about such weddings between the two families, and the biggest problem for the bridegroom was getting a description of the bride he was never permitted to see. Certain old women served as intermediaries in this task, bringing back full descriptions to the suitor. Sometimes they were corrupted by the bride's family to describe her charms in enthusiastic terms, and on the wedding night the bridegroom might suffer an unpleasant surprise. Second, the wedding was extremely expensive, and the bridegroom had to come up with a considerable dowry.

I had a particularly interesting conversation with one of these young friends about the sexual mores of Moroccan youth, which I quote from notes made at the time.

> They are precluded from marriage until they are in their thirties and can get enough money together — and yet can see no women outside their own households. They can't get away with visiting "maisons de plaisir" — everyone would know. The only unrelated women they see are the family servants — and if there happens to be one of the right age things are bound to happen if the father hasn't already appropriated her. If they go around with European women they are ostracized. And if they marry them — as have a few — they are also snubbed. He told me that the fact that he dated some European girls caused a great scandal in the family and the matter was even brought before the Pasha. His cousin had married a European and nobody received them until she died and he married again.
>
> Thus he said many turn to homosexuality — which often starts in the Koranic schools and causes many problems in Moslem society, not the least of which is venereal disease. He also spoke against bigamy — his father had two wives, a cause of constant quarreling — and the evils of the concubinage system. Little girls are sent from the country to work as servants — they grow up — and one day the master of the house notices one.
>
> "Children result, who are somewhat looked down upon — more conflicts. The young people are very much for monogamy, and even among the generation of my father's age you find few in the North, at least, with more than one wife.
>
> "It really is a terrible thing if anybody whistles or sings in the street — or smokes. Nobody can smoke in the presence of his elders. And as for the women — what a life! And how can you expect a Moslem to grow up completely rational when he is brought up in his most formative years by an illiterate mother, amid a household of tribal servants and black slaves."

A big event occurred during this period — the visit of President Roosevelt. I attended a great parade outside the forest of Mamourah where the president addressed the troops. (Afterward, I had some awkward moments with my Arab friends, who inquired how my meeting with my uncle Franklin had gone — Siblini had told them all that the president was my uncle.) To the dismay of the French authorities, not only was the sultan with his oldest son (now King Hassan) invited to dine with the president and Prime Minister Churchill, at the Hotel Anfa, in Casablanca, but they had a private conversation afterward. The sultan spoke frankly of his problems with the French and Moroccan aspirations for independence, and the president indicated that there would be "changes" after the war. This vague remark encouraged the sultan to think that FDR understood the Moroccan situation and intended to do something about it.

Meanwhile Mehdi had been making sure that at least FDR's lowly cousin gained some understanding. He arranged for me to meet with the key leaders of the Istiqlal party, Hadj Ahmed Balafrege, Hadj Omar ben Abd-al-Jalil, and Mohammed el-Yazidi. I wrote reports based on these conversations, which naturally contained information unfavorable to the French authorities. A constant irritant to the Moroccan population was the fact that the lion's share of food and clothing supplies from the United States, in this sternly rationed country suffering from the deprivations of war, went to the French population. The French did not hesitate to make disparaging comments about the Americans to their Moroccan contacts, pointing out that our presence was temporary, and our influence transient. They tried to prevent, as much as possible, American contact with the "natives."

My DAP liaison officers now began to ask leading questions, which showed their awareness of my contacts, and they made their unhappiness about them known to the U.S. military. Had I not been on the point of leaving Rabat for Casablanca, to take a more circumscribed assignment, they might have made more of an issue of it.

In early February 1943 I was finally transferred and found myself in a room full of mirrors in a luxury hotel on Casablanca's main street, leading to the port. It had formerly been occupied by the Italian Armistice Commission, and the officer who had lived in my room had left a number of steamy love letters behind, many of them to the wife of a member of the German Armistice Commission who had visited him two nights a week. According to a French police officer, all his other nights were occupied by visits from various ladies, and as the officer said, he had "a satisfactory love life."

The street outside was a tree-lined avenue — I could have imagined myself in a French provincial city except for the picturesque street scene, with constant processions of French and Moroccan soldiers in their variegated uniforms and Arabs from every walk of life with their horses and carts. The Arab city began on the other side of the avenue, with a few food stands in front fragrant with roasting lamb.

The office was almost next door, and was like nothing I have worked in before or since. My contemporary description:

> This is inhabited by a number of people of varied nationalities, all rushing around madly in a very small space. Jay [Allen] has a special inner sanctum, inhabited only by himself, and there are always 16 people waiting outside to see him. I have not yet managed to find a desk for myself, as every one of our rooms is chuck full, so I generally perch in the antechamber to the great man's reception hall, either discussing things with some Arab or other, or laboriously working my way through an Arabic newspaper, or dictating a report to somebody else's secretary, if I can ever find one.
>
> The head secretary goes around trying to find out who will be there for lunch. All but six say they will be out. At 12:30 one of the offices is cleared, a table set, and some hors d'oeuvres put on it by our chef — a real artist who looks like Napoleon — but nobody comes. Then around 1:15 twenty people appear, some of whom are guests — all of whom have violent political opinions. Many have spent most of their time either in a concentration camp or escaping from one.

Shortly after my arrival we had a visit from Bob Sherwood, the playwright. He was a friend of Franklin Roosevelt's, and FDR had entrusted him with the leadership of the Office of War Information. A Lincolnesque figure, wearing a moustache instead of the beard, he had the mournful look of someone who carried the woes of the world on his shoulders. Upon his arrival everyone added their own cares to his load.

I remember a long night session at the hotel when I explained to him the situation of the Arabs in North Africa. He took these world problems so seriously, he said, that sometimes when traveling on a plane over the sea, he felt like jumping out and ending it all.

In Casablanca I met two officers of the Office of Strategic Services (OSS), both of whom shared my views on the Arab situation in Morocco. One was Captain Frank Holcomb, stationed in Tangier. There he served as one of the vice-consuls who had been posted in various parts of North Africa under an agreement signed in Vichy between General Maxime Weygand and the counselor of the U.S. Embassy there, Robert Murphy. This provided for the assignment of U.S. consular officers to different North African cities to oversee the distribution of American relief supplies. Murphy then proceeded to Algiers to supervise them in carrying out this task, as well as the secret one of working with the French Resistance under General Henri Giraud to prepare for an Allied landing.

The other OSS member, also from Tangier, was the great anthropologist Carlton Coon, who had made the Rif tribe his particular specialty. These were my first friends in the organization that, in a later form, was to be a large part of my life.

Another officer, who was not actually in any of our programs but attached to the air force, was Vincent "Jimmy" Sheean, once a great news reporter and by then a well-known author. He had been with Abd-el-Krim during the rebellion of his Rif tribe against the Spaniards in 1925, and recounted this experience in his book *Personal History.* In it he alludes to "the murderousness, hypocrisy and stupidity of imperialism." He was a tall man with a ruddy, merry Irish face. We became boon companions and located a restaurant in Casablanca that became our favorite evening hangout. It was owned by Papa Gouin, a southern Frenchman who, despite all the rationing problems, managed to put together savory meals. He occasionally enlivened our dinners by coming out from the kitchen and singing Provençal songs. We would all then join in with songs of our own.

A number of war correspondents made our office their home during their stays in Casablanca. One of them was a bearded Russian, a *Life* photographer of enormous energy and charm, Eliot Elisofon. One day I arranged with Elisofon to accompany him to a photographic session with the sultan. He had heard about me by reputation, and we had a few words together in which he clearly showed that he was aware of my contacts with the nationalists and approved of them.

The reader might be excused for assuming that during my stay in Morocco my contacts were exclusively Moslem, but this was decidedly not the case. It is true that I did not find my liaison contacts *sympathique,* and had no social relations with them. The Vichy French military establishment never liked us, but it was U.S. policy to work with and through them.

Bob Murphy had established working contacts with the French authorities in advance of the Operation Torch landing — and they understood that at some point such an operation would take place, although they were not tipped off before it actually happened. The commander in chief of the Vichy French armed forces, Admiral Jean-François Darlan, was in Algiers on December 1 and arranged the armistice, remaining in charge of the French North African government until his assassination on December 24 by a young royalist who was executed the following day. General Giraud, who had worked with Murphy organizing resistance before the landing, succeeded Darlan, and had to depend on the forces he inherited.

Some of my French friends were military but not part of the establishment. A Spahi warrant officer liked me enough to invite me a couple of times to his home to enjoy a meal with his pretty wife and well-behaved child. A young French officer assigned to Radio Maroc, André Gérard, became a friend and invited me to meet some of his acquaintances. The wife of a French army officer, a prisoner in Germany, asked me for bridge a couple of times. I even went to a Corsican wedding. But no, I never had any romantic involvement with any of the attractive French women I ran into during my stay in Morocco. I had made a pact with my wife before I left home that I would not go out alone with a woman, and held myself to that promise.

In fact, I was tempted to break it only by a constant attraction in my office, my secretary. Her name was Miriam; she was from a Tunisian Jewish family, educated in England, with a flawless English accent. She had classic Sephardi features and the appealing femininity common to many Near Eastern women. Besides this she was efficient, intelligent, and had the sense of humor so necessary in our work. It was through her that I met the only Moslem woman I talked with during my stay in Morocco. One day Miriam brought into our office a small bundled-up figure who pulled off her headgear to show a girlish Moroccan face. "This is my friend Fatima," Miriam said. "She's in school here preparing to go to college. She has to do it in secret as her family would punish or even disown her if they found out."

"Yes," said Fatima, "I pretend to be Jewish at school. *Hélas,* it is impossible today in Morocco for a Moslem woman to get an education. But I plan to go on to college and hope some day things will change here with *le progrès.*" I admired her spunk and hope she fulfilled her dreams.

Miriam never introduced me to her family, although several times she spoke of doing so — perhaps she would have had I been single and Jewish. But she did arrange for me to meet some of her Jewish friends. However, my work did not involve Jewish questions, which were the responsibility of others. One was Captain Paul "Piggy" Warburg, a member of that old New York Jewish family, who was yet another friend of my father's and was with Colonel Percy Black. Robert Schuman of our own Psychological Warfare Branch office, himself a French Jew by origin, followed Jewish affairs. Many French and other European Jews sought us out and told us unpleasant stories about the French authorities, most of whom were thoroughly anti-Semitic.

I did, however, make one interesting Jewish contact on my own. Maurice Vanikoff, a Frenchman of Russian-Jewish origin, managed the Centre de Documentation et de Vigilance, which attempted to coordinate the activities of all Jewish organizations in France and the colonies opposing racism and anti-Semitism. Vanikoff and his associates assembled a mass of documentary material to support their activities, and after the fall of France, Vanikoff fled with the whole of this material, amounting to five tons, to Morocco. He hid this for a time in his apartment, but the French police got wind of it, confiscated it, and held it under guard. Vanikoff persuaded them to return it, claiming it concerned only educational matters, and opened up just the right crate to disarm their suspicions. Since much of the documentation contained material that would have compromised anti-Fascists still in Europe, he mixed up all the papers so that only he could reassemble them.

After our landing, he had tried without success to interest American military authorities in his library, and had now turned to the Gaullists, who had suggested he join a group in Algiers.

I thought his material would be of great value to our Psychological Warfare Branch, as it contained much information that could be used in anti-Nazi propaganda. Also, I thought he could produce features on Nazi racial theories and antireligious views, and on German colonization in Africa.

I suggested that PWB maintain liaison with him if he went to Algiers, or even hire him outright, but don't know if these suggestions were acted upon — or what became of Vanikoff, since I was transferred shortly after delivering my report.

In the course of my assignment to Casablanca I had occasion to make a couple of trips to Marrakesh. I had the best kind of introduction to that town from one of my Arab friends in Rabat, Sherif el Guennouni. With a charming smile half-hidden in his beard, he combined an almost childlike simplicity with great native sagacity. He had a kind heart and his deep religious faith encompassed tolerance and love of humankind. He used to stay awake at night worrying about the terrible things happening to his brothers — "all humanity throughout the world."

A true citizen of the world, he had no real home of his own, and a couple of times he came to stay with me in my hotel in Casablanca. He had traveled much in the Middle East on ships and caravans. He was once attacked in Arabia and still bore saber scars from a Bedouin he eventually killed (and probably felt sorry about).

The Sherif did, however, have a wife and eight children, all of whom lived with one of the great lords of Marrakesh, the Caid el-Ayadi. The Caid's great rival was the famous Glaoui, the Pasha of Marrakesh. The Caid was chief of the Arab tribe of Rahamna, which occupied the territory immediately north of Marrakesh, and the Sherif brought me a number of times to the Caid's palace near that city.

I saw quite a bit of the Caid, a large dignified figure with a white beard to match his white robe. Although in repose his face was reserved and stern, he had a sense of humor that allowed him to break out into an occasional smile. Yet from his features I could see the craftiness and cruelty that were part of his nature. He had often looked on impassively as a captured enemy begged for mercy, then calmly ordered his execution. One enemy, at least, had managed to lop off a couple of the Caid's fingers first.

In winter of 1943, shortly after General Mark Clark arrived in Morocco to organize the army that was to invade Sicily and Italy later in the year, the Caid el-Ayadi staged a "fantasia" for him in Rahamna tribal territory by the Casablanca-Marrakesh road. As an invited guest of the Caid, I witnessed the great spectacle, at that time still in its traditional form: tribesmen armed with old flintlocks charging down on us, firing into the air with wild battle cries, their white robes flying behind them framing their dark bearded faces.

I remember two very different visits to Marrakesh itself. The first was in spring, in the company of my friend the Sherif. The road south from Casablanca was flanked by fields green with wheat sprouts, and sprinkled with flowers of every kind — some yellow, some blue morning glories, but mostly red poppies scattered over the plains and hills like dandelions on a suburban lawn. As we went south the wheat fields gradually gave way to pastures filled with sheep, goats, and many cattle that lethargically stood in the middle of the road until they were chased away by frantic little boys with sticks and stones.

Just this side of Marrakesh the son of the Caid el-Ayadi intercepted us for lunch à la Omar Khayyam — under a few shade trees, in the middle of sun-baked fields, carpets were spread, with cushions arranged around a small table. Black slaves appeared with large, flat baskets covered with pointed leather hats. They lifted the hats one by one to reveal a large roast lamb, then pigeon pie, chickens in several succulent styles, and ending with the usual flourish of couscous, followed by fruit.

After lunch we drove on to the city, entering directly into the *souq,* or market, outside its walls. Here are my first impressions, written immediately after our visit:

> Its streets are narrow, tortuous and dark — covered with reeds. They are lined with tiny shops — like five-foot-square boxes stuck together and raised above the ground. Their inside walls are covered with fine cloth, leather goods or brass. The owner squats cross-legged in the middle, patiently waiting until God sends him a customer — if such is His will. He may be leaning his bearded face in his hand, or reading his accounts, or poring over a book of Traditions of the Prophet, or the Koran, which he intones, rocking gently from side to side.
>
> Every shop in each particular street sells the same thing — streets of brass workers, melodious with the sound of the small brass hammers; the leather merchants, the weavers — where

little boys stand in front of the shops holding two long strands of string in their hands, while the owner weaves — or the smiths, where boys work on goatskin bellows, while the smith hammers the red-hot iron.

The street itself is like an anthill that has been opened by a shovel. There are donkeys, lots of them, heavily loaded, usually with grain, each followed by a man with a stick crying "balak" — watch out — to which warning nobody pays the least attention. We hear a brass bell, rung by a water-carrier, a "black Moor" from the Wadi Dra', with a hairy waterskin bulging over his shoulder. He clicks a couple of brass cups in his right hand, occasionally bending to ladle out the precious liquid at the summons of passers-by. A few Jews pass in the procession, their little black fezzes perched on the back of their heads, distinguishing them from the red-fezzed Moslems. Masses of lower-class women crowd by, shapeless in their layers of garments, while their high-born sisters peer down on you stealthily from the lattices of their cloistered bowers. Many children of all shades, thin, ragged, pluck at our sleeves, begging. Professional beggars, too, sit against the wall and chant over and over, in the same tune, "One franc for the love of Abd-el-Qadir, the servant of God" — or any other saint.

Every other person we came across greeted the Sherif like a long lost brother. "La bas aleik? Kull shi be kheir? Anta bi kheir? Al-hamdu lillah!"* etc., going on interminably until one of the parties became exhausted!

About 90% are barefoot, while the remainder have yellow babouches or slippers — how these stay on the feet is one of the eternal mysteries. We passed by the meat souq where I have never seen anything so fantastic in the way of flies! Then we went to the baboush street. It was so packed with Arabs that we had to squeeze our way through them. Most of them were engaged in walking solemnly up and down carrying large piles of babouches, while others bargained in furious voices in the middle.

It was a relief to emerge from the souq to the great square of the city, the Jama'a al-F'na, framed on the opposite side by the crenellated red walls of the city. First we had to thread our way through a mass of squalid mat huts. We passed a native

---

* "Is all well with you? Is everything all right? Are you all right? Praise God!"

doctor — who sat in front of a decaying animal skull or two, an old horn, and some very wicked-looking powders — I saw him sell a bit of decayed flesh off the skull. The open space of the square was filled with people gathered around various performers. These included a snakecharmer and his men, from the religious brotherhood of the Aissaua in the Sahara; card-manipulators; a ballad singer from the mountains, accompanying himself on a two-stringed instrument — monotonous beyond belief; a primeval drama, in which the actors are a man and a boy — the latter always bright as a button; and dancers from the hills — always male homosexuals — with mincing steps.

Later on in the evening I whispered to the Sherif, "What about the Koran you promised to lend me — and the wine." For I had asked if he couldn't find some wine for the three-and-a-half-hour trip back home. As it was Sunday he had to send two people with connections with bootleggers in the Mellah, the Jewish Quarter.

The Sherif said, "Wait," putting his finger to his lips and we drove out with him to a lonely part of the country, with the Caid's son following. There they presented us with the wine, hidden in a basket of straw, and the Sherif gave me the Koran, carefully wrapped in paper — for the Caid would have disapproved of his giving a Koran to an unbeliever — and also to save it from contamination. He was very worried about the latter — was terrified I might put the Koran next to the wine, and insisted on seeing just where I put it, so as to be sure it didn't rest on the floor. "You don't understand now," he said, "but you will after you have studied it." (An Arab will never leave a piece of Arabic writing lying on the ground, in case it contains the names of God and his Prophets.)

The other visit was in the company of Jimmy Sheean, when we were invited to stay at the Villa Taylor, where Roosevelt and Churchill spent a weekend during the Casablanca Conference. It belonged to an American lady living in the States who had lent it to Kenneth Pendar — one of Bob Murphy's vice-consuls. Pendar had been asked by prominent residents of Marrakesh to make the villa available for a party for Josephine Baker, the noted black American singer and dancer who was a refugee in Morocco from Nazi-occupied France.

She was a striking figure, tall and coffee-colored. Fed up with second-class citizenry in the United States, she had gone to Paris to triumph in dance acts that made her famous — she was known as the Banana Lady for the three bunches of bananas strategically placed to hide her charms. I had met her before in Casablanca and found her indeed a warm, attractive human being. I was especially pleased to see that she wrote of me in her memoirs, in connection with that fantastic evening in that dreamlike villa.

It was a motley party, Moroccans of every hue, a few French, American officers, and some war correspondents. Josephine Baker, in a red dress, was a proper star — very Parisian, but still showing that she had not forgotten her roots, especially with her throaty laugh. Native boy and girl dancers alternated on the floor. Emboldened by the generous flow of wine and hard liquor, some black American officers, flouting local custom, coaxed giggling dancing girls to try Western-style, cheek to cheek. Some of the less dignified Moslems joined both in the drinking and the even more sacriligious ballroom dancing, their robes flying shamelessly behind them.

Many of the Arabs were very dark — Marrakesh is the northernmost of the "desert ports" of the Sahara and much black blood from its southern border flows in the veins of those on its northern edge. I recall a couple of them sitting with me and Josephine, saying they understood black Americans because *"Nous aussi sommes gens de couleur."*

Recovering from the party the next day, Jimmy and I were given a tour of this beautiful villa, a tasteful blend of European and Moorish. Its large reception room on the ground floor was embellished with carved cedarwood and its six-story tower in the same red-ocher plaster as the walls of Marrakesh the Red. We looked out over the great square, already clouded with reddish dust to match the long walls that bordered it. The ancient minaret of the Koutoubia rose from its midst, the twin of the Tour Hassan — and the snowy Atlas Mountains framed the panorama. A month before, Winston Churchill had fallen in love with this view, called for his paints, and recorded it for posterity.

Back in Casablanca, I had one of my last dinners at Papa Gouin's with Jimmy Sheean. He was ecstatic because he had just received a copy of his new book along with good reviews and a clipping from "The Suppressed Desires Department" of a movie magazine in which Betty Grable said her suppressed desire was to have a date with Sheean, "who could tell her about so many interesting things, places and people."

It was not long after my last visit to Marrakesh that I received orders transferring me to Allied Force Headquarters in Algiers; after a brief period there I would be going on to Tunis. By then I was beginning to tire of Morocco, where I felt I had little more to contribute. I had written a monumental report on our propaganda and political position in the Arab world. In this I pushed two major proposals — one, that we establish a higher educational facility in Morocco (where education for the Arabs was limited) similar to the American universities in Cairo, Beirut, and Istanbul; two, that we provide some special accommodation for the Moslem pilgrimage to Mecca, which had been interrupted by the war.

I saw that U.S. interests in the Arab world lay farther east, and was glad at least to be heading in that direction. I was much stimulated by a meeting in mid-April with the British minister to Morocco, Hugh Stonehewer-Bird. He had previously been consul general in Jidda, Saudi Arabia, and this "remarkable old fellow," as I termed him then, spoke of his admiration for another remarkable old fellow, King Ibn Saud, whose picture I had clipped from a newspaper at Groton almost ten years before.

On June 8, 1943, I was on my way for a brief temporary duty in Algeria, en route to Tunis.

8

The Maghreb from West to East

IN MY MANY TRIPS crisscrossing North Africa, I had plenty of time to ponder the history of these lands — and indulge in another of my hobbies, anthropology. As I gazed at the crowds I passed on the roads and in the souqs, I often observed how North Africa's past was reflected in the varied faces of its people.

They are largely descended from ethnic groups that have inhabited the region since the Stone Age, despite invasions from Europe and Asia and the importation of thousands of slaves. Though some originated in Europe, the dominant strains come from the Middle East, speaking languages distantly related to the Semitic group that includes Hebrew and Arabic. These developed into the various dialects of Berber, a word derived from the Arabic term for barbarian.

Racially, the North Africans were originally a mixture of Middle East and European types, many of the latter fair-haired and blue-eyed. The Egyptians depict some of the Libyans on their tomb monuments with blond hair; although this type has disappeared from Libya, it is still reflected in a proportion of fair-haired and blue-eyed individuals among the mountains of eastern Algeria and in the Rif Mountains of northernmost Morocco.

The Romans who occupied the northern strip of Morocco, the province of Mauritania, left no permanent imprint on the Berbers, whom they called Mauri (Moors). When the Arabs took over the area at the end of the seventh century A.D., these

Moors furnished most of the troops for the Moslem conquest of what became "Moorish" Spain. While Arabs and their language eventually dominated North Africa, most of the population is of Berber origin, and more than 50 percent of Moroccans still speak a Berber mother tongue.

The Sahara was a racial barrier between the Berbers and the black population of West Africa until late Roman times, when the camel was introduced among the tribes. These people developed into camel nomads who roamed the Sahara and started a slave trade between black and Berber Africa that lasted until the last century.

Later rulers sometimes found it useful to enlist blacks into their armies when they could not trust their fellow tribesmen. The best-known example of this was Sultan Moulay Ismail, who enlisted an army composed entirely of blacks recruited throughout Morocco. Ismail was the son of a black slave mother, and actually promoted the mixture of races by forced intermarriage. While this policy was not continued by his successors, the tradition of a black army survived. The Sultan Moulay Hafid, when he needed an army at the beginning of this century, invited all the members of a black religious fraternity, the Genaoua (the Guineans), to his palace for a celebration — and forcibly converted them into soldiers. Their descendants still form the royal Black Guards. Yet despite all these accretions from sub-Saharan Africa, the dominant strain in the population is still Berber.

The Moroccans until recently did not call themselves Arabs or even consider themselves part of the Arab world. In the Arabic language, North Africa and more specifically Morocco are known as the Maghreb, which means simply the West or Place of Sunset. In my day the Moroccans referred to themselves as Maghribis, or simply "the Moslems."

Unlike most of the countries of the Middle East and Africa, Morocco has a long history as a national entity. It was originally founded in Fez by Idris, a descendant of the Prophet, some twelve hundred years ago.

The present Alawite dynasty of Morocco was established in 1666 by a family reputedly descended from the Prophet, and named after his son-in-law, Ali. One of its first rulers was the powerful and ruthless Sultan Moulay Ismail, founder of the black army. Unfortunately, many of his successors were comparatively weak men, ruled by their viziers. As there is no primogeniture in the Moslem world, each time a sultan died, his sons and brothers fought for the succession. In 1912 one of these domestic battles resulted in the French occupation of Fez under General Louis Lyautey, who established a protectorate over Morocco. The sultan of the time, Moulay Hafid, abdicated in favor of his brother, Moulay Yusuf, grandfather of the present king (the title of king was considered to be a pagan one by Moslems until recent times, and was only reintroduced into the Arab world after World War I).

The sultan became a French puppet. The French controlled Morocco's foreign relations, and most of its internal government, through Moroccan governmental and tribal officials. Except for continued resistance by scattered tribes in the southern Atlas Mountains, there was no real resistance to foreign rule until the rebellion led by Abd-el-Krim, which began in the extreme northern zone administered by Spain. In 1920, when the insurrection spread south into the French zone, and tribal forces began to threaten Fez itself, the French military became involved. The rebellion was finally suppressed in 1926.

Abd-el-Krim surrendered and was exiled, but his gallant effort triggered the foundation of the Moroccan nationalist movement. The movement was formed separately by Ahmed Balafrege in Rabat and Allal al-Fassi in Fez, and eventually merged to form the Istiqlal party. Despite efforts by the French administration to contain the Istiqlal movement, it spread and in 1937 was able to mount large-scale demonstrations, as a result of which both of its principal leaders were exiled.

The party was decapitated, but among its younger members who came to the fore was my friend Mehdi Ben Barka, a brilliant young university graduate who taught mathematics to Moulay Yusuf's successor, the young sultan Mohammed the Fifth.

Mohammed the Fifth was not the complaisant ruler the French authorities assumed they would be dealing with. He was in close touch with the Istiqlal at the time I met him, and Mehdi spoke of him with reverence. Inspired by his talk with Franklin Roosevelt, the sultan thought that the United States would favor Moroccan independence at the end of the war. In this he was to be disappointed, but with the support of his own people, after being deposed and exiled, he finally led Morocco to independence in 1956.

Mehdi Ben Barka became president of the National Consultative Assembly that year. However, the Istiqlal party split between a conservative wing, loyal to the monarchy, and a more nationalist socialist wing under Ben Barka, who broke off from the party and founded his own in 1961. Later in the year he prudently went into exile in France, where he continued to lead the principal opposition to the monarchy. While he was still part of the radical wing of Istiqlal, he was invited to the United States on a leadership grant and I saw him briefly at breakfast at my house in Georgetown. He was much changed from the person I knew, now self-important and arrogant. I had considered informing him of my CIA connections, but I decided against it and he clearly thought I was merely a junior officer in the State Department. We had no substantive discussions and I saw him no more; I was distressed to learn of his murder in France later in the decade. The question of exactly who was responsible in this murky affair has never been established.

Unlike Morocco, Algiers has had no national existence — in fact, the country did not even have a name until the French occupation in 1830, being lumped by the Arabs in the general area of the Maghreb and by the Europeans as part of the Barbary Coast. The Romans, following the Carthaginians, occupied all the arable north of the country, which, with Tunisia, became the breadbasket of the western Roman Empire. The Arabs not only overran the whole country but imposed their language on most of it, although there are sizable Berber-speaking populations in the eastern provinces and the arid south. Black Africa contributed less to their gene pool than in Morocco, and Europe more, not only from the Roman Empire and Moslem Andalusia, but also from European slaves and renegades brought in at the time of the corsairs.

The Algerians were simply a mass of warring tribes, occasionally tamed by rulers from Morocco or Tunisia, until the Ottoman Turks took over the coastal area in the sixteenth century. But it was not really unified until the French landed in 1830 and over the next twenty-five years subjugated the entire country.

With Algeria, unlike the later cases of Morocco and Tunisia, there was no question of a protectorate. It was annexed to

France and organized into three departments of the French state. Many of the best lands were parceled out to the French colonists — the *colons* — and immigrants from southern France, Spain, Italy, and Malta formed a large part of the urban population. Although all the Europeans were or became French citizens, very few Algerians were offered this privilege, with the exception of the large Jewish population, all of whom were enfranchised in 1870.

The Moslems, deprived of their elite, became a nation of peasants, bazaar merchants, and an urban proletariat. There were only a few large landowners and businessmen. Arab culture suffered, and French became the language of all educated people — even the Algerian nationalists used it as their first language. The Algerians, at the time of my visit, never called themselves Arabs, although the French referred to them as such. Among themselves, and in conversations with me, they were always "the Moslems."

Conversing with Algerians, I soon discovered that they had become denationalized. Their own heritage had been replaced by an inferior, secondhand European one. It is hardly surprising that the Algerian character reflected this. They struck me as a dour, sullen people, without the assurance and openness of their Moroccan and Tunisian neighbors.

These barriers of distrust were quickly breached for me, and Algerians of today are losing the inhibitions inherited from their gloomy past. They have found a proud national identity of their own, tempered by the terrible war of independence that blazed from the ashes of World War II.

But at the time *"Alger la Blanche"* — the famed White City of Algeria — made a poor impression on me: "dirty, squalid, and horrible," I pronounced it.

I was sharing a room with my old boss Ferny Auberjonois and was immediately contacted by Mohammed Siblini, now broadcasting the Koran for Radio Algiers. That same day I had my first contact with the great world outside in a lunch with the head of my section — also attended by Randolph Churchill, son of Winston. I found him brilliant but flippant, cynical, and amusing. He had little use for the Arabs, whom he termed an inferior race, and was very much in favor of the Zionist experiment in Palestine.

Shortly after this lunch, I was brought by my chief to meet

the great Robert Murphy, now in charge of all civilian matters in Allied Force Headquarters. I was extremely pleased to find out that he knew all about me and had read my reports, including the monumental one about Morocco that I had composed before my departure. A big Irish-looking fellow radiating charm, he handed me a scotch — liquid gold in these parts — and asked Socratic questions about how I would react to various situations. My outpouring of ideas, such as providing U.S. support for the pilgrimage to Mecca or founding an American university in North Africa, brought only cryptic, noncommittal responses.

While in Algiers I was fortunate enough to meet a person I had long admired, Dr. É. Lévi-Provençal, a professor of the Sorbonne and the University of Algiers, a great scholar of Moslem Spain whose comprehensive works on this subject — alas, not completed before his death — are still a major source for scholars. We were engaged in related work, as he was active in French propaganda aimed at the Arab population. We took to each other at once, and I am sorry that we never had occasion to meet again.

I met few Moslems during my week-long visit to Algiers, which with its large French military and civilian presence was not hospitable to Algerian nationalists. These were now head-quartered in the city of Constantine, where I stopped en route to my ultimate assignment in Tunis. I reported in to John Whittaker, the chief of Psychological Warfare Branch in Con-stantine. My mission: to look into the question of Axis propa-ganda among the Arabs in that very political city. The Psychological Warfare Branch was a joint operation in which the British were major participants, and from this point on my superiors were British — my first experience in working with our cousins across the Atlantic with whom I was to be linked during many future years.

At first I was enchanted with Constantine — then known as Shangri-La to the Anglo-Saxon soldiery — perched on the edge of a deep ravine. My room gave me a fine view down into its depths. But disillusion set in when I approached the impressive ruins of a Roman bridge and aqueduct spanning the chasm and found the view ruined by huge signs and arrows pointing to a "Pont Romain." What remained of Constantine's beauty was completely destroyed for me when I descended to

the bottom of the gorge. The fetid atmosphere stank horribly
of the sewage of the city, dumped in by disgusting fat pipes
attached to the sheer wall of the cliff.

This squalid town was the center of Algerian nationalism and
the home of Ferhat Abbas, the leading figure of the moderate
majority of that movement. Its radical element was led by
Messali Hadj, who had become a Communist after marrying a
French Communist party member in Paris. There he led an
organization of Algerian workers called Étoile Nord-Africaine,
which he eventually developed into the leftist nationalist Parti
Populaire Algérien. Messali was under house arrest in Algiers,
and the PPA was dormant, leaving the field to Ferhat Abbas.

Ferhat had started his political career as president of the
Muslim Students Association at Algiers University. In those
days he was French-oriented (French remained his first language) and was not yet really an Algerian nationalist. All he and
his followers sought was Moslem equality with the French in
French Algeria — and even infuriated the nationalists by declaring that "the Algerian nation does not exist." He welcomed
the initiative of Léon Blum's Popular Front government in
France to institute reforms in Algeria, which died aborning.
Ferhat and like-minded intellectuals in Algeria looked not to
the Arab nationalism of the East for inspiration, nor to Islam,
as did the religious leaders who had once dominated the
nationalist movement, but to the secular European-oriented
nationalism of Mustafa Kemal of Turkey. Also many, perhaps
most, of the Arabo-Berbers of Algeria still wished to identify
with the French. But every initiative by the French government
to grant citizenship, even when limited to those qualified by
French education or military service, was thwarted by the *colons*.

One of the few Moslems I met in Algiers was a certain Dr.
Benjelloul, from Constantine, who had heard about me and
offered to introduce me to Ferhat Abbas in Constantine. The
day after my arrival there he met me at my hotel and led me to
meet Ferhat at the little pharmacy he owned. A tallish man with
a lean, moustached face, he greeted me with a warm smile and
introduced me to a small circle gathered to meet me. These
included two brothers-in-law and a nephew, Alaoua Abbas,
who acted as his special assistant.

Ferhat led me and his group into the back office of his scruffy
pharmacy — I noted a picture of Stalin in a prominent position

on the desk — and we had an animated day-long conversation about the problems of Algeria. I was struck by their openness and fearlessness. Unlike the Moroccans, they seemed to be observing no security precautions with regard to the French authorities. In this they were probably ill-advised, as subsequent events were to prove.

We discussed the problem of Axis propaganda in the Constantine area, the official reason for my visit. A number of anti-Allied leaflets had appeared and we had a considerable debate as to their authorship. My interlocutors quite naturally tended to believe that French Fascists were responsible, but there was also a theory that they were produced by Messali Hadj's PPA. Ferhat and his friends said that many Algerians had been pleased about German victories, since they originally hoped that the Germans would help them against the French colonialists, but this did not prove to be the case. Ferhat's group had advised their friends to avoid pro-German activity, saying that the Germans were going to lose the war and there was nothing to hope for in that direction. They were all impressed by the Atlantic Charter, and asked whether it applied only to Europe. They felt that so far Allied policies had simply strengthened the hold of the French. As was the case in Morocco, one of their greatest concerns was the distribution of American supplies of food and clothing, which benefited mainly the French population.

Ferhat and the others were not particularly impressed with what they had seen of the British, who seemed indifferent to them. American soldiers were generally liked, "especially for their generosity to children." The human qualities of our GIs, despite occasional lapses, generally left a good impression in North Africa.

Concerning the French they were ambivalent. They expressed hatred and scorn for the French of Algeria, whom they considered to be a different breed from those of France, yet they admired French civilization. (I was struck by how de-Arabized they were — they hardly used the Arabic language even among themselves.) I asked them if they would accept Algeria's being a part of France and become Frenchmen, were they to be given equal privileges as French citizens. They said that this was not their stated goal, which was an autonomous Algeria, but should full French citizenship be offered, they would "forget the past and be content, but that won't happen — the *colons* will stop it." They recounted how in 1936 they had been considering with Léon Blum's Popular Front government a plan for enfranchisement of at least the educated Moslem Algerians but were disillusioned when this was defeated through the efforts of the *colons.*

Now their hopes had been renewed, particularly since the Gaullists had effectively taken power in North Africa at the beginning of the month, fired Governor-General Marcel Peyrouton, and replaced him with General Georges Catroux. Peyrouton, who had earned a bad reputation with the Arabs as resident general of Tunisia, had shown the same inflexible tendencies during the few months of his administration of Algeria, while Catroux had a totally different reputation as a colonial officer in North Africa and more recently in Syria.

They presented me with a manifesto they had submitted to the governor. It summarized the position of the Mouvement Revendicatif, of which Ferhat was the prime mover. They called it their Atlantic Charter. The manifesto began by stating that the Algerian people would not remain indifferent to the problems of the future now being debated as a result of the Anglo-American occupation and the war for justice and liberation. Yet the actions of the Vichy government since the fall of France and of the French in Algeria since the Allied landings had demonstrated that they intended to maintain the separation of Algerian society.

While praising French culture, spiritual values, and the tradition of liberty brought by the French colonization, it listed the evils of repression, exploitation, and confiscation of land in favor of the *colons.* "Today, after 113 years of colonization, there are two Algerias — 700,000 Europeans, plus 130,000 Algerian Jews given French citizenship by the Cremieux Decree of 1870, exercising full sovereignty, and 8,500,000 Arabo-Berbers officially termed 'Native Moslem French subjects' still in a conquered and subordinate status."

The manifesto pointed out that the time had passed since Algerian Moslems would be content with French citizenship; the solution was now Algerian citizenship —

In response to the declaration by President Roosevelt assuring the rights of all peoples, the Algerian people demand an end to

colonization, with self-determination and a constitution providing: Liberty and equality for all without religious or racial
discrimination; Agrarian Reform; Recognition of Arabic as an
official language, co-equal with French; Liberty of the Press and
Assembly; Free education; Freedom of Religion; and Separation
of Church and State.

The manifesto then called for immediate participation by
Moslems in government, freedom for political prisoners, and
fulfillment of its demands now, not promises for postwar times.

Former governor-general Peyrouton had agreed to the appointment of a commission to study the manifesto and make
final recommendations, in which Ferhat's group played a
dominant role. Meanwhile (as I found out later), they had been
in touch with the Gaullists, who had since taken over the
Algerian government. Charles de Gaulle's position was that any
recommendations to be acceptable would have to provide for
continued ties with France. Abbas's group presented a reform
project based on the manifesto to the commission on May 26,
1943, and it was adopted by the commission after my departure,
on June 25.

The document provided for a sovereign Algerian state in
which Europeans and Moslems would be equal under the law.
A constituent assembly would provide a constitution for the
new state after the end of hostilities. Meanwhile the governor-
general's office would be replaced by an Algerian government
with an equal number of European and Moslem ministers. The
document concluded by stating that acceptance of these provi-
sions would result in full participation by Moslems in the war
for humanity, followed by a new dawn after victory.

Both the manifesto and the project based on it assumed the
French population to be a permanent sector of Algerian
society, with both peoples, religions, and languages having
equal status.

How different the future might have been could this dream
have been realized, and Ferhat Abbas and his associates been
partners with the French population in creating a new Algeria.
But it was not to be. Shortly after the reform project was
presented to the French authorities, Ferhat and some of his
associates were placed under house arrest. And the end of the
world war, VE-Day, was marked not by a new dawn for Algeria,

but by a bloody massacre that ended forever the possibility for an Algerian binational state.

In Sétif, about eighty miles west of Constantine, VE-Day celebrations on May 8, 1945, turned into violent nationalist demonstrations by Algerian Moslems demanding democracy and the release of their imprisoned leaders. The police fired on the crowds, who then overwhelmed them and attacked the small European population of the area, killing about one hundred people. But retribution by army troops, navy guns, and air force bombs was deadly, causing perhaps as many as fifteen thousand deaths. This terrible event led, step by cruel step, to the beginning of the revolution on November 1, 1954.

Ferhat, released from house arrest in 1944, was rearrested after Sétif. A more liberal French government again released him, and, still a believer in the French connection, he was elected to the French National Assembly. But it was too late for his brand of moderation. The Front of National Liberation (FLN), a merger of nationalist groups, adopted an increasingly radical position — already Ferhat's nephew, Alaoua Abbas, whom I met in Constantine, had been murdered for collaboration with the French by an FLN mob.

Nevertheless, Ferhat was still respected as one of the original leaders of the movement, and when the FLN formed a provisional government in Tunis in September 1958, Ferhat was made its first prime minister. From that moment on his moderating influence waned as he was thwarted in his efforts for compromise. He was deposed in August of 1960; at the end of the war in 1962 he played no role in the new government, and his humiliation was complete with his expulsion from the FLN the following year for his pro-Western attitude. After passing years of exile in Europe, he was allowed to return to Algiers by the present Algerian president, Chadli Benjedid, to pass the remainder of his life in obscurity.

9

Always a Little Further

I WAS ONLY TOO HAPPY, on June 16, 1943, to leave Constantine and the depressing Algerian scene, where I could see no new dawn coming — only gloomy, stormy weather. But of course that day the hard-burning North African sun blazed overhead as I set off for Tunis across a rolling plain covered with wheat and vines. In our truck we carried leaflets to leave for pilots at airfields along the way to drop over enemy lines in Italy.

Driving on into Tunisia we passed clusters of Roman ruins, some of them remains of fair-sized towns, reminding us that this was once the rich Roman province of Africa, which eventually gave its name to the whole continent. The Arabs, who drove the Romans out at the end of the seventh century A.D. and Arabized most of the population, still called the country Ifriqiyya at the time of my arrival. Halfway to Tunis we stopped off for a time at a Royal Air Force base to drop our pile of leaflets, which I hoped were worth distributing along with the bombs these courageous British airmen risked their lives every night to deliver.

I had seen a number of combat officers, mostly from the British Eighth Army, while in Algiers and Constantine. Now, talking with these RAF officers, I felt guilty that I was not in a combat unit, especially since my father had once more become a war hero.

As recounted earlier, Father, along with his other efforts to shape me according to family tradition, had done his best to get me some military training while I was in college. Strangely enough, one reason I was not a combat officer sprang directly from something he did himself. Before that fateful cruise when we were detained in Nantucket and I fell in love with K.W., I had been slated to attend summer camp with the Massachusetts National Guard. Father really wanted me on that cruise, so he uncharacteristically called on our family doctor and strongly hinted to him that he hoped a physical examination would reveal a problem that would necessitate excusing me from attending the training course.

The doctor's report, stating that I had a systolic heart murmur and should not undergo the physical strain of camp, produced the desired result. I had always thought it slightly fraudulent, but later I discovered — as Father might have known all along — that I did indeed have this heart defect, which was to put me in serious danger more than once in the future. However that may be, this doctor's report changed my life. Without it I probably would not have married K.W., and might indeed have become an infantryman — though clearly lacking the physical and psychological makeup that made my father such a good one.

Father had really been happy to see me involved in the early fighting in North Africa. In getting me into this operation, he had told his friend Colonel Truman Smith that "Archie wants to sniff gunpowder." Of course, the fact is that he himself had a hankering for that gunpowder aroma. He referred to himself as "an old soldier," and looked back on his World War I infantry experience with nostalgia. He always boosted the infantry, deprecating the less dangerous artillery his brother Kermit had joined. He had pulled every string to become an infantryman once again. He succeeded and soon found himself a lieutenant colonel, commanding a battalion of the 162nd Infantry of the Forty-first Division in the Pacific. Sometime in June 1943 news reached me in Algeria that he had been slightly wounded in action in the area of Salamaua, in northeast New Guinea. He was now recovering from this, along with a bout of malaria, and expected to return to action again soon. In the Salamaua campaign, he had been conspicuous in personally leading his troops and drawing Japanese fire in recon- naissance — and had a ridge named after him.

Now my encounter with the RAF led me to ponder all this as

we bumped along the road through the night. I was full of doubt about the real value to the United States of what I was doing, worried about Father, and aware that he really would not approve, or would think that I should be in the infantry. He never could accept the idea that his son should be so different from himself: neither an outdoorsman, a good shot, nor now an infantryman.

Exhaustion soon spared me from further gloomy reflections and I was dozing when I arrived in Tunis in a garage at 2:30 A.M. I lay down, still in a daze, in a pile of hay and soon got back to sleep, despite the swarms of mosquitoes and fleas that fed on me the rest of the night. Waking up with bites and scratches, I found myself looking at the face of Captain Cosgrove, one of my British superiors in Tunis. He stared at me in some dismay as I brushed the straw off my stained and crumpled uniform; he, in contrast, was totally dapper, down to his newly polished brass buttons. "Spruce up," he shouted cheerfully, "we have got to load up to go to the royal palace. The Bey has asked to see you right away!"

Blinking my eyes, I quickly recalled the salient facts about the history of the beys, and how the Bey I was about to see got his job, such as it was. They were the descendants of Levantine corsairs who had taken over the country in the sixteenth century, and, assuming the Turkish title of bey, paid loose allegiance to the Ottoman sultan in Constantinople.

The beys of Tunis were, by and large, not an admirable lot, depending on a mixed bag of ministers, civil servants, and soldiers, mostly of Turkish or Levantine blood, to run the country. The Bey was a typical oriental potentate, complete with slaves, harem, a royal guard, and a courtful of obsequious ministers.

In the early nineteenth century the ruling beys got rid of the Turks and Levantines and tried to bring in European innovations. They abolished slavery and attempted, without lasting success, to create a modern army and apparatus of government. But these actions also led to an increased European presence, which became ever more threatening and ended up with the French and Italians jockeying for control.

The contest was really decided by Otto von Bismarck, who wanted to turn the attention of the French to Africa after their defeat in 1870, hoping to drain off their impetus for revenge against Germany and for recovery of Alsace-Lorraine. The fate of Tunisia was settled at the Congress of Berlin, in 1878, and a financial crisis provided the pretext for French occupation three years later. The French made the Bey sign away all his effective domestic and foreign power in the Treaty of the Bardo, in May 1881. He retained the trappings of power, overseeing a grand vizier, a chief of protocol, and a "minister of the pen," an antiquated title; this official's pen was mainly used to write decrees dictated by the French resident general.

Tunisia became, in effect, a French colony and, as in the case of France's other protectorate, Morocco, quickly received a European population, including the classic *colons,* who acquired some of the best agricultural lands.

While the Tunisians, unlike the Moroccan Berbers, were a peaceful nation of tradesmen and farmers, and bred no revolutionaries like Abd-el-Krim, they were far more sophisticated and better educated than their counterparts to the west — as the French would tell me, *"Ils sont plus évolués."* Thus there was a more fertile field for the growth of modern nationalism, which derived its origin and inspiration from Woodrow Wilson's Fourteen Points at the end of World War I. The new movement coalesced under a religious leader, Sheikh Abd-el-Aziz Thaalebi, and became known as the Destour (Constitution) party. Its ideology was conservative, based on both Islam and Arab nationalism. Its members were mostly derived from the old bourgeois families.

The movement was disrupted by the secular revolution of Mustafa Kemal in Turkey, which provided a different ideal to younger Destourists, mostly of more modest social backgrounds. These elements became more active in exploiting the social discontent of the Tunisian townsmen, and in 1933, the repressive measures of a tough French resident general, the Marcel Peyrouton who later went to Algeria, brought about a split in the Destour.

A young firebrand, Habib Bourguiba, was the moving force behind the Neo-Destour, as the new splinter party was called. An inspiring speaker, with expressive hands and piercing blue eyes, Bourguiba, along with his associates, was promptly exiled by Peyrouton to the southern desert. But Peyrouton went too far in his repression and the French recalled him in 1936. The Popular Front government came to power that same year, and the new liberal governor of Tunisia allowed the Neo-Destour to organize itself effectively under the presidency of Bourguiba, with Salah Ben Youssef, another firebrand of whom we shall hear later, as secretary-general. But, as has been observed by de Tocqueville, among others, it is liberalization, not repression, that opens the way to revolution.

In 1938 bloody riots led to renewed crackdowns, and Bourguiba and company were again imprisoned, this time in France. After the Allied landings in Algeria and Morocco, the Germans occupied the part of France loyal to the Vichy government and liberated Bourguiba. Steering a careful course of neutrality in the war, Bourguiba made his way back to Tunis with his associates, and did his best to restore the Destour (some of whose members had turned to the Germans) to safe neutrality until the Allies arrived.

During this entire period the nominal sovereign had been a liberal reformer, Moncef Bey, who inherited the throne in June 1942. He immediately did away with the absurdities of oriental potentatehood — the ceremonial kissing of the beylical hand was replaced by a democratic handshake. He toured the capital to hear the grievances of his subjects. The Bey had been, in effect, restricted since the 1881 Treaty of the Bardo from touring the provinces, but Moncef Bey did the next best thing by receiving provincial delegations. When the Vichy authorities began making difficulties for Tunisian Jews, Moncef Bey received Jewish delegations and said he would treat them as his country's subjects without distinction, refusing to permit Vichy to force on them such indignities as the wearing of the yellow Star of David.

In August 1942 the Bey sent Marshal Philippe Pétain a list of suggested democratic reforms. While Pétain responded favorably, his attitude was not shared by the French resident general, Admiral Jean-Pierre Esteva, with whom relations became increasingly tense. They deteriorated still further when, at the time of the Allied landings, President Roosevelt asked the Bey's permission for U.S. forces to pass through Tunisia to fight the German army, commanded by Field Marshal Rommel and then entrenched in Tripolitania.

Although the Vichy government had ordered resistance to the Allies, the Bey sent a courteous reply to the president spelling out his desire to keep the war out of Tunisian territory, along with similar letters to Winston Churchill, the king of Italy, and Adolf Hitler. This was, in effect, an act of rebellion, since, according to treaty, foreign policy was controlled by the French.

The Bey's prime minister and cabinet had advised against this show of independence from Vichy. They urged him to follow a policy of resistance to the Allies. Instead, he dismissed them all, replacing them with young nationalist professionals.

Admiral Esteva bided his time. In April 1943 he asked the Bey to give decorations to a number of German and Italian officials. The Bey replied that he would do so provided the admiral gave him assurances that this did not constitute a violation of Tunisian neutrality. The admiral gave the requested assurances, and after three weeks' delay the Bey presented the decorations with the Allies practically at the gates.

This gave the admiral a pretext to portray the Bey as an Axis supporter, and when the Allies, on May 9, actually reached Tunis, the admiral had his revenge. The French had broadcast from Radio Algiers that the Bey had fled to Rome, and the BBC picked up the item. The Bey was actually in his palace at Hammam Lif, east of the capital, and the British were sufficiently convinced of the Bey's complicity with the Axis to take him away briefly from the palace in a jeep to the resident general's office in Tunis. Then they agreed to release him at the request of U.S. vice-consul John Utter. Admiral Esteva, however, demanded his immediate abdication, and when the Bey refused to comply, the French hustled him off on May 14 to the Algerian Sahara.

Although the Bey still refused to abdicate, the French installed a new ruler, Lamine Bey, the most senior available member of the beylical family — an old-fashioned seignorial type who brought back the old court ceremonial, with a powerless and sycophantic cabinet.

All this had happened just one month before my arrival in Tunisia, but I had not felt its impact further west, where everyone — Allies, French settlers, and nationalists — was too preoccupied with their own crises to worry about this one. Hence, I was not prepared for the turmoil among the nationalists awaiting me in Tunis.

*　　*　　*

I was still brushing myself off as I rode with Captain Cosgrove up the hill to the Bey's palace. Waiting for us at the gates was an impressive figure in a magnificent red uniform, with a chestful of decorations. The golden epaulets on his shoulders proclaimed him to be a general or a field marshal. He had a ruddy complexion and huge mustachios, which moved up on his cheeks as he smiled a welcome to me; then he saluted and shook my hand. The troops behind him clicked to attention and trumpets rent the air.

We passed on to be greeted by the chief of protocol, who led us into a small room where Lamine Bey rose from his throne to shake my hand. He was tall and lean, with reddish gray hair and whiskers, which reminded me of a similarly adorned cousin. The protocol chief then introduced me to a half-dozen ministers flanking him. Their titles indicated the restricted fields of their responsibilities; besides the grand vizier, I remember the minister of *habous* (religious bequests) and the minister of the pen.

Overwhelmed by this reception, I was at a loss for words, but the Bey opened the conversation by asking, "How is your father? I hope he is in good health."

Replying to what I thought was a conventional opening, I truthfully responded, "I am afraid that the last news is that he is not well. He is in the hospital now in the South Pacific. He was wounded, though not seriously, and also suffers from malaria. They tell me, though, he will be back in action soon."

The Bey was visibly disturbed. "That's terrible news!" he cried. "Wounded — how can that be?" Turning to his ministers, he demanded, "Why was I not told?"

I then realized that the Bey was under a misapprehension, recalling that FDR's son Elliott, a lieutenant colonel in the air force, was in North Africa. Clearly, the Bey had mistaken me for my cousin. What to do? I could have left things as they were, but I felt I had to tell him the truth.

"I fear, Your Majesty, that there has been some mistake. I am not the son of President Roosevelt, only a cousin. His son Elliott, I believe, is expected here in a few days." Then I quickly added, hoping to save the Bey's dignity and a smidgen of my own, "But I *am* a grandson of President Theodore Roosevelt."

The Bey was crestfallen — my addendum had not really salvaged the situation. His ingrained politeness came to the rescue as we finished our coffee, exchanging a few courtesies before I could withdraw with whatever grace I could muster. Upon our exit, the general and the guard, not yet informed of how the mighty were fallen, gave a salute with a fanfare equal to the one that had greeted our arrival.

There was a sequel to this event. A week later Elliott did indeed appear at the palace and received a duplicate of the welcome I had stolen. Elliott duly expressed his good impressions of Tunisia, mentioning his admiration for the horses he had seen stabled near his billet, and the Bey remarked that these were his own, promising to put one at Elliott's disposal.

Elliott then said he was sorry not to have been able to present the Bey with an appropriate gift. However, he said he would like to present him with a few American cigarettes, which he knew were hard to obtain, and some candies and chocolates for his children. He then gave the Bey a carton of cigarettes, and a large quantity of chocolates and other candies.

Present at the time of the visit was a French liaison officer. The French then spread the story, which found a ready audience among gossip-loving Moslem society, that Elliott had treated the Bey "like a black tribal chieftain" — fishing an open package of cigarettes from one pocket and a bar of chocolate from the other, which he gave to the Bey. The French also at first wanted to veto the horse but later relented; however, they gave the Bey to understand that no more foreign personalities were to be presented at court without consultation with the French residency, and specifically directed that Lieutenant Colonel Roosevelt not be received again.

It was downhill all that day after the high point of the beylical reception. I went on to the second-rate hotel where I was billeted. I gratefully sank into the sheets of the rusty old iron bed, heedless of peeling walls and shoddy furniture, only to be rudely awakened after a few minutes with stings in a dozen places. Throwing off the blankets, I found the bed crawling with ugly black bugs, which left bloodstains as I swatted them angrily. The management was most apologetic, I was soon given another room, but it was an unpromising beginning. From then on matters could only improve, and they did!

Tunisia turned out to have many more surprises for me, most of them pleasant. The people I worked with were stimulating and I took to the Tunisians at once, a gentle people, friendly and charming. The men in the street had a custom of wearing a red hibiscus behind the ear, which proclaimed their benevolence. The educated ones I met soon after my arrival were lively, outgoing Mediterraneans, quite different from the dour Algerians and the self-contained Moroccans. Tunis itself had much to offer. I awoke to the sounds of its souq every morning, a medley of shouts, of hawkers, the raucous tones of bargaining, and the background murmur of ordinary speech. Sometimes I had only time for a quick walk through those markets, but when I had an hour or so, there were the treasures of the Bardo Museum, or the trolley across the lake to Sidi Bou Said, with a glance at some of the then-unexcavated ruins of Carthage.

But I was not there for sightseeing. I had, as in Algeria, introductions to nationalist leaders and decided to begin with the Old Destour party, then fading into history. I started out one day on the trolley to a suburb on the coast to find the man to whom I had been given a letter of introduction, Mohammed Munsif al-Mestiri. Arriving in the village, I was shown to the house of a man who admitted his name was Mestiri, but not Mohammed Munsif. He appeared fearful and at first denied that there was any such person as Mohammed Munsif. I later found out that he was frightened by my uniform, in itself a political commentary. Finally convinced of my benign intention, he admitted he was a cousin of the man I sought and led me to his door.

Mohammed Munsif was a patriarchal figure with the bushy moustache of the older generation of Tunisians. We settled down to chat in a cluttered room opening onto a dusty patio, from which a chicken wandered in to visit us. He knew no French, or did not admit to knowing any, so we talked in Arabic — the Tunisian dialect was closer to the classical language I had learned than those farther west. He spoke of the history of the Destour, how he himself had been inspired by President Wilson's Fourteen Points after World War I, and of his years of exile imposed by the French. He arranged for me to see the founder of the movement, Sheikh Thaalebi, who received me a few days later on a sofa at his home, enormously fat, crippled, and, I think, terminally ill.

After seeing the dying Old Destour and before visiting with the new one, alive and struggling, I reestablished contact with

Hooker Doolittle, the American consul general whom I had first met in Morocco. He is still remembered with affection in Tunisia, where a street is named after him; forty-two years later Habib Bourguiba brought Doolittle's picture to show President Ronald Reagan at the White House during his official visit in June 1985.

Hooker and I took to each other immediately. With his full head of white hair and a matching moustache, he looked like the perfect ambassador, and would have been had Tunisia been independent. He had a keen understanding of Tunisia and was doing his best to educate those in Washington and Algeria who lacked the knowledge or will to accept anything except the official French line.

Doolittle was ably assisted in his task of representing American interests by his charming, motherly Russian wife, and his vice-consul, John Utter. I confided to him the plan I was formulating to wander back and forth among the three countries of the Maghreb, reporting through my own channel the problems of French colonialism common to all, with recommendations for an independent U.S. policy. He thought that I should abandon this project and concentrate on Tunisia, which I was certainly about to do for the time being.

My first item of business was to get in touch with the leaders of the Neo-Destour — the principal ones had been released from their prison and exile in Marseilles and made their way to Tunis via Italy during the German occupation of Tunisia. They had managed throughout this period to maintain the policy of neutrality enunciated by Moncef Bey, but now the French authorities were threatening to close in on them once again.

I was introduced to them by an engaging young activist, Abdelaziz Hassine, active in the performing arts under the name of Slim Driga. Like other Destour activists, he had suffered the rigors of prison in France, including beatings and torture, but was jolly and plump and appeared none the worse for it. He became my political guide in Tunisia, as had Mehdi Ben Barka in Morocco, though politics for him was an avocation — he later devoted himself to his real vocation, producing movies.

Through him I met a number of activists in the Neo-Destour. First, there was Mohammed Badra, director of the Tunisian Chamber of Commerce, who had been private secretary to

Moncef Bey's last prime minister, Mohammed Chenik. He filled me in on all the details of the removal of Moncef Bey, the national hero still steadfastly refusing to abdicate under pressure from his French jailers in the Sahara. I took depositions from Chenik himself and from all concerned with the matter and submitted full reports on it to my office and to Hooker Doolittle for transmittal to Washington.

Another Destourist I met was party secretary-general Salah Ben Youssef, a dynamic activist from the island of Djerba in the far south. His features, half-hidden by thick glasses, were like those of the ancient Egyptians and betrayed his Berber heritage. He poured out his sentiments in a constant stream of rapid, almost violent French, with many gestures, often relieved by a bubbling sense of humor.

I shall never forget, however, my first visit with Habib Bourguiba, the president of the Neo-Destour, in his tiny second-story apartment off a Tunis side street. At first glance he struck me as a visionary, a modern prophet, with his startling blue eyes staring out of an Andalusian face marked with suffering. He and his followers had spent five and a half years in solitary confinement in Marseilles — the first half without books. When he left for prison his son was eleven; now he was almost seventeen. Since the boy's mother was French, he had been forced to take a French name, but was called by the Moslems after his father, Habib — not customary in the Arab world — and so he is still known today. Also at the apartment I met Bourguiba's wife, Mathilde; perhaps once attractive, she had become an old woman during his imprisonment. He eventually divorced her to marry his present wife, Wassila. Bourguiba was a very different personality from Salah Ben Youssef — deadly serious, tense, destined for greatness.

The message conveyed to me by the Neo-Destourist leaders was more like that of the Moroccans than the Algerians. All three groups had identical views on exploitation by the French *colons* and the government that backed them. But although the Tunisians, unlike the mass of Moroccans, were much influenced by French culture, they had no desire for continued political association with France. They remained loyal to Moncef Bey, condemned French treatment of him, and despised his successor. They subjected me to so many diatribes that I reached the point of saturation.

I took the bold step of asking Bourguiba, Ben Youssef, and the rest to meet with me, and told them I had heard enough lectures, that the time had come to summarize it all for the American authorities. For a start, I suggested that each of them write a report on the facts known to him, the history of the past month including the actions of the Germans, the French, the Destour, and the whole drama of the Bey; then I planned to submit them all and combine their information in a comprehensive summary for presentation to all U.S. military and civilian channels available to me.

I realized that the French were by now well aware of my activities, that they would certainly see my report, and could only hope that I would get it done in time before I was removed from the scene. I was also risking my promotion to first lieutenant, which I knew was being processed, and might, as I recorded in a letter to K.W. at the time, "even get stuck in censorship or something." But I felt passionately that the situation had to be brought to the attention of our government, which was blindly following an oppressive French policy completely contrary to the ideals for which we were fighting in the present world conflict.

Having thus put all the Destour leaders to work writing reports, which must have given them some satisfaction, I set off at the end of June with Hooker Doolittle in his consular car, a magnificent open gray Mercury, on a tour of the Sahel — the coast and the coastal plain south of Tunis, the heartland of the country. We were accompanied by Slim Driga, who provided a running commentary as we made our way through olive groves, wheat fields, and mountains to the Mediterranean coast. It amused Doolittle and me how every negative aspect of nature on our trip was ascribed to the French. If it was hot and dusty, Slim would say, "You know who's responsible, don't you? If the French had planted trees, it wouldn't be so hot, and if they paved the streets in the native villages, it wouldn't be so dusty!"

We drove to Moknine, Slim's village, to spend the night at his father's house near the sea. Our host seemed to bear no physical resemblance to Slim, whose smooth brown face looked Mexican. Paris, where he had spent all his recent years, had marked him for life. His father, Hassine Ben Hadj Ahmed, however, was the typical Tunisian patriarch, complete with fez, silver whiskers, and an ample midsection disguised under flowing white robes. Slim's son, half-French but with the gravity of Arab boys, awaited him. The women were invisible, confined to their own quarters. A little black boy named Sa'adullah completed the family. Various portly relatives wandered in and out of the house to greet Slim.

Everything was prepared for our coming, and several Arabs were waiting to see Doolittle. This, even to one who was acquainted with the *"telegraphe Arabe"* (the Arab grapevine) was amazing; every place we visited, the Arabs were waiting for us, and yet we informed nobody ourselves and traveled certainly faster than any Arab could.

After completing the reception niceties, we gratefully retired to the beach to wash away the heat and dust in the Mediterranean. As the Moslems at the time did not go in for swimming — considering display of the body unseemly — we were accompanied by friends from the Jewish quarter.

We went through a couple of native villages to a shoreline that could not have changed much since the Carthaginians. Behind us were olive groves; along the shore were white Arab houses, and on the sea little fishing boats with triangular sails. An old cart was in the water, and also a camel being washed by some Arabs. We sat on mats after our swim and sipped tea with our Jewish hosts. I noticed a white water jug on the brink of the sea — exactly the same type as that used by the Carthaginians. Two philosophic old Arab teachers came up and joined us, and we exchanged oriental compliments. Hooker Doolittle and I felt like Connecticut Yankees, transferred to an earlier, more tranquil century.

That evening we sat in Hassine's garden, on a carpet on the edge of the cistern, drinking Doolittle's whiskey or a vodka-like liquor made of figs and grain. All present — Slim, a local judge, and ourselves — drank, except our host, who had gotten religion. Afterward we all went to eat in the courtyard under millions of stars. One of the uncles served. Slim's son, ten years old, had just been circumcised, with great ceremony and presents, but was still sore — a fertile subject for discussion.

In the morning we awoke to find a breakfast waiting for us in the courtyard — coffee, sweetmeats, and cakes dipped in honey. Also, great excitement. Little Sa'adullah had been told once too often that he mustn't eat the berries on the garden wall, a sort of locoweed. He had tried them the day before, and now his eyes were rolling, his white teeth were flashing, and weird sounds issued from his coal-black face. He would be "loco," I was told, anywhere from one day to a week.

We passed the morning in the Jewish quarter. People of all ages surrounded us and led us to the synagogue while crowds on the balconies and rooftops cheered and yelled: *"Vive l'Amérique! Vive Roosevelt!"* (Though we heard isolated cries of *"Vive l'Angleterre, l'Italie!"* and even *"Vive Daladier!"* — the last prime minister before the fall of France.) The rabbi welcomed us in the synagogue, where we sat for a while exchanging formalities before an equally triumphant procession back to the Moslem quarter.

We were very sad on departing the next day for Mahdia, an ancient fortress jutting out into the sea; then we went on to the extreme point of our journey, Sfax — our route always following the Mediterranean. The entire country seemed one mass of olive groves, beautifully cared for.

The following day we took a detour away from the coast on our road back to Tunis to see a little of Tunisia's heartland. The late June heat was almost unbearable and the flat countryside, bare except for wheat stubble and an occasional olive grove, uninteresting. We arrived at the holy city of Cairouan, the goal of our journey, only to find that its famous mosque was closed to infidels. We gladly left its white walls, glaring in the devastating summer sun.

We were not unhappy to turn back toward the sea, and after a few kilometers' drive the monotony of the plain was suddenly blocked by the ruin of an enormous amphitheater. A twin of the Colosseum of Rome, it stood isolated in the middle of the tiny Arab village of El-Djem surrounded by olive groves. It was awesome to realize that once this must have been the playground of a thriving Roman town, teeming with toga-clad citizens of the province of Africa.

Back in the reality of Tunis, buoyed by a notice of my promotion to first lieutenant, I hurried around to collect the reports assigned to my Destour friends. Then I frantically went to work composing my comprehensive report, knowing I was on borrowed time.

As it was nearing completion, on the evening of July 4, a quarrel between Senegalese and Algerian soldiers in the red-light district led to a riot, with stones as the principal weapons. The Senegalese went to their barracks for reinforcements, returning with about a hundred of their comrades, armed with rifles, bayonets, tommy guns, and hand grenades. They were accompanied by black noncommissioned officers. They proceeded to bayonet, club, and shoot Arabs in the Bab Sadoun area, and even entered houses to beat up, club, and murder Arabs regardless of age or sex. French NCOs and officers followed and not only made no attempt to stop their men, but encouraged them; according to some witnesses, certain of them even joined in the fray.

American and British military police were instantly summoned, but, ascertaining that no British or American troops were involved, they merely stopped all vehicles from entering the zone.

At 9:45, one or more superior French officers appeared, a bugle sounded the call to cease firing, and the Senegalese assembled and marched back to their barracks in good order.

Meanwhile, Senegalese troops and their French NCOs were stopping trolley cars coming from the Bardo to Bab Sadoun and making all Arabs descend. They then beat up the Arabs, often to unconsciousness, and dragged them to their barracks, where they beat them further.

At least twenty Arabs were killed during the riot, and three times as many wounded. There were no Senegalese casualties. I concluded my report on the incident with evidence of French complicity in the massacre, based on the fact that Senegalese troops were usually restricted in their access to weapons. These were always kept padlocked on a chain in the barracks, the key to which was held by an NCO. But on Sundays — and July 4 was a Sunday — arms were not normally permitted to be distributed at all, and an exception to this would require permission from higher authority.

The day I was writing this report, I wrote my wife,

I can't tell you — because of censorship — the interesting things which make up my whole life at this time. Really what I pass my time doing is struggling against a lie — which is, unfortunately, believed by nearly everybody. I am gradually converting a few people here and there, as I get the spotlight turned on a certain section of the lie. But meanwhile people are

using the darkness to do things you read about in Jan Valtin.*
And I have these things on my conscience, as I feel the faster I
turn on the spotlight, the sooner they will stop doing these
things. There is probably little ground for my guilty conscience,
however, because even when I do get the thing all lit up, nobody
will look at it. But I do my best to make them look at it, by
talking, orating, beating the table day and night, so that I am
known as a veritable fanatic and people say — "He's talking
about his Arabs again!" However, don't think I'm losing my
sense of proportion — as with one side of me I have a clear view
of the whole thing and its present unimportance. But it also has
some interesting future possibilities and may be important some
day.

The Allied landings in Sicily in the next few days underscored
the comparative unimportance of it all. Having completed my
reports, feeling my work in Tunisia was done, I wondered what
I might be doing next.

I did not have long to wonder — within a few days Hooker
Doolittle was recalled to Washington, and in an obviously
related action, I was ordered to Algiers. The French authorities
were, of course, well aware of our contacts with the Destour.
They were probably getting my reports directly from our
Psychological Warfare Branch, which worked closely with its
French counterpart. They were evidently sufficiently concerned about me to raise my case with the highest Allied
authorities. Somewhere in old files in the Pentagon, there is a
cable reading something like this: "General de Gaulle requests
that Lt. Archibald B. Roosevelt, Jr., Serial No. 885630, be
immediately returned to the U.S." — signed "Eisenhower."

The evening before I left Tunis, Slim Driga organized a
party for me and my friends from the Psychological Warfare
Branch in a fine old villa on the shore, owned by a gray-bearded
gentleman of the old-fashioned Moslem type. He wouldn't sit
down to dinner with us, not only because it was the tradition for
a host to remain standing to wait on his guests, but also because
we were drinking wine.

All the Neo-Destour leaders were there, and after a sumptuous banquet, a Bedouin girl danced for us, with great poise

---

* His book *Out of the Night* is the autobiography of a Comintern agent who suffered at
the hands of both Communists and Nazis.

and queenly gestures, yet with a wildness in the flash of her black eyes. A magic evening by the sea, lit by the crescent moon — we sat drinking coffee, rose-flavored wine, and muscat until they finally let us go home at four-thirty.

That was my last experience of Tunisia, which I was not to see again for thirty years. After arriving in Algiers, I learned of my enforced return to Washington, and was hurried onto a troop ship, carrying German prisoners from the Afrika Korps, back over the ocean on which I had come nine months before.

A few days before I left Tunisia, Moncef Bey, finally giving way to his French captors deep in the Sahara, abdicated. And the Destour leaders once more suffered imprisonment and exile. Bourguiba himself was on the loose for a while, making his way across the desert to Cairo to gain pan-Arab support, then across the Atlantic to the United States in a mostly fruitless bid for our sympathy. He was involved in a scheme to free Moncef Bey from his French exile, which was doomed from the start, as Moncef Bey did not want to be freed!

But the Tunisian resistance to French rule continued, with increasing violence on both sides, until a liberal government came to power in France. Bourguiba returned to Tunisia in triumph, leading his party in negotiations that finally brought independence in 1956. Habib Bourguiba became Tunisia's first president, a post he held until November 1987.

PART THREE

Arabian Nights

10

To the Nile

UPON MY RETURN to America at the end of August 1943, I reported to Office of War Information headquarters in Washington, accompanied by Lieutenant Mohammed Siblini, whose removal from North Africa had simultaneously been demanded by the French. Siblini and I worked together at OWI headquarters, making a number of recommendations for U.S. propaganda aimed at the Moslem population of North Africa and the Arab world in general. We gave general and specific advice on films, radio broadcasts, and publications. We composed a general report on "the political situation of North African Arabs with reference to propaganda."

I also promoted my pet projects: the establishment of an American university in North Africa and U.S. sponsorship of a pilgrimage to Mecca, interrupted by the war, for Arab notables.

Although Bob Sherwood and many members of his staff were sympathetic, in general all our efforts came to naught. The pilgrimage proposal, for instance, submitted by us months before, had been passed to the French by someone on our staff a while earlier, and they had preempted the plan — though I never heard that it had been implemented.

While I was in Washington I usually stayed at the Virginia home of my cousin Kermit Roosevelt. He had been a couple of classes ahead of me at Groton and we both went on to Harvard. "Kim" and his wife, Polly, were by far the closest to K.W. and me of all the cousins. Kim knew of my interest in the Arab

world, and listened to my views that the Arab world would be
of great importance after the war and deserved more attention
now. Kim was in the OSS and I had hoped to get in touch
through him with this glamorous organization, but he did not
respond to my overtures. I never did make contact with
operational units of the OSS, but I did see the leading Middle
East figures in the OSS Research and Analysis Sector and had
interesting exchanges of views with a number of its members —
particularly Dr. Ephraim A. Speiser and Dr. Ralph Bunche.
R and A was sufficiently interested in me to request that I be
transferred to that organization.

But the fact was I belonged not to OWI, to which I was
seconded, but G2, which claimed my body. One day when I was
in New York, enjoying a respite from all the flattering attention
I was getting from Washington, I was contacted by telephone
and ordered to report once more — to Camp Ritchie. I recall
the very moment when the call came, early the day after K.W.
and I had seen *Oklahoma!,* and I came out of the shower singing
"Oh, What a Beautiful Morning," to be stunned by this message.
Ever since, I have avoided this song as an omen of bad luck.

I arrived in Camp Ritchie as the fall was turning cold, to find
that they had no clear instructions as to what to do with me.
When it was obvious that I was going to be stuck there for some
time, I rented a little apartment in Waynesboro, Pennsylvania,
a few miles from the camp, and put K.W. and Tweed in it. This
made up, in part, for the somewhat surreal military stint I
underwent that winter.

Camp Ritchie was filled with soldiers of various foreign
backgrounds being trained for field intelligence work, and they
made me an instructor. The training site was not Camp Ritchie
itself but a rough jumble of barracks and other facilities
bunched in Camp Sharpe, an installation near Gettysburg
known as the Salt Mines and the Russian Front. There I found
a varied collection of interesting human beings whom I was
supposed to convert into soldiers in two weeks, a task for which
I was patently unfit. Some were Spanish Civil War veterans;
others were Slavs, Italians, and Filipinos, but the majority were
German Jews, many of them intellectuals even less suited than
I was to be field soldiers. (I was delighted to discover an Iranian
Jew from Meshed who spoke Arabic!) A number of them were
destined to serve in reconnaissance teams in the Pacific, and I

remarked in a diary I kept at the time that I thought this "criminal," virtually sending these barely trained, miscast intellectuals to their death.

In charge of the camp was a schoolmasterish martinet captain, seconded by another kind of martinet, a lifetime cavalry lieutenant — complete with cavalry brimmed hat, boots, and swagger stick — and a sadistic buck sergeant, reputedly busted from staff sergeant for rape. I was a platoon leader, teaching the enlisted men firing and bayonet practice, and close-order drill. The drill was generally disastrous, as all were confused by the random introduction of cavalry drill by the lieutenant. For example, my column ended up on the wrong side when we passed in review and nobody knew in which direction to salute.

We were only too happy after our two weeks were over to take the twenty-mile hike back to Camp Ritchie, where some of us were assigned to a Section Nine whose function we termed organized gold-bricking.

I made good use of this windfall of leisure time, reading many classics about the Arab world: W. G. Palgrave's *Central and Eastern Arabia*, Alois Musil's *The Bedouin*, R. A. Nicholson's *Literary History of the Arabs*, Ibn Jubair's *Geography*. After my San Francisco experience as a newspaperman I had decided that I really wanted to be an orientalist, and since in those days there were no specifically Middle East studies in universities, this meant Semitic studies. I had therefore taught myself the rudiments of Hebrew and while in New York made the acquaintance of a leader of the Sephardic community, David de Sola Pool, whose family, like my own, had come from Holland to New Amsterdam. He had given me a Hebrew Pentateuch, and I dutifully read ten lines a day from it.

During this limbo of "between assignments," in addition to reading and study, I had time for reflection. Had I really been right in the path I had followed in North Africa, which had led to my present impasse? Had I not violated the main principle that should guide a true intelligence officer — to seek the truth without embellishment — by becoming emotionally involved in the issues, losing objectivity?

The answers were yes and no. I had become involved with the Arabs of North Africa, reporting how the French were taking advantage of our military occupation to tighten their grip on the Moslem population, denying them a fair share of consumer goods provided by the United States, and suppressing nationalist movements on the pretext that they were aiding the enemy.

On the other hand, our intelligence and hence our policy (such as it was) on the Arab situation were deficient in that our military and civilian authorities relied almost completely on the French view of North Africa. I thought it my duty as an intelligence officer to point out the distortions of this view, and give my overall estimate that the French would, after U.S. troops left the scene, be unable to contain the forces of nationalism.

The military strategist Karl von Clausewitz said that war is a continuation of diplomacy. The converse is also true — that diplomacy is the continuation of war. But the United States was acting as if the war would be forever — that it was almost unpatriotic to think of postwar until the war was over. The Europeans, who are more conscious of history than Americans, all were conducting their policies with the postwar world in mind.

In addition to thinking about the future of the world, I was also concerned about my own immediate prospects. G2 had turned down a request for my services from OSS but apparently had no immediate plans for me. But Colonel Truman Smith was trying to find a place for me in the Middle East — my ultimate goal. On January 29, 1944, at the Camp Ritchie post office, I found a letter from him saying there was still no vacancy for me in G2. Yet two days later I was told to go to G2 in Washington the next day for an interview.

On my arrival at the Munitions Building, I was sent to see Lieutenant Colonel McKay of the South American Department along with another lieutenant colonel from G2, both of them extremely well informed. They questioned me very closely on what I would like to do.

I told them about my aspirations, my interest in the Middle East and my thoughts about its importance, my qualifications for an assignment there, as well as my problems with the French in North Africa. I could see that Lieutenant Colonel McKay had a report about me on his desk, but was unable to get a peek at it. Neither of them was sympathetic with the Arabs in North Africa; when I mentioned the massacre in Tunis, McKay turned to the other officer, saying, "We have seen many massacres, haven't we? Some people would call them legal executions."

I remarked, "When women and children are killed I think this amounts to a massacre — besides this incident, there are certainly plenty of other examples of executions."

McKay said that he did not want officers to be pro-Arab but only pro-American and for this reason did not send Americans of Arab origin to Arab countries. "Do you really consider yourself impartial on Arab questions?" he asked.

"I think I am as impartial as possible, but as an aspiring orientalist I naturally have some sympathy with the Arabs."

"What about Jews — how would you feel about the Palestinian question?"

"I'm just as interested in Jews as in Arabs and am now studying Hebrew. Since I haven't been to Palestine, I can't say what my feelings would be about that situation, although I have been following it in the news."

McKay said, "It's too bad that you're no longer useful in North Africa, and so many months have been wasted at Ritchie."

"I couldn't help that — I saw the people in North Africa I felt it my duty to see, and the French know that I saw them."

Then Lieutenant Colonel Haynes came in — I already had made his acquaintance — and McKay asked him if he would recommend me for the Middle East.

"Yes," said Haynes. "His Arabic would do anywhere after a month or so. I would only make one provision, to speak frankly — we would have to keep him away from the French. Assign him anyplace but Syria."

As the interview was clearly over, I took my leave, but asked if they could not use me in military intelligence, to be released to the OSS. They said they would see what could be done, and on that uncertain note I returned to Camp Ritchie. I passed most of February in suspense, but on February 24 orders came transferring me to Washington, and I left the next day.

Reporting to G2 headquarters, I was told only that an overseas assignment was imminent, and was placed under the tutelage of various members of the Middle East section. They were kindred souls with personal experience of the Islamic world. Major Henry Snyder, who knew Saudi Arabia; Captain Ogden, a missionary; Mary Crane, a Persian expert; and Mrs.

Thomas, a historian who had lived in Iraq. They told me that I had influenced Colonel Smith to take a greater interest in the Middle East. Mrs. Thomas arranged for me to meet the Iraqi ambassador in Washington, Ali Jawdat, who invited me to dine at their embassy — my first exposure to the country that was later to engulf me.

On March 15 I was told I would be assigned to Cairo to the Joint Intelligence Committee, Middle East (JICME), an organization that was supposed to coordinate all intelligence activities in the area. I was directed to report immediately to General Russell Osman, responsible for the military attaché system of which JICME was a part.

Entering his office, I was greeted by a live-wire type who looked like a businessman in uniform. He came right to the point.

"Well, what do you know?"

I told him I had experience in political intelligence among the Arabs of North Africa and in Middle East studies.

"We need experts out there!" he said, and then abruptly changed course to tell me of a meeting he had just had with Zionist leaders Moshe Shertok (later Sharett) and David Ben-Gurion.

"They are tough boys," he said. "If they'd been born in Chicago, they'd have been part of Al Capone's mob. Shertok told me, 'General, we're always glad to help with information — if there's anything I can tell you, just ask me and I'll oblige!' I said, 'Well, then, how many guns you got?' "

A colonel entered the office and asked, "When can I see you, General?"

"In three minutes and twenty seconds."

I took my leave as quickly as possible, giving him a few seconds to spare.

Now that I had my official blessing, I started on my shots and got passport photos. I had a last session with a dentist and a doctor in New York; the latter told me that I had a systolic murmur in my heart, which he considered of no significance but which, if heard by an army doctor, would bring a medical discharge!

I had reunions with comrades-in-arms Jimmy Sheean and Fernand Auberjonois. My aunt Alice had me to dinner with Freya Stark, the traveler and writer — we "took to each other beautifully," I noted in my diary. I found her "not as homely as pictured, with black hair queerly arranged to cover her missing ear." And my auntie Belle, Kim's mother, also did me a favor. Uncle Kermit and she were the only members of our side of the family close to Franklin. She was staying at the White House and asked me to tea with Cousin Eleanor.

Cousin Eleanor greeted me upstairs in her usual kindly manner. There was a young black clergyman there and they discussed racial problems. I wrote, "She seems more moderate politically than I had thought but I found their discussions amazingly impractical. She said the whole problem is economic."

She spoke of her overseas trips. She had recently made one to the Pacific, and received many abusive letters from women saying, "Why should you go there, and I can't." Undaunted, she was about to set off for the Caribbean. The other night, she said, when she suggested to Franklin that she visit European hospitals during the coming invasion, "to my surprise, he said it's the best thing you could do." She then showed us around the White House, and pointing out Grandfather's portrait, she told us stories about "Uncle Ted."

As we were about to take our leave, Cousin Franklin himself came wheeling in from the hall, smoking from his cigarette holder as in the newsreels.

"Hello, Archie — how's the boy?" he said, on this, our first and last face-to-face meeting.

On April 4 I was on my way, with a two-week stopover in Miami to wait for a plane. This time was not entirely wasted, as I found companionship with several others of similar interests who were similarly marooned. One was an OSS man, Donald Downs, a former history teacher who had been in Morocco and involved in Arab affairs just as I was, and shared my views. Another was Moses Hadas, a Greek Sephardi, professor of Greek at Columbia University, with whom I had discussed at length possible openings there for postwar Semitic studies. He gave me a lot of practical advice, one piece of which was to undertake the translation of one of the many important Arabic classics not yet available in English. Then there was Dan Dennett, a Harvard instructor in Arabic who also had taught at the American University of Beirut. "I imagine he will take Thomson's place [as professor of Arabic] some day at Harvard," I wrote. Alas, he died in a plane crash less than three years later.

Finally, I was off to Cairo, via Natal, Brazil; Accra; and Khartoum, arriving on May 21. As soon as I reported to the office, I knew I had landed on my feet. The other officers in JICME were all experts in their fields. Despite my lack of local expertise, I was assigned to the vacant position of officer responsible for Palestine and the Levant States. My immediate supervisor was Major Edwin Wright, a former missionary and later an archaeologist in southeast Turkey, Iraq, and Iran who became my mentor and, as it turned out, a benefactor who years later did me a good turn that transformed and enriched my life.

Hooker Doolittle was in Cairo and we had a good talk about Tunisia. He had managed to get a hearing with OSS chief Bill Donovan and made quite an impression. He seemed to have sold him on the American university idea, which eventually led to the establishment of an American school in Tangier. He passed through Tunisia en route to Cairo and I wrote, "He and I are considered saviours of the country. All this is very gratifying and I feel as if my work has been some good after all."

Although Egypt was not my responsibility, I was eager to make some Egyptian connections. Ed Wright had a relationship with the American University, and I attended a commencement ceremony where the speaker was Egypt's most revered writer and philosopher, Taha Hussein. Blind from birth, wearing dark glasses, he was still a tall and commanding figure in his eighties. At an alumni dinner there, I sat next to a newfound friend, Mustafa Amin, city editor of Cairo's leading newspaper, *Al-Ahram*. We got bored at the dinner and sneaked out together. His newspaper was getting out a new edition, and I was interested in the comparison of their fine offices and new equipment with the traditional dinginess of their American counterparts. I talked politics with the newsmen there, as I did off and on throughout my stay in Cairo with Mustafa Amin. A giant of a man, with a go-getting temperament that seemed more American than Middle Eastern, Mustafa Amin might have become my political guide, as Mehdi Ben Barka and Slim Driga had been farther west, had I stayed in Egypt longer.

My situation in Egypt had its good and bad points. I lived in a back room of a nineteenth-century princely palace on the east bank of the Nile, where I loved to walk in the morning and look across its waters teeming with boats and people. The bad part was that I was the most junior of the thirty officers sleeping and eating there and, knowing the language, was naturally put in charge of food, liquor, and servants. The senior officers were a crusty lot, not used to Middle Eastern life, frequently complaining in the midst of this comparative luxury because things were not like home.

This was the only time in my life I spent more than a few days in Egypt. It was interrupted by two trips to Palestine and the Levant States, so I was scarcely touched by the political, social, and cultural life of the country. Like everyone involved in the Middle East, I have paid many visits to Cairo, and I have met all three of the outstanding figures who have led Egypt during the last three decades — Gamal Abd-al-Nasser, Anwar Sadat, and Hosni Mubarak. I have admired most of its ancient and Islamic monuments and enjoyed my many contacts with its lively people. But I have never explored the byways of the country and its complex society.

I have known Cairo more as a crossroads of the Arab world, and made good contacts there during my first exposure to it. Doolittle introduced me to the new American minister, Pinckney Tuck; I met the great brigadier Iltyd Clayton, Middle East veteran since World War I, whose brother Gilbert figures prominently in T. E. Lawrence's *Seven Pillars of Wisdom*.

Through Katie Antonius of Jerusalem I had an introduction to her brother-in-law Sir Walter Smart, oriental secretary to the British embassy. After dining with him I wrote, "It was wonderful to be able to talk to somebody like that, with a wise and tolerant knowledge of the people of the Middle East, so badly misunderstood by so many in so many different ways."

Cairo was the center for the Arabs of North Africa as well as the Middle East, and I had a nostalgic reunion there with my Tunisian cicerone, Slim Driga. He had had many adventures in Tunisia, escaping from a French prison and then traveling in a small boat to Tripoli. Doolittle arranged for him to come to Egypt.

He was his usual ebullient self, and expressed contempt for all the Tunisian and Moroccan leaders then in exile in Cairo, with the exception of the veteran Moroccan tribal leader Abd-el-Krim, whom he took me to see. Jimmy Sheean had often mentioned him to me in Morocco, and he emerges in Sheean's book *Personal History* as a man of courage tempered with a sense of humor, with "the mark of greatness."

I was surprised to find him so tiny, though he did have a certain majesty in his white turban, grizzled beard, and traditional Moroccan dress. He had the broad face and small eyes one sees in many Berbers. He spoke in quiet, pleasant tones in classical Arabic and good but hesitant French. Speaking about imperialism, he contrasted French imperialism with that of the British. "Think what would have happened to the Irish if the French had been their masters!"

He thought the Egyptians unduly violent in their criticism of the British. "Egypt suffers only economic squeezing, nothing compared to what the Latins do in North Africa," he said, lumping the French with the Italians in Libya.

But aside from its interest as a center for Arabs and Arabists from all over, I found Cairo depressing, and debilitating in summer, now well on its way in June of 1944.

Hence I was delighted to receive orders early in the month transferring me to Baghdad as assistant military attaché to the U.S. Legation there. (In those days only the most important foreign countries housed a U.S. embassy and ambassador. The rest had to make do with a legation headed by a minister.) I was thrilled and elated by this development. Both the country and the nature of the assignment were a new challenge, and I eagerly questioned Ed Wright, who had been a missionary in Iraq in the twenties, drawing upon his vast store of knowledge in the area.

My earlier knowledge of Baghdad was derived from *The Arabian Nights,* and I had read much about it in my more recent studies. Iraq had an ancient past as glorious as that of Egypt, and its more recent history had far greater allure for me than the chronicles of foreign conquerors ruling the patient subject peoples of the Nile.

Ed Wright warned me, during those last couple of weeks in Cairo awaiting finalization of my orders, not to expect too much of Baghdad. The city of the caliphs had turned to dust, he said, and he hoped I would not be disappointed by the diminished city of today. But nothing could contain my enthusiasm. I had a premonition that today's Baghdad would turn out to be full of wonders, even if the caliphs were long gone. And I believed in premonitions.

Baghdad the Beautiful

"We gnaw the nail of hurry. Master, away!"
"O turn your eyes to where your children stand.
Is not Bagdad the beautiful? O stay!"
"We take the Golden Road to Samarkand."

To THOSE who have read of the splendors of Baghdad under the caliphs, the modern remnant of the capital of Haroun al-Rashid and the setting of the *Thousand and One Nights* provides a depressing letdown. It is true that nothing remains of the magnificent "round city" destroyed by the Mongols. But for someone like myself, who had read deeply into the country and was not expecting very much, Baghdad turned out to be a magic city after all.

I arrived, along with Ed Wright, on July 14, 1944, at the British air base at Habbaniyya, west of the Euphrates. We drove to the Tigris across a bare desert whose only feature was the high walls of abandoned irrigation canals, sad remnants of a vanished civilization, and rattled across the river on the old bridge to the mud bricks of Baghdad the Beautiful.

We pulled up at the steps of the Zia, an unprepossessing hotel on the riverbank. A porter hoisted my bags up to a dingy, square room with a minimum of furniture, and turned on a fan standing on a bare wooden table, which feebly stirred the hot, dusty air.

Far from depressed by these drab beginnings, I went down-stairs full of anticipation — I felt I had started at last on the Road to Samarkand. Ordering a drink from the bartender, known to all visitors by the name of Jesus, I sat on the terrace with Ed Wright, my kindly guide and teacher during my first days in the city. I asked him about Jesus. "He's a Chaldean, like most restaurant and hotel workers — the Arabs won't do that kind of work. They come from Tell Keif and other Christian villages north of Mosul."

Descendants of the people living in the Land Between Two Rivers when the Arabs conquered them in the seventh century, the Chaldeans still speak their Aramaic dialect. Many of the other inhabitants of Iraq, now thinking themselves descendants of the noble Arab nomads of the desert, are really Chaldean cousins who took on the faith and the tongue of the Bedouin invaders.

I remember vividly that first evening sitting with Ed on the banks of the Tigris, the desert breeze cooling us after the ride in the dusty heat. The stars seemed to be reflected by sparkling lights from the boats floating on the bosom of the great river.

A boatload of young men passed by our terrace singing, and for the first time I heard the strains of the melody that became for me the theme song of Baghdad:

> *Mu kull warid, isma'l-warid*
> *B'idi zara'ata, b'idi,*
> *B'idi shittalta, b'idi.*

"Not every rose with the name of a rose have I sown with my own hand, transplanted with my own hand" — it sounds banal in English, but its melody, enriching that starry night, still haunts me today.

I sat back and breathed the fragrant air of the first of my Baghdad nights, still redolent of the nights of Haroun al-Rashid, enjoying this bewitching lilt of Arab melody rising from the waters. Here I had found myself at last, on the site of the splendor of Old Islam.

My musings on its vanished glories were cut short by the arrival of my future boss, Colonel Paul Converse, who was joining us for dinner. As he came up to the terrace, Ed Wright absentmindedly introduced me as Lieutenant Robinson.

"Glad to meet you, Robinson," Converse said. "Now perhaps one of you can tell me when this fellow Roosevelt is getting here!"

Almost at once, after this unpromising beginning, a relationship grew up between us. It might have seemed an unlikely combination. Converse was a crusty, spick-and-span cavalry officer, with close-cropped white hair and granite features. But his eyes were kind and friendly, and his gruff voice could not disguise his good and generous heart. He had an open, naive nature and the best qualities of a gentleman.

He might have been initially disappointed at the sight of this sloppy, unprofessional lieutenant come to replace the also spick-and-span professional army captain who had preceded me. But he adopted me almost at once, and our relationship developed into that of an outwardly stern, actually indulgent father and a promising, if somewhat unruly, son.

The next morning he took me to my new office, a small building of mud brick like everything else in Baghdad. Across the street stood the large but hardly imposing edifice that housed both the residence of the minister, who headed the American mission in Baghdad, and the legation offices. We were a tiny group compared with American embassies today. The military segment included the colonel, myself, a warrant officer, a military censor, and five enlisted men. The legation proper included a minister, an administrative and consular officer, a political officer, an economic officer, an OWI officer, and three male clerks.

We spent the morning making protocol calls, first on the embassy, then on the Iraqi chief of staff, Lieutenant General Ismail Namiq, and the various British elements who were our principal liaison contacts. These were PAIFORCE, the organization responsible for the flow of military personnel and material to Iran and the Soviet Union, headed by Lieutenant General Sir Arthur Smith; CICI (Counter Intelligence Center Iraq), headed by Squadron Leader Dawson-Shepherd; the political adviser, Lieutenant Colonel Charles C. Aston, responsible for a network of British military advisers to the Iraqi government in the provinces; and General J. M. L. Renton, chief of the British military mission to the Iraqi army.

We had lunch with the minister, Loy Henderson, whom I termed in my first letter home "a very intelligent fellow." As I soon learned, he was a great deal more than that; he was, in fact, one of the most brilliant American diplomats of his time.

He was an expert on the Soviet Union and the Baltic States, where he worked in 1919–20 before joining the State Department. There he served in the Eastern European Division under veteran Sovietologist Robert Kelley, and was second in command in our Moscow embassy from 1934 to 1938. Then he returned to the department as assistant chief of the Division of

European Affairs, which by now included Eastern Europe as well.

During all this period he fought for a realistic approach in dealing with the Soviets, in the face of a naiveté on the part of many U.S. officials that now seems incredible. When he was sent back to Moscow in late 1942 as counselor of the embassy, the Soviets expressed their unhappiness with him. He was relieved after a few months and shunted off to Baghdad.

Henderson was understandably bitter, as well as deeply concerned about a foreign policy committed to cooperation with the Soviets far exceeding the requirements of the war. As we got to know each other, he shared his wealth of experience with me in facing the Soviet problem, soon to be the major one of the next half of the century.

Meanwhile he had Iraq to handle, and for the first few months he was clearly delighted to have me on his staff as someone who seemed to understand the Arab scene. He was promoting a state visit to Washington by the Regent of Iraq that fall and decided that I should accompany him (it was later postponed till the following year).

While we became somewhat estranged later in my tour, when my relations with the local power structure caused him to feel that I was getting too big for my britches, Henderson always held me in high regard, and showed this in tangible ways after he returned to Washington and, finally properly appreciated, strode in the corridors of power.

After our lunch with Henderson, Colonel Converse told me that he was putting me in charge of the office immediately, as he was leaving the next day on a three-week trip. He dropped me that evening at the Semiramis Hotel, supposedly more comfortable than the Zia. I hardly noticed. My head was buzzing with my new status as a military diplomat, although I was also worried about carrying out my duties as a mere lieutenant. That morning I had been acutely aware of my lowly status as the colonel presented me to the British lieutenant general. But I'd been more than a year in grade and was clearly in line for promotion, virtually a necessity since, as I wrote, "This is an expensive business and I'll be living right on the brink of bankruptcy, in spite of my efforts to save by living in a cheap hotel room!" (Because the colonel was under the impression that I had come to him freshly promoted, he did nothing about it until I found this out late in the fall — and I didn't make captain till after the first of the following year.)

A couple of days later I was rudely awakened from this new, exciting world. It was a dream world I was living in, in the midst of the world at war. My father was slugging it out in the South Pacific, while farther north the marines had made their historic descent on Iwo Jima; and the Allies had just landed in Normandy. On July 17 I received news of a family tragedy in each of these war theaters. My father had been wounded again — I could not find out how seriously. My wife's cousin, Harry Blaine, the brother of my college roommate, had been killed in Iwo Jima. And my uncle Ted, who had been warned by the medics about his heart before insisting on participating in the Normandy landing, had died a couple of days later when that brave heart failed him. I wrote my wife:

> It seems that every day brings some new tragedy. I just got through writing Auntie Eleanor, and I remembered the dinner we had at Uncle Ted's house just after we were engaged, the Christmas dinners, the hockey games, and how he was the one who told me to go into newspaper work. And he was right. I can see Auntie Eleanor alone in that house they had only just put together, thinking there were twenty years ahead — sitting looking out on the apple orchard with his books and his trophies all around. Of course, it's worse in a way about Harry, with a life of hope ahead of him, and the darling of the family. And what in hell has happened to Father? The fact that it was evidently announced in Cold Spring also made me think it couldn't have been serious. I don't know why nobody told me. In fact, I feel completely cut off from the world and wish to hell there were some way of my taking a trip to the States to find out what is going on.

Summers in Baghdad are not pleasant. Daytime temperatures often rise to 125 degrees Fahrenheit, and in those days we had to endure it without air-conditioning; from time to time the misery index is considerably increased by dust storms. My boxlike room was hot — the very bed sheets were hot — and when I took refuge outside, the tiles on the terrace were hot, even after dark. But the dryness of the desert air makes the heat more bearable; late at night the thermometer drops sharply, and early mornings are a joy. And I put these torpid summer months to good use.

First, I got a regular instructor and worked at mastering the local dialect. In the Maghreb and Egypt I had concentrated on the classical tongue, but in Iraq the spoken language is much closer to the classical. Also, with the end of the war approaching, I was thinking more about my postwar future, and my ideas were already changing. Dr. Speiser of the OSS and others had pointed out that if I wanted to devote my life to Semitic studies, this would involve not only Arabic and Hebrew, but boring Syriac — with mostly ecclesiastical literature — and the cuneiform texts of ancient Babylonia.

Better still, I thought, would be to find a place as a modern orientalist, and I decided to take advantage of Baghdad's large Iranian community to learn Persian. Also, taking seriously Professor Hadas's advice to translate a major classical Arabic work into English as a way of entry into the academic fraternity, I selected *Muruj al-Dhahab* ("Prairies of Gold"), by the tenth-century historian Mas'udi, known as the Herodotus of the Arabs, hitherto not translated into English. It is one of the primary sources of Arab history. I had found an Arabic edition of it in Cairo, and started work on it during these ample stretches of spare time.

While office work was not on the fast track that summer, especially since Iraq was politically and militarily dormant, there were foundations to be laid. Legation and liaison contacts could be solidified, and the basis established for reaching the political and intellectual leadership of the country. Also, I needed to discover what was of real importance to the United States, militarily and politically, in Iraq and map out a program for myself in contributing to our overall intelligence picture.

The only truly important development in Iraq at the time involved the Kurds, about a seventh of the population inhabiting the northeast corner of the country, who engaged in sporadic rebellion against the authorities along with their cousins across the Iranian border. My predecessor had completed a definitive report on the entire Kurdish situation shortly before his departure. The Kurds in Iraq were comparatively quiescent at the moment. Therefore I decided to leave the Kurds until later, except for reporting on occasional local developments, and devote a major effort to a comprehensive report on the Arab tribes, still a militarily significant element of the population at that time.

In the legation I found another kindred soul, Donald Bergus — then a clerk, later a vice-consul — at the beginning of a distinguished diplomatic career. He shared my love of classical Greece, being half-Greek himself, along with a compatible sense of humor. In August we moved in together for a while in the house kindly made available to us by a British couple on leave, which made Baghdad summer life much more bearable. "It's a dream," I wrote, "to get out of that hotel — I've lived so much in shabby hotels in the last two years but have never gotten used to it."

My principal official contact at the legation, by coincidence, I already knew, though our acquaintance was a distant one: The political secretary, Walter Birge, had been a sixth-former at Groton when I was a "new kid." He was tall and handsome despite a touch of premature baldness, and much more attached to our Groton ties than I. He recalled how he, the tallest sixth-former, had led the choir in chapel, followed by me, the school runt. Recently divorced, he was starved for female company, not easily available in Baghdad. But he knew how to make himself charming to the few ladies one could meet, and it was he who introduced me to what there was of Iraqi society in the Western sense of the word.

The center of this society was the salon of Iraq's only prominent woman, the extraordinary Badi'a Afnan, the widow of Hussein Afnan, a diplomat and government official who died in 1940. He was a grandson of Baha'ullah, the Iranian founder of the Baha'i religion. Badi'a herself came from the distinguished Husri family, originally from Aleppo, Syria. She was the first Moslem woman in Baghdad to take off the veil and take part in social life, and at the time few had yet followed her example. She was also one of the very few women in government, an inspector in the Department of Education.

To her house flocked the few Westernized, "liberated" people of Baghdad, like the Ali Jawdats, whom I had met in Washington; the Askaris; the Pachachis; and others, including, occasionally, the great Nuri Pasha Sa'id himself, the prime minister. Badi'a's teenage daughter, Furugh, attended the dinners.

The principal language of these gatherings was Turkish, dating from the days of the Ottoman Empire, and on the occasions of lapses into Arabic, Badi'a had a Turkish accent. Frequently at her house was her brother-in-law, Hassan Afnan, and his family, whose language was Persian; the Iranian minister and other Iranians were occasional guests. This further stimulated my interest in the Persian language. I had already started on its very easy grammar and was beginning to read the Gospel of Saint John in the language.

Badi'a took me under her wing and I was often at her house, sometimes with just a few friends to play bridge. Others began to invite me to their homes, where the wife could sit at the dinner table. These were drawn from the few families who constituted Westernized society in Baghdad, either Christian or the handful of Moslem couples who joined Western-style dinner parties.

Such couples were entirely Sunni — the rare Shi'ite guest never brought his wife, with one notable exception, Fadhil Jamali*. His wife was an American, and they occasionally invited Americans to their home, and entertained us with a musicale after dinner. These evenings tended to be somewhat stiff, since alcohol, so helpful when guests do not know each other well, was banned, as was tobacco! This was not because of Fadhil's religion but hers — she was a Presbyterian Prohibitionist. He rather liked to sneak a drink with us, away from home, when she was not looking.

Yet this rather formidable lady had made a romantic marriage with Fadhil, himself no figure of romance either, with eyes bulging under his glasses, and mouth hidden behind a bushy, mouse-colored moustache.

She had been on the night shift as a librarian at the University of Chicago when she noticed one of the exchange students, an Arab, staring at her. She found his gaze sinister, and asked another girl to accompany her home. But one night they got to talking, and he turned out to be a mild-mannered idealist with a burning desire — to reform Iraqi education. Long talks and long walks followed.

Soon her family, who had probably resigned themselves to her perpetual maidenhood, were horrified to learn that their daughter was about to marry a Moslem from Baghdad. They persuaded her to settle for going to Baghdad to teach for a year

* Later prominent in the Iraqi government in the 1950s, notably as foreign minister.

before deciding. She agreed, and then decided in his favor. Now they had three little boys who looked American, but spoke only Arabic.

British guests, generally those involved in cultural rather than political or military affairs, were not uncommon at Baghdad social gatherings. There was nothing here resembling the gulf that separated the French from the Moslems in North Africa.

The French in North Africa had replaced independent states with a colony and two semicolonial protectorates. The British *created* the states of Iraq and Transjordan, replacing Turkish rule with progressively more independent governments. Iraq had advanced by a series of small treaties from a British mandate to at least nominal independence in 1932.

But the 1932 treaty between Iraq and Britain left the British with a dominant political and military position in Iraq, with advisers throughout the government, a British military mission, and a base agreement. It was signed over the objections of many nationalists and never fully accepted by a majority of educated Iraqis.

In April of 1941, when Britain was on her knees after the fall of France, a former Iraqi prime minister, Rashid Ali al-Gailani, led a coup that deposed the monarchy, then in the hands of the Regent, Abd-al-Ilah. The British air base of Habbaniyya was overrun and its garrison killed or captured. But the British, not as supine as Rashid Ali assumed, within a few weeks had landed troops at Basra, and sent a column across the desert to retake Habbaniyya and Baghdad. The rebellion had lasted less than two months.

As a result of the rebellion, and the need to establish a secure base for operations in Iran — which Britain and the Soviet Union occupied in August 1941 — the British not only reestablished and greatly strengthened their military presence in Iraq, but also expanded their political advisory system. A senior political adviser was appointed to the British embassy in Baghdad with representatives in every province.

British advisers were found also in all government departments, their authority stretched far beyond their titles, and the monarchy and the cabinet maintained a close partnership with the British embassy. But little in their dealings with Iraqi affairs reminded me of French oppression in North Africa — no *colons* settled in their countryside, no foreign bureaucracy, no prison camps.

Nonetheless, the British were much resented by my Arab friends, many of whom had sympathized with Rashid Ali, though not with his German backers, whose racial theories were abhorrent to them. My friends never expressed hostility toward their Jewish fellow citizens, although they strongly opposed further Jewish settlement in Palestine.

On the other hand, since the troubles in Palestine in the 1930s, anti-Jewish sentiment had grown up in the streets of Baghdad. During the last hours before the British took Baghdad from the forces of Rashid Ali, mobs attacked the Jewish quarter. British officers later told me they could hear the screams of Jewish women in the night as they waited on the west bank of the Tigris for dawn to break. The event was still referred to as the *Farhoud,* the "Looting."

Soon after my arrival in Baghdad I met at the Semiramis the local representative of the Haganah, the military arm of the Jewish Agency. Leopold "Ari" Chill, a small, intense European whose piercing blue eyes in his bronzed face reminded me of Bourguiba, was a passionate Zionist who despised all Arabs.

During that summer of 1944, he took me a couple of times to dine with leaders of the Jewish community. They told me that during the Farhoud some one hundred Jews were killed, and many women raped and kidnapped.

I heard later from various Christian and Moslem Iraqi friends about the horrors of the event: the Jewish quarter echoing with screams, how many women were murdered after being raped, or returned weeks later pregnant. Some Jewish households escaped by bribing policemen to guard their houses and say they were Moslem. Others took refuge in neighboring quarters with Arab friends — occasionally even with tribesmen — in accordance with the tribal tradition that you must protect a guest or anyone who takes refuge in your house.

My Moslem friends had mostly forgotten about the Farhoud until November 1, 1945. This was the anniversary of the Balfour Declaration and, as I wrote in my diary, "The Jews were petrified. All the poor Arabs had counted on a day of looting and raping, and the students on a nice demonstration." But the government had lined the streets with police and troops, and all gatherings were dispersed before they could grow threatening. The day passed without incident. But the Jewish community never did recover from the Farhoud and took the opportunity to flee en masse when Israel became independent.

The Christian community, numbering about 100,000, slightly smaller than the Jewish population, got along with the Moslems reasonably well, and there was some social mixing, particularly at the sophisticated level of the Afnans and their friends. Nevertheless, lower down in the social scale the communities did not socialize, and the Christians spoke a distinct dialect of Arabic.

As that first summer ended, my life in Baghdad began to fall into a pattern. The colonel and I would be driven to the office together at seven o'clock, when office life began, to take advantage of the morning coolness. I found myself quickly assuming the role of reporting on all substantive matters of interest to G2, as the colonel was not concerned with what was going on in Iraq. He confined himself to the routine liaison functions of the job, and consequently did not have enough to do. He filled his time by involving himself in details such as long-winded correspondence, prolix office memoranda, guest lists, and meticulous study and application of regulations. He wasted quite a bit of my own time in trivia, but on the other hand, with his passion for minutiae he kept us out of trouble, and represented us well in high-level functions and contacts with British and American brass.

Meanwhile I expanded my own contacts, and in contrast to my pattern with the French in North Africa, many of the most important of these were with the British authorities. I was a frequent visitor at the mud-brick headquarters of CICI and with our common interests the barrier of our different nationalities melted away. My New England background had conditioned me to be an Anglophile in any case. We formed those easy friendships of wartime, and their help was invaluable in all my projects.

I also got to know the more senior British political advisers reporting to Her Majesty's Embassy, such as Lieutenant Colonel Aston and the oriental secretary, Stewart Perowne.

Outside these strictly official circles I met with other local

Britons, semi-official in the sense that most British private citizens abroad traditionally have a closer connection with British officialdom than do their American counterparts with their own embassies.

On the Iraqi side I found contacts with the military establishment sterile and nonproductive and soon learned that they would be of little assistance in carrying out my project for a study of the Arab tribes.

More interesting were the civilian contacts, such as Salih Jabr, the finance minister and only Shi'ite in the government; Tahsin Qadri, the foreign minister; and the off-and-on prime minister Nuri Sa'id, the wily veteran who managed to keep the helm of Iraq to himself so many years. He did this by keeping the various factions and the British in balance, apparently invulnerable until his grisly end at the hands of the mob in the revolution of 1958. The same mob would also murder His Royal Highness King Feisal II, only a small child when I was in Baghdad, and his uncle the Regent, Abd-al-Ilah.

While my office hours and evenings were often devoted to these contacts, outside the office I gradually found an enjoyable personal life in this city that I came to love.

Between one and two in the afternoon the sun and the heat brought Baghdad to a standstill, and we all went home for a siesta. I often had post-siesta tea with my Persian teacher, an engaging young man named Ali Loqmani who lived, along with most Baghdad Iranians, in the Shi'ite suburb of Kadhimain, around the gold-cupola'd mosque dedicated to Ali Asghar, one of the Shi'ite imams. He knew no English, and his Arabic was not particularly good, so he was the best possible Persian teacher. As that language has hardly changed over the centuries, I learned it almost entirely by reading with Loqmani the *Gulistan* of Sa'adi and the odes of Hafiz.

After that it was back to the office, comparatively quiet in the early evening, as most government offices remained closed for the day after lunch. Then I often worked on my translation of the "Prairies of Gold" when there was no report to write. At nightfall, in accordance with the colonel's decree, I cleared my desk bare — not a natural habit — and set my books standing straight, "like soldiers at drill," following a recent order after he made a late surprise visit to my room. (I am what is known as a "messy desk person" and, alas, the colonel's discipline had no permanent effect on my habits.)

Then I would generally walk back to the Regent Hotel, which became my permanent home. (Don Bergus and I had established ourselves there after our British friends returned from leave.) It was a nice walk, first to the Bab al-Sharji or the eastern gate of the now-vanished city wall, next to the Gailani Mosque, then along Rashid Street, the town's principal thoroughfare parallel to the river. Sometimes when I was in a hurry I would hail an *arabana,* a one-horse carriage, to take me home, joining the many others that filled the road.

The Regent was the newest and best hotel in town, run by an efficient manager, a Jew from Vienna. He had an attractive wife, a petite, zaftig woman with a twinkle in her eyes. She was rumored to exchange flashlight signals across the river with a lover among my CICI friends. His colleagues envied him for this supposed — though certainly fictitious — liaison. It would have been almost an impossibility in the highly visible world of the Regent Hotel, where this pleasant and lively woman knew all about the rare amorous escapades of her guests; none of us ever saw any evidence for suspicion that she had strayed from the reservation herself. But such gossip was natural among the unwillingly celibate expatriate males of Baghdad, which was still off-limits to Western women because of the war.

Local Christian girls who risked going out unescorted with British or American men found that they were no longer accepted by men of their own groups, because their virginity would then be forever in doubt. One of my friends who found a Moslem girl of good family willing to go out with him was visited thereafter at his office by a couple of young thugs who administered a severe beating.

Thus in the hotel dining room and reception chambers our company was entirely male, with a variety of guests to liven up the noontime hours and those evening ones where there was nothing else to do but eat in. One of the most amusing was "Doc" Hoff, the Viennese psychologist, liked by everyone, whose jolly, rotund figure was a frequent presence at Arab homes. His services were often called upon by aging tribal sheikhs who were always worried about declining virility. I remember him telling me one day about his experience in this field. "Amazing," he said, in his pronounced Viennese accent, "the standards they set for themselves. They go to their wives morning, noon, and evening after prayers, and then worry because they cannot do it that last time at night!"

As for ourselves, at night during the hot months we dined late and went to bed at midnight, when the desert air cooled down. While the rooms seemed cool enough for sleep in the afternoon under overhead fans, at night they were unbearable, and we all went to mosquito-netted beds on the roof, with the star-studded sky for our ceiling. The sun woke us before six, in time for a breakfast in the fresh morning air on the banks of the Tigris, already alive with boats sliding through the mists.

Often we went out in those Baghdad nights to dine with friends, and sometimes one of us would organize a *masgouf* party. We would travel down the river on boats to picnic on one of the islands, with plenty of beer to accompany the ritual dinner of *samach masgouf* — flat river fish roasted in a circle around a fire.

Also, one could dine at the Alwiyya Club, near the embassy on the outskirts of town, where we swam in the pool or played tennis on weekends. Sundays we sometimes took a picnic in the gardens on the other side of the Tigris.

There were many fascinations in Baghdad itself, especially in the variety of people on the streets in those days, both in costume and physical type. One time I said to my Armenian driver that when they wore Western dress it was difficult to pick out Baghdadis of different religions and races. "Oh, no," he said, "it's easy. I could never make a mistake."

When I challenged him, he showed me. "What is that man?" — "An Assyrian," or "A Kurd," or "A Jew," or "A Moslem," he would reply, and then shamelessly — and to my embarrassment — he would stop and ask. He was never wrong!

Along Rashid Street many passersby wore rather shabby Western dress, topped by that sorry invention of King Feisal's, a brown forage cap called the *sidara*. It was an Iraqi compromise between the brimmed European hat decreed by Mustafa Kemal for his people (anathema to Moslems, since it impeded the prostrations of prayer) and the fez and turban, considered old-fashioned. The sidara had looked all right on King Feisal because that tall figure and distinguished, regal face could carry anything, but it was dismal on anyone else.

But the religious men and those from all parts of the country still wore mostly the costumes and headwear of their ancestors — robed Bedouins in their kufiyyas, Kurds with their tasseled turbans, cummerbunds stuffed with daggers, and tobacco pouches, Assyrians in their plumed *kepis,* old-fashioned Moslems in their fezzes, and religious sheikhs in white or green turbans.

Most city women were enveloped in black veils, but country women went barefaced, displaying tattooed cheeks and chins, often with turquoise nose rings. This did not add to their charms, but at least they did not bear the scars of the Baghdad boil, which disfigured the faces of the unveiled Christian and Jewish women (and, indeed, of most Baghdadis I knew). At that time this affliction, also found in other Middle Eastern towns, such as Aleppo, struck almost all Iraqis in childhood. It was supposed to result from the bite of a sand fly and, mysteriously, seldom affected Europeans.

Of Baghdad's many ethnic and social strata, one of the most distinctive was the Sabians, who occupied a small corner of the souq reserved for silversmiths. They etched in antimony on silver boxes scenes from their ancestral homes on the Lower Euphrates. A few thousand are still scattered there in tiny colonies, working metal and fashioning riverboats for the marsh tribes.

The Sabians have striking, aquiline features, the men tall and grave with long beards, their heads covered with red-checked kufiyyas, and their open-faced women are famous for their beauty. They still speak an Aramaic tongue, Mandaic, which is the language of their holy books. They are really the descendants, lineally and ritually, of the Babylonians, but call themselves Sabians, because the Koran uses this mysterious term to designate one of the three Peoples of the Book, along with the Jews and the Christians. The Koran require toleration of the Peoples of the Book, as opposed to pagans, for whom the alternatives offered by conquering Moslems were conversion or death.

The Sabians' religion is a mishmash of paganism and monotheism, with a dash of Christianity thrown in. They were happy to be known as the Christians of Saint John when Europeans first appeared among them. However, old Babylonian beliefs form the basis of their faith, especially a reverence for running water, which is part of their religious services. Their holy texts are written on both sides of their manuscripts, so that they can be read simultaneously by priests sitting opposite one another along a narrow stream.

I first learned about the Sabians from an extraordinary Englishwoman I sought out in Baghdad, Lady Drower, a Middle Eastern scholar and traveler of renown. She had managed to gain the confidence of their priests, who for the first time turned over to an unbeliever parchment rolls of their sacred writings, which she was translating. She showed them to me; in a letter I termed them "peculiar things, done up like rolls of toilet paper, full of magic diagrams."

While we were looking at them, one turned out to be missing. Frantic search while I made sympathetic noises. "I know who has stolen it, his reputation is none too good," said Lady Drower. "I left the room while he was looking at them — well, he shan't be allowed in there again, that's for sure."

The suspect was one Père Anastase, an ancient French Carmelite monk. Everyone had been telling me to see him if I could, but this was very difficult; everyone went to see him on Friday mornings, and there were usually several dozen people waiting to ask him questions on Arabic, mostly Moslems. As his life work, he was preparing a huge Arabic dictionary. He was also reputed to have no patience with ignorance or lack of intelligence, and though several people had offered to take me to him, I hadn't pressed it.

I mentioned my desire to see Père Anastase to Lady Drower — she had found the "missing" manuscript and now felt guilty about having suspected him.

So we met in her house. As I entered the door he was huddled with Lady Drower over a Mandaic manuscript, wearing a brown robe with a cowl turned down over his collar. He turned to face me, bullet-headed, with a flowing white beard that covered his whole chest. He gave me a beneficent smile, clearly delighted to see me. It turned out that he had met my uncle Kermit when he was serving with the British in 1920 in the Mesopotamian campaign.

We had a wide-ranging discussion about our mutual interests in this part of the world, in the course of which I told him about my project for translating Mas'udi's "Prairies of Gold." When I told him I was using the recently printed Cairo edition, he was horrified.

"There is only one decent edition," he said, "done by two Frenchmen, with a translation, nine volumes long, and eighty years old, and impossible to find."

I knew this, but had discovered for myself that it was unobtainable. It turned out that Père Anastase had a few volumes of an extra set — *"Ils m'ont volé les autres"* ("They've stolen the others from me") — it seemed that scholars around here were without shame in such matters. He offered to sell them to me at cost, and this gave me an excuse to go and see his library.

We drove through most of Baghdad, and got out at the entrance of the Christian quarter. There was a funeral going on and the narrow, winding streets were full of priests, with their black robes and tall, cylindrical black hats with red tops. We sneaked past, by the church, into a small room, like the cell of a medieval monk, with a squalid bed, a pitcher or two, and an old toilet article here and there — and walls lined with ancient books. I scanned them with fascination and happily took the Mas'udis — they turned out to be just the ones I needed the most.

Then he showed me his dictionary. Fifty fat volumes — looking somewhat like the *Encyclopaedia Britannica* — though inside they were quite different, covered with scrawls and scratches.

"The government doesn't want to publish it because I'm Christian — people without greatness of spirit," he said.

He fished out his edition of the well-known medieval history of pre-Islamic Yemen, the *Iklil*. I mentioned the recent edition of this published by Professor Nabih Faris of Princeton. "I know him," he cried, "he's a brigand — a great thief. He stole my *Iklil* without saying a word, and didn't even write my name in his introduction!" I refrained from remarking that this highly respected professor did indeed make extensive reference to Père Anastase's work in the preface to his English translation of the *Iklil*. What probably enraged the venerable Carmelite was Faris's critical comments on Père Anastase's work, which he said should be superseded by "a critical and complete edition"!

The Land Between Two Rivers

BAGHDAD held so many fascinations it was difficult to tear myself away, but an entire country had yet to be explored and understood. In the task I had set for myself of making a definitive study of the tribes of Iraq, I had tentatively mapped out eleven tribal areas and hoped to make eleven separate expeditions. But besides this more ambitious undertaking, I wanted to see everything within easy reach of Baghdad, and then the principal cities of Iraq — Mosul, Basra, and the holy cities of Kerbela and Nejef.

My first trip, only a month after my arrival, was south over the dusty desert to the Arch of Ctesiphon, the old palace of the Parthian and Sassanian shahs. Alas, it was rather a disappointment, as one entire side of the palace had dissolved into mud in some particularly violent flood of the Tigris a few years previously. I tried to imagine the Arabs bursting into its halls after their victories in the seventh century, when wild tribesmen cut up the priceless carpets studded with gems, to parcel them out democratically. Nothing remains of the twin Sassanian cities on either side of the Tigris except piles of sand.

Hearing the mournful lament of the doves circling the palace ruins, I thought of the lines of Omar Khayyam: "Upon that castle rising to the sky/Towards which the kings set their faces/We saw a ring-dove sitting/Saying 'coo-coo-coo' " (meaning "where, where, where" in Persian). In other words, where are these mighty ones today?

My most rewarding one-day excursion from Baghdad was an

expedition to Samarra. This had been the seat of the Arab caliphate during the latter half of the ninth century, when Baghdad was in turmoil, but the vast city that flourished during those days has vanished. Its only remnant is an imposing mosque, uniquely built in the form of a Babylonian ziggurat, a cone with a stairway winding around it.

The golden dome of a new mosque honors the tombs of the last of the Shi'ite imams, who perished during Samarra's heyday — including al-Mahdi, the very last, who has no tomb, as the faithful believe he disappeared in the cave of the Great Mosque. According to the True Believers, somewhere in the depths of the earth he remains hidden, to emerge once more someday to restore the true religion throughout the world in preparation for the Day of Judgment.

We came to Samarra not to view religious monuments, but to observe a ceremony by living devotees of another sect, the Sufi followers of a latter-day saint, Ahmed ar-Rifa'i. Crowded into a courtyard surrounded by high walls were silent watchers. In a niche in the wall an orchestra of cymbals and drums accompanied a dozen or so bearded dervishes chanting *"Ya Muhammed, Y'Allah, Ya Rifa'i,"* over and over. I described their faces in my diary as "gentle, fanatic, kindly and simple."

As they whirled slowly around, we saw them take long skewers and ram them into their bodies, continuing to chant without changing expression. I could see the points of the skewers breaking the skin after passing through their bellies and backs, and even their necks under the chin — with no sign of blood.

One of our party, a consul, fainted. Nothing daunted, some dervishes came up to our group and offered to kill a man and bring him back to life, but Colonel Converse put his foot down at this point. A policeman accompanying us assured me he had seen them take a running jump at the wall. "You can hear their skulls crack — but then they get right up good as new."

All the way back to Baghdad we speculated. Our eyes could not have deceived us; these miracles were genuine. Doc Hoff offered the view that they knew how to miss vital organs, and controlled the flow of blood by self-hypnosis — not a very satisfying explanation, but the best available.

The only "must" to see in reach of Baghdad was, of course, Babylon. I paid this duty call soon after my arrival — and what a disappointment it proved! There was nothing left of the great city and palace of Nebuchadnezzar except a pile of crumbling bricks, since the Germans had carried away the glazed lion gates to Berlin.* The tower of Babylon — the seat of the hanging gardens — had mostly been demolished by the Turks, who used its bricks to build the nearby dam.

More impressive was the nearby ziggurat of the ancient Babylonian city of Borsippa, called Birs Nimrud by the Arabs, who associate it with Nimrod, "a mighty hunter before the Lord." The Sumerians are supposed to have built these high brick structures surrounded by circular staircases out of home-sickness for the mountains whence they came to this flat and monotonous plane. On our climb to the top we passed huge piles of brick fused into rock by heat, supposedly by a bolt from heaven to scatter the nations in punishment for their arrogance. This was the Tower of Babel. Beneath us stretched the desert plain, relieved by a few green fields, and a cluster of black Bedouin tents, bounded by the faint line of the Euphrates on the horizon.

Shortly after my Babylon expedition I made my first foray into tribal Iraq, to the Dulaim tribe of the Upper Euphrates. In our company were Don Bergus and Walter Birge, my friend from Groton, and we took along Badi'a Afnan and her daughter Furugh — not a successful idea but one that at least served to illustrate the gulf between Baghdad and tribal society.

After crossing the Euphrates on a makeshift ferry near Ramadi, we were greeted first by a magnificent array of horsemen armed with obsolete rifles lined up on either side of the road leading to a house. There the sheikh, accompanied by a half-dozen tall and handsome sons, received us with becoming gravity.

After being led into a large but crudely built stucco house, we stood awkwardly on the Persian rugs covering the vestibule until the sheikh ushered us into a small dining room. In the center of the table was a huge dish filled with a black mass of unfamiliar food. A swish of towels caused thousands of flies to rise from the plate, revealing a mountain of white (but fly-

* The Iraqis have since managed to excavate and restore enough to make the trip worthwhile.

specked) rice, surrounded by fried eggs, kidneys, dried fruit, and bread.

None of our party except myself and an accompanying Iraqi army officer had the courage to attack these dishes, and I wrote, "I cannot remember ever having been to a stiffer repast." Hardly a word was spoken, but the mutual disapproval of the Afnans and our host was palpable. The sheikh professed surprise to hear Furugh speaking Arabic, and polite astonishment when informed that she was "a daughter of the Arabs" — in fact, the daughter of the famous Hussein Afnan. "Why were these women allowed here, not even veiled?" you could see him thinking. "And why are we sitting at the table of this feudal savage?" thought the Afnans.

For the only time in my entire Iraqi tribal experience we were served beer. When Madame Afnan refused it, the sheikh said, "Perhaps you would prefer whiskey?" — this and the "mistake" as to Furugh's national origin being veiled barbs at what he considered the loose habits of the townspeople.

But the Dulaim were really a settled and somewhat detribalized people, and I wanted to seek out a traditional Bedouin tribe in the north before pursuing my most important objective, the great tribes of the south, particularly the Marsh Arabs. The nearest at hand were the Shammar, the nomads who roamed the Jazirah — the "island" between the Tigris and the Euphrates.

I had already had one intriguing glimpse of them on my visit to Babylon, when I had passed a section of the Shammar migrating south, in a long single file of camels. The men, healthy-looking and fine-featured, rode beside the column, their rifles strapped to their backs. The women were borne in litters covered with blankets, swaying slowly on the camels' backs.

Fortunately, the brother of Sfuq al-Ajil, paramount chief of the Shammar, lived in the Regent Hotel. He was Sheikh Ahmed, an intelligent and likable graduate of the American Jesuit College in Baghdad, and about my own age. One day early in the new year, he invited me to lunch with his brother, Sfuq, and a leading member of the tribe, Mish'an al-Faisal. Hardly a Rudolph Valentino type, Sfuq was fat, his coarse, hairy face half-hidden by blue-tinged hexagon glasses. He took no part in the conversation. Mish'an, on the other hand, was a real tribal warrior who had killed a dozen men, shooting from the saddle during desert skirmishes.

His eyes lit up as he told me the history of his tribe, how they had migrated to Iran long ago, but left that country when the Shah had demanded tribute. Most went off to Nejd, Saudi Arabia, but a section, the Shammar Jerba, split off and ranged in Iraq. I laid the groundwork for a visit to them in the early spring — the best time in the desert — and set out the following April with the colonel. There were some disadvantages to these trips with the colonel despite my affection for him. With the local officials and tribal leaders, he would often lead our conversations into irrelevant byways — trivia such as geegaws he might have glimpsed in the souq, or some detail about clothes or uniforms, cutting down the amount of time for any substantive talks I wished to have. He hated local food, terming shish kabob "flies on a stick." He preferred to eat army rations in the car!

The colonel insisted that we travel in a horrible old crate he called the field car, which he claimed was the only thing "for heavy duty." Actually it was almost useless. Originally a reconnaissance car — a model abandoned by the army — it was a large steel cube with one door on which the colonel had painted the initial of every country he had traveled in. After one trip he cheated by adding *K* for Kurdistan, a country unrecognized by anybody. Inside, he put a huge radio, a map table or two, first-aid kit, a bag of kitchen utensils, racks innumerable, a box of hand grenades (some Colonel Blimp had told him that was the best defense against attacking tribesmen) — and about a dozen cans for water, gas, and oil.

On the back was tacked a trailer with tents, beds, canned goods, and various instruments for surveying and finding one's location (which nobody knew how to use). So much weight had practically ruined the body of the car, which rattled and shook at every bump, and the tires gave out every few miles. The car traveled a mere thirty miles an hour even on a flat, hard surface, and broke down three times a day. It took the better part of a day to load and at least an hour to get started. After every trip the old heap was laid up for a month!

Before every expedition all of us in the office would try to persuade the colonel to go the easy way, in the sedan. But this field car was the colonel's pride and joy (though everyone in the Middle East laughed about it) and he wouldn't hear of our leaving it behind. Thus much time on every trip was spent in struggling with the car under the hot desert sun.

On this particular expedition we drove first to Mosul, and after exploring the ruins of Nineveh, set out for the Jazirah. We made a short detour north to visit the mixed villages on the edge of Kurdistan, especially those of the Yazidis, a syncretic sect of Kurdish-speaking people, distrusted and persecuted of old because of their unorthodox rites and beliefs. These include a certain respect for Satan, on the theory that it is wise to propitiate both sides in disputes between powers. They avoid using his name, Shaitan, or even words beginning with the Arabic letter *shin,* so as not to offend him!

We passed over the Khosh River to the Yazidi village of Ba'shika. On its edge we found a religious feast in progress, with Yazidi girls and men dancing arm in arm — in itself enough to shock orthodox Moslems.

They spoke Kurdish, as did the inhabitants of the next little town, Dohuk, in a green mountain valley. We passed on through these charming hills to Zakho, spectacularly perched on an island in the middle of the Khabur River, with an ancient bridge spanning its rapids. Half of the people there were Jews — fine-looking men with kind, pleasant faces and long black curly Assyrian beards. There were also Armenian refugees from Turkey as well as Chaldeans.

The following day we turned east and south toward Bedouin country, passing through the Turkoman village of Tell Afar, and on to the Yazidi center of Balad Sinjar. Its souq was full of Bedouins as well as Yazidis, as we were on the Shammar border, and a short way out of town we were met by one of Sfuq's black slaves. He led us to Sfuq's desert camp not far away, in a valley full of spring grass and flowers, crowded with grazing sheep, camels, and horses.

Sfuq, and a number of his sheikhs, received us and led us to three multicolored pavilions that dominated the black tents surrounding them. They offered me my first ride on a horse without stirrups — sackcloth was used for a saddle — and then my first fried locusts (tasting a bit like crunchy shrimp) as an hors d'oeuvre for the usual tribal dinner. Despite their show of hospitality they were obviously preoccupied. A tribal meeting was clearly in session. Our hosts kept slipping in and out of the guest tent to confer, often with the closemouthed Mosul chief of police, who was also visiting, with two carloads of his forces. I later found out that my previous hosts, the Dulaim, who paid tribute to the Shammar, had been robbed by the traditional enemies of the Shammar, the Ageidat from across the river in Syria. Retribution was called for.

They were probably relieved to see us leave accompanied by one of their sheikhs, Daham al-Turki, small, dark, and fierce-looking except when a smile flashed across his face. He clutched his rifle throughout the trip, scanning the horizon and once calling us to a halt when he sighted a dust cloud, perhaps enemy horsemen, in the distance.

Very soon the meadows turned deep red, covered by a rustling river of larval locusts in the hopping stage, ready to be transformed into lethal swarms. After passing many Bedouin tents and flocks we started to cross a *wadi,* or streambed, still damp from the winter rains, and the colonel's famous truck just couldn't make it. There we sat for five hours. A Bedouin appeared on the horizon, looked at us for a minute and, not liking what he saw, turned away. Daham shot a pistol at him, without persuading him to change his mind and come back.

Finally Daham climbed out of the wadi and wandered around the desert for a time waving his rifle with his kufiyya attached to the muzzle. At last he found a mounted Bedouin, borrowed his horse, and galloped after help, while the Bedouin stared at us and our gear with childlike wonder. He asked us if we were English, saying, "The Ingleis are our cousins!" and wanted to know just who was at war with whom in the wide world outside.

Daham returned with a truckload of cheerful Shammar locust exterminators to pull us out. We went on to look over the ruins of Hatra, in Roman times a flourishing town on a river (now long gone dry), before rattling our way back to Baghdad.

Luckily I was able to visit on my own, unencumbered with the colonel and his dreadful vehicle, three cities of the south, beginning with the holy city of Kerbela. I was accompanied by one of my buddies from CICI, Captain Christopher Hohler, an earnest Oxford graduate my own age with my kind of sense of humor; he was tall, with a huge British colonial moustache. On the way, in Hilla, we were joined by Major Robert Ellis, the area liaison officer, a bluff, heavy, hard-drinking irrigation expert with no pretensions to real involvement in the area. I think he was mainly responsible for making my pilgrimage to Kerbela one of the more sacrilegious ones in its history.

After the obligatory calls on various officials, we drove to the summer house of the hereditary sheikh of Kerbela, Hamid Kamuna, in a dark palm grove on the banks of a canal, where we had been invited to spend the night. Meeting us at the door, our host settled us on the top floor, then led us down to the veranda.

He was a short, rather plump, elderly man with hair dyed a deep black, evidently some time ago, as an inch of whitish hair grew from its roots. His face was twisted in a servile, artificial smile, and when he got up to offer cigarettes or drinks, he moved in an affected, mincing manner.

We sat for at least two hours, sipping various gin concoctions, until lunch finally appeared around four in the afternoon. The food was stone cold, as it had to be carried over from the main house some distance away. After lunch and what seemed like endless dull conversation, we were finally allowed to go for an evening walk around the town, under the guidance of Sheikh Hamid's house poet, Abd-ul-Amir Kandarchi.

A short, sturdy figure in Arab costume with a tarbush circled by a turban, he had some knowledge of Arabic and Persian literature. Shortly after our arrival he declaimed a poem specially composed for the occasion, in classical Arabic, with many grand phrases about Anglo-Iraqi understanding, and allusions both to Eisenhower and Major Ellis.

Most amusing was the introduction, in English, of which Abd-ul-Amir did not understand a word. This had been written out for him in Arabic characters by a friend who thought he knew English — to me it sounded rather like Hindustani. Later Sheikh Hamid said that Abd-ul-Amir, who doubled as a steward in his household, gave him reports on his date crop written in verse!

Kerbela had the aspect of an old Arab town, with only a few paved streets bisecting its maze of narrow, winding lanes. The inhabitants were a picturesque lot — *seyyids*, descendants of the Prophet through his grandson Hussein, with green bands around their tarbushes; descendants of Hussein's half brother Abbas, wearing black bands instead; and the ordinary members

of the community with bands of gold-embroidered silk. Occasionally a huge white turban of one of the *ulema* (religious
sages) wove its way majestically through the crowd. Among all
these one heard Persian spoken as much as Arabic, and bands
of tribal pilgrims in their kufiyyas wandered like strangers
among these holy men.

Pushing our way through this motley throng, we arrived at
the square fronting the Mosque of Hussein, and cast a furtive
sideways glance through the mob pushing in and out of this
holiest of shrines. A large chain hung at the gate, beyond which
no unbeliever was supposed to pass, and I saw the faithful
touch it as they moved in and out. We had to content ourselves
with a glimpse of the walls of Persian tiles within, framed with
arabesques, before turning back to the hospitable compound of
Sheikh Hamid.

We had been promised an evening of entertainment, which I
hoped would enliven the banal group of guests who began to
appear in the summer house after our return. They were
obviously Kerbela's secular establishment, portly middle-aged
officials and businessmen in European dress. Fortunately there
was no need for much stilted conversation, for shortly after
their arrival, when we were slightly mellowed by some of the
sheikh's precious whiskey, an ill-assorted troupe of entertainers
presented themselves.

First came three instrumentalists: one was a merry black
armed with a drum, next a seedy-looking Arab with a *rababa* —
the Arab fiddle — and finally a shriveled old man, nearly blind,
with his flute. Soon they set up a rhythmic but, to my ears,
unorchestrated series of sounds; the flutist seemed to be paying
no attention to what the others were doing, but struck out
feverishly on his own.

Then into the room tripped a sallow pockmarked youth with
long stringy hair. He simpered lewdly as he walked, swinging
his hips. He wore a shabby brown jacket of European make,
and a drab silk tunic, known as a *zaboun,* of neutral shade
swinging around his ankles. Dancing in the same manner as the
gypsy girls I had seen in the Lower Tigris, he shook his
shoulders and threw his lank black hair about. So this was one
of those dancing boys mentioned by the poets!

After a good long stretch of this, he paused for a rest, and his
place was taken by Abd-ul-Amir, who in spite of his stout figure

danced rather gracefully, embellishing his performance with lascivious movements of the head and eyebrows. He followed this by an act with a glass of *arak* perched on his head — in the course of which he lay down on the floor, and leaped about the room, without losing a drop of that ghastly fluid. But even this was not the limit of his performance. Next we were treated to a comic song, with a spirited accompaniment by the orchestra, the refrain of which ran:

> *Tuwankel, tuwankel lettlee star,*
> *Major Ellis al-Khattar.*

In spite of the outlandish sound of this verse, it contained just one Arabic word, *al-khattar,* meaning guest; the rest was adapted from a well-known English rhyme about a twinkling star!

Abd-ul-Amir disappeared for a while, and the orchestra relaxed. All at once into the room stepped what appeared to be a learned *mulla,* or cleric. He had the huge white turban on his head, all right, with the white nightshirt and the gigantic potbelly characteristic of his breed. But what at first glance seemed to be his outstretched arms upon closer inspection turned out to be two long boards wrapped up in his robes — and his big belly looked suspiciously like heavily stuffed pillows. He came in and squatted cross-legged on a chair placed for him with mock respect by one of the orchestra, and twitched his moustache and his mouth in a self-important manner. It was only then I realized that he was none other than our friend Abd-ul-Amir the poet.

He began to speak classical Arabic in the rapid, perfunctory manner of a priest uttering a formula repeated too often to have any trace of meaning. The recital was frequently interrupted by impressive coughing. I gathered he was telling something about the life of Hussein, and that the whole performance was highly blasphemous.

After this had gone on for a while, he raised his heavy figure from the chair and, singing in a loud voice and shaking his tremendous frame, he danced around the room. His artificial arms swayed up and down, while his real hands, concealed beneath his robes, one before and one behind, flapped back and forth in unison, one hand emphasizing the most honored part of man's anatomy, and the other the most despised!

This was the climax of the evening. After that I would have been content to settle down to a good dinner and bed. But, alas, that was not the custom. That sallow youth resumed his unseemly dance while the orchestra droned on. Everybody but Hohler and myself began to get rather drunk and to disport themselves around the room. A figure I had not noticed before, a big handsome youth in clean tribal dress, hovered about our host. He came from Sheikh Hamid's country estate and acted as a highly privileged servant. All these men, Ellis told me, were bisexual; and our host obviously preferred dancing boys to the company of his secluded and uneducated womenfolk.

Meanwhile the whiskey had run out and they poured a glass of brandy for me. I certainly did not want to add brandy to the whiskey I had already consumed, so each time the sheikh raised his glass in a toast I merely pretended to swallow. Of course they soon noticed and assumed it was because only whiskey was good enough for me. So Sheikh Hamid sent out to his country estate, eighteen miles away, to fetch another bottle of whiskey, and when it arrived, I had to accept it with feigned gratitude. Accompanied by that infernal orchestra, the black drummer went on singing for my benefit, including a composition that had found its way from Harlem to the holy city of Kerbela, "Chicky-Chicky-Boom-Boom." Finally, after two in the morning, a huge meal was served, again stone cold — and at last came the hour for sleeping.

Not surprisingly, we felt terrible in the morning. Hohler and I had hoped that a Turkish bath — our first experience of this fabled delight, which had been promised the night before by the sheikh — would revive us. A servant led us into a dirty, shabby little building, where we were accosted by an even dirtier, shabbier little old man. He wore a ragged garment so patched that it was hard to discern the original material.

Leading us along a dingy passage to a narrow room with a bench and hooks, he presented us with some wooden clogs. He told us to undress, and gave us a piece of cloth apiece for decency. After undressing, he said, we were to go into the next room and wash. We obeyed, and proceeding through a short passage made unpleasantly odoriferous by an Arab toilet, we entered the bathroom: a dark room with a dirty tiled floor; walls covered by green fungus from which the plaster had fallen away to expose the moldering mud beneath; a low bench; a few basins on the floor; a couple of showers separated by a wooden partition; and a steam jet dejectedly spouting a wisp or two of vapor, like a tired smoker. Shades of Caracalla and Haroun al-Rashid!

Hohler and I washed, and stood around waiting for something to happen, preferably for the traditional shiny black slaves to rush in, seize us, and pound us into human shape. But nobody came, and we were beginning to get cold. So we proceeded to the next room, took a few towels from the shabby old man, and sat awhile wrapped up in them, then dressed and went away. That was all.

Somewhat disappointed in my stay in the second holy city of the Shi'ites, it was not without a certain feeling of relief that I found myself, along with Hohler, Ellis, and a rather unsavory taxi driver, bounding over the desert to Nejef, smaller in size than Kerbela but first of the holy cities in rank.

Compared with our visit to Kerbela, our brief stay in Nejef was sedate and uneventful, in keeping with the sacred character of the town. The approach to it, on the edge of the desert that stretches all the way to Arabia, is the traditional pilgrim road, and we saw busloads of them, and some, too poor or too pious to take the easier way, on foot. On either side was a vast cemetery, dreary in the uninspired stony disorder of such establishments — for Moslems do not believe in chiseled tombstones. Here and there its monotony was relieved by the blue-green dome of a minor saint's last repository. It was thronged with relatives of the dead.

Unlike Kerbela, Nejef had broad thoroughfares swarming with nomads from the desert. We passed through the center of town to the home of our host for the night — and what a pleasant relief after the excesses of the previous evening.

Our host, Hajji Muhsin ash-Shallash, was a pious Moslem of the old school, dignified, gray-bearded, with an aquiline face and a benign smile. We discussed religion, religious education, and Old Islam. No liquor was served, but both lunch and dinner were delicious and hot. In the afternoon his sons walked us to a high mound west of the city to admire the fine view of its old houses surrounding the golden dome of the holy mosque of Ali, the Prophet's son-in-law. After an early evening we went to bed, ready to resume our travels the following day with improved disposition and conscience.

Basra, the other great town of southern Iraq — its only true city — is not holy at all. In fact, many of its inhabitants are Sunnis. It is the commercial capital of the south, as well as the port for all Iraq.

I set out on this expedition on the night train from Baghdad in late February 1945. The first-class compartment I shared with a British captain was not exactly deluxe — I slept on a hard bench, shivering between two army blankets. But I awoke to a glorious sight: The flat, naked desert had been turned by the winter rains into an endless green meadow, spangled with yellow and purple flowers.

This changed abruptly when we approached the dreary mud flats north of Basra. The captain pointed out to me the salt pans. In summer, he explained, women came from Basra to collect the salt in burlap bags. After scraping the salt from the bottom, they placed it in the bags and trudged back the many miles to the city with brine dripping down their backs and caking in the fierce desert sun. "One would think it would sear their flesh, but, as far as I know, they suffer no ill effects," he said.

From Basra I set out in the U.S. naval observer's launch down the Shatt al-Arab to Khorramshahr. It was a beautiful morning, with a cold breeze blowing over the water. The date palms stretched along the shore in a solid line of dark green, broken by a few clearings in which stood old-fashioned mansions with blue-rimmed balconies, date-packing plants full of milling coolies, or clusters of reed huts. Here and there a canal left the main stream and wound its way among the palms.

The river was filled with mostly traditional craft, but one did see an occasional launch, and even a freighter or two. However, one was hardly ever out of sight of the long, graceful *mashhuf*, the canoe of the Marsh Arabs. Each carried anywhere from one to fourteen persons. It was astonishing how many Arabs could be packed on one mashhuf and still stay afloat. The water often reached to within an inch of the gunwales, and when we passed them in our launch, our waves drenched the passengers, who took it with good-natured grins.

Often a woman sat paddling in the stern and a man in the

bow, but their positions were never reversed. The Arabs thought that if the man sat behind and the woman in front, his eyes would always be resting on her — which might prove damaging to male virtue.

Eventually we arrived at Abadan Island, and then at the mouth of the Karun River, filled with dozens of dhows. On its banks stands the great city of Khorramshahr, or, as the Arabs called it, Muhammarah. This was then nothing more than a squalid collection of mud and corrugated iron huts, with a narrow, unpaved slough for a main street, swarming with wretched coolies. From there we drove back to Basra, where I spent the afternoon.

Basra has three main suburbs: Old Basra, Ma'qil, and Ashar. I quote from my trip report:

> The city presents a squalid and untidy appearance. Most of its streets are unpaved and hence muddy in winter, and probably dusty in summer. Its outskirts consist of dirty huts constructed of mud, petrol tins, or pieces of corrugated iron; its main part consists of a jumble of ugly buildings of decaying yellow bricks. Most of the British army installations are in Ma'qil, the port of Basra; the name means "tethering-place of camels" — and one wishes it were still what its name implies.
>
> Ashar is the residential and commercial section — but it possesses little to boast about; its drab public buildings seem perfectly at home in their dreary surroundings. Ashar Creek, however, still retains something of the picturesque, with dhows and footbridges. The bazaars north of the creek are not entirely devoid of charm, nor are the old Moslem houses lining the bank.
>
> Old Basra, which lies near the tail of Ashar Creek, is a tumbling heap of mouldering brick, swarming with filthy humanity. As one drives past it on the main road, one can catch a glimpse of the large rickety structure known as the Beehive, Basra's famous house of prostitution. The bazaar of Old Basra used to be fairly prosperous, but trade has been gradually moving to Ashar following the sacking of the Basra bazaar during the Rashid Ali rebellion.
>
> Many of the inhabitants of Basra are of African descent. Not only does one see many blacks in the street, but most of the Arabs, even those of aristocratic families, are of mixed origin.

The following morning we drove through the dreary salt flats south of Basra — which air observation shows once to have been irrigated fields — to Busairah, ancient Basra, the city of Sindbad. Our first sight of it was a crumbling tower in the distance, popularly known as the Tower of Sindbad, but which, an Arab servant told me, was formerly the Mosque of Ali. As we drew nearer, we could make out the tumbled heaps of mud and loose bricks where once stood the great city.

Of the mosque itself only a corner was left — a few falling walls the local Arabs had made into a shrine. In the shelter of its crumbling roof they had built a *mihrab*, or prayer niche, and covered its moldering walls with the marks of their hands, dipped in manure: the age-old protective symbol of the hand of Fatimah, the Prophet's daughter.

Far more impressive than the mosque were the low mounds of rubble, stretching for acres and acres, the hollows between them covered with green grass and bright little desert flowers shivering in the spring breeze. I longed to pause there and think about the glories of the past; the great merchants and their wares and ships; the generals, *wazirs*, and caliphs; the camel drivers, the porters, the slaves. I could imagine its streets, looking much like those of Fez, only more bustling, broader, and cosmopolitan. Of all the ruins I have ever visited, these gave me the deepest feeling, although there was nothing there to mark the dead city but the bare ground, and two forlorn piles of bricks. In the back of my mind floated formlessly the many passages I had read in Arabic literature about the passing of all earthly things. I recalled the sonorous sentences beginning the tales of *The Arabian Nights:* "*Balaghani annahu kana fi qadimi 'z-zaman, fi khilafati amiri-'l-mu'minina Haruni-r-Rashid. . . .*"*

From the Tower of Sindbad we went on to the walled town of Zubair, at the edge of the high desert, whose inhabitants were known for their strong Sunni convictions. Like Nejef, Zubair had the feel of Arabia — streets lined by blank, buttressed gray walls, featureless except for an occasional wooden gate with a heavy bronze knocker in the shape of a hand; its clean, sandy streets; its muffled figures — all these made me feel that I had

---

* "I have heard that in olden times, in the Caliphate of the Commander of the Faithful Haroun al-Rashid. . . ."

reached the confines of the austere and holy "Island of the Arabs," as they call the Arabian peninsula.

Before leaving, we visited the flat ground outside the walls on the far side of town where the Bedouins came in to sell their wares; a boy was showing off his desert horse; camels stood on three feet, the fourth being flexed and tied up; and women were selling truffles. We only had time to glance and speed away, as I had to catch the train back to Baghdad.

13

The Tribes of the South

AFTER THESE FORAYS to the holy cities, it was time to focus on what would become the major accomplishment of my mission to Baghdad, a definitive report on the Arab tribes of Iraq. The most significant of these were in the Shi'ite country of the south, and I made three extensive trips to study these tribes, most of whom could be grouped under the loose classification of Marsh Arabs.

Southern Iraq was once mostly dry, dusty desert alternating with marshland, where its two great rivers, fed by spring floods, had burst their banks. Its inhabitants were primitive nomads and fishermen.

Then appeared, about 3000 B.C., that talented people, the Sumerians, bringing with them the art of irrigation. Under the strong rule of their priest-kings, they turned the deserts and marshes of the Lower Euphrates into a garden. But hungry tribes of nomads were still prowling the desert, waiting their chance to burst in on the smiling country at the first sign of weakness. At their savage hands the farm population perished or melted away. Dams broke, canals silted up, and the rebellious rivers escaped from the levees that imprisoned them. What the rivers could not turn to swamp, the nomads made a desert.

The wild tribesmen, in their turn, were tamed. Strong kings appeared who changed them into toiling masses of *fellahin*, clearing canals, building dams, and piling up bunds, or embankments. The rivers, too, were tamed, and the country smiled again.

Thus it has been throughout the history of the Land Between Two Rivers — periods of tribalism and desolation, followed by periods of settlement and prosperity.

During its peaceful interludes, the land enjoyed a series of great civilizations, such as that of the Babylonians two millennia before Christ, and the Persians, who ruled it for the thousand years straddling the Christian era. But they, like all before them, fell prey to desert nomads, this time the Arabs.

While the great caliphs of Baghdad brought most of the land back into civilization, after a few centuries their empire deteriorated, to be destroyed by the Mongol invasion in the thirteenth century.

From that time until late in the last century, southern Iraq was a tribal country of deserts and swamps; only the riverbanks here and there were green with nonproductive willows and poplars. In the vicinity of a few large towns, permanent cultivation lingered on, but in the rest of Lower Mesopotamia, agriculture was dead.

Then, under the vigorous rule of a reformist Turkish governor, Midhat Pasha, the land began to awaken from its long sleep. In spite of the corruption and ineptitude of the Turks, the waters of the two rivers began to be put to use, old canal beds were cleared, and little pieces of the land became green again. Most of the modern towns of Mesopotamia were born during this period.

But the country was still largely desert and marshlands, fought over by unruly tribes, when the British arrived on the scene in World War I. The British political officers who then took control of the tribal areas, many of them with prior experience in Arabia and especially India, proved much more adept in bringing order to the area than their Ottoman predecessors. Civil order and security led the way to yet another conversion of the Mesopotamian countryside to agricultural prosperity. The tribes as I knew them are today vanishing from the scene — with the Iran-Iraq War perhaps dealing the final deathblow to the way of life of the Marsh Arabs.

Just who are these inhabitants of the marshes? The Bedouins do not consider them Arabs. The nomads of the desert, People of the Camel, view themselves as the only true Arabs.

During periods of prosperity, the camel nomads settled on

the Land Between Two Rivers. In the first stage of settlement they abandoned their camels as the source of food, cloth, and transport, for sheep and donkeys, and moved in and out of the riverbed in search of pasture. They were looked down on by their brethren still in the desert, who called them Sheep People — Shawiyya.

After a few generations the Shawiyya settled down to farm rice on the banks of the river, moving east until they reached the edge of the marshes, losing the last remnants of their Bedouin nobility. Beyond them are the Ma'adan — those who actually spend their whole lives in the depths of the swamps, living off fish and their herds of water buffalo. They already bore this name in the time of the early fourteenth-century Arab geographer Ibn Battuta, who wrote:

> Then we travelled along the Euphrates by a forest of reeds in the midst of the water, inhabited by Arabs known as the Ma'adi, who are brigands, and Shi'ites by faith. They have fortified themselves in this jungle and are inaccessible from attack in it — and there are many lions there.

Since Ibn Battuta's day the lions have disappeared — the last lion was seen around 1920 — but the rest remains as he describes it. The country between the Euphrates south of Nasiriya and the Tigris south of Amara down to the Shatt al-Arab, and west of the Tigris from Amara south, is almost entirely freshwater swamp. These vast marshes are covered with reeds, up to twenty feet high, towering over the channels that wind through them. These are usually only a few feet wide, navigable only by canoe.

The Ma'adan are mostly of non-Arab origin, perhaps descended from the ancient inhabitants of Mesopotamia. They live in the middle of the marshes on mounds of earth, called *ishan*, which are generally the remains of ancient cities and castles. They also construct for themselves mounds of mud and reeds, called *chuba'ish*, which have to be renewed every year in the flood season.

In their canoes, or *mashahif* (the plural of mashhuf), which have high tapering bows like gondolas and are made of reeds or wood and covered with bitumen, they paddle or pole their way through the marshes. If floods or enemies drive them from their mounds, they simply bundle their possessions into their mashahif and take to the swamp, leaving behind their easily replaced reed houses without regret.

They make their living by cutting and selling reeds, making rush mats, trapping otters and wild fowl, fishing (with nets or curious, five-pronged fish spears), or by selling the milk, butter, and cream produced by their water buffalo.

While the Marsh Arabs still live very much in the style of their ancestors, the tribal system in which they were organized at the time of my visit has now almost disappeared. The gradual encroachment of the ways of the townsmen and the more abrupt changes following the revolution of 1958 have all but destroyed it.

Before all this, Arab tribes, nomad and settled alike, were organized in much the same way. Each tribal unit was headed by a sheikh, generally the most senior or strongest personality of the recognized sheikhly house. On the sheikh's death his office generally passed to a brother or one of the sheikh's sons. This was usually decided by a family conclave — as in the Kingdom of Saudi Arabia today — with, possibly, the participation of tribal elders.

The sheikh supervised all activities of the tribe requiring collective effort. Tribal life centered on his guest house, or *mudhif,* which was always open to everyone. Among the qualities expected of a sheikh were generosity and hospitality, and the huge amount of coffee and food served in the mudhif could deplete the sheikh's resources considerably. For this reason the rest of the tribe usually contributed to the upkeep of the mudhif.

The sheikh was, in most cases, illiterate. He had in attendance, therefore, a scribe, or mulla, to take care of such reading and writing as had to be done. This individual's title and office did not have any religious implications, but in his position as the sheikh's confidential secretary he sometimes was the power behind the throne.

The household of a big sheikh was likely to be an organization of some size, including not only his wives and children, but relatives of various degrees of proximity who acted as advisers, stewards, or attendants according to age and dignity. He had a varying number of black slaves who often enjoyed considerable personal influence, and were generally treated with indulgence. He often had a personal bodyguard, called *hashiya,* composed of slaves or young tribesmen, sometimes several hundred in number.

Among the special servants attached to the sheikh's household, there was one who held a special position: the *gahwachi,* or coffee man, who had charge of the mudhif, and especially of the preparation and serving of coffee. It was considered good form for a guest at a feast to send a few choice morsels on a plate to the gahwachi.

It must not be supposed, however, that all this organization was used by the sheikh in dictatorial fashion; the sheikh originally was only the first among equals. The ordinary tribesman showed him respect by rising when he entered a room and kissing his hand, but he also showed his independence by calling the sheikh by his first name and freely expressing his views before him, whether called for or not. The closer a tribe was to the desert, the stronger was this democratic tendency, whereas among settled tribes the sheikh tended to become more of a feudal lord.

Although the tribal system was broken up by the socialist policies initiated in the revolution of 1958, the mores of tribal society have not changed with the system of government. The most important possession of the tribal Arab is not his wife, nor his son, nor his camel — nor, as some romanticists would have us believe, his horse — but his *sharaf,* a word that summarizes the three notions of honor, nobility, and integrity. He often makes an oath by his sharaf, and acts almost as if it were something one could hold in one's hand, but which could be very easily lost.

The opposite of sharaf is *aib* — the Arabic word for shame and disgrace. If an Arab does something, or fails to do something, that incurs aib, he loses caste. Other tribesmen avoid all social contact with him, refuse to give their daughters to him in marriage, and lose no occasion to cast the reproach in his teeth. "His face is blackened," they say.

There are several principal obligations for the upholding of sharaf. First and foremost, the inviolability and chastity of the women of one's family must be maintained. Any departure from chastity must be punished with death for the woman herself, and the guilty man if caught — the only possible exception being rape, when the man only is theoretically liable. This is, however, a very rare crime among rural Arabs. If a husband should suspect his wife, he returns her to her father or brothers for punishment. Even a whisper against a woman, however unjustified, can bring death. The woman's virginity must on all accounts be preserved, and should her husband discover that she has had some previous experience, he will return her to her parents, either to be killed, sent away, or treated as a pariah.

This code was sometimes carried to fantastic lengths — as in the case of the noble family of the Sa'adouns who would even kill a woman of their family whose face was seen by a stranger. On one occasion a Sa'adoun girl came near to putting this to the test when a strong wind whipped away her head covering as she was climbing into the litter of her camel. In the nick of time, however, she swept the rest of her garments around her head — and although this exposed the whole of her body naked to anyone who cared to look, her honor was saved because her face was covered.

One of the greatest insults is to have the honor of one's women impugned, and at the time of my visit the Albu Muhammad tribe of the Lower Tigris was despised because they occasionally let their women off with a scolding. On the other hand, tribal Arab women were, on the whole, much freer than those of the cities. Bedouin and peasant women did not veil — although they might draw their head cloth over their face at the approach of a stranger. Only the wives of sheikhs veiled and were subjected to the restrictions of city women.

The second obligation in maintaining sharaf is to exact blood in retaliation for blood. This is an absolute obligation except under two conditions: first, in the *yom el-kebir,* or day of open pitched battle between tribes, deaths in action do not count in the blood feud (at least among the settled Arabs); second, upon the payment of *fasl,* or compensation, which may be paid in money, in kind, or in women (at the rate of two women for every man killed). The idea of this last alternative, forbidden by law but still in practice during the time of my visit, was that women would bear sons to replace the slain men.

At the time of my wanderings among the tribes, there was a slight amount of aib attached to accepting compensation; it was considered more honorable to exact the full penalty in blood. The blood feud probably preserved at least as many lives as it took, for fear of the blood feud made many a tribesman hesitate before taking a life, and often made tribal disputes comparatively bloodless. Although less common than before, still today such feuds sometimes lead to killings, even among detribalized Arabs of the villages.

Hospitality and generosity are an important part of sharaf. It is a sacred duty to receive the guest well, and to protect him during the three days in which one's food is supposed to remain in his belly. The guest house of the sheikh was always open to fellow tribesmen and strangers alike, and no one was refused coffee and food. Still today the poorest peasant will give you a drink of milk — even if that is all he has. Formerly, one of the worst insults to a tribesman was to call him *labban,* seller of milk, for milk is given, not sold, and to sell milk was a terrible aib.

When an honored guest appeared, no trouble seemed too great for a sheikhly host to incur; he would not, as a rule, sit at table with him, but would stand and help serve him. He would attend him like a servant, and when he left, accompany him to the border of his territory.

Dakhala is an Arab institution whereby a man may, under certain conditions, throw himself under your protection, saying, *"Ana dakhilak."* Your sharaf then demands that you protect him against his enemies. If anything happens to him, your "face is blackened"; and vengeance must be taken on those who have blackened it, or you must obtain compensation from the offending party.

Until comparatively recently, a tribal Arab could engage only in certain activities if he wished to maintain his sharaf. A Bedouin thought it was aib to do anything but keep camels. Agriculture was shameful; it was a terrible thing, also, for a Bedouin to allow his camels to carry loads for hire. The agricultural tribes thought that it was aib to cultivate vegetables for sale, own buffalo, manufacture reed mats, sew *abas* (cloaks), or be a blacksmith.

This description of their moral code applied, and to some extent still applies, to all Arab tribes alike. The tribesmen of the south are Shi'ites (except for the Bedouin and a few noble families), converted centuries ago by religious leaders from the holy cities of Kerbela and Nejef. Their priests, the *ulema* (also called *mujtahids*), are represented among the tribes by lesser holy men, the *muminin,* or faithful. Also, scattered among them are the seyyids, held in veneration as supposed descendants of the Prophet. Not only are they considered authorities on religion, but also possessed of healing powers — and powers to harm. All fear the curse of a seyyid.

In tribal warfare the seyyids used to enjoy immunity, and to be sure there is no mistake about it, they still fly a small black pennant above their houses. There are so many of these that one has to admire the reproductive powers of the seed of the Prophet. Also, seyyids and muminin long ago discovered that holiness is a good investment, and many acquired wealth with a minimum of effort. Real estate comes from bequests by those hoping for happiness in the next world, and tribesmen enrich them with annual gifts of rice, grain, butter, and other good things of life.

While the political hold of the ulema on the tribesmen had already weakened at the time of my visits (and in the current war the tribesmen have failed to respond to appeals from the Shi'ite hierarchy in Iran), religious feeling remained strong. While I was in Iraq, all the sheikhs of the Middle Euphrates and their retinues made a pilgrimage to Nejef, and wept as they viewed the annual passion play about the death of Hussein, grandson of the Prophet.

The tribes with their traditional ways were in fundamental conflict with the partly Europeanized people of the cities. Baghdadi officials and schoolteachers generally looked down on tribesmen as yokels, and tried to change their ways, while the tribesmen considered the Baghdad *effendis* — as they called them, after the Turkish word for mister — people without sharaf, unworthy of the name "Arab."

The tribesman coming to the wicked city found it difficult to adapt to its mores, especially its system of punishment of the type of crime, particularly murder, that a tribesman was bound by his sharaf to commit. Hence, the British authorities in 1916 drew up a special law for people of tribal origin along the lines of those established for dealing with Northwest Frontier tribesmen in India. Under this law, for instance, a tribesman who shed blood for his honor was given a light sentence of perhaps three years' imprisonment. This *Qanun al-Ashair* — "Law of the Tribes" — was greatly resented by my nationalist friends in Baghdad.

This law was also beginning to become an anachronism as the tribal system gradually broke up. As tribes acquired land, and the free tribesman gradually became a peasant and his sheikh a landlord, the tribal system became a feudal one, to be swept away in revolution and reform.

Yet while I was in Iraq the tribal system was alive and well, and the tribesmen still lived up to the romantic ideal. In the marshlands they blended in an idyllic scene for the rare visitor like myself. I can still vividly feel the spell of the mysterious passage through the tall reeds, and the aroma from the mat huts woven from their substance, as I read from my faded summaries my impressions of that lost world.

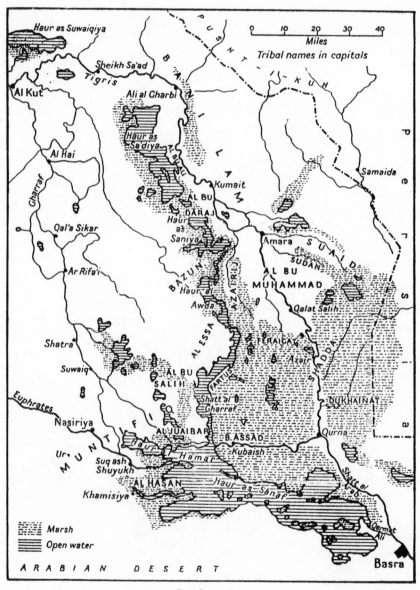

Southern Iraq

14

Waters in the Wilderness

TRIBAL IRAQ during World War II was largely under the control of British political officers who, despite their modest ranks, were really kinglets in their domains. The Lower Tigris was the realm of Captain Francis Grimley — deputy assistant political officer, Amara — a stubby young man with a merry, open face under fair hair either flying in the breeze, or confined by a kufiyya. He often wore Arab clothes, which won him the disapproval of some of the old colonial hands, but while I was with him I followed suit.

In November 1944, Grimley and I set out from his house in Amara to the large Majar al-Kabir canal and embarked in a sheikhly mashhuf rowed by five servants, two in front and three behind. They propelled the boat either with long bamboolike poles from the inner marshes or by short, blunted paddles that they wielded with amazing speed, changing sides frequently. When they had to go upstream they jumped out and ran along the bank, pulling the mashhuf by rope. They were well-muscled young men, slaves of the sheikh we were to visit, and dressed to kill, in the literal sense, covered as they were with daggers and cartridges. As was customary, we passengers sat in the middle on a rug, covered with a sheet, stretched between two cylindrical pillows. I, as guest of honor, faced the bow, with Grimley graciously taking the second-rank position in the stern.

Finally we arrived at the house of the senior sheikh of the Albu Muhammad tribe, Majid al-Khalifa, feared and hated, but generally listened to by the whole of the tribe. He met us at the landing, and his immense bulk, stub nose, loose lips, and round face covered with straggling white hairs gave a first impression of a rather jolly Silenus. But his family history was a dark one.

Only a few years before, his favorite son, Khuraibit, married a cousin famed for her beauty named Chasbiyya. Khuraibit was very much in love with her, and she soon also became the favorite of Majid. Of course, it was whispered that Majid's feelings were not entirely platonic!

Now Sharifa, wife of Majid, was most displeased by the ascendancy of Chasbiyya. She had always been jealous of Khuraibit, who was not her son, and thought Chasbiyya was using her influence on the old man to advance Khuraibit's interests.

One day, on some pretext or other, Khuraibit was induced to leave his wife, now far advanced in pregnancy, to go to Amara. That night Sharifa's slave woman stole into Chasbiyya's tent.

The following morning the village was awakened by the cries of Chasbiyya's slave woman, who had found her mistress lying on the bed in a pool of blood, quite dead. Opinions differ as to how she died — according to one brutal version I heard, she was kicked to death.

When Khuraibit first heard of the murder, he was inconsolable. Naturally he did not return to his father's house, but lived with some friends. One day one of these reproached him for his lack of spirit. Stung by the rebuke, Khuraibit took his pistol, went to the house in Amara where Sharifa was staying, and shot her.

He made no attempt to hide the crime. And in spite of the fact that he was tried under tribal law, lenient in such matters, his father saw to it that he spent two years in prison.

It was this terrible old man with the jovial facade who met us at the landing of the canal, with the usual words of welcome — *"Ahlan wa-sahlan wa-marhaban! Shlonak, zein? Al-hamdu lillah"* ("Welcome! How are you, all right? Praise be to God").

We were conducted to the sheikh's guest house for effendis and foreigners, his *cherdagh* — a primitive structure of brick with a large porch, the roof of which was supported by rough-hewn wooden columns. Inside was only one large room, gloomy and sparsely furnished with a few loud carpets and some cheaply upholstered armchairs. Of course, there were no pictures, since Islam prohibits representations of figures.

These structures seemed to be a requirement of every sheikhly establishment. They were rarely used, all the tribal Arabs and religious people being received in the mudhif. A cylinder-shaped structure about sixty feet long, a mudhif is made entirely of reeds the pale gold color of cornstalks. The four corners of the mudhif are marked by tall tapering columns, with two more framing an arched open doorway at one end. Supporting the roof are thicker columns made of hundreds of bundles of tightly packed reeds covered with matting.

The importance of the sheikh is measured by the number of these columns, arched over the building like giant horseshoes. The columned form of the mudhif is thought to have evolved into the Babylonian and hence the Greek temple. The Palace of Ctesiphon, which I had visited earlier in the year, with its great hall, resembled an oversized masonry mudhif.

As we were changing into warmer clothes for the chilly winter night we were presented with a bottle of whiskey — a welcome sight. Nobody joined us in our libations, however, as it would have been political suicide for a member of the sheikhly family to indulge openly in the forbidden delight. But alas, this was not followed by the hearty Arab meal I had anticipated. Instead, there were dancing girls.

Let us pause here for memories — memories of our youthful imaginations as we pored over the delightful pages of *The Arabian Nights,* or listened to the strains of *Sheherazade,* or watched Hollywood at its best in *The Thief of Baghdad.*

Then let us return to the reality I faced. The girls were dark-skinned gypsies, with coarse, tattooed features. Their figures — perhaps fortunately — were hidden under billowing robes during their interminable dances, neither sensual nor artistic.

The orchestra was composed of a gypsy or two, and some of the sheikh's slaves. Their instruments consisted of a rababa — a sort of fiddle; drums — hollow wooden cylinders with a skin stretched across one end; and tambourines. I rather like Arab music, which has a hypnotic cadence; I also enjoy the songs they sing in chorus. But when one of the gypsy men sang one song after another alone, in a half-strangled, whining voice, I soon found it unbearable. Most of his songs contained an oft-repeated phrase, *"Ya galub wai"* — which means heart of woe — and soon I heartily hoped that some enemy would cut his *galub wai* right out of his chest.

This dancing and drumming and caterwauling continued until after midnight. Even then we would not have had any dinner had I not hinted that I was dying of hunger. It seems that they put off dinner as long as possible, so that if any stray guest turned up, he wouldn't have to go without his supper.

Afterward we slept on the porch, and were awakened at six-thirty in the morning by a huge colony of sparrows nesting in the rafters above, who devoted that hour to lovemaking and certain other bodily functions. We hurriedly rose to perform our ablutions in the portable family washbasin, under the scrutiny of a dozen pairs of tribal eyes. (Everything one does at these affairs — in fact, one's every move in Arab countries — is zealously observed. Of course, this means that any gaucherie will be endlessly discussed and passed on to everyone in the tribe.)

Grimley and I had breakfast with Majid — consisting of a tea-milk-sugar mixture, fried eggs, chicken, flat unleavened bread, and buffalo butter, a white, rather tasteless substance that they pressed down in the plate evenly with their fingers.

After breakfast we embarked in Majid's mashhuf toward the lands of the Azairij, where we were to lunch. On our trip we had a chance to talk to the boatmen, delightful fellows, with loud, hearty voices.

I asked about the turquoise necklaces worn by the little children of the tribe to protect them against the evil eye. They all believed implicitly in the powers of the evil eye. They have a proverb, *"Thulthain al mujabir min 'uyun"* — "Two thirds of those who are buried die from the evil eye." An evil eye can stop your cow from giving milk. You mustn't praise a child — he will think you are putting the eye on him.

It was fun listening to them. Every sentence was preceded by a phrase such as *"Abus idak"* — "I kiss your hand" — and lots of blarney was handed out.

Finally we came to the boundary between the Albu Muhammad and the Azairij. In the old days these boatmen would never have been allowed to cross into the territories of their neighbors, but raiding and warfare between tribes were now prevented by the government. Grimley, for my benefit, asked our boatmen what they thought of the Azairij. "Oh, *kullish mu zeinin* — very bad people — we hate them; *wallah,* we'd kill them if it weren't for the government. They killed our fathers and our uncles and our brothers."

Grimley asked them if it wasn't better now that there was no more raiding back and forth, and they admitted that it was. "They'll tell you what you want to hear," Grimley said, remarking that they gave mostly lip service to this traditional enmity. Indeed, when we arrived at the house of the Azairij sheikh, our boatmen were well received, and I saw the son of the sheikh squatting on the canal bank talking with them.

Whatever opinion the Albu Muhammad had of the Azairij, it must be said that the Albu Muhammad themselves enjoyed a most unenviable reputation among neighboring tribes. It was said that their women were sheikhs and their men very much like women. Their women were considered immoral as well as uppity, and the slaves of the Albu Muhammad sheikhs were said to enjoy the favors of their mistresses. Furthermore, outraged husbands, fathers, and brothers, instead of throwing their erring wives into the canal, as tribal custom required, were reputed to punish such slights to their honor with at most a mild rebuke.

Our host was Mutlaq al-Salman, the most important sheikh of the Azairij. He was fairly young; I should have said not yet forty. His appearance was at first unprepossessing — he had one bad eye, his complexion was yellow from liver trouble, and he seemed nervous, always jumping up and sitting down, never still. But after a while I got used to this and ended up liking him. He was a straightforward, intelligent fellow. One of the few sheikhs in the district who had married only once, Mutlaq led an exemplary home life.

Mutlaq's cherdagh faced his mudhif, so we could see that the large group which sat all day long in the mudhif included a seyyid and two men with enormous turbans, one being the local mumin, and the other a visiting mulla from Kerbela. This was the period just before the Feast of Muharram, when the murder of Hussein (the grandson of the Prophet whom Shi'ites consider his legitimate heir) is reenacted throughout southern Iraq. At this time the religious men of the holy cities go out to the country, each to his special district, and collect the rice, clothes, and other worldly goods due them because of their holiness and wisdom.

The seyyid can pass most of his life in the mudhif. No labor is required of him except to propagate the blessed seed of Hussein and produce a son of whom no other task will be required. The mumin, however, must perform some labor; he must learn enough about the interpretation of the Koran and the traditions of the Prophet at least to mystify the people who support him. And he himself must support the huge white turban on his head — quite a task on a hot day. Furthermore, he must pray long and conspicuously at the all too frequent hours of prayer, provided somebody is around to see him.

Sheikh Mutlaq's mumin, apparently pricked by curiosity, joined us for lunch. He was a plump, jolly fellow, with a bushy black beard and twinkling black eyes, introduced as Sheikh Hashim. We asked him how he happened to be called sheikh. He replied amiably that he had no tribe, but that the title was an honorific one bestowed upon his father when this worthy first came from Nejef to live with the Azairij. We asked him what were his duties. "I teach the people," he answered, "the difference between good and bad."

"How do you know the difference?" I asked.

"I have books which tell me."

He lived half the time in Amara and half with Sheikh Mutlaq, and had solved the domestic problem this entailed by placing a wife and family in both places. He showed his high religious standards by declaring that for a boatman to sing was *haram* ("forbidden by religion"). We asked him why. "Because women on the banks of the canal might hear, and these songs about love might give them sinful thoughts!" However, he laughed as he said it. He was very anxious, as were others of this class, to show us he was not *asabi* — "fanatical."

Another holy man joined us, the *Rauzakhon* — Sheikh Baqir as-Sa'idi, a handsome man with delicate, spiritual features. He knew and loved his Moslem and Arab traditions, history, and literature. His title is a Persian word that means reader of the eulogy, as his principal function was to direct the passion play of Muharram and chant emotional oratory between the acts. He was supposed to incite the audience to tears and lamentation.

This Rauzakhon had the resonant voice required by his calling, and sang the songs of the old Arab poets, which seemed familiar to the more cultured of the assembly, who urged him to sing again and again. (Later in the year, the Rauzakhon walked into my office in Baghdad unannounced. He told me that on his trip to his hometown of Nejef he assured religious dignitaries that the Americans were good people, citing his friend Archie as an example!)

During the late afternoon we had enjoyed the Rauzakhon's singing and discussions on ancient lore and tribal affairs, and I looked forward to a stimulating evening.

But alas, we had no sooner settled down in the guest house after dinner when in trooped the gypsy girls from the night before. May Allah curse their maternal uncles! What's more, the man who sang about his *galub wai* was with them, and they danced while he sang most of the night. At least this time it was on a carpet under the stars, with the circle of listening Arabs like an orientalist painting in the flickering lamplight.

Grimley and I passed our next overnight visit with Majid al-Khalifa's rival and brother-in-law, the other leading sheikh of the Albu Muhammad, Muhammed al-Uraibi. Our mashhuf bore us to him on the Chahala, the largest canal in the country, which carries more water than the Tigris itself. It was very high, and we could see into the reed houses, where the women were pounding rice with huge mortars and pestles. They grunted as they pounded to avoid rupturing their abdominal muscles. The interiors looked surprisingly clean, and were brightened with piles of brilliantly colored rugs. Outside, against the walls, I saw pancakes of cow dung arranged in symmetrical rows. The citizenry were healthy specimens, but dressed in rags and sackcloth. Many of the children were naked.

In the fields the tribesman wore only a loincloth, or at most a long cotton *thob* tucked around his waist. But under more formal circumstances he wore a brown or black woolen cloak, the aba, which served as a blanket. On his head he wore a kufiyya — *chefiyya* in the local dialect — generally black-and-white-checked, except for the Sunni Bedouins and a few Sunni notables, whose chefiyyas were red-checked. An oversized double strand of wool-covered rope, the *agal* (originally a camel hobble) kept it in place.

The women universally wore black abas as outer garments with a bright-colored silk or cotton dress underneath. They sometimes wore black cloth around their heads as well, but often went bareheaded and always barefaced — as opposed to their sisters in the towns. Their animals included dirty pie-dogs, cows, scrawny chickens, and, a pleasing contrast, big healthy-looking water buffalo, their passive faces raised in the air, standing in rows as if posing for an ancient Egyptian tomb painting.

As we slipped peacefully along the canal, it grew dark, and the stars came out. Venus appeared first, and I asked our boatman for its name — they call it Zina. They do not realize that it is the same as the morning star, for which they have a different name.

Sheikh Muhammed met us at the water's edge. He was a quiet, meek, rather uninspiring old fellow who had the reputation of being a good, simple soul.

Muhammed al-Uraibi was married to Majid's sister, herself almost as huge as her brother. But according to gossip, her lover was none other than the sheikh's spiritual mentor, the locally notorious Mulla Lazim. When word of this reached the ears of Majid, he is supposed to have dispatched a spy who caught his sister and the Mulla in flagrante delicto. Majid happily informed Muhammed but Muhammed intended to hang on to the Mulla as long as Majid was alive, because the Mulla was the only one smart enough to keep his tyrannical brother-in-law in check.

I could well believe all this after meeting Mulla Lazim — a great smiling bull of a man, with a wicked brown face, a deep booming voice, and sudden sweeping motions of his hands. He radiated strength and craft and charm, and we took an instant liking to each other. At least he seemed to take to me and I was delighted with the old *shaitan* ("devil"), to whom I could credit any depravity. He had inherited his position of Mulla from his father. The Mulla of a sheikh is often merely his secretary, but if he has a strong personality, he becomes the real sheikh, as in this case. In tribal conclaves the Mulla waved aside poor old Muhammed's feeble comments and interruptions and laid down the law. This position was not without its advantages for Muhammed, for every bad decision could be attributed to the Mulla.

Sheikh Muhammed's cherdagh was little different from that of other Arab sheikhs. We received the same whiskey and soda, and I feared that the dancing girls would soon make their appearance.

Mulla Lazim bent to whisper in my ear, "You must excuse us for not offering you real entertainment here — music and dancing girls — we are in mourning for the loss of one of

Muhammed's grandsons." It required great effort to assume a mournful countenance.

Shortly after our arrival a man ran in to tell us that the warrior chief of the Beni Turuf, a tribe located across the border in Iran, had fled into Iraq under bombardment by the Iranian air force. He was now on an island in the huge marsh to the east of us that spanned the border. My hosts readily agreed to take me to see him on the morrow, though Grimley had to return to town.

The next morning the sheikh and I embarked in a mashhuf for the marsh, through rice fields filled with men and women harvesting, until we came to the reeds, gradually increasing in size to the height of a man. The marsh was teeming with ducks, loons, cranes, and herons, and the surface of the water was sometimes broken by a rising otter.

After an hour and a half's paddle we came to a clump of houses on some raised land, topped by a mudhif on a high mound — the only part of the village not inundated in flood time. We descended here and walked up to the mound, entering the mudhif to drink a cup of tea, while the Arabs clustered around the entrance.

This was the first time I had been inside a mudhif. Passing through the arched doorway from the bright sunlight into semidarkness, I felt as if I were stepping into a churchlike cavern, its sides lined with enormous columns of bound reeds as large as the stone ones of a cathedral, each gradually tapering to join seamlessly overhead with its opposite. I inhaled the balmy aroma of reeds, spiced with smoke from a fire of cow dung smoldering in the crude stone hearth in the middle of the floor.

The gahwachi was standing by the hearth, which was surrounded by a large number of copper coffeepots ranged in order of size, headed by a giant one called the *gumgum*, which stored a couple of gallons. The sheikh led me past rows of silent guests seated on mats along the walls on both sides to the end of the hall. There, I sat on the right of my host in the gloom, with the only light filtering in from the door opposite.

The gahwachi poured coffee from a medium-sized pot into cups for the sheikh and myself. After we had sipped, and shaken our cups to show we had finished, he passed the same cups around the circle of guests, beginning each time with me as guest of honor. Thus I shared a loving cup with the tribe.

At first I tried to make conversation but answers were perfunctory, and it was embarrassing having my every word listened to by those long rows of squatting, robed figures. Then I fell into the Arab habit of simply sitting in silence, presumably in deep contemplation. Loud talk, and especially laughter, are unseemly in these gatherings, and silence is not embarrassing, but correct behavior.

Suddenly outside we heard women *yu-yu*-ing, and in stalked a magnificent figure in a gold-trimmed brown aba over a black well-tailored jacket. He was stocky and of medium height, with a face broader than that of most Arabs, a strong, clean-shaven jaw, and a short, well-trimmed moustache. He moved like a lord and in his greeting to Muhammed it was obvious that his station was in no way inferior to that of my host. He was the kind of person about whom one says to oneself, "There is a man."

It was Yunis ibn Asi.

He sat down and talked eagerly to Muhammed, so rapidly that I could only catch fragments — "the Iranians" — "betrayal" — "people without honor" — "if we gave up our rifles we should be at their mercy" — "the Iranian army machine guns" — "we fought" — "killed." I cursed myself for not knowing the dialect better.

Then he turned and looked at me, asked the sheikh who I was and if I understood Arabic. When the sheikh told him, he turned to me, smiling, and said, *"Shlonak? Zein?"* ("How are you? Well?") Muhammed excused himself for a few minutes and I invited Yunis over to sit next to me. I asked him when he had left Iran, and he said two days before. I asked him a few questions about the situation in general and the fight with the Iranian troops, and if he ever intended to go back to Iran. He said of course he missed his native land, but that as long as it was subjected to such an oppressive government, he could never return, adding that he hoped England and the United States would do something about the situation.

On our way out Muhammed drew Yunis aside for a private chat, and I had a short talk with the villagers. They were pleasant, simple folk who had never seen an American before and had never heard of New York. But they evidently had heard of Uncle Sam's reputation for largesse, because they immediately asked me why the Americans and the British didn't do anything about the clothes situation. They pointed to their own rags, and said that the women had so little to wear that they had to stay indoors. I asked them how it had been before, and they said that two years ago there had been plenty of cloth, mostly from Japan, and from England, and — they quickly added — the United States (without the slightest regard for truth, as Iraq imported no American cloth).

Muhammed and Yunis were soon back, and we said good-bye and left. When we came out of the marshes, we found ourselves fighting a strong current, and instead of paddling, the boatmen got out and ran along the bank, towing the mashhuf behind. When we arrived at higher land, some horses were waiting for us, tended by Muhammed's son Uraibi — a clever little boy of around seven, with a passion for riding, who soon became a fast friend. We cavorted together, while the old sheikh rode slowly and steadily back home. The boy was obviously the household pet in a family so large that neither the sheikh nor Uraibi could tell me how many brothers he had; all they could say was *"chethir"* ("many").

Grimley returned that night, and the following afternoon we set out to visit the most important of the sheikhs of the Beni Lam, Alwan al-Jandil. The rain had converted the once-dusty road into a morass but our little jeep got through, though we often had to leave the road to travel on the fields alongside.

On our way, we passed the guest house of a son of the famous Ghadhban bin Bunayya, "a sort of local Napoleon," as Grimley put it. In Turkish times the Beni Lam were a proud tribe of camel Bedouins, very *asil* (pure-blooded). They despised the rice-growing and marsh tribes, over whom they usually maintained a precarious suzerainty, which paid dividends in the form of tribute.

At the time of the coming of the British, Ghadhban controlled not only the Beni Lam in Iraq but the sections of the tribe in Iran, along with kindred tribes there with proud ancient names, dating back to the days before the Prophet. He made war from time to time with Sheikh Khaz'al of Muhammerah, the Persian government, and the Albu Muhammad. During World War I he joined the Turks or the British as convenience dictated. But with the establishment of a strong government in Baghdad, Ghadhban's days as a conqueror and despot were over.

The old man didn't take to the change. He began to deteriorate mentally. Some said that his *farrasha* (the female slave who made his bed and took care of his apartments), annoyed because his affection for his wife blinded him to her own allure, placed a charm under his pillow. Others whispered that he suffered from a venereal complaint.

Ghadhban went up to Baghdad to see a doctor. The story doesn't say whether this was a newfangled *franji* (foreign) physician or one of the time-honored prescribers of rolled-up verses of the Koran, which, when swallowed, are considered most effective. In any case, he recommended a most unusual remedy: He told the old man that he must marry, one after the other, seven virgins, and relieve each one of them of that inhibiting condition.

Ghadhban thought the advice good, and as soon as he returned to his tribe, he began to cast about to find virgin number one. Now it happened that one of the local landowners had several marriageable sisters, of personable appearance and unquestionable virginity, whom the landowner had stubbornly refused to marry off in spite of many attractive offers. For years these sisters wandered about the house, spouseless, albeit somewhat less personable with the passage of time.

Ghadhban, ignoring their brother's intransigence, took the landowner for a ride in his car and demanded one of his sisters. The landowner hastened to say, "Take her."

"It's lucky for you," said the old tyrant, "that you gave your consent, for I was prepared to smite you on the head and take her anyway."

So they were married, and Ghadhban lost no time in chalking his first maidenhead off the list. But, as is sometimes the case with elderly grooms, the effort was too much for him, and he died shortly thereafter.

Ghadhban's sons were not the men their father was, and thus the position of paramount sheikh and deputy fell to Alwan al-Jandil, who was their great-grandfather's first cousin. (Such discrepancies in generations should surprise nobody who has read the last related story and has thus gained a keyhole view of the private life of superannuated sheikhs — a sheikh's first-born son may be fifty years older than his youngest.)

Alwan al-Jandil, whom I met twice at Grimley's house, had a

crafty, inscrutable face covered with deep, strong lines, and I should have liked to know him better. But it was not to be. When we arrived that evening at the ferry landing to cross to the sheikh's house, we found no arrangements had been made for our reception. Grimley, furious — or pretending to be — at this want of consideration, told the man at the ferry landing, "Go, tell Sheikh Alwan that his guests arrived, and found no ferry, and nobody to receive them, so they went on to spend the night with Gourjis."

After we arrived at Gourjis's house — Gourjis was not a tribesman, but a Baghdad Christian landowner — Grimley confessed to me that he was somewhat relieved at not having to spend the night with Sheikh Alwan, as he was suffering, like myself by this time, from a temporary surfeit of sheikhs. I had another reason for rejoicing: I had heard rumors that Alwan occasionally entertained his guests with gypsy dancing girls.

The Beni Lam had declined seriously since the British occupation. Cut off from their Persian lands by an artificial boundary, deprived of the right to raid and take tribute from the settled tribes, they found themselves reduced to grazing their animals and farming on poor lands without water.

At that time a few of their black tents and the open mudhifs of their sheikhs were still to be found scattered over the plain from Amara to Kut, but every year there were fewer of them, as more and more of the tribe wandered off to neighboring districts or the cities, attracted by the relatively high wages. The Beni Lam have now slipped away into history — mostly unwritten history depending on the vanishing pages of human memory.

My next trip was to visit Major Michael Berkeley, deputy assistant political adviser in Nasiriya, on the Lower Euphrates, capital of the Muntafiq, the most interesting part of tribal Mesopotamia.

The Muntafiq (meaning federation) was founded by the noble Sa'adoun family, seyyids from Mecca. In the time of the Turks they ruled in almost complete independence, but after the arrival of the British the tribes gradually shook off their yoke. While some were still found along the Euphrates as landowners, many, including the leader of the family, Abdullah

Falih Al Sa'adoun, withdrew to "high desert" west of the river. The Sa'adouns had always been at home there and were known as the Hawks of the Desert.

The Muntafiq was the tribal province par excellence — in no other were the tribesmen so independent, both of their own sheikhs and the government. They were almost all armed, and the government did not even dare enforce conscription on them. Their only real authority was Major Berkeley (pronounced Barclay, of course). All the chief personalities had been his friends since the time when he was political officer there at the end of World War I. In 1941 many went to Baghdad and asked the British ambassador to reappoint him.

He was frankly colonial in outlook, and so sure of his superior qualities as political officer that he was disliked by most of his colleagues. As an uncrowned king of the Muntafiq, he kept CICI from appointing an area liaison officer, as he wanted to rule without interference.

Late one night at the end of February 1945, I arrived at Major Berkeley's house after a cold drive over the slippery salt marsh from Ur Junction. He was waiting up to see me with a whiskey ready. A short, spare man who looked and acted much younger than a World War I veteran, with a full head of hair and short brown moustache, Berkeley was one of a kind.

Nervous, impatient, executive, he talked a great deal, and was an excellent raconteur. His stories and turns of speech gave one the impression of a whimsical sense of humor, though he rarely laughed at another person's jokes. He was outspoken in his criticism of superiors, equals, and inferiors, with an occasional word of praise for somebody who happened to have met with his approval. Berkeley was a vain man, but I did not find his conceit offensive.

He was neither well educated nor well read. Son of an Indian army officer, he took part in the Mesopotamian campaign, then transferred to political work, serving on the Lower Euphrates. Then he went to New Zealand and raised sheep and a family. He loved the tribal Arabs, whom he called "charming people." His Arabic was fluent, though he used the verbs in the third person only. We took to each other soon after I arrived, and by the next day he was telling me that I was one of the few people he knew fitted to be a political officer.

In the morning we proceeded to Berkeley's office, where he

was holding a *majlis,* or council, of the sheikhs in my honor. The government might easily have raised a row about these sessions over which Berkeley presided — reminiscent of mandate times, and by then obsolete in the rest of the country.

I was placed next to Berkeley's desk at one end of the room, while the sheikhs came in one by one, shook hands with me, and sat around in a circle saying nothing. I blurted out one or two awkward phrases, and was answered by the usual chorus of polite formulas; tea was passed around, and then another group of sheikhs appeared. I breathed a sigh of relief when these had gone and the room was empty except for Berkeley and me and an old petitioner or two who had remained behind.

I must have met forty or fifty sheikhs that morning, including a number of the Sa'adouns and their retainers, wearing the handsome red-checked chefiyyas. Notable among them was Wabdan Al Sa'adoun, a true movie sheikh in spite of the fact that he was beardless — for not only was he strikingly hand-some, but he had two long braids half-covered by his red headdress. He was one of the family who still lived in the desert.

We made a side trip to have tea with the famous paramount sheikh of the Abudah, the first man of the Muntafiq, Khayyun al-Ubaid, a clean-shaven, plump, rather comical-looking char-acter. Berkeley was a fountainhead of anecdotes about his tribal friends, and one was about Khayyun in the first days of British occupation, about 1919. Once, contemplating a tribal uprising, Khayyun evidently decided to trigger it by a direct confronta-tion with Berkeley. British political officers then expected the tribesmen to rise, as they did in the presence of sheikhs. One time when Berkeley passed by Khayyun and a number of Arabs sitting against a wall, none of them rose. Berkeley realized that if he let it pass, he was finished — and yet he could hardly go up to the group and fly into a rage. So he said, *"Salaam 'aleikum."* Following the inviolable custom, Khayyun rose and said, *"Wa-aleikum es-salaam."*

Berkeley had a number of stories to tell about the Sa'adoun. He told me how they had come from Arabia broken in battle and almost finished, and had gradually become the first family of the Muntafiq and, indeed, of all Iraq. Once one of the great sheikhs of the Sa'adoun was killed; the tribe responsible finally made submission. But compensation for a sheikh of such importance was out of the question; it could never honorably be received. So the head of the family stipulated that henceforth the Sa'adoun would not rise to receive any other sheikh and that all should kiss their hands.

Berkeley took me to the southern desert west of Ur to call on the head of the Sa'adoun family, Abdullah Falih. Shortly after crossing the Euphrates, we passed our first Bedouin, wrapped in sackcloth, holding a camel stick; we noticed his beard, his long, matted hair, and wild, bewildered eyes. After a few miles of driving we found ourselves in the high desert, struggling along under a sky darkened by dust. The violent, freezing wind prevented us from admiring the flowers raised by the early rains — "the best in forty years!" They were of all kinds — Berkeley said a botanist had told him there were five hundred varieties — all small and close to the ground. The most common types were poppies, miniature irises, and black-eyed Susans.

Soon the country lost its flat character; we came over hills, and across wadis. We got stuck in the soft sand and had to dig our way out. Buffeted by the wind, we finally arrived at Qal'at Neb'ah, a ruined castle that used to be the capital of Falih Al Sa'adoun, father of Abdullah. Close beside the ruins were two pavilions and two "houses of hair," as the Arabs call their black goat's-hair tents. We were ushered by a black slave to one of the pavilions — a tent of canvas lined with red cloth. The inside was completely bare except for the Persian carpets, which covered the sand. A servant brought in some camel saddles, and we made ourselves comfortable against them.

"Here he comes," said Berkeley, and we rose as a fine-looking old man entered the tent to greet us, our host, Abdullah Falih Al Sa'adoun. He was a tall, gracious figure clothed in a red chefiyya and a fine aba, under which we could glimpse flashes of red and gold. His proud but gentle face, with its hawklike nose and white goatee — giving him somewhat the appearance of Richelieu — marked him as a noble and a prince. He was so courteous, gentle, and kindly that it was hard to believe this was the man who, a dozen years ago, went up to Baghdad and shot and killed Abdullah Sani, director general of the interior, who had dared to marry a girl of the Sa'adoun family, in spite of repeated warnings. None but a Sa'adoun — or one of equal rank, if such existed — might marry a Sa'adoun, and Abdullah Sani was descended from servants of the Sa'adouns and had African blood in his veins.

The Sa'adouns are the most noble family in Iraq, and had it not been for their numerous tribal enemies they would have been chosen as Iraq's royal family. Although they are Sunnis, whereas all the settled tribes of the Muntafiq are Shi'ites, they were looked upon with veneration by all as descendants of the Prophet. If you get bitten by a snake, an Arab assured me in all seriousness, all you need to do is to get one of the Sa'adouns to read some of the Koran to you, while drinking a certain potion, and you have no cause to worry.

Given all this background, I was fascinated by this dignified old man. Leaning against the camel saddles, we talked about the old days when the Sa'adouns still ruled the tribes. We sipped endless cups of tea, which helped drive the chill out of our bones, for the wind was still whipping around the tent; it was evening before it died down. When the darkness had settled, the sheikh excused himself, and tactfully sent over a bottle of brandy — not such an extraordinary concession as it might first appear, for in spite of his holiness, he was rumored not to be averse to an occasional sip of the forbidden liquid.

After we had had time to increase our slender store of internal heat, the sheikh reappeared with the remainder of his guests, followed shortly by a huge dish of roast lamb and rice, and many dishes of yogurt and vegetables. Best of all, not long after dinner the sheikh left us, and we were allowed to stretch ourselves and make a quick passage to the land of Nod.

Awakened several times during the night by the cold, I stepped out of my tent into the desert, and stood a long time gazing around me in the semidarkness, for the night was brilliant with stars as one sees it only in the desert and on the sea. As I took deep breaths of purest air, surrounded by the bones of the earth stretching far into the darkness, I sensed that aloneness in the universe, under the eye of God, which has inspired men of the desert through the ages. From these Arabian wastes came the procession of tribes of Semites through the millennia, and the prophets raising their eyes to the stars, alone before God. A sense of man's littleness, in the vast wilderness of space, fills one not only with awe, but with something like fear. The sad little ruins in the foreground only reinforced the loneliness, and I shuddered, sensing the ghosts of the past sliding through them, just as I had in Basra.

After breakfast Abdullah Falih took us around these ruins,

where sheep were grazing in the early morning sunlight. He pointed out the foundations of the mosque, fast crumbling into the desert, the rubble heap that marked the site of the souq, and the place where the well used to be, from which water was drawn by camels to irrigate a garden outside the walls. I found myself catching the mood of the old man, as he mournfully surveyed vanishing remains of his ancestral home, especially when he went to his tent and returned with a fragment of fine china. "This I found in the ruins," he said. "It belonged to my fathers — once they ate from the bowl from which this fell." He put it back in the folds of his aba. "I would not sell it," he said, "for a million dinars."

Later, we set out with Sheikh Abdullah and his hawk to have a try at falconry. Soon in the distance, we came across some bustards — *habarah*. The sheikh, who was standing up in the backseat of Berkeley's car, his head and flying red chefiyya sticking out of the open roof, took off the falcon's mask, but the bird refused to look at the bustards. We followed them and tried again, with the same result. Finally we gave it up, feeling sorry for the old sheikh's loss of face.

Fortunately, four gazelles appeared at this awkward moment, and glad of the distraction, we quickly gave chase. We soon caught up with them, and got a shot or two. Then the buck dropped behind and, with us in swift pursuit, changed his course — while the others escaped in another direction. It is evidently quite common for a gazelle buck thus to sacrifice himself for his family. He ran along slowly for a while, then put on a magnificent burst of speed, and in our admiration for his spirit, we let him go — which astonished but at the same time pleased the Arabs.

I had expressed a desire to see truffles growing in the desert; I had eaten them for the first time in Berkeley's home, and had seen donkeyloads of them being driven in. There are two main varieties, red and white. Berkeley's Bedouin guide, although half-blind, was an expert at finding them, like all Bedouins. All one sees above ground is a slight swelling of the soil; the Bedouin digs them out with his camel stick. After prolonged and diligent search, we found a couple of undersized ones — fortunately for the sheikh's face!

We returned to the camp for a hasty lunch and took our leave of the old man. I felt sorry for him — a forlorn figure. He paid me a visit in my office in Baghdad later in the year, before my departure. He seemed old and feeble and left after a few minutes, with nothing said but greetings and farewell. Not long afterward he died.

On my last trip, in November of 1945, I paid final visits to Grimley and Berkeley, driving down from Baghdad and arriving in time for lunch with Grimley in Diwaniyya, on the Euphrates. He had been transferred to this less active and interesting post because of complaints that he was too involved in tribal politics. Enthusiastic and idealistic, he felt compelled to intervene on the side of the oppressed both in tribal quarrels and troubles with Iraqi officialdom.

I found Grimley in a rather fey, absentminded mood. He talked about his plans to go into business in Hilla after his imminent retirement, and I put his mood down to distraction caused by worry about his future. But when I went on to join Berkeley for dinner in Nasiriya, he lost no time in recounting the real reason for Grimley's moodiness.

Grimley did not live the austere, asexual life common to British political officers, and was obviously not suffering from sexual deprivation. On one of my previous visits he had provided some evening entertainment by inviting in a dancing girl to perform for us after dinner. This was no ugly, graceless gypsy girl, but a rather pretty Christian who did not hesitate to uncover most of her attractive figure. She clearly had an intimate relationship with Grimley.

On a later occasion, when I went to wake Grimley in the morning, I found another girl in his bed. It later turned out that she was his cook, and their relationship had now led to serious consequences. They had been in Baghdad, staying in the house of Grimley's absent boss, Colonel Aston, when, in a fit of rage, she left him, taking with her the key to the colonel's safe. Grimley had just sent the safe to the souq to have it blasted open when the colonel returned. This probably had some bearing on the urgency of his retirement plans!

Berkeley — an old-fashioned officer who kept his distance and dignity among the natives — thoroughly disapproved of Grimley's too-familiar manner, "going native." He mentioned how the tribesmen had danced when the news came that Grimley's mare had produced a filly — and Grimley joined them, wearing Arab dress. "Grimley had T. E. Lawrence's ridiculous habit of dressing up like an Arab — very bad for prestige!"

Berkeley and I set out by boat across the great open lake in the midst of the marshes, the Hor al-Hammar, to Chubaish, capital of Sheikh Salim al-Khayyun, the turbulent chief of the Beni Asad. The sheikh was then, as several times before, in exile in Baghdad. The first time he was banished was after publicly insulting King Feisal and rebelling in 1924. Every time he returned to Chubaish trouble ensued, the last time being earlier in the year of my visit. He was quite anti-British and his son was one of the few tribal leaders to support Rashid Ali al-Gailani, while most of the tribes, inclined toward the British, stayed on the sidelines.

I knew Salim al-Khayyun as a frequent visitor to the Regent Hotel. On a couple of occasions he brought a whole roast lamb into the dining room, which he invited me and other friends to share. He was short but distinguished-looking with his fine brown beard. Courteous and genial, he was also outspoken in his views. He visited me and the minister at the legation to tell us that we and the British should get out of Iraq and then we could "reach an understanding" with the Jews of Palestine.

Chubaish was an undistinguished but pleasant little village of reed huts amidst the palms, with streets of water. The best part of the visit was the fifteen-mile boat ride there and back, on the calm surface of the shallow lake with its flocks of waterfowl, and the boatmen joined by rice farmers and fishermen on the way singing mournful songs.

We left the lake in the evening to visit a tribe who were among the few remaining camel nomads in the desert between the rivers, the Albu Salih. Their late chieftain, Badr al-Rumayyidh, was one of the last of the old-fashioned tribal warriors in the days of World War I and its aftermath.

Tribal horsemen came to meet us on the gallop, brandishing their guns, and finally Badr's son Muhsin rode out of the night on a splendid horse. He led us through a reed-hut village to a rise in its midst where stood a huge tent of black camel hair, the pride of the tribe. Muhsin and his brother Smeir, storybook Bedouins in the red-checked chefiyyas that distinguished the Sunnis of the desert, motioned us into the tent, and we reposed on its carpeted floor for the traditional feast.

We spent the night stretched on rugs alongside our hosts in

the great tent. The next morning we returned to Nasiriya, where I sadly took leave of Berkeley, guessing that I would never see him again.

The next day, my last among the Marsh Arabs, I passed in tribal travel — by horseback on fields and desert and on a boat by canal to the Euphrates. There at Hilla, I said my final good-byes to Grimley, concluding my wanderings in the marshes and deserts of the Land Between Two Rivers.

15

The Lonely Prince

WITH THE DEATH of Franklin Roosevelt, the lives of all of us took a new direction. At 3:30 A.M. on April 13, 1945, Armin Meyer — newly appointed Office of War Information representative at our legation — woke me with the news. All the following day people streamed into the legation to offer condolences, and the British were obviously deeply moved.

I wrote at the time,

> Our first reaction here was personalities scattered around in the government will have a chance to prove their mettle; it is no longer a one-man government, and we shall now see if democracy can really compete in this present world. One good thing occurs to everyone — at least the advisors like Harry Hopkins and the men of small stature who have been around the President will no longer count — and we hope the new president will listen to the responsible people.
>
> Nobody knows what the new man is like — he certainly has been a Throttlebottom so far — but we all have hopes that he'll be OK. Some of the local people, including the Saudi chargé d'affaires, expressed sympathy to me instead of the Legation, for to them the death even of a distant relative is a more important event than to us, personally. We are all in mourning for 30 days, can't be seen in public gatherings, and wear mourning. Our big worry is who are the Big Three now?

On May 8 came VE-Day and I wrote, "Nobody is very thrilled about it, and we are faithfully obeying the order not to celebrate with the Japanese War ahead and a Russian one coming up someday if they continue along the course they seem to be following, a celebration seems hardly in order." (VJ-Day, on August 14, caused scarcely a ripple.)

What really brought me back to the world outside, however, and refocused my priorities was my trip to the United States to accompany the Regent of Iraq on his first official visit.

The Regent, Abd-al-Ilah, had taken over the responsibility for the throne on the death of King Ghazi in 1936. Ghazi's father, King Feisal, founder of the Hashemite dynasty in Iraq, had never been popular with the people. It was the British who decided that Iraq should be a monarchy, an institution that had not existed in the Arab world since the Prophet Mohammed, who had been basically opposed to kings.

The British had considered selection of a king from one of the prominent local Iraqi families, such as the Sa'adouns and the Namiqs, but both of these families were unpopular and even hated by large sections of the population. While Feisal had good religious credentials, being the oldest son of the Sharif of Mecca, he was considered a foreigner from Hejaz, Arabia, an associate of Lawrence, and a creation of the British.

Feisal had qualities of leadership and won considerable respect in the course of his reign, but many young Iraqi nationalists rejoiced when his death brought Ghazi to the throne; at the beginning of his brief reign he showed signs of seeking independence from the British. In April 1939, however, Ghazi was killed in an accident while driving his own car.

There is no such thing as a genuine accident in the view of many Middle Easterners, who almost always jump to the conclusion that such events are the result of murder conspiracies. The British were held responsible for Ghazi's death — there was an anti-British riot in Mosul in which the British consul was assassinated. Thus, the rule of the Regent had an inauspicious beginning, and with his strangely aloof personality he could never be popular.

I first met him at the home of Stewart Perowne, the British embassy oriental secretary, who had kindly invited me for an intimate evening. The two men were obviously on good terms and shared a quality that I can only describe as epicene.

The Regent was hardly the virile Arab type. His mother was

Circassian, and he himself, as I remarked on seeing him the first time at a ceremony, "looks less like a nephew of that old Afrit [demon] King Hussein than a degenerate Bourbon, with a weak face and vacant eyes. He gave the appearance of not being sure of himself, of not really knowing who or what he was and he spoke in low tones without animation and little seemed to arouse his interest or enthusiasm." However, from the beginning he was friendly to me, and I think he had probably heard about me and my family from our old friend Prince Muhiddin, his cousin.

Prince Mooi lived in Baghdad, where he was very much at home, with his Turkish background and common language, among the old Baghdad aristocracy. I sometimes had lunch or tea with him and would also see him at Iraqi social gatherings. He told me how an old and ugly heiress tried to marry him but, fortunately, died before she could succeed. He said, "I get offers from young and pretty ones too, but I couldn't take care of both my music and a wife." (When we saw him in Istanbul some years later, he had married a part-black dancing girl from Medina, his hometown!)

In all our contacts before, during, and after the state visit to America, the Regent always treated me as his equal; possibly as a result of what Prince Mooi had to tell him, he thought of me as a sort of fellow member of a royal family. Thus it was that when, comparatively early in my tour, plans for a trip by the Regent to the United States were discussed, both Minister Loy Henderson and the Regent himself wanted me to be the Regent's escort officer.

The trip finally began on May 21. Our party consisted of Nuri Sa'id; Daud Pasha al-Haideri, a Baghdadi notable; the Regent's aide, Colonel Ubaid al-Abdullah; and the royal physician, Dr. Sir Harry Sinderson. This last, a great, beefy Scot, had a sort of hypnotic influence on the Regent, who called him Sindbad. All official Baghdad, including the young king Feisal, came to bid us farewell and we took off barely in time to make lunch at Lydda, Palestine.

There we were met by High Commissioner Viscount John Standish Gort, Glubb Pasha, and Amir Abdullah of Jordan himself, who invited us to lunch. I sat on the Regent's left, opposite the Amir, who seemed to take a special interest in me — he probably hadn't met many Americans, and those he had doubtless did not resemble me!

We spent one night in Cairo and the next in Casablanca, at my old perch the Hotel Anfa, eating in the same VIP mess. I couldn't help feeling that I had come up in the world, thinking back on the first night I slept there, dirty and depressed, on November 10, 1942.

Arriving in New York we were put up at the Waldorf, where K.W. joined me, and the next day, as I recorded, "I take the whole party to see Sagamore Hill. I think they were impressed. Grandmother was fine but looking very old and tiny. At Mother's insistence and somewhat to my embarrassment we visit T.R.'s grave and the bird sanctuary. At Cold Spring Harbor we had them all to lunch. On the way back the Regent wants 'Sindbad' Sinderson in the car — fascinated by him."

The following day we took a special train to Washington, where I parted from the Regent and reported to G2. There I met many of my old associates, ending with my original patron, Truman Smith. Later I had tea with him and his wife in their Washington home, and he briefed me on Soviet expansion into the heart of Europe, with a great wall map as a prop. In my farewell visit to his office he said he was retiring, completely disgusted with the supineness of the United States in the face of Soviet expansion, stating that "the Russians have their people high in G2." (I heard this last opinion echoed in other conversations with my friends in that organization.)

I also touched base several times with Loy Henderson, who had just been brought back from Baghdad to take over Middle Eastern affairs in the State Department. He expressed the same concerns as Truman Smith, both about Soviet expansion and the extent of their penetration of our government. He hinted that one of his new staff might be involved with them.

I had another most interesting meeting in Washington. My brother-in-law, Bill Jackson, son of Supreme Court Justice William Jackson, took me to lunch with Justice Felix Frankfurter, who had expressed an interest in seeing me. Frankfurter was short, white-haired, bespectacled, with sharp brown eyes and a kindly manner.

At first he sounded me out to see if I was "romantically attracted by the Arabs," or considered myself a Middle East expert. "A man is not an expert on Chicago, just because he lives there," he said pointedly. His reason for seeing me obviously sprang from an interest in the Zionist cause in Palestine, which he had just visited.

"What do you think of the future of the Middle East — and our own position there?"

"I think that since we do not appear to be too interested in playing a role, we should back the British, rather than see the French and Russians divide it up," I replied.

"I agree," he said. "Though some people consider me too pro-Russian, I hate to see any more of the world abandon democracy for the Soviet system."

I returned to Baghdad at the beginning of July, but the Regent remained abroad until September 20, when, along with the diplomatic corps, I went to greet him on his return. The streets were lined with soldiers holding back the crowds; in the greeting party were several hundred sheikhs and religious people. As he got off the plane, he shook all their hands with a stolid, rigid expression but he didn't return my salute — only smiled and said a few words.

A month later he invited me to dinner at his palace, attended by Prime Minister Nuri Sa'id, Defense Minister Ismail Namiq, and various other dignitaries. He sat me on his left — quite an honor for someone of my lowly rank. During dinner he talked about his cousin Amir Abdullah, whom we had seen during our stop in Palestine, remarking how "he had always something to say to everyone in the group but I, myself, can't find a word to say when I am with strange people." My heart went out to this shy, miscast man.

My next meeting with him was on December 5, 1945, just before my departure from Baghdad, when I called at the palace to make my farewells. I was taken to a small anteroom where three tribal sheikhs were standing. The Regent came in, seemed awkward and ill at ease, but he wore a smile. Shyly he approached me and pinned a medal on my chest — the Order of Kadhimain. I thanked him and asked him if there was anything he wished me to tell the authorities in Washington about Iraq's requirements from the United States. He said, "Yes, we want help in irrigation and agriculture. We have asked Great Britain for advisers, as we must do in accordance with the treaty, but have not yet received a reply. We will ask for

American ones if the British can't supply them." He also wanted to send three young men to America to study agriculture so they could run his own personal estates. "There is no use in advising people about these things unless you set an example yourself." It was ten years before I saw him again.

16

The Bear Comes to the Tigris

WHEN I RETURNED to Baghdad after my trip to America with the Regent, my perspective was greatly changed, and while I was determined to complete my report on the tribes, it no longer seemed terribly relevant or important. I had long believed that with Allied victory certain, the Western Allies were bound to have an increasingly hostile confrontation with the Soviet Union. My conversations in Washington had brought home to me the extent of Soviet penetration of our government, the Soviets' determination to hold on to and establish their rule in Eastern Europe, and their obvious designs on Iran and Turkey. Developments in Iran, especially Azerbaijan and Kurdistan, were beginning to attract more of our attention in Baghdad, notably after some ominous signs of trouble in Iraqi Kurdistan. Also, the Soviets had already made their first appearance in Baghdad itself.

On January 12, 1945, in the lobby of the Regent Hotel, Don Bergus and I had met the newly arrived Soviet representative, Nikolai Klimov, just transferred from Kermanshah, Iran, where he had been consul. He told us in halting English that he had come to Baghdad to open a Soviet legation and asked us up to his room for a vodka after dinner.

He was waiting for us in a dimly lit little room on the top floor of the hotel. He invited us to sit at a tiny table in the center of the room, on straight chairs. On the table rested a basket of oranges, two bottles of Moskovaya vodka, and three jigger glasses.

He was a small, slightly built, dapper man, with pale brown hair, pale blue eyes framed by Slavic cheekbones — a pale lean face reflecting a deep, brooding, spiritual character. But the initial impression of pallor evaporated in the course of the evening. An occasional twitch in his features and the tremor of his hands betrayed supercharged nerves and inner fire, force, and energy.

He filled the jiggers and, standing up very straight, proposed a toast to President Roosevelt. We followed his example and drained our glasses to the bottom. He refilled them ritually and we reciprocated with a toast to Stalin. This was followed by a series of toasts to the victorious American army, the victorious Red Army, Soviet-American friendship, and a whole list of other things we still half believed in. It was very solemn, more like a state ceremony than an evening of drinking.

But as the evening wore on and the vodka took hold, Nikolai began to loosen up a little. One reason for our limited conversation up to that time had been his barely rudimentary English — but now he took out a dictionary we had not noticed lying on the table beside him, and in stilted, heavily accented English, interrupted by shuffling pages of the dictionary, he talked about the war.

He told us of how the Germans occupied his hometown in Russia and about the atrocities they committed. He choked and the tears ran down his face as he told how they killed an old man in the village. "We will never forget," he said. "After three generations we will never forget."

I tried to lighten the conversation by saying how much Americans had liked the Soviet airmen who came to Alaska to ferry planes to Russia. "You used to send Soviet aviators to Alaska to ferry out American planes," I began.

He gave me a hard and suspicious glance. "Perhaps," he said cautiously. I left his room feeling that while the man reflected the strength of his people, he also mirrored the terror under which they lived.

When I told Loy Henderson about it the following day, he was obviously intrigued, reminiscing about the old days in Moscow, and then said, "You had better be careful or you'll get him shot."

A little later Don Bergus and I invited Klimov to a large cocktail party we gave to pay back the many Iraqi and British friends who had been nice to us. The party was supposed to last from six to eight o'clock, but at ten o'clock we were all going strong and doing improvised folk dances. We were enjoying enormous prestige by introducing Klimov, and even he loosened up a bit and accompanied us to a name-day party of an Armenian-American from the legation from which we did not return until two in the morning.

After that I saw a great deal of Klimov, generally having lunch with him at the Regent Hotel. Far from being nervous about becoming too friendly with an American military officer, he appeared to welcome our talks, and I attributed this to his dedication to the study of our language.

He borrowed books from me — not novels, but political and sociological volumes — and it was obvious that he was staying awake nights slaving at the language. But also he borrowed magazines like *Time,* which gave him more problems than the more sophisticated material: He would show me an occasional page covered with underlined phrases and ask me questions like "Just what is meaning of 'behind the eight ball'?" and insist on a detailed explanation.

He was also both fascinated and horrified by the depiction of America he gleaned from these magazines. He saw a frivolity and lack of awareness of the problems of life, its many meanings and its essential tragedy, which amazed and repelled him. His attitude toward sex contrasted with what I had always understood to be a relaxed Soviet view of such matters — the sexy pictures and stories in the *Esquire* of that period shocked him.

All this was in line with what he thought about American popular music, which he considered degenerate, overcharged with sex, and empty of feeling. "It has no soul," he said. "Have you ever heard songs Russian people sing? They are so different, so deep. When you hear them, they go right through chest to heart. They make you feel happy, proud, but other times sad, you feel all sad things of world, you cry."

There grew between us the relationship the Spanish call *confianza.* I had been shy about trying my Russian on him, which was as bookish as his English, but I was rewarded when I overcame this timidity. When I tried my first tentative phrases on him his face lit up, and he was delighted to hear that I had read most of Pushkin. After exchanging a few words I asked if he would help me improve my Russian, to which he readily agreed. I thought this surprisingly unselfish of him, as it would rob him of his opportunity to practice his English.

By then we had started going for walks along the riverbank in the afternoon, and during these strolls we talked mostly in Russian. This made for slow-going conversation. But then I thought of telling him the half-remembered story of Pushkin's "Golden Fish," and he produced a book of Russian fairy tales he had bought for his children, who were to join him shortly. We'd work on them together, and sometimes, as a great favor, he'd tell me a story he'd learned in his childhood. Long before, in my own childhood, I'd read some of these stories —inherited from Grandfather — and loved their exotic simplicity that touches the heart.

Every now and then we passed an Iraqi acquaintance, which clearly embarrassed him. Iraqi friends teased me about our association. But it had its limits, clearly defined. We never discussed politics or current events after I made one early mistake. I had asked him some question about Poland, then very much in the news. He was silent for a moment and then said in English, "Shall we go back to hotel? Is late — you speak enough Russian today."

I probably should have known better, guided by the experience of Don Bergus and a British colleague, who had hoped to smoke him out in the course of an evening of drinking whiskey, which they assumed he was not as well prepared to handle as vodka. One or the other would bring up a political subject and they would argue about it together. Klimov would remain silent, and whenever they turned to him to ask his opinion, he would only say, "Is interesting." Just as the evening was breaking up, and they had concluded that probably his English was too weak to join their discussion, Klimov said in his thick Slavic accent, "I am sorry, gentlemen, that I make no comments." Then he looked Bergus in the eye and added, "You see, for us these things secret."

If we rarely spoke English, or talked politics, why did he seek my company? I later discovered that he was, in fact, an officer of the NKVD (now called the KGB). Certainly when reporting on our contacts he also cited valuable insights our association might have given him on U.S. official attitudes. But he respected the unspoken pact now established between us never to bring up substantive matters.

True, he was lonely, as the only declared Soviet in town, with the common Soviet inability to relate to Third World people. The rest of our little world saw a totally different Klimov. Those of his colleagues who dealt with him on official matters found him cold, humorless, and rigid in negotiations. I myself caught a glimpse of this side of Klimov after my return from my visit to the United States with the Regent, full of forebodings about the Soviets. After the German surrender, the Iraqi government concurred in an Allied request to inspect the premises of the German legation, closed since the failure of Rashid Ali's revolt, under the auspices of a neutral power. Accordingly, in the company of the Swiss minister, the newly arrived U.S. political counselor Bob Menninger, myself, a British embassy representative, and Klimov paid an official visit to the old German legation. During our inspection of the musty files and library of former German minister Dr. Fritz Grobba, we found a bottle of champagne along with some glasses and tasted the rather stale wine from it.

Klimov looked grim, refused to drink the champagne, and threw it into a corner of the room, a sudden violent gesture that would have been merely gauche from an Iraqi, but was frightening from Klimov, ominous in its implications. We then went back to the Foreign Office and Klimov made a furious scene with the Swiss; afterward he told me, "I hate Swiss," and demanded, "Why did no one inform me in advance about all this?"

As we spoke it dawned on me that he was aware of telephone conversations the rest of us had had about the German legation before contacting him. This meant that he had some kind of telephone intercept capability — the only direct indication I ever had in Baghdad that he was an intelligence officer.

Now, even after many years of experience in Soviet intelligence matters, I do not consider I was naive in thinking he was a friend in spite of everything. Perhaps I stumbled once on one of the reasons for his warm feelings toward me. It was, I think, on the occasion of Easter. He had left the Regent Hotel when his family arrived to occupy a permanent residence, and invited me to visit him in his newly established legation. It was already guarded by a doorman, a lackey or two, and an efficient-looking, close-cropped, barely female secretary who led me into a big room, furnished with grim stuffed leather chairs. He was alone behind a huge desk, and jumped up to greet me with a broad smile.

As soon as the door closed behind me he brought out a bottle of Georgian cognac — to my dismay, as it was only mid-morning. I resigned myself to a lost day, and we drank a couple of conventional toasts. Then he said, "I miss you, now that I've left the Regent. You know, you remind me of my brother — let's drink to him." We solemnly raised our glasses as he said, "You look a bit like him, even talk like him. He liked to laugh and joke like you, but also he was like you a serious man, a scholar. When the war came he became an army officer to fight the Germans. They killed him at Gomel — a fine, brave man, but now he is gone, my brother."

There were tears in his eyes as he refilled our glasses. "Let's drink to the end of wars where they kill brave men like my brother. Let's drink to peace between our two great countries."

We drank, and with one accord hurled our glasses against the wall.

After I returned to Baghdad on July 4, 1945, I did not see Klimov for many weeks. He was probably very busy with the arrival of the new Soviet minister, Grigori Zaitsev, and a couple of other officers, and I was preoccupied with many transitions, both in our Baghdad legation and in my career.

17

Farewell to Baghdad

"Open the gate, O watchman of the night!"
"Ho, travellers, I open. For what land
Leave you the dim-moon city of delight?"
"We take the Golden Road to Samarkand!"

THE U.S. LEGATION changed hands during my 1945 visit
to the States, and the morning after my arrival back in Baghdad
I met with the new minister, James Moose, whom I had seen for
the first time in Washington. A very different breed from the
old-school diplomat represented by Loy Henderson, Moose
was a pioneer Arabist whose last post had been minister to
Saudi Arabia.

He later told me how he had instigated the historic meeting
between Franklin Roosevelt and King Ibn Saud. It all began
when King Ibn Saud, having heard from Prince Feisal that FDR
was a stamp collector, sent him some sets of Saudi stamps. The
president in his thank-you letter said, "I hope to pay you a visit
some day." The king took this literally, and asked Moose when
he could expect the president.

Moose was home in the State Department at the time and
heard that a cruiser was in the Dardanelles preparing to take
the president home from the Yalta Conference. He
buttonholed everyone in State concerned with the president's
trip, urging that the president stop off in Saudi Arabia on his
way home, but no one seemed interested. Finally, he got
someone to send a memo to the White House, and when it
reached the president, he jumped at the chance for this exotic
encounter.

Yet the meeting, while making a deep impression on the
king, who thought he had obtained a commitment from the
U.S. government, remained without sequel after FDR's death

soon thereafter. Moose — a pessimist by nature — was even more pessimistic about the future of the Arab world. I think his interest in the Arabs and Arabic faded early. He once said that he had spent years studying the language so that he could read the literature, and then "found myself in an empty room." When I took a tribal sheikh in to see him one day, I was surprised to find his conversational grasp of the language so faded that I had to fill in the gaps.

There was certainly much to be pessimistic about, not only in the greater world of Europe and Asia, where the Soviets were proving ever more aggressive in expanding both their own territory and the Communist system of government, but next door in Iran.

At four in the morning on August 14, 1945, as I came down from the roof of the Regent Hotel after a short night's sleep, I learned that the Japanese had surrendered. The war was over and I lost no time planning for my future.

That same day I wrote my wife that I had enough points under the system established for release from the military, had asked to be relieved, and expected to be home by Christmas. I said I was writing Philip Hitti at Princeton, Dr. Ephraim Speiser in Pennsylvania, and someone at Columbia to enquire about the prospects for a Ph.D. and possibly an instructor's job to see me through. Also, *Reader's Digest* had shown an interest in me in connection with the Arabic edition they were about to launch in Cairo. Then I said I had "no intention of closing other doors in case the University thing does not work out" — such as the State Department!

> Strangely enough I shall now have more work to do than ever here. The Middle East is at its busiest after a war — and trouble always comes. Yesterday the papers came out with an announcement that plainly showed that there is a war on in Iraq — one that nobody in U.S. will ever hear about — between the Iraqi army and Mulla Mustafa of Barzan, a wild and woolly Kurd who has the most ideal set of mountains just made for ambushes and pot shots. We are all wondering if the Mulla's scientists will dig up the secret of the atomic bomb!
>
> I intend to have a last fling around the country — see every part of it I can while the seeing's good — as soon as I can get away from Baghdad.

The most enthusiastic reply I received to my letters came from Hitti, who discussed how I might fit into the Middle East Studies program. I even suggested to K.W. that she start looking for a house in Princeton. But in the back of my mind my reservations were growing about pursuing an academic career, as opposed to playing an active part in an expanding American role in the Middle East. It was becoming clear that we would have to supplement, and to some degree even replace, the power of a fading British Empire.

During the last six months of my tour in Baghdad I cemented even closer ties with the British intelligence community. Those I worked closest with continued to be the young RAF intelligence officers in CICI, my most important source of intelligence, my boon companions and friends in off-duty hours.

The British really had two intelligence systems, with representatives in the provinces (*liwas*) of Iraq. CICI was strictly a military (air force) intelligence organization represented in the liwas by area liaison officers (ALOs). The other system, which was civilian and had a political as well as an intelligence mission, was a network of deputy area political advisers reporting to the political adviser to the British embassy, Lieutenant Colonel Charles Aston. These positions were modeled on those of the British Indian political service, and most of the advisers were of an older generation, steeped in Arab lore. Some of them had been political advisers in Iraq under the mandate.

Their official function was to advise the British embassy on policy matters in the light of provincial conditions. Although they were under orders not to interfere in the internal politics of their liwas, in fact they often played an important local role, sometimes virtually as proconsuls. As the "eyes and ears" of the British embassy, they were bound to "cross lines" with the ALOs of CICI. They looked down on the raw young officers of CICI, who often depended on paid informants and seldom had as much understanding of the local scene as the veteran area political officers.

In addition to my CICI and British embassy contacts, Aston, and Oriental Secretary Stewart Perowne, I had another key British contact. He was C. J. Edmonds, adviser to the minister of the interior. He was, like Aston, an old Iraqi hand, but one whose younger days had been passed not among the Arabs of the south, as in the case of Aston, but with the Kurds. He was of the same school as a few other Kurdish experts stationed in the north as ALOs and assistant political officers, and indeed of the ambassador himself, Sir Kinahan Cornwallis. Cornwallis had been involved in Kurdistan in the 1920s as counselor to the British High Commissioner. It was he who negotiated with Sheikh Mahmoud, who for a time was lord of the province of Suleimania in defiance of the central government.

As ambassador, Cornwallis pressed the Iraqis for reforms in Kurdistan, which was restive under bad administration combined with nationalist and tribal resistance, especially in the northeast corner, where Mulla Mustafa Barzani was in open rebellion. Cornwallis urged the government to withdraw officials from this area and win over the rebels with an offer of amnesty. The government resisted, and complained about the pro-Kurdish attitude of the British provincial officers.

In February 1945 Cornwallis retired from his post, to be succeeded by Hugh Stonehewer-Bird, whom I had met in Rabat as British minister to Morocco. Before that he had served in Jidda, Saudi Arabia; thus he was essentially Arab-oriented. A few months after his arrival the British government began actively to side with the Iraqi government in putting an end to the Kurdish rebellion. Whether the new policy stemmed directly from the British government, or resulted from Stonehewer-Bird's own recommendations, or both, I am not sure. Certainly the British were concerned with the threat of the expansion of Soviet influence emanating from the Kurdish nationalist center of Mahabad in Iran.

I first ran into the new ambassador at the British embassy reception for VE-Day on May 13. "We have met before," he exclaimed. But, what with my trip to the United States with the Regent and the faster pace of events after my return, I had no occasion to talk to Stonehewer-Bird till the following October. We started out, of course, talking about Morocco. "The Moor is only an Arab for political purposes," he said, "not at all like these people."

Then he launched into the Palestine situation, expressing the usual British irritation with Americans at the time, "criticizing the British from three thousand miles across the ocean." After we got through that, he turned to Kurdistan: "The Anglo-Saxons are always falling in love with strange peoples," he said. "The Assyrians are a typical example."

The new British policy in the north was reflected, soon after Stonehewer-Bird's assignment, by the replacement of British interior ministry adviser Edmonds by Major R. H. Ditchburn, who had spent his entire career with the Arabs. He had played a role during the rebellion of the southern tribes at the time of the World War II occupation of Iraq by the British.

Ditchburn and I soon became friends and I savored the stories he told me about the old days in Iraq. Unlike some of his colleagues, he believed that "the British must loosen control and give real independence." He took issue with the low regard British provincial officers held of Iraqi administrators, saying most of them were making the best of a difficult situation. He was most critical of the French in Syria, where, he believed, resistance to their rule sprang largely from their "bad, untrained political officers who take bribes."

This is a good time to bring up the markedly different reaction I had to the British in Iraq as opposed to the French in North Africa. The British intelligence establishment in Iraq included a large number of Arabists generally sympathetic to Arabs and Islam, without an adversarial attitude toward them. The French for the most part considered "their" Arabs inferiors, fit subjects for *"la mission civilisatrice de la France."* This was, indeed, generally a relatively benevolent policy when they were dealing with more primitive societies in sub-Saharan Africa, without a national or religious identity, but not in the Islamic countries of North Africa, heirs to an ancient civilization. (It is true, however, that at the time of the arrival of the French in North Africa, Morocco in particular had degenerated into semibarbarism from the glorious times of Moorish Spain, and undoubtedly benefitted initially from French occupation.)

American troops entered North Africa against armed resistance by the French, who then exploited our presence to reinforce their authority, weakened by their defeat by Germany. They tried, with almost complete success, to prevent us from making contact with the local population, and to establish themselves as the sole intelligence and policy channel to the Moslems.

In Iraq, to the contrary, we came as allies of the British to support the Allied presence in Iran as an entrepôt to the Soviet Union. The British were almost invariably friendly to our intelligence mission, respecting our right to see things for ourselves, at the same time honestly providing us with undistorted information. Philosophically I found them congenial; we were the same kind of people. Ever since that time I felt that I could have my own special relationship with British intelligence, which was to be crucial later in my career.

In my expeditions to the tribal areas I always had British support, based on the historic British relationships with the tribes. I tried once to get the Iraqi military to help me in this connection — they spoke of including me in a camel patrol in the southern desert, but nothing came of it. As I have remarked, there was a deep cultural gap between the provincial officers of the government and city Arabs on the one hand, and the tribal people on the other, who contemptuously referred to these city-dwellers as effendis.

I was told in Morocco by a French friend that I would have had a totally different impression of the French "native control" establishment had I got to know the dedicated French officers who worked with the Berber tribes in the mountains, which was probably so. The gap between tribal and city people in Morocco was exacerbated by the fact that the Berbers were a separate ethnic group.

As I wrote K.W., I did have a final fling in Iraq, but not as extensive a one as I hoped — there simply wasn't time. For one thing, the last part of my tour was interrupted by a trip to Palestine and Transjordan, and another to Tehran. I squeezed in two forays to Kurdistan, and one last trip to the south to complete my coverage for the report on the Arab tribes, the crowning achievement of my assignment to Baghdad.

Unexpectedly early, on October 22, I received orders from Washington relieving me from duty in Baghdad. I was unprepared for this unusually prompt reply to my request. Not only were my plans for my future still unsettled, but the Great Report was nowhere near completion. I had to ask for a few weeks' delay of my return, and this gave me barely enough time. I worked all the daylight hours — usually contending with a hangover, as every night there was a good-bye party for me given by Iraqi, British, or American friends.

The most memorable of these was a huge affair attended by a hundred and fifty of my best friends given by the OWI chief in Baghdad at his offices. This was Armin Meyer, later to be ambassador in Tehran, Beirut, and Tokyo, a lively, genial man who had come to Baghdad just in time to replace Don Bergus as my closest American companion there. I still have the guest list of that party today, with a few pictures to remind me of the people I saw so much of those days and hardly ever again, and it brings back nothing but good memories. I had come to love Baghdad, and the year and a half of my assignment there was one of the best times of my life.

During my last months in my beloved Baghdad, the international scene was looking increasingly grim, as the Soviets tightened their iron grip on Eastern Europe. I noted in my diary how they nullified the results of the election in Hungary by arresting opposition leaders.

On November 19, 1945, came the news that Soviet-sponsored separatists had taken over the northwestern Iranian province of Azerbaijan. None of this was reflected in the friendly atmosphere of my good-bye call on Nikolai Klimov, who received me once more in his legation, this time in the company of the Soviet minister, Grigori Zaitsev, who had come to take over. After pressing on me the customary vodka, Klimov presented me with a book, *Arab Historians,* by the Soviet orientalist I. Iu. Krachkovski. "If you want to correspond with Academician Krachkovski, I can arrange it," he said.

I assured him we would be meeting soon again, as I somehow felt we would. By now plans for a scholastic future were fading away. I felt our first real trial of strength with the Soviets might be looming directly east of us.

I had never believed the Germans could defeat the United States, that they ever could succeed in conquering *die ganze Welt,* as they boasted they would. Their ideology, based on German nationalism, appealed only to isolated segments of other populations. They could not possibly have won the war, once faced with the overwhelming might of the United States, added to British grit and the vast lands and unexhaustible millions of Russia. I had, indeed, expected it to be over long before it ended, and I felt the Japanese were doomed after their first brief months of triumph.

But the Soviets had a philosophy that transcended national boundaries, appealing to millions throughout the world, especially intellectuals. At that time many of our own intelligentsia were attracted to Communism. And now the Red Army was in control of Eastern Europe, maintaining its battle strength while Western armies were hurriedly demobilizing. The Soviets had abandoned their wartime fellowship with us as they pursued an aggressive policy of expansion. The war-weary population of Western Europe was not in a mood for new confrontations. And such resolve as it had was weakened by the growing power of Communist parties, reinforced by many who refused to believe that the Soviets were now their enemies.

I thought that the Soviets had a capability of winning "the whole world" such as the Germans never possessed. The only power that could effectively block them was the United States, and I felt there might be a role for me in the struggle that lay ahead. I was focusing increasingly on Iran, a country for which I had developed a fascination in Baghdad, and which seemed destined to be the testing ground for a worldwide confrontation with these new aggressors.

I had already visited the country, for the first time with Major Carl Garver, air attaché in Tehran. He came to Baghdad with his plane at the beginning of 1945 to formalize his accreditation as air attaché in Baghdad as well.

Garver was my first real contact with the American air force. Previously I had known only army and navy officers — a very different breed. Carl was a quintessential air force officer: brash, outspoken, even tactless, and completely impervious to the complications of foreign politics and the nuances of foreign cultures. Yet he had a certain rough charm and both the Iraqis and Iranians probably thought he typified the American character as they imagined it, based on Hollywood.

It was in the course of a flight with him to Iran that I experienced a mental transformation which was to decide the course of my life. En route we stopped at Abadan for the night and the following morning took off from the flat yellow desert and climbed fourteen thousand feet to pass over the mountains on the Iranian side of the border. At that moment the thought came to my mind, "How can I go back from this to a university to study dead languages and old civilizations? Now I am a part of something new, something exciting, and perhaps I should make this the beginning of a career." I didn't realize it at the time, but at that moment I started the process of becoming a committed intelligence officer.

It took me eight days to reach home from the time I left Baghdad on December 12. In those days everyone was competing for air space home. I traveled on battered transport planes with bucket seats via Cairo, Rome, Marseilles, and Stephenville, Newfoundland. In Cairo I met an eccentric Christian sheikh from Es-Salt, Jordan, plus Musa Alami and a gaggle of Palestinians, and a charming young Egyptian princess. En route were a number of the world's new wanderers — correspondents, former and future scholars in transit, and fellow officers of U.S. military and civilian services — as well as Rabbi Abba Silver and another Zionist leader.

But at least I arrived in time for Christmas at Cold Spring Harbor, to find my angelic baby boy Tweed turned into a boisterous four-year-old, and a K.W. unhappy to learn that my ideas about the future had changed.

The day after Christmas I hurried down to Washington, where I had morning appointments to brief General Clayton Bissell, the G2, followed by meetings with General George Marshall and Eisenhower. They each had time only for a quick briefing, and I neither recorded nor remember anything about my meetings with these titans of history — perhaps because I was so much involved in negotiations regarding my future career. For by now I had made my decision not to pass my life in study at a university. My future lay in the Middle East, as a participant in the drama now unfolding there.

It turned out that the now-powerful air force, underrepresented in the past, had grabbed many of the most desirable military attaché assignments. An empty slot I had hoped to fill in Tehran had been taken by an air force ground officer whom I thought — rightly, as it turned out — completely unqualified. They offered me Rabat and Ankara, and friends in the State Department said they would try to get me a Damascus posting. But I stubbornly persisted in seeking a place in Tehran. I was put on hold, but at least did not get a firm turndown. Full of hope, I spent my leisure hours boning up on my Russian and reading books on the Kurds, who would surely be a concern of mine in Iran.

In my few days in Washington I found myself bombarded from both sides by early skirmishes in the Judeo-Arab battle for American public opinion in the burgeoning Palestine dispute. My friend Eliahu Epstein was there, and invited me to cocktails to meet some of his supporters, including General Orde Wingate's widow, dark-haired, Scottish, attractive, fanatical — carrying her late husband's flame. On the other side there was Badi'a Afnan, arrived from Baghdad along with Furugh, who testified at the congressional committee hearings then going on — the first of so many.

I heard another echo in Washington from a more distant past. Henry Villard of the State Department told me that my old proposal for an American college in North Africa had been brought to the department's attention by one of Bob Murphy's vice-consuls reassigned from Morocco — and this had also been brought to the attention of the White House by Bob Sherwood. Paul Alling, then U.S. minister in Tangier, had written to our legation in Baghdad asking that I stop by on my way home. They were thinking of assigning a cultural attaché there to start working on the project.

But my heart lay farther east of all this and I started brushing up my Russian at Berlitz on January 9. I never completed the course — a week later I was called into G2 and informed that somehow they had found for me another military attaché slot in Tehran. I was given three weeks' leave before departure.

They were not the happiest in my life. K.W., with her New England roots, insisted on spending them at her aunt's New Hampshire cottage. We were alone there, buried in the snow, and I found it depressing after becoming so accustomed to sunny lands. And she was depressed, after spending a happy year at Sarah Lawrence getting the degree she had missed by a year in marrying me too soon. She liked the life of academe, and had been looking forward to being a faculty wife. Although she gamely set about planning to bring Tweed to join me in Tehran once I got settled, her heart was not in it. And the ties of our marriage, weakened by our many months apart, showed increasing signs of strain.

She had taken several courses on psychology at Sarah Lawrence, and expressed the view that a psychologically guided education for all would curb man's warlike and antisocial tendencies. I wrote her, at a stop in the Azores on my way to Tehran:

> Perhaps if everyone had devoted a 100% effort on it thirty years ago it could have stopped this last war. But no amount of it now will stop the one that threatens to come. Stalin, the Soviet leaders and the whole Russian people would have had to have been given a totally different environment — but they weren't, and the thing is here — and you *can't* get anything in their country to change even the next generation, even if it weren't too late for this one.

K.W. was a great admirer of T. S. Eliot's, and in New Hampshire she had argued with me about the virtues of the contemplative life, saying that she felt at one with Eliot rather than with crass participants in international politics like myself — and Loy Henderson.

In that same letter I wrote,

> I don't think your comparison of T.S. Eliot vs. Henderson, K.W. vs. ABR is fair. T.S. Eliot and K.W. can do nothing about Russia and the aggressive force in the coming crisis except to whistle in the dark — or like King Canute, bid the waves to stop and the tide to go down (— he had to move, remember?). The only thing one could do along your lines is educate Americans to foresee this crisis — but they would have to be taught from childhood and I doubt there is time.

My worry about my differences with K.W. was buried in a golden haze of expectation as I winged my way eastward on a "plush job" plane with real seats.

PART FOUR

Iranian Days

Northwestern Iran, 1946

18

The Russian Bear
and the Lion of Iran

AFTER A FEW STOPS along the way, I arrived in Iran on March 9, 1946, on a British Airlines flight that barely made it through a low cloud ceiling. Gendarmes and soldiers lined the airport and the road to Tehran in anticipation of Prime Minister Ahmad Qavam as-Soltaneh's arrival home from Moscow — but the more cautious Soviet pilots decided not to land, returning instead the next day.

It was a damp, shivery day, and through the fog I couldn't see the dramatic mountain backdrop that was Tehran's most striking feature — I say was, because now, alas, you can hardly ever see those mountains always covered with snow. Like Mexico City's Popocatepetl and Ixtaccihuatl, the Elburz Mountains are hidden in smog poured out by thousands of superannuated exhaust pipes.

My chest was bursting with the thrill of my arrival in this magic country at one of the most dramatic moments of its crowded history. The Russians appeared to be on the verge of realizing a centuries-old dream, the conquest of Iran, which had endured so many other conquerors in history. I believed that I could somehow be a part of an effort to block them.

Since the time of Peter the Great, the Russians have sought an outlet to the warm waters of the south, both the Bosphorus and the Dardanelles, and the Persian Gulf. They first devoted their efforts to nibbling away at the Ottoman Turkish Empire; they won a long stretch on the northern side of the Black Sea by seizing and colonizing Crimea and the adjacent provinces.

Then their armies helped win independence for the Balkan
States, especially Slavic Bulgaria adjacent to Thrace, the last
European province of the Turks, fronting the Straits of the
Dardanelles and the Bosphorus.

Also, in bloody wars they crushed the independent Moslem
peoples of the Caucasus, assisted by the Christian Georgians
and Armenians on the southern flanks of the great Caucasus
Mountains. Early in the last century, they seized from Persia the
northern part of the province of Azerbaijan with its oil fields at
Baku.

After the Bolsheviks had triumphed in Russia itself, they,
too, turned their attention south. They easily overthrew the
nationalist governments that grew up in the Transcaucasus in
the wake of World War I, and fostered revolutionary separatist
regimes in the Iranian part of Azerbaijan and the neighboring
province of Gilan, supported by the Red Army.

But there was a shift in Soviet policy as a result of the failure
of Soviet attempts to establish Bolshevik regimes in Eastern
Europe, notably Hungary. In 1920 Lenin decided to change
the focus of Soviet revolutionary efforts, under the aegis of the
newly founded Communist International, to the Middle East
and India. That summer the Congress of Peoples of the East —
mostly Moslem representatives from twenty nationalities — was
held in Baku, presided over by Comintern chief Grigori
Zinoviev. He called on the assembly to oppose "English imperialism" by launching a "people's jihad" — a strange blend of
Communism and Islam.

In accordance with this new direction, Lenin decided that
larger Soviet anticolonial goals would require a temporary
retreat from Iran. This was formalized in a peace treaty,
ratified in early 1921, ending Soviet occupation in Iran but
giving the Soviets the right to intervene once more in circumstances they considered threatening to their southern frontier.

That year also saw the coup in Iran by Sayyid Zia-ed-din
Tabatabai, a conservative nationalist, with the military support
of Reza Khan and his Persian cossacks. Reza Khan gradually
took over power, and institutionalized himself as Shah, giving
himself the title Reza Shah Pahlevi, while Sayyid Zia had to go
into exile (but we shall see him again).

Turkey, prostrate after World War I, also fell into the hands
of a strong leader, Mustafa Kemal, or Ataturk, in time to hold

on to both the Caucasian border and the Straits. Turkey's control over the latter, subject to rights of freedom of navigation, was confirmed by the Montreux Convention of 1936, signed by Britain, the Soviet Union, and the Balkan States. The following year Turkey signed the Sa'adabad Pact with Iran and Afghanistan providing for cooperation against foreign (i.e., Soviet) interference.

Reza Shah imitated Ataturk in imposing a secular regime in Iran. Women were induced to remove the veil, and Western dress was imposed — with the whole population, except exempted priests, exchanging their turbans and other brimless headgear for battered European hats and caps, and their robes for tattered secondhand clothes, many of them from Manhattan! The tribes were subdued and, with great resentment, forced to discard their distinctive traditional costumes, though many hid them away, awaiting better times. However, these changes were both physically and spiritually superficial; tribal and religious sentiments were suppressed, but the embers were buried, not extinguished.

In the late thirties Reza Shah developed especially close relations with Germany, as a foil to British and Soviet encroachment; relations became even warmer after the outbreak of war, when it looked as if Germany might win. Iran brought in hundreds of Germans to provide advice and assistance to the government, especially the military. When, in August 1941, the Shah turned down a British and Russian demand for expulsion of the Germans, the two powers in concert invaded Iran and occupied it with negligible resistance. The Soviets occupied the north, and the British the south, divided by a line drawn through Tehran, which was under joint occupation. The Shah went into exile, leaving the throne to his son, Mohammed Reza Pahlevi.

The young Shah had just completed his second year on the throne of his enfeebled nation, helpless under occupation by the great powers, when their leaders — Roosevelt, Stalin, and Churchill — held a summit meeting in Tehran.

From the beginning they all but ignored Iran and its chief of state. The British and Soviet embassies had informed the Iranian government about the summit a few days before it took place, but American minister Louis Dreyfus was forbidden to do so until his hand was forced by the action of his colleagues.

Then the pleas of the minister of court, Hussein Ala, that the conference be housed in one or more of the royal palaces were rejected. The honor guard drawn up by the Iranians at the airport was bypassed. FDR refused to call on the Shah in the course of the visit, although Stalin and Churchill both did so. The Shahinshah of Iran endured the humiliation of himself having to call on FDR at the Soviet embassy, and of being kept waiting in an anteroom for a twenty-minute interview that left little time for matters of substance.

Yet the matter of Iran was one of the few raised at the summit that could, in the light of history, be regarded as favorable to the interests of what would afterward be known as the free world. In other respects, although the cause of winning the war may have been advanced, the summit was disastrous for the prospects of winning the peace.

After the three leaders arrived in Tehran on the evening of November 27, 1943, FDR moved from the American legation to the Soviet embassy, where he remained throughout the conference. There all his conversations were audible to Soviet listening devices, and his servants were NKVD personnel, several of them high-ranking officers. Stalin, in nearby quarters, thus had almost instant access to him, and had two face-to-face meetings with him, a favor FDR denied Churchill on the basis that it would give "Uncle Joe" grounds for believing Churchill and FDR were consorting against him. Throughout the conference FDR tended to side with Stalin against Churchill in controversial matters.

The disaster of Yalta has been attributed to the fact that FDR was a dying man at the time, but that conference mostly ratified decisions and processes already covered in Tehran, when he was in good health.

Various reasons have been cited for FDR's concessions to the Soviets at a time when the United States held the trump cards. The subversion theory can be dismissed at once — no American official under Soviet control had any significant role in policy-making. The answer lies in the character of FDR himself, and indeed, he thought that he alone was best qualified to deal with Stalin, whom he felt he could handle through the power of his personality and charm.

FDR was brought up as a country squire, an indifferent student who did little studying or reading in his youth and who

knew Europe only in terms of the Grand Tour enjoyed by
generations of Anglo-Saxon gentlemen; his ideas about world
politics were superficial until the end. He was a lightweight in
all things before his devastating polio attack in 1921, which
called forth the reserves of courage, character, and greatness
previously hidden in his core. He then went on to become one
of America's finest politicians, and a magnificent war leader,
but he lacked the depth of knowledge and experience to be a
world statesman in planning for the peace to follow — and we
have been paying for it ever since.

He viewed Europe as a nuisance, a contentious conjuncture
of nations, breeding ground of wars, and foresaw a world
dominated by two great powers, the United States and Russia —
although he admitted that he did "not understand the Russians"
at all. He actively promoted, even in conversations with Stalin,
the decolonization of the British and French empires, without
appearing to perceive that the Russians reigned over one of the
world's largest empires, no less so simply because it was
contiguous and not divided by oceans.

Apparently unaware of past Russian empire building, he did
not realize that the Soviets would simply follow the expansionist
policies of the tsars. In the Middle East this meant pushing
toward domination of the Straits of the Bosphorus and the
Dardanelles, and a warm-water port on the Persian Gulf.

Fortunately, other Americans in the government were completely aware of this particular Soviet goal. FDR had no briefing
by the State Department before the Tehran summit and gave
no serious study to any briefing papers they may have prepared.
He had frequently expressed a low opinion of the State
Department and the Foreign Service. But those responsible for
Iran in the State Department — this time supported by the
amateur foreign-policy buccaneer Patrick Hurley, whom FDR
did trust — pushed for a summit declaration on Iran. The final
version was drafted by my friend Jack Jernegan, former Iran
desk chief, then a third secretary at the legation, with Hurley's
help and the backing of Averell Harriman, then U.S. ambassador to Moscow. It was crammed into the agenda of the closing
session of the summit, the dinner meeting on December 1.

The communiqué summarizing its decisions committed the
three nations to "the maintenance of the independence, sovereignty and territorial integrity of Iran" and withdrawal of

occupation forces six months after the end of hostilities. Stalin signed it without demur despite previous rejections by the Soviets of similar proposals. He had, after all, essentially "won" the summit, and furthermore, FDR was suggesting a free port on the Persian Gulf under the trusteeship of the great powers, with a railroad connecting it to the Soviet Union. And the agreement could also be broken — as others were after the war when their terms did not suit the Soviets.

When Soviet troops first entered Iran in 1941, they showed little interest in establishing political control of the area assigned for their occupation and did not even permanently occupy all of it. They continued to rely on Iranian civil authorities and the police to administer the provinces. They even allowed fifteen hundred Iranian troops to reenter the Soviet zone.

This period of comparative inattention came to an end after the victory of Stalingrad, at the end of 1942. The Soviets then began a two-pronged political offensive, one directed at the separation of Azerbaijan from the rest of Iran, first under an autonomous Communist regime, which eventually would bring the province into the Soviet Union. The other, more ambitious prong was the absorption of the whole of Iran by the instrument of the Tudeh (Masses) party.

The Tudeh had been organized in January 1942 after the release of Communist leaders jailed by Reza Shah following the British-Soviet occupation. The party became increasingly active, expanding with Soviet support after Stalingrad, especially in Azerbaijan, where Tudeh candidates with Soviet support were able to win eight seats in the Iranian parliament in 1943.

In September of 1944 the Soviet Union moved to expand its influence in Iran by sending its vice commissar for foreign affairs, Sergei I. Kavtaradze, to negotiate an agreement for oil concessions in the north of Iran. Faced with opposition from the government of Prime Minister Mohammad Sa'ed, which in October decided to postpone oil concessions until after the war, Kavtaradze publicly denounced the Sa'ed government. The Soviets assisted the Tudeh in organizing demonstrations — sometimes using Soviet trucks to transport demonstrators, who were even openly supported by Red Army soldiers. Although the Iranian government held firm on oil concessions, the Soviets were able to effect the removal of Sa'ed as prime minister. He was replaced by a colorless figure, while opposition to the Tudeh — and the Soviets — began to coalesce around the figure of Sayyid Zia-ed-din Tabatabai, returned to Iran after twenty-three years of exile.

VE-Day, on May 8, 1945, when I was still in Baghdad, marked not only the end of the European war but the beginning of the Cold War. In an earlier chapter I mentioned our muted reactions in Baghdad to VE-Day and my own premonitions about the coming confrontation with the Soviets. During my subsequent visit to Washington, although I found Loy Henderson and a few others shared these concerns, the nation was already looking forward joyfully to "bringing the boys home."

On May 19, when the Shah sent a note to the "Big Three" Allies requesting the evacuation of Iran, the United States was already rapidly dismantling its military facilities there. The mission of the thirty thousand supply troops — keeping open the lifeline to the Soviet Union, pumping more than four million tons of U.S. equipment to that beleaguered country — had been rendered obsolete by the opening of the Dardanelles at the end of 1944. The U.S. Persian Gulf Command was deactivated on June 1, 1945.

The British responded to the Shah's note by proposing a staged withdrawal by British and Soviet troops, but the Soviets refused to commit themselves, and the question was not even addressed in the communiqué agreed upon in the Potsdam Conference of July-August 1945. The British, however, unilaterally began troop withdrawal from the southern sector.

Meanwhile the Soviets singlemindedly continued to pursue a Near East policy identical with that of the tsars, driving toward the warm waters of the south. This drive had been blocked between the wars by the rise of strong governments both in Iran and Turkey. Iran now lay almost prostrate, with British troops withdrawing from the south. Turkey's position had been weakened by the war, in which it had, of necessity, remained on the sidelines, so Iran was isolated, with the Red Army in control of all its northern and eastern borders. Iran represented the last hard obstacle blocking fulfillment of the dream of Peter the Great, and the Soviets long before VE-Day had been planning its removal.

Already in 1939, at the time of the Nazi-Soviet pact, Foreign Minister Vyacheslav Molotov had tried to get the Germans to agree to the establishment of a Soviet base near the Bosphorus.

Also, in addition to their designs on the Straits, the Soviets wanted to regain the territory the Russians had ceded to the Turks in 1878, the regions of Kars and Ardahan. The Soviets appear to have been obsessed with the idea of regaining all territory lost from the tsarist empire, as demonstrated by their insistence on restoring roughly the old Russian boundaries in Eastern Europe. It has also been suggested that Stalin and his police chief Lavrenty Beria had, as Georgians, a particular interest in regaining these ethnic Georgian provinces.

In March 1945 Molotov gave the Turks a statement denouncing the twenty-year-old treaty of friendship between the two countries, and on June 7 indicated that the price of a new treaty would be a revision of the Montreux Convention on the Straits, calling for the establishment of Soviet bases there and the return of Kars and Ardahan. The Soviets followed this up with a note on August 7 declaring the Montreux Convention obsolete, and in September demanded a "return" of western Thrace to Bulgaria, which had held it briefly prior to World War I.

But the doughty Turks were not about to yield to threats, and the Soviets knew they would have to fight a bloody war to fulfill the Turkish part of their grand design. The easy way to those warm waters lay through Iran, and already Soviet troops occupied the northwest province of Azerbaijan. There lay the key to the rest of Iran, and perhaps Turkey as well, on its flanks. Not long after VE-Day, the Soviets started to turn that key.

Their task would have been easy but for the United States, at long last beginning to wake from the cherished dream of Franklin Roosevelt for harmony with the Soviet Union. While President Harry Truman was facing the difficult problems of transition, and as yet was unable to construct a new policy to "contain" Soviet expansion, the State Department's Division of Near Eastern Affairs was not indifferent to events in Iran and Turkey.

The division was headed by Wallace Murray, a crusty old-school diplomat who was under no illusions about the Soviet Union. Iranian affairs were the direct responsibility of Jack Jernegan, who made it his business to try to get the U.S. government involved in Iran, and to save it from annexation. With the support of Murray, he prepared a policy paper outlining aggressive Soviet moves in Iran and suggesting means for the United States to support its interest in maintaining the integrity and independence of Iran. It was sent on to U.S. minister Louis Dreyfus for his enthusiastic concurrence.

Dreyfus, ignored at the Tehran Conference, was dismissed from his post in December. After a six-month hiatus, a full-fledged ambassador was assigned to Tehran, Leland Morris. The inexperienced Morris did his best during his brief tenure to support the Iranian government in resisting Soviet demands for oil concessions.

In May 1945 he was replaced by the formidable Wallace Murray. Murray left his job as director of Near Eastern affairs to Loy Henderson, whose expertise on the Soviet Union and experience in Iraq fitted him for the task awaiting him at this point in history. He played a key role in halting the Soviet drive against Turkey and Iran, for which the free world should be eternally grateful.

19

The Azerbaijan Crisis

THE AZERBAIJAN CRISIS was the first scene of the first act of the Cold War, and I was fortunate to be on the set, playing a minor walk-on role, among the actors in this tumultuous drama.

I had witnessed the beginning of the scene as a spectator in Baghdad, where shock waves from events in Azerbaijan had brought about the British change in attitude toward the Kurdish problem.

The Soviets' intentions became clear when, two weeks after VJ-Day, on September 2, 1945, the Shah sent a note to the Allies reminding them of the terms of the Tripartite Treaty providing for removal of Allied troops six months after the end of hostilities. The Soviets refused to affirm their intention to comply, and their troops remained in place.

Azerbaijan now became the object of a systematic Communist takeover. The Tudeh had been strengthened by the Soviet occupiers, staffed and supported by "refugees" (*muhajirin*) from Soviet Azerbaijan who had arrived in Iran in 1936, supposedly fleeing from Stalin's purges. Almost all of these had joined the Tudeh, headed by Ja'afar Pishevari, an old-time Communist. Though born in Iran, he had lived most of his life in Baku, in Soviet Azerbaijan, and participated in the government of the short-lived Soviet-backed Gilan Republic in 1920. After returning to Iran as a "refugee" under a false name in 1936, Pishevari was arrested and imprisoned until his release in 1941.

In July 1945 armed members of the Tudeh party temporarily occupied government buildings in Azerbaijan, and in August, under Soviet instruction, Pishevari organized the replacement of the Tudeh by a newly formed Democratic party of Azerbaijan. In mid-November he launched a revolution with arms supplied by the Red Army, forming a militia composed mostly of muhajirin, giving them the name of *fedayin,* meaning devotees.* The Iranian army was blocked by Soviet troops from sending reinforcements and its Tabriz garrison fell on December 10. An Azerbaijan national assembly then proclaimed the autonomy of the province.

Meanwhile, Ambassador Wallace Murray had been alerting Washington, and on the advice of Loy Henderson and Secretary of State James Byrnes sent a note to Molotov protesting Soviet actions in Iran and urging compliance with the evacuation agreement. The Soviet reply was equivocal, with an ominous reference to the 1921 Soviet-Iranian treaty. This was followed up by a visit by Byrnes, along with British foreign secretary Ernest Bevin, to Moscow in late December to try to iron out Allied disagreements.

The Soviets not only stonewalled them in their attempts to discuss Iran, but intensified their pressure on Turkey and their campaign in Iran. The Soviet press reported demands by Georgian representatives for the annexation of a large strip of northeast Turkey, including the Black Sea port of Trabzon. The Azerbaijan "Demokrats," with Soviet logistic assistance, captured Rezaieh from the last Iranian garrison in Azerbaijan on Christmas Eve.

On Christmas Day, 1945, Henderson warned Dean Acheson — acting secretary of state in the absence of Secretary Byrnes, who was in Moscow — that Soviet moves in Iran threatened world peace, and President Truman reacted strongly, saying that there should be no more compromise. The stage was set for the first real confrontation. The United States supported a series of efforts by the courageous Iranian representative to the UN, Hussein Ala, to get the United Nations to

---

* The singular is *fedai,* a term derived from the fanatics dispatched by a heretical Shi'ite leader in the Middle Ages to murder opponents. They were often under the influence of hashish and known as *hashashiyin,* from which comes the word "assassin." The fedayin of Pishevari were the first of a series of revolutionary groups who have taken the name in this century.

condemn Soviet acts in Iran and to insist upon Soviet evacuation.

But the Soviets undermined these efforts by bringing about the fall of the Iranian government in January and the appointment to the premiership of Ahmad Qavam as-Soltaneh. He owned estates in the Soviet zone and, perhaps opportunistically, had supported the Tudeh-sponsored Freedom Front in the past. He believed in appeasement of the Soviets, hoping that this policy might be more effective in inducing them to withdraw their troops, and gave no support to Ala at the UN. On February 19 Qavam went to Moscow to negotiate an agreement with the Soviets.

It was not an auspicious moment. Stalin had begun making statements about "encirclement" of the Soviet Union and the rights of intervention they had by virtue of the 1921 treaty, which he told Prime Minister Qavam justified the retention of Soviet troops in Iran. On his trip to Moscow Qavam failed to budge Stalin from this position, at least with regard to Azerbaijan. The Soviets did agree to evacuate the Iranian provinces south of the Caspian and the eastern border, and to the partial reintegration of Azerbaijan in Iran as an autonomous province.

Thus, on March 2, the date agreed on for the withdrawal of Allied troops from Iran under the Tripartite Declaration of 1942, Soviet troops still occupied Azerbaijan. Muzaffar Firuz, Qavam's official spokesman, blandly characterized this as a "friendly Soviet gesture," for which he was roundly criticized in the Iranian parliament the following day by nationalist leader Mohammad Mosaddegh.

It was this Soviet move, among so many others, that inspired Winston Churchill to make his historic speech on March 5 in Fulton, Missouri, when he told of the iron curtain "that has descended across the continent" of Europe. And while he was alerting the free nations to this new danger, threatening all the freedoms for which they had just shed so much blood, ominous rumblings of imminent aggression came from Azerbaijan.

The day of Churchill's speech, Robert Rossow, U.S. vice-consul in Tabriz, reported Soviet military movements that presaged an attack on Turkey's eastern borders.

Rossow was one of a handful of men whose efforts halted Soviet expansion southward that ultimately could have been fatal to the West — as well as the Middle East. Twenty-seven years old, he had a military school background, though his wartime experience was confined to a brief tour in the OSS. He had arrived in Tabriz on Christmas Day to replace a weird old gentleman completing a preretirement assignment.

The brief history of our wartime consulate in Tabriz reflected American naiveté about the Soviet Union. The consulate had been reopened, after many years' lapse, by an old Soviet hand, an acquaintance of mine, Bertel Kuniholm. He was a hard-bitten Finnish-American with a thorough understanding of Soviet methods and intentions who set about uncovering them in his blunt, undiplomatic manner. The Soviets were starving the province by exporting most of its grain and livestock, and Kuniholm began surveilling and reporting on this and their other activities. They demanded his recall and he was sent out to pasture as a visa officer, though I later encountered him as deputy chief of our Beirut legation.

His replacement, Rossow's predecessor, was given the brief of getting on with the Russians, which he fulfilled only too well. He took ballet lessons from a Russian teacher and was occasionally seen dancing around the consulate. He found the company of Krasnik, the Russian consul and real ruler of Azerbaijan, charming, although I knew him as a bull-like, coarse-featured man with a mouthful of steel teeth.

When the secretary of state opened his *New York Times* one day in the late fall of 1945, he was surprised by an item about an uprising in Azerbaijan, since he had received no report on it either from our Tehran embassy or the consulate in Tabriz. An "immediate" cable to Tabriz prompted the reply, "All is quiet in Azerbaijan." This was followed by a bill from the consulate for repairs to the consulate building caused by gunfire. Orders relieving the consul from his retirement post followed, and Rossow took his place.

Rossow spent January and February of 1946 struggling to keep the flag flying in this state in the midst of Communization. In March came the crucial test.

On the fourth of that month, Tudeh demonstrations took place around the Iranian parliament, or Majlis, in Tehran, preventing it from meeting and forcing an end to its term because of failure to achieve a quorum. This left Qavam in charge without the restraints of the Majlis.

That same night Rossow reported that Soviet armored forces

had started crossing the borders in numbers into Iran. Soon Tabriz was glutted with Soviet troops, while the famed Soviet wartime tank commander, Marshal Ivan Bagramian, arrived to take command of the force, some of which moved toward the Turkish and Iraqi frontiers. Other units moved south, with one detachment taking up a position in Karaj, only twenty miles west of Tehran.

Qavam denied that any troop movement had taken place. Newspaper pundits in the United States, still enamored of the Soviets, were casting doubt on Rossow's alarming reports from Tabriz. However, the mounting crisis had brought experienced news correspondents to Tehran, and just before my arrival there, Air Attaché Carl Garver took some of them on a flight over Karaj to have a look at the Soviet tanks.

Secretary of State Byrnes immediately sent a strong message demanding clarification from Moscow, and prepared to back Iranian UN ambassador Hussein Ala in a presentation to be delivered to the Security Council when it met on March 21. Ala was acting against the instructions of Prime Minister Qavam, then apparently collaborating with the Soviets, who continued to increase their forces in the face of front-page U.S. press reports, which they denied.

It was just after this dangerous week that my bold British pilot landed me through close, thick cloud cover in the caldron of Tehran on the same day Qavam had been expected back after his dubious performance in Moscow.

As I drove to the middle of town with its broad avenues sparsely filled with cars, donkeys, and *droshkies,* I was struck by the distinctly Russian look of it all, with the ragged black suits of its inhabitants and their tattered wool caps. Some wore the lambskin caps common to the Turkic peoples as well as Russians, and their faces seemed to have a strong Tatar slant of eyes and cheekbone. The bright *chadors* of the women were the only cheerful aspect of the scene — the houses were drab and dreary, and the poplars lining the streets leafless in winter.

That evening I met Jack Jernegan, the embassy political officer, formerly head of the Persian desk in the State Department: a tall, thin man with receding sandy hair whose role I knew was an important one in the scene then approaching its climax.

The following Monday I made my first visit to my future

office. My heart sank as I entered the grubby little building on the southwest corner of the square where Boulevard Shah Reza and Avenue Ferdowsi met. The military attaché's office was crammed into the dingy second floor and even scruffier third floor, where Colonel Joseph K. Baker, my new chief, showed me the tiny back storeroom full of boxes that was destined to be my office.

Then we went on to visit the somewhat less grubby but still unimpressive American embassy. I could not fail to be impressed, however, by Ambassador Wallace Murray, a wise and weighty career diplomat who appraised me with shrewd eyes. Hardly less imposing was his deputy, Angus Ward, a magnificent figure with a mixed red-and-white beard, an old Moscow hand who shared Henderson's views on the Soviets.

The next morning I spent in the office learning about my future role. Colonel Baker had no substantive knowledge of the Iranian situation and was the figurehead, responsible for official liaison. One of the assistant attachés, the air force ground officer who had first got the slot I had hoped for myself, was patently unqualified either by education or experience. Carl Garver's responsibility as air attaché, with the plane assigned to him, was largely concerned with reconnaissance of Soviet forces. The other substantive officer was Captain Alexis Gagarine, who had arrived the previous year. He was a tall, husky man of about my own age, with strong Russian features and a slight Russian accent, and we soon became fast friends. He had the principal responsibility of reporting on the Red Army, and in his dealing with them proved brave and resourceful. This meant also that his attention was concentrated on Azerbaijan.

Thus my role was clearly going to be that of the Iranian expert, covering activities in the country as a whole, and soon, because of prior experience in Iraq, I also became the Kurdish referent.

The military attaché's office was most primitive by today's standards, having only one bathroom, and one large safe for all our classified documents. The key to the safe was hung in the bathroom by the last to leave the office, cleverly concealed under a towel — where perhaps a Soviet agent found it at night.

Across the street was the Ritz Hotel. To imagine it, banish

from your mind the picture of glamorous establishments of that name in international capitals. It was a grubby little place with a cozy bar and one of the few European-type restaurants in town, though nowhere near even one-star quality. Often we had a meal there consisting only of vodka and dry bread with a large bowl of caviar in the middle of the table; caviar was cheap in Iran in those days and not much liked by the locals.

The bar became the headquarters of the foreign press corps, and my first day at the office I had lunch with three of them: Harry Zinder of Time-Life, Gene Markey of the *New York Times,* and Joe Goodwin of the Associated Press. I met Sam Souki of the United Press later — he was something of a loner in the press corps, perhaps because he had more background and hence better contacts than the others. He was an Egyptian of Lebanese descent whom I was to see, off and on, from that time forward.

I have always had great respect for foreign correspondents and felt a certain kinship with them, as our objectives were similar — to find out the truth about what was going on. We were one in "buying the night flight," as Georgie Anne Geyer expresses it in the title of her recent book describing her life as a foreign correspondent, traveling from one country and milieu to another, in pursuit of the truth around the world. I often found it useful to exchange impressions and views with correspondents, to the profit, I think, of both sides. None of them ever betrayed a confidence, and when in my later career they knew my position in the CIA, none of them ever gave me away.

During my first days in Tehran I also found myself thrust into another role — that of Carl Garver's assistant in reconnaissance missions over Russian lines — and duplicated the correspondents' own flight of a few days before. For now the Soviet evacuation crisis was in full swing.

I took my first reconnaissance flight with Garver on the morning of March 19, my assignment being to observe and list all Soviet units. First we headed northeast over the Caspian coast, ascertained that the Soviets had indeed fulfilled their promise to Qavam to evacuate that area, then swung back over Karaj. As we dipped down to almost three hundred feet I saw the white faces of Soviet soldiers looking up at us beside some twenty tanks.

All activity was brought to a momentary halt by *Naw Ruz,* the Iranian New Year, which announces the beginning of spring on March 21. Headed by the ambassador, the entire embassy went to the royal palace for the traditional salaam to the Shah. The palace was a combination of splendor and Coney Island. The walls of the reception hall were covered with many-faceted panes of glass, with the Peacock Throne in its midst. Many of its jewels were false and some missing — when a shah needed money, he took the obvious course. Court officials in gold brocade helped us to line up behind our mission chiefs — each embassy, in order of seniority, with the Afghans first. The Shah, a weak, washed-out-looking young man, read an answer to our greetings in an inaudible voice, then shook hands with us all. Yet it was the lot of this unimpressive figure to save his country, and this time he proved equal to the challenge.

The Soviets, apparently worried about world reaction, decided to evacuate Iran after all, abandoning any plan they might have had to attack Turkey. After having arranged the dissolution of the Majlis, they evidently thought that they could in a less blatant fashion take over Iran through manipulation of Prime Minister Qavam. While they probably had no more faith than we did in this devious Iranian politician, they had a more reliable instrument with which to control him, his political counselor, Prince Muzaffar Firuz.

Firuz was a member of the Qajar royal family deposed by Reza Shah. A tall, lanky figure with a long, sallow face and tiny moustache, by his very appearance he inspired all of us Americans with mistrust. He had once served in the Iranian legation in Washington, and left under a cloud. Always at Qavam's elbow, this unpopular man had a sinister influence over the prime minister, the reasons for which no one professed to know, although there was no lack of theories. One of the most frequently heard — at least by me — was that it stemmed from a bond between Qavam and Firuz's attractive wife.

It was Firuz who announced at a press conference on March 25 that the Soviets were leaving Karaj and would be out of Iran within five weeks. I was having lunch at the Ritz with a representative of *Reader's Digest* when Joe Goodwin of the AP rushed in with the news. Soon the correspondents and myself were headed for Karaj by car.

The Soviet checkpoints and guards had indeed vanished,

and we saw Soviet soldiers dismantling local houses, taking furniture, bathroom fixtures, windows, and even floorboards and loading them onto horse carts and trucks. As we went on to observe similar activity at the railroad station, Soviet soldiers ran up and started shouting questions at me — I was in uniform. I pretended not to understand them, but they ordered our driver to leave. They were menacing, dirty, and brutalized. I felt sorry for the people of Eastern Europe who had just undergone "liberation" by the Red Army.

It turned out that the sudden announcement by Firuz resulted from a meeting the evening before between Qavam and the new Soviet ambassador, Ivan Sadchikov, in which Sadchikov had informed the prime minister of Soviet plans to evacuate, along with an obvious quid pro quo: a proposal for a Soviet majority-owned joint oil company. The arrest of conservative politician Sayyid Zia-ed-din Tabatabai the same day was evidently part of the deal.

Garver continued to monitor Soviet troop movements and concentrations from the air, and I generally accompanied him to count trucks and tanks. Occasionally the Soviets would rotate their guns in our direction, and often we could see the upturned faces of the soldiers. Otherwise they simply went about their business and ignored us, and Garver got overambitious. One night he told me that he planned to take some correspondents with him on a flight to the Soviet border, crossing to Astara, in Soviet Azerbaijan. I thought this was extremely risky, but he made the trip without incident. A *Life* photographer with him even sent back shots taken above Astara, which duly appeared in the magazine the following week.

But while he was actually in the air, a Soviet assistant military attaché marched into our office in a white uniform and handed us an unsigned three-paragraph note in Russian. It said that an American plane had been buzzing Soviet troops, disturbing them while they were completing their evacuation, and ended by stating that if this provocation did not cease, the Soviet government could not take responsibility for the consequences. Colonel Baker decreed that this was to be Garver's last Soviet reconnaissance. For some reason the Soviets did not follow up with a protest about Garver's daring exploit — doubtless they had immediate intelligence information on Baker's prohibition.

As the Soviets evacuated Azerbaijan, they turned over their occupation duties to the Azerbaijan Demokrats, and Alex Gagarine and I decided on April 26 to drive north to Tabriz and have a look. We were stopped at a Demokrat check post at a place called Sharifabad. It was manned by thirty or forty tough-looking fedayin. They wore nondescript clothes, and spoke Russian among themselves. Their commander greeted us in a friendly manner and, after checking with his headquarters in Zenjan, gave us an escort and waved us through.

Sixty miles farther on, in Zenjan, we were taken to the governor's office. There we met General Ghulam Yahya Daneshian, commander of the fedayin, who happened to be in town. He looked as villainous as his reputation. He politely asked us our business in Turkish, with an interpreter to translate it into Russian for Gagarine, trying to maintain the pretext that he did not know Russian — although he came from Soviet Azerbaijan! Gagarine explained that we were making an official visit to Tabriz. After some heavy palaver, punctuated by lengthy pauses as Ghulam Yahya puffed on a pipe and scratched his shaggy head with it, he let us go to bed, promising to clear our trip with the Tabriz authorities during the night.

The next day we were allowed to proceed north past the next town, but were blocked at the provincial boundaries by fedayin. Returning to Zenjan, we tried to call Ghulam Yahya, but were told he had left town. We had to return to Tehran, frustrated and furious, but admitted that it was a relief to see the central government frontier post in "Free Iran," as our Armenian driver called it, with its "good old inefficient gendarmes."

The first overt sign of the new direction of Soviet policy came with the mammoth May Day celebration, organized by the Tudeh, which I attended a few days after our abortive car trip. Its participants — numbering about thirty thousand — cheered as a party leader harangued them in a hysterical, cracking voice, waving his arms.

"Down with Sayyid Zia!" he yelled, to the responding echoes of the crowd. "Long live Free Iran! I am a son of Azerbaijan — we are four million of whom three hundred thousand live in Tehran. We have won our freedom in Iran! We shall make all Iran as free as Azerbaijan."

The crowd roared in unison after every phrase, raising their fists in the Communist salute, in drill order. Apparently many

of them were Azerbaijanis, and insisted that the party leader
continue his speech in Turki. He ended it with renewed calls of
"Down with Sayyid Zia! Down with the *Mostarja'in* [Reaction-
aries]!"

An embassy officer asked one of the crowd what was Mostarja'in. "That's the brother of Sayyid Zia" was the reply.

This was the first of a series of demonstrations during the
whole of that spring. The Tudeh, with Soviet help, extended
its influence throughout central and southern Iran, since in
the northern corner the Demokrats were in charge. The
Soviets slowly withdrew their troops from Azerbaijan. Ja'afar
Pishevari, the Azerbaijan Demokrat prime minister, came to
Tehran and negotiated an agreement reaffirming Azerbaijan's
status as a province of Iran, but leaving its government, army,
and police forces intact. The form had changed but not the
substance.

Unfortunately, during this transition period, Ambassador
Wallace Murray was stricken by a cardiac crisis and had to be
brought home. George V. Allen arrived at the beginning of
May to take his place. While Allen had only had one previous
post — in Athens — he had served for several years in the
Office of Near Eastern Affairs in the State Department, most
recently as Henderson's deputy.

Highly regarded by all his superiors at State, Allen was the
youngest ambassador ever appointed. Even I, at the advanced
age of twenty-eight, found him surprisingly young and rather
naive in his opinions — except about the Russians. He came
from North Carolina, so probably had not been brought up
with the fantasies of our northeastern intelligentsia.

During this comparative lull I took time off to go to Cairo
and pick up a car, passing through Baghdad on my return
drive. There I had lunch with Nikolai Klimov, and he immediately asked me, "Has there been a change in American public
opinion about the Soviet Union?"

"I'm afraid so, Nikolai," I said. "Your people seem not to be
able to meet us halfway. We find the Soviets secretive, suspicious, not able to deal with us in the open manner to which we
are accustomed. This will have to change — we must have
mutual understanding."

He was upset. "There can never be trouble between our two
great countries. You must understand that individual, personal

relations are not important in my country. All this trouble seems to come from individual politicians."

He was moody and sad throughout the meal, and as we parted tried to show that he still felt personal friendship for me. I felt his distress was genuine. It was the last time we met, and I don't remember anything about his career from then on, except that he served for a time as KGB resident in Mauritius in the sixties.

My relations with Soviet officials in Tehran were of a different kind. Our ambassador had been outwardly cordial with his adversary, Soviet ambassador Ivan Sadchikov, but my contacts were with my opposite numbers, the Soviet military attachés. These were headed by Lieutenant Colonel Boris Razin, so my normal contacts were with his assistants, Majors Veniamin Maligin and Konstantin Zasorin, and Lieutenant Colonel Vladimir Krachkovski.

Garver, Gagarine, and I had several get-togethers with them at dinner, with innumerable vodkas, in a Tehran hotel of their choice, run by a suspected Soviet agent. Conversation was not exactly substantive, except for a few not too vehement exchanges of opinion. Generally, I spoke Persian with Zasorin — and found it strange to be uttering courtesy phrases in stilted, book Persian with a Soviet officer. Gagarine spoke Russian, mostly with Maligin, and Krachkovski tried his broken English on Garver.

Early in the evening I would say that my doctor had forbidden me to take much alcohol, and Alex would also beg off as the evening heated up, leaving Krachkovski — a big, red-haired Ukrainian — and the smaller Carl Garver alone in the contest, for that was what it was. There were the usual tests of whether each jigger was drained to the bottom, with demands that the glass be emptied over the head to be sure there was no liquid left. The rest of us cheated by substituting soda for vodka, and were sometimes exposed by a demand for exchanging glasses. The penalty for cheating was an extra jigger.

Garver always bested Krachkovski despite the difference in their size — Krachkovski would finally say "Enough," and American honor was upheld. Neither our military attaché, Colonel Baker, nor Colonel William T. Sexton, an infantry officer from the Third Division who succeeded him in June, took part in these affairs. Both were mainly concerned with dealing with the American military.

During this June lull I had occasion to meet Prime Minister Qavam, along with Firuz, at a lunch he gave for our new ambassador. I noted at the time:

> Qavam is quite an impressive figure — a largish man with a stoop, a round face with thick glasses and reddish hair painted on his head. His manner is dignified, but shows that he feels the burden of his office. Muzaffar Firuz — face of a fox, movements of a snake, resembles both. Nervous, shifty eyes as he talks with Soviet Ambassador Sadchikov — of medium height, thinning blondish hair, in a baggy gray suit — contrast with the impeccably dressed British Ambassador with aristocratic features and military moustache.

The day after this lunch I flew with Garver to Tabriz. With us was Colonel Sexton, who, like his predecessor, had no experience in the Middle East. Passing over Zenjan on our way, we buzzed some Demokrat troops standing by their trenches. They waved at us, and apparently reported us as an unidentified aircraft, because when we arrived at the Tabriz airport, we were greeted suspiciously by a group of military officers in nondescript uniforms who told us they were not informed of our mission. When we explained who we were, they said they would check with their headquarters, and a group of pilots asked us to have tea.

After tea, they said we were free to go on to Tabriz. But as we returned to the plane and a waiting car, we were surrounded by officials who informed us we were not going anywhere.

The head of the delegation, a little round man called Mahtash, who had a high-pitched voice and an oily manner and who turned out to be the minister of agriculture, said, "I am truly sorry, but you do not have written permission from the government in Tehran. We are sending a telegram now — meanwhile why don't you fly back to Tehran and return with proper documentation."

As the Persian speaker of the group, I protested, "We have Prime Minister Qavam's personal permission to come here. You must permit us to proceed" — but to no avail.

Then a thunderstorm burst over us — it was Bob Rossow, the American vice-consul at Tabriz, ordinarily a slight, bespecta-

Grandfather, Mother, and infant Archie, 1918.

Left to right: Archie, Mother, Theodora, and Father at the Acropolis.

Archie and Tweed at Camp Ritchie, winter 1943–44.

Archie and three U.S. Army officers in Moroccan costume,
with the son of their host on Archie's knee.

Minister Loy Henderson and his wife in Baghdad, 1944.

U.S. Legation staff in Baghdad, 1944. *Left to right:* Don Bergus, vice-consul; Archie, assistant military attaché; William Moreland, second secretary; Walter Birge, third secretary; Minister Loy Henderson; Armin Meyer, OWI; Colonel Paul Converse, military attaché.

Dr. Harry Sinderson, the Regent of Iraq, Colonel Ubaid al-Abdullah, and Archie en route to the United States, 1945.

Qaimmayam of Qal'at Sikar, Oriental Secretary Stewart Perowne, Archie, and Major Berkeley, 1945.

Interior of a *mudhif* with coffee hearth and seated guests. (Wilfred Thesiger)

Abdullah Falih Al Sa'adoun before his tent in the desert.

At the Regent Hotel. *Standing:* Armin Meyer and Archie.
Seated, left to right: Sheikh Salim al-Khayyun, "Doc" Hoff,
Sheikh Ahmed al-Ajil of the Shammar.

Prime Minister Ahmad Qavam, seated, with Muzaffar Firuz, his *éminence grise*.

Archie flanked by Azerbaijani *fedayin* in Zenjan, 1946.

Pusho, with Armin Meyer and Archie.

Amr Khan with Shikak tribesmen in Zindasht, 1946.

Qazi Mohammad shares a watermelon with Archie.

Archie at the Voice of America, as Lucky first met him.

Archie toasting Lucky at their wedding.

Ambassador George Wadsworth on his golf course near Ankara.

Saudi Foreign Minister Yusuf Yasin, Archie, and
Finance Minister Abdullah Suleiman in Dhahran, Saudi Arabia.

Archie with Lucky in the Oval Sitting Room in the White House before a state dinner. (Mary Anne Fackelman-Miner, The White House)

Archie with President Ronald Reagan in the East Room of the White House, with King Fahd of Saudi Arabia and Lucky. (Mary Anne Fackelman-Miner, The White House)

cled, balding young man of deceptively mild appearance. But now he was a dynamo of fury, berating the hapless Mahtash.

"How dare you arrest diplomats of a friendly power? I demand that you release them at once!"

"But they are not under arrest," Mahtash protested, "they are free . . ."

"This is outrageous," Rossow interrupted. "Tomorrow the whole world will know about this, and that you are responsible."

Mahtash drew him aside as he continued to try to appease the inexorable Rossow, and a nasty-looking fellow appeared, with a wet, open sore on one cheek and a sarcastic smile twisting his lips. He was a Soviet Caucasian named Dadar, and his sinister appearance betrayed what I later found out to be his calling, chief of the political police. He motioned us all to join him in the nearby telegraph office, where, after Rossow had delivered another tongue-lashing, the Demokrats settled for a brief phone call to another official, and let us go on to the consulate.

There we met Rossow's newly assigned assistant, Gerry Dooher, a redheaded Irishman not long out of the Emerald Isle. We all went out that evening to the Pars, Tabriz's premier restaurant — unless it was the other one! With us were Bob's British colleagues, and we celebrated our reunion with Russian champagne. An orchestra regaled us for a while with American and British wartime ditties, and several times we saw Demokrat officials, including the repulsive Dadar, crack the door open to stare at us. We asked the orchestra to play a popular Russian tune, but a fedai stepped up to stop them, demanding that they play the Demokrat national anthem, "Hamishalugh Yasha Azerbaijan" ("Live Forever, Azerbaijan").

Rossow, Dooher, and I, full of Dutch courage, grabbed our champagne bottles by the neck and advanced on the offending fedai, who hastily acknowledged his mistake, as our British colleagues suggested it was time to go home.

Bob Rossow told me that he had given Mahtash the impression that I was President Roosevelt's son, producing the effect intended. Not surprisingly, the following day a political police official appeared at the consulate to say that a telegram had arrived from Tehran approving our mission and apologizing for their summary treatment of us. On his heels came a Tass man to interview "the President's son," who had to be satisfied with a brief word while we paid the obligatory call on the gross but powerful Soviet consul.

After lunch with our British friends, Rossow took me around town and showed me the places where, sometimes accompanied by Alex Gagarine, he had counted tanks in the dark during the last month's Soviet troop movements. He rode with us on our plane back to Tehran, where he had just been appointed third secretary in the embassy, in charge of political affairs. (Since the Tabriz post was no longer considered quite as crucial, an inexperienced junior officer was appointed to replace him.)

While in Tabriz I became a full-fledged member of the Azerbaijan Club, originally founded by Bob Rossow as the Flying Wedge of Azerbaijan. One qualified for membership by a point system. There were points for days spent in Azerbaijan, hours under arrest, being targets of gunfire. Twenty points were required for membership, which could be attained at one stroke if you were killed trying out for it.

I had acquired a house, just above Carl Garver's, in the town of Tajrish, north of Tehran, complete with an Assyrian couple to take care of me, and K.W. and Tweed, whom I was expecting shortly.

It was a nice little white stone cottage with a swimming pool, usually numbingly cold. Our porch overlooked the village square and, far below, Tehran itself, nestled down in the valley, with the white mountains rising starkly behind us. I used to enjoy taking my breakfast on that porch, looking down on the stone walls of a village that seemed central Asian. I was really not that far from Samarkand.

At the end of June, K.W. and Tweed arrived to take up residence, and immediately came down with Tehran tummy. K.W. recovered quickly but Tweed — then four and a half years old — could not shake it off. The American military mission doctor's prescription did not seem to help. Desperate, as he was losing weight and becoming dehydrated, I called on an Iranian doctor, who ordered a diet of yogurt and pomegranate soup at alternate intervals. Within forty-eight hours he was cured. (I have always found yogurt an excellent preventative against bacterial dysentery.)

The political doldrums in Iran began to end at the time of K.W.'s arrival with the announcement by Qavam of the formation of a new party, the Democrat party of Iran. None of us could fathom what lay behind this move by that unfathomable politician. Was it a move to preempt the Demokrats of Azerbaijan, or was it another face of the Soviet drive for control of all Iran? The active participation of Firuz gave a bad signal, and soon there were ominous developments in the southwestern province of Khuzistan, pointing the way to the realization of Soviet plans.

There, in mid-July, the Tudeh-controlled union called a strike of the workers in the great British oil installations. The British, however, were quick to react. The Marsh Arabs of Khuzistan, who had no use for the Tudeh and were in close touch with the British, attacked the Tudeh. The British immediately brought in a sloop and a cruiser to Abadan and, as rioting continued, imported four thousand Indian troops to Basra "to protect British lives and property." Qavam and the press denounced the British, and sent Firuz to settle the strike. It was settled, but on much the Tudeh's terms — hardly surprising, as the Tudeh were now in the government.

On August 1, Qavam formed a new cabinet including three Tudeh ministers plus a member of the collaborationist Iran party and a former dragoman at the Soviet embassy. George Allen, optimistic by nature, whipped off a telegram putting the best face on the move, interpreting it as a ploy to control the Tudeh. He did not consult Bob Rossow, who was furious, looking on it as a move closer to the Soviets, who would soon subvert the entire government.

Many Iranians shared this fear, and the powerful Qashqai tribe of Fars province rose in revolt, demanding the resignation of the Tudeh ministers. The Azerbaijanis, meanwhile, were far from being appeased and became increasingly truculent. Qavam began at last to be worried enough to ask George Allen what the United Nations, and by inference the United States, would do if a clash occurred with Azerbaijan. He did not get a commitment at that time, nor in response to a number of feelers he put out in August and September.

What brought matters to a head was the necessity of holding elections to replace the recently dissolved parliament, and on October 5 the Shah signed the decree authorizing them. This was followed by massive demonstrations, complete with marches, banners, slogans, and cheers along familiar lines. The Democrat party of Iran held its own demonstration, and we all noted that the same rented crowd that had wildly cheered the Tudeh was now yelling "Death to the Tudeh" and "Azerbaijan — inseparable part of Iran."

Muzaffar Firuz took an active part in this demonstration, carried on the shoulders of his followers, who distributed propaganda sheets extolling their hero. Those idealists who hoped for true democratic government in Iran would have found all this discouraging; the fact is that Iranians have no democratic tradition and have only the experience of three millennia of being ruled by a shah or khan.

The demonstration battle was finally won by the Shah. He had no party, but he had the loyalty of the army. For the first time since the occupation of Iran in 1941 he held a mammoth military parade.

Following an ancient custom from before the advent of Islam, bulls were sacrificed in the big square in the center of the city; then two full infantry divisions and a cavalry division passed in front of crowds screaming "Long live the Shah!" — yes, the same crowds. The loudest applause came when two companies of ancient tanks rumbled across the square, with a few prewar Hinds fighter planes precariously doing stunts overhead. Yet, despite the fickleness of the crowd, all of us felt there was an element of pride, so long offended, being demonstrated by the Iranians in their troops and their shah. It was the Shah who carried the day.

Henderson in Washington and Bob Rossow in Tehran had been urging Allen to press Qavam to reconstruct his cabinet without the Tudeh and take a firmer attitude toward Azerbaijan. When Qavam equivocated, on October 17, Allen went to the Shah and encouraged him to force on Qavam a change of government. Assured of at least a degree of American support, and sure of the military, the Shah had a showdown with Qavam — who backed down. Qavam dismissed the Tudeh ministers and finally yielded to the Shah's order that he remove Firuz, who was appropriately bundled off as ambassador to Moscow.

Preparations were now complete for the holding of elections in all provinces of Iran — and Azerbaijan (by the terms of the July agreement) was once more a province. The stage was set for confrontation.

In preparation for this, Garver once more took to the air in reconnaissance flights over Azerbaijan, this time to monitor Demokrat troops, with me along as observer. We took various routes but I have particular reason for remembering the last flight, which took us as usual over the rugged pass of Qaflan Kuh, where the Demokrats were dug in; we saw their anti-aircraft guns pointing at us. We were the only plane in the air, and the Iranian troops had orders to let us pass. We hoped that the Demokrats had the same kind of orders.

We flew low over the Azerbaijani city of Mianeh. It was the Day of Ashura, and we saw the tents, horsemen, and soldiers with waving banners lined up on the square performing the passion play of the death of Hussein.

Turning back home, after happily passing over Qaflan Kuh and the Demokrat lines, we suddenly saw the ground below us puffed with smoke, and shells exploded around us in the air. Someone in the Iranian army had not passed on the word! We were struck a couple of times on the wings, and the plane wavered, but got us safely back to Tehran. The Iranians on the ground were most apologetic, and a week or two later the Shah summoned us to his palace and, in a private ceremony, pinned medals on our chests, the Order of Merit (Third Class, in the case of Captain Roosevelt!).

Meanwhile the climax was approaching. George Allen, now able to offer more concrete support from a stiffened U.S. government, galvanized Qavam into action. He at last hurriedly put together the underpinnings of his Democrat party, no longer merely a facade. For whatever motives, this devious intriguer decided at last to turn on his erstwhile allies, the Tudeh, and face the Demokrats of Azerbaijan.

In late November he openly stated that elections in Azerbaijan, as well as those in other provinces, would have to be supervised by Iranian police and military units. On the night of November 25–26, Iranian troops reoccupied the town of Zenjan.

The fedayin fled, and Demokrats were attacked by a mob. Some three hundred muhajirin ("refugees" from Soviet Azerbaijan) and their families, huddled around the railroad station awaiting a train north, were saved from the mob by the intervention of a newly arrived Iranian army colonel.

Qavam followed this move by arresting Tudeh leaders in Tehran. The Soviet ambassador made repeated demarches to the prime minister, protesting these actions and referring to the terms of the 1921 treaty providing for Soviet intervention in event of a threat to Russia's southern boundaries. But meanwhile, George Allen stated to the press that the decision to send security forces to *all* provinces of Iran was "normal and proper."

In the early morning of December 10 the Iranian army entered the forbidding pass of Qaflan Kuh, and the defenses we had viewed from above crumbled after a short battle with the fedayin, who then started a headlong flight north. Meanwhile, there was a popular uprising against the Demokrats, whose cruelty and oppression had made them hated by every section of the population. One has to conclude that the Soviets, in deciding to leave the Demokrats to defend themselves, had been victims of their own propaganda, greatly overestimating the strength of their regime, and contemptuous of the Iranian army.

On December 12, with government forces now occupying Mianeh and advancing rapidly forward on Tabriz, the Demokrat governor-general, Dr. Salamullah Javid, telegraphed a declaration of loyalty to the Shah and ordered provincial officials to cooperate with the Iranian army.

That day George Allen called a staff meeting at the embassy and addressed us gravely: "Gentlemen, the Iranian army is advancing in Azerbaijan and we have no information on what is happening in Tabriz. Apparently all communications have been cut, and we have no word from our consulate. I can only hope that all of our colleagues are safe."

While the ambassador was speaking, I noticed Gerry Dooher, who had been reassigned to the embassy shortly after Rossow to follow Azerbaijani affairs, looking at me. He turned his eyes skyward, and after the meeting I took him aside and asked him, "What gives?"

"Well, I haven't dared show it to the ambassador, but we *have* just received a telegram from our consul in Tabriz — God bless him!"

He showed it to me. It read, "Flush toilets urgently needed here!"

I hope that young consul acquired more insight into international affairs in the course of his diplomatic career.

Meanwhile, Joe Goodwin and the newly arrived *New York*

Times senior correspondent, Clifton Daniels, asked our office if we could lend them a military vehicle to observe these events — which it would not have been politic to view for ourselves. With Allen's consent, I lent them my own car, whose American flag painted on the fender offered some protection.

The Iranian military apparently had no qualms about letting them drive north on the road to Tabriz ahead of the advancing troops. When the correspondents arrived at the first village past the front, and told the villagers that Mianeh had fallen and the Iranian army was on the way, they sacrificed a sheep, with cries of *"Zindeh bad Shahinshah!"* ("Long live the Shah!"). The American flag on the fender of a military vehicle gave rise to a rumor that American troops were accompanying the Iranian army, which may have encouraged general participation in the uprising.

The correspondents continued their triumphant journey all the way to Tabriz, where the Demokrat officials and the muhajirin took a hasty departure. They filed a story on the evening of their arrival in Tabriz reporting the flight of Pishevari. A couple of days later he and General Daneshian crossed the Soviet frontier with scores of their followers and more than a hundred truckloads of furniture and other possessions — or dispossessions, as the general apparently emptied the bank vaults of Tabriz before his departure.

Thus ended the battle for Azerbaijan, of which I was a firsthand witness, and perhaps could even qualify as a minor participant.

The first battle of the Cold War was over. The Soviet advance south of the Caucasus had been checked — the pressure on Turkey eased as well. With the Truman Doctrine, proclaimed and formalized in the early part of the following year, the United States finally drew the line at the boundaries of Greece and Turkey.

The fall of Azerbaijan brought to an end my reason for serving in Iran, and I was anxious to get on with the next phase of my life — whatever that was to be.

I had already taken the Foreign Service examination at the end of September 1946, having prepped myself as much as possible, with my greatest problem lying in the field of international law. This was the only part of the general examination I found really difficult — the others, the sections on international politics and geography, and preparation of reports on imaginary situations, came easily.

I was even more fortunate in the language exam. One had the choice of French, German, or Spanish, with added credit for passing points if you took two of them. So I took French as my first language, and with my book knowledge of German took it on as well, and received 100! Two days after Pishevari and Ghulam Yahya Daneshian passed the frontier, I received a telegram, authorized by Loy Henderson, saying that I'd passed the Foreign Service exam with a grade of 94, the highest ever recorded.

I was away from the office when the telegram arrived, and somebody told K.W., who by now had lost any illusions she might have had about my future career. Her only comment was an unladylike expletive!

I myself had some reservations about a career as a Foreign Service officer. Two weeks after receiving the telegram, I wrote similar letters to my friends at the Arabian American Oil Company (Aramco) — whom I had visited several times over the previous two years — as well as *Reader's Digest,* which was starting an Arabic edition in Cairo; C. D. Jackson of Time-Life; and Cliff Daniels of the *New York Times:* "I feel a growing reluctance to bury myself in a lifetime career in the Foreign Service, offering so many opportunities for stagnation. My principal reason so far has been my interest in the Middle East and the promise of State Department officials" — Allen and Henderson — "that I shall be able to start right in as a Middle East specialist. In my search for some other outlet I thought of your organization . . ." etcetera.

I also considered the possibility of continuing my career in military intelligence, but this route was rendered less promising by events occurring just after New Year's of 1947, when we were honored by a visit from my mother-in-law, Countess Eleanor Palffy.

She was an extraordinary woman, the fifth wife of the much-married Hungarian count Palffy. The count eventually broke up with my mother-in-law in a dramatic scene in which he struck her on the head with a pistol.

The countess was one of the more enjoyable people I have known — although my parents strongly disapproved of her. She preferred to live in Paris, where she knew "everybody," including the literary establishment. She counted Somerset Maugham among her friends, took us to spend an evening with him in San Francisco, and vainly tried for the honor of figuring as a character in one of his stories.

She was a great conversationalist, cynical and bawdy, and I got on with her famously — better than did K.W., who in no way resembled her. The countess had a sharp and witty tongue, given to speaking unpalatable truths, which was sometimes loosened even more when she had been drinking. We didn't worry much about this, however, at the time of her visit to Tehran, for after Hitler invaded Paris she swore off alcohol for the duration and had almost become respectable. We did not take into account the fact that the duration was over!

A week or so after her arrival we invited the French and Belgian ambassadors to lunch with a few of their fellow officers and wives. The French ambassador was a good friend of mine whom I had first met in Tunis. We agreed to ignore protocol — I would not invite our own ambassador and our military attaché to this luncheon, or even inform them of it. Not speaking French, they would have detracted from the intimacy of the occasion.

We had ordered the best food we could find, and plenty of wine, including champagne, and our refrigerator was stuffed full when a driver arrived from Colonel Sexton's house. The colonel's wife needed to borrow the transformer to my refrigerator.

I had to give it up, but no sooner had the driver closed the door than, enraged by the prospect of the deterioration of my food and wine, I made a number of uncomplimentary remarks about the colonel in my mother-in-law's hearing. Then I forgot all about it as we found a way to keep things cool until our guests arrived.

We had a jolly lunch, accompanying brilliant, witty French conversation with lashings of wine. My mother-in-law was at her best, full of the novel she had just written, a roman à clef about Paris; she had great hopes for its success.

After lunch we all retired for a Sunday siesta, to recover in time for a cocktail party Major Garver was giving in his house down the street.

I woke up to find the house empty — K.W. and her mother

had already gone to the cocktail party, leaving me to complete my snooze. I hurried down to be greeted at the door by Garver, who pulled me into a side passage. He had a frown on his usually jovial face.

"I'm afraid your mother-in-law has just had a scene with the colonel. It was really bad — she's gone now, but the damage is done."

"What on earth did she say?"

"She started out by asking how did he dare borrow the transformer for your refrigerator just before an important lunch with two ambassadors. The colonel said he knew nothing about any lunch with ambassadors — he was obviously already pissed that you hadn't invited him!"

"Oh, my God," I said, clutching my head, "I hope that's all — I'll try and explain."

"But that isn't all. She went on to say that he was obviously just a figurehead, a dumb colonel taking credit for the reports submitted by her brilliant son-in-law. He was speechless with rage, and before he could think up a reply she was gone. But I think he's probably blaming you, and thinks that's what you told her."

I groaned and went into the next room. The party was grim — K.W. must have left with her mother by the back door. The colonel did not speak to me, and I departed as soon as I decently could.

I had no sooner arrived at the office the next morning than the colonel's secretary told me he wanted to see me. He sat at his desk, his face white and tense.

"Your mother-in-law insulted me last night."

"I'm sorry about that, Colonel, but I can't be held responsible for everything my mother-in-law says."

"Well, I do hold you responsible, Captain, and I won't forget it."

It was the very week he was preparing our annual fitness reports. Thus I was not too surprised when later, in Washington, after appearing before a G2 board, I was not offered a regular commission in the army. To be fair to my mother-in-law, the army's lack of interest may not have been entirely due to a bad mark or two on my last fitness report, but to the fact that I insisted on a career in the Middle East, saying I was not interested in an assignment to another area.

We took off on the first stage of our trip home to America in Garver's plane a month after this incident, in mid-February 1947. We just made it to Dhahran, Saudi Arabia, after a very bumpy trip over the snowy mountains covered with clouds, with two gallons of gas to spare. There I was offered a definite job as a "head specialist" in the Government Relations Department of Aramco at the then-respectable starting salary of five hundred dollars a month, and filled out the application forms. Then we set out for Paris via the Air Transport Command, planning to take advantage of our stopover there to see K.W.'s mother.

After settling down at the Hôtel Meurice, we went to the countess's apartment. She said that she had planned a dinner party for us, but we would be eating alone that night.

"After my book appeared," she explained, "everyone said they recognized themselves and their friends in it, all hopping in and out of each other's beds, and they're all hopping mad at me. They say they won't set foot in my home again!"

But I couldn't be mad at her, despite her faux pas with the colonel. The fact is that I enjoyed the extraordinary character who was, for a time, my mother-in-law. And the fact is that she did me a favor by helping to close my military career. A better choice was awaiting me.

20

The Kurds

BEFORE FATE was to unveil the path of my future career, however, there was a special facet of my role in the opening battle of the Cold War in Iran that came to a tragic conclusion during my last days in Tehran. This was my involvement with the Kurds, which began during the latter part of my assignment to Baghdad.

There, it will be recalled, I had decided to concentrate on the Arabs, especially the tribes, as my predecessor had just completed an exhaustive study on the Kurds, the most turbulent element of the population at that time.

But I had to be mindful of intelligence priorities dictated by the march of events in Iraq and beyond its borders in Iran, and the role of the Kurds became increasingly important. Therefore, especially beginning in the summer of 1945, I became, willy-nilly, involved with the Kurdish problem.

Because my experiences with the Kurds in both Iraq and Iran are linked together, it is better to treat them as a unit, and Kurdistan as a separate country — though its name is found on few maps. Maps concern themselves not with ethnic groups but with political boundaries, and there is no nation called Kurdistan. But this is the name by which the Kurds know their mountainous homeland, shaped like a crescent, with one horn in northeastern Syria, stretching through the mountains dividing Turkey, Iran, and Iraq, and the other horn passing through the Zagros Mountains toward the Persian Gulf.

Although Kurdistan is divided among five nations (as there are a couple of pockets of Kurds over the border in the Soviet Union), and recognized by none, its people are united by blood, language, and sentiment — a sentiment often manifested in violent rebellion, which even the most brutal suppression has failed to stamp out.

There are few places in the world more fascinating to the visitor than Kurdistan. Its rugged mountains — sometimes bare, sometimes covered with scrub oak and pine — are broken here and there by broad valleys. Scattered everywhere are the stone and mud villages of the Kurds. I saw my first Kurdish village some forty-three years ago, draped on a mountainside overlooking a deep gorge, at the bottom of which, barely visible, was the silver line of a brook winding its way down to the plains. As I read my impressions at the time, I believe they would still be valid today.

> The costumes of the villagers and their hats gave me a feeling of being in Shangri-La. The men wear big, blue-gray turbans with innumerable tiny tassels falling over their eyes, and bright-colored vests crossed by bandoliers filled with cartridges, the copper shells gleaming in the sun. Their brown, baggy trousers hang down from a huge waistband made up of several yards of bright-colored cloth, knotted many times in front. This serves as a pocket — filled with curved daggers, leather pouches of money or tobacco, and the characteristic long, clay pipes, which they smoke incessantly. Many villagers are also carrying rifles, for in Kurdistan it is wise to be armed to the teeth.
>
> The women, almost as picturesque as the men, walk along with the proud, easy gait of mountain folk, with water jugs on their heads, their erect figures wrapped in blue-gray turbans. The young ones, almost invariably pretty, will probably smile at you — but don't look too long, for the Kurd is jealous and proud of the honor of his women.
>
> The life of the Kurdish villager is a hard one. Those that cultivate the fields must struggle constantly with the dry and rocky soil. They must dam the tiny streams bursting out of the mountainside, carefully husbanding each drop of water to irrigate their crops of rice, fruit, poplar trees, and the tobacco that is the main staple of Kurdistan. In the border valleys, they scratch large stretches of soil with crude wooden plows to grow

wheat, barley, and tobacco in the rich bottomland, which still keeps some moisture from the winter rains.

Others live a harder life still. These are the nomads who carry their black tents with them as they move, with their flocks, following the grass that springs up in the wake of the melting snow or retreating down to the valley in the fall to escape the blizzards. [By now, these nomads are mostly settled but they were still important in 1945, when I wrote these lines.]

The Kurds are of Iranian stock and have been settled in their present homeland for more than two millennia. While references to them in ancient cuneiform are open to dispute, there seems to be little question that these are the Kardoukhoi whose murderous attacks on his troops are recounted by the Greek general and historian Xenophon during the March of the Ten Thousand to the Black Sea. The Romans also had their troubles in the region then known as Corduene, and when, in the seventh century A.D., the Arabs converted its inhabitants to Islam, they found the Kurds as difficult to control as do modern governments today.

Yet, through their history, only one Kurd, Saladdin, managed to build an empire. He is proudly remembered by Kurds today as the savior of Islam. It was he who drove the Crusaders from Jerusalem and almost out of the Middle East altogether. French and Arabic chronicles recount stories of his chivalry and generosity, traits shared by some Kurdish chieftains in modern times.

After prosperous petty kingdoms in Kurdistan had been broken up by the terrible Mongol invasions of the thirteenth century, the country became a battlefield between the rival Persian and Turkish empires. Not until 1639 did the Ottoman sultan Murad IV and the Persian shah Safi divide up Kurdistan between them, setting the boundary approximately where it is today.

Drawing a line on a map is one thing but governing the country is another. Neither empire was able effectively to control the innumerable tribes who acknowledged no rule but that of their own chiefs. But the tribal system made it possible for a central government to deal with them, setting one tribe against another.

Until the last century, there was no sense of nationalism as we know it today, and Kurds did not think of themselves as a separate nation. It was not until the 1830s, when a petty Kurdish chieftain named Badr-Khan threw out the Turks and managed to hold on for some years to a kingdom of his own, that Kurdish nationalism was born. The banner was taken up later in the century by a religious leader, Seyyid Taha of Shemdinan, at the time of World War I.

Yet it was in Turkey, birthplace of Kurdish nationalism, that the movement was to be sternly repressed. The Turkish national philosophy enunciated by Mustafa Kemal left no room for other nationalities. Teaching of the Kurdish language was forbidden, and nationalist leaders were forced to flee to Syria. Kurdish revolts between 1925 and 1930 ended with the elimination of the last corner of resistance — the Republic of Ararat, whose forces were led by former Turkish army major Ihsan Nuri. Reprisals and repression were stern; villages were wiped out, whole populations transferred to the western plains, and the Kurdish language and costume forbidden. The Kurds became, in government eyes, "Mountain Turks."

In Iran, the Kurdish tribes coexisted with the Qajar shahs in semi-independence until World War I, when northwest Iran became a battleground for the Turkish and Russian armies. Although in some areas the Kurds suffered much from the destruction wrought by Russian troops, elsewhere they were able to reassert their independence, plundering and robbing their neighbors in the time-honored manner of tribes everywhere.

Chieftains were able to carve out small kingdoms for themselves — among them the notorious Simko of the Shikak, whose name is still a byword for the Kurdish ideals of bravery and chivalry, as well as for ferocity and cruelty. The story of how Simko kept his word according to the tribal code, and yet obtained his desired revenge, is told in every Kurdish hut to this day. Some Shikak subchiefs who had rebelled against him promised to surrender on condition that their lives be spared and they be left in freedom. Simko reluctantly agreed to these conditions, but no sooner did he have them in his power than he effectively forestalled further trouble from that quarter by having his retainers smash the bones of the right wrist of each of them to a pulp and then cut their neck tendons. Then, according to his word, he set them free — and a pitiful sight they were, with their heads lolling about helplessly on their shoulders.

Simko once concluded that the new generation of Kurds no longer had the warlike quality of their fathers, and decided that the breeding stock of the tribe needed strengthening. An American officer was passing through the area — a big, broadshouldered, bull-like man whom all the Kurds held in great respect. Simko called him in one day and made him a singular proposition: to marry him, for a brief period, to every girl in the tribe.

This would, he hoped, produce a crop of babies of a superior hybrid variety, heroes of future raids and wars. The American officer unfortunately had other duties that prevented him from acceding to this request.

Simko's reign was short. Iran found a new leader in Reza Shah, who began systematically to restore order throughout the country, bringing the tribes under a rule of iron. Simko was high up on the list. In 1922 the Iranian army drove him out of the country. He was foolish enough to accept an invitation to return to Iran in 1930 and was speedily executed. Simko's fate was shared by many other Kurdish chiefs, who either fled the country, were liquidated by the Shah, or, if they were lucky, were kept in forced residence in Tehran. By 1925, all Kurdistan was under control and the government began trying to break up the tribes, settling them on the land and forbidding them to wear Kurdish dress, so that they conformed to the Iranian model in secondhand Western clothes.

In Iraq, meanwhile, the 650,000 Kurds in the northeast were faring considerably better, mainly because of British protection. When Iraq was recognized as an independent state and admitted to the League of Nations in 1932, she declared to the league council her intention of recognizing Kurdish as an official language and appointing Kurdish or Kurdish-speaking officials in the Kurdish areas. While this promise was faithfully observed, the Kurds were not content. They claimed, with some justice, that they were discriminated against in such matters as the establishment of schools, communications, health facilities, and development of their natural resources and crops. They were particularly annoyed at the way in which their main crop, tobacco, was handled by the government — most of the profits went to cigarette manufacturers in Baghdad and other cities.

This resentment found expression in several revolts. The first Kurdish leader to raise the standard of rebellion was Sheikh Mahmoud — a religious leader from Suleimania, a rich tobacco-growing area in the northeast corner of Iraq. Not satisfied even by his appointment as governor by the British, Sheikh Mahmoud began calling himself king of Kurdistan — and acting the part. The British in 1932 deposed him and he fled to Iran. He was later pardoned on condition that he retire to his farm and stay out of politics, a promise he kept until his death.

In typical Kurdish fashion, the Kurds of the northwestern mountains of Iraq waited until Mahmoud had been suppressed before starting a revolt of their own. It was led by Sheikh Ahmed of the tiny Barzan tribe, a religious leader deified by his superstitious fellow tribesmen. The British forces, stationed in Iraq under the mandate, subdued the Barzanis, who were then taken over by Sheikh Ahmed's more forceful younger brother, Mulla Mustafa. The two brothers were sent into exile with their immediate followers to southern Iraq. In 1936, they were allowed back into Kurdistan but were kept in forced residence in Suleimania.

Kurdish nationalism was at its nadir when World War II broke out in 1939. On August 25, 1941, as British and Soviet forces occupied Iran, the Soviets — in occupying the northwestern part of the country — established control only of the towns surrounding Lake Rezaieh,* while British influence did not extend farther north than Sanandaj. This left a no-man's-land for the Kurds between the two areas of control and the mountains along the Iraqi and Turkish borders. The tribes were left to govern themselves, although Iranian police were still located in the towns and villages.

A virtually independent state gradually grew up around the only sizable town in the area, Mahabad. Mahabad was originally called Sauj Balagh, from the Turkic words *soghuk balagh*, meaning cold spring (a name symbolically connected with my childhood home!). Reza Shah changed the name to Mahabad, meaning city of the Medes, based on the supposed Medic origin of the Kurds.

---

* The town of Urmieh and the lake that took its name were renamed Rezaieh in honor of Reza Shah. After Khomeini's revolution, they once more became Urmieh.

Mahabad had an almost completely Kurdish population, while the inhabitants of the other towns surrounding Lake Rezaieh were Azerbaijan Turks. Mahabad had a nontribal bourgeoisie, the leading figure of which was Qazi Mohammad, a member of a respected judicial family.

Qazi had only a religious education, but from his father, who had proceeded him as a religious judge, and from his library containing books in seven languages he acquired a broader education on his own. In his early forties, he had gained a dominant position in the town by virtue not only of his judicial position but his intellectual superiority and strong personality.

At the end of 1941 the Soviets began to show an interest in the Kurds by inviting a group of thirty of them to Baku. Almost all were tribal leaders, but Qazi Mohammad represented Mahabad. After touring farms and factories, the group was received by the prime minister of the Azerbaijan Soviet Socialist Republic, Jafar Baghirov. He spoke of Soviet friendship for small peoples and of Kurdish-Azerbaijani brotherhood, but only in the vaguest terms of the future political arrangements in the area. After the end of the visit, there was no Soviet follow-up, presumably because the Soviets were primarily concerned with the German invaders knocking at the gates of the Caucasus.

However, this visit may have given an impetus to greater nationalist activity. In September of 1942, a dozen citizens of Mahabad met with a captain in the Iraqi army named Mir Hajj, who was the Kurdish representative of a nationalist organization recently formed in Iraq called Hewa, meaning hope. The local Kurds then decided to form a nationalist society of their own, Komala-i-Zhiyan-Kurdistan — the Committee for the Revival of Kurdistan. It gradually expanded its membership and influence among the local community, and in May 1943 a Kurdish nationalist mob destroyed the police station — the last symbol of Iranian authority in Mahabad.

In late 1944 Qazi Mohammad took control of the Komala, aided by his younger brother Abol-Qasim Sadr-i-Qazi, a deputy in the Iranian parliament, and his cousin Mohammad Hussain Saif-i-Qazi, a former gendarme officer. With Soviet assistance, the Komala issued a weekly periodical, *Nishteman* ("Native Land"), which began to circulate across the border to Iraq.

This upsurge of Kurdish nationalism was not without its echo in Iraq. In 1943 Mulla Mustafa with his followers escaped from forced residence in Suleimania and made his way home to Barzan. Soon after his arrival, trouble began with the local authorities. In October, Mulla Mustafa's forces — then numbering only a couple of hundred — won a battle with the local police. A month later, with an increased following, he defeated an army brigade.

At this point, British ambassador Sir Kinahan Cornwallis began to take an interest in the situation. He was a veteran of Iraqi politics, having been King Feisal's closest adviser at the beginning of the British mandate in the 1920s. Later, he played an important role in negotiating with Sheikh Mahmoud in Suleimania, where he gained considerable experience in Kurdish matters and probably some sympathy for the Kurds. He suggested that Iraqi mismanagement had led to their troubles with Mulla Mustafa and urged reform, including Kurdish participation in the government.

At the end of 1943, Iraqi prime minister Nuri Sa'id appointed a Kurdish minister without portfolio, who arranged for Mulla Mustafa to visit Baghdad in February of 1944. Not much came of the Baghdad meeting nor of Nuri Sa'id's visit to Kurdistan the following May. There was an impasse on the question of amnesty for the rebels, especially for the military and civilian officials who had deserted to Mulla Mustafa's forces. Despairing of finding a solution to these problems, Nura Sa'id withdrew temporarily from the government. A period of uneasy truce followed, which was the situation when I arrived in Baghdad in July 1944.

There I began to educate myself about the Kurdish situation, both through CICI and personal contacts. These latter included a number of Kurds in Baghdad.

One was Sheikh Mahmoud's son, Baba Ali, a handsome man-about-town. Another was "Pusho," whose given name was Mohammad Siddiq, son of Seyyid Taha. Seyyid Taha had been a great admirer of General Ferdinand Foch at the time of Pusho's birth and his name was as close as Kurdish pronunciation could get to that of the French general. Pusho cut a colorful figure in the Regent Hotel, where I saw him almost daily, in his white tunic and baggy pants held together by a cummerbund. A white felt hat bound by a turban cloth perched on his head. He made no bones about his hatred of the Arabs and was in close touch both with Mulla Mustafa and with

Kurdish nationalists in Iran, where his relatives were located.

A third contact was former assistant chief of staff General Baha-ud-din Nuri, whom I met two weeks after my arrival. He was an imposing figure with a large belly and drooping moustaches, recently ousted as governor of Suleimania. I was taken to meet General Nuri by Doc Hoff, who started out the conversation provoking Nuri by stating that Kurdish was nothing but a hodgepodge of dialects.

"Oh, no," protested Nuri, "it's an independent language."

He showed us pictures of ragged children in Suleimania before and after his government had provided them with clothes. He said he saw one woman wearing nothing but a mat she threw on whenever she left her tent. He expressed his frustration in trying to get money from the central government to improve the impoverished, isolated villages of the province.

A year later I was to get a firsthand view when I visited Suleimania in October of 1945 with the area liaison officer, James Shotter, the best kind of young political officer, well liked by the local Kurds. He joined me in Kirkuk for the three-hour drive to Suleimania.

We entered the Kurdish mountains via a pass with the picturesque name of the Donkey's Fart — whose origins Shotter could not explain — through barren hills. Next we drove through Bazian Pass, a deep cleft between two high mountains, and Shotter pointed out the foundations of a wall Sheikh Mahmoud had erected in 1919 to keep the British out — to no avail.

Then we were in green tobacco fields and, just after the harvest, great tobacco leaves were hanging up to dry outside peasant huts. When we arrived in Suleimania at Shotter's house, we were joined by Kurdish dignitaries and heard much local political gossip, beginning with the case of Baha-ud-din Nuri. They confirmed his own account given to me in Baghdad, saying he was an excellent activist governor, ousted by the intrigues of high officials in Baghdad. Neither Shotter nor his guests had any use for the other governors, and blamed them for the flight of Mulla Mustafa in 1943. They told me the following story.

Mulla Mustafa and some eighty members of his family were in exile there in Suleimania, living on a government stipend whose value gradually diminished due to inflation. With his family and little band of retainers reduced to starvation, the Mulla began selling the tribal rifles — an almost unendurable necessity. Then his wife took an even more drastic step and began secretly to sell her gold ornaments, the family fortune.

One night, when the Mulla was affectionately patting his wife's head, he noticed that her large golden headband had a strange, rough feel to it. Snatching it out, he found that she had substituted a horseshoe!

He flew into a terrible rage. "By Allah, I will avenge this humiliation of my family," he cried. Summoning his little band, he spirited them away during the night across the Iranian frontier. Following the high crests of the border to the north, he then led them back to Barzan. Now the Barzanis were in Iraq as leaders of a rebellion, and the Kurds of Suleimania province were one in their sympathy for them.

Exploring the city and souqs of Suleimania, I was struck by the fine appearance of the Kurds. Most wore beards — now almost vanished from Baghdad — and were comparatively well dressed. But what made the deepest impression on me was a little school in the bazaar, where a white-bearded venerable was teaching nine-year-olds to recite, of all things, the *Bustan* of the Persian poet Sa'adi. I later ascertained that the cultural language of the Kurds in Iraq as well as Iran was Persian, the language closest to their own. This may also reflect the fact that Persian literature — and even the language — was once the Latin of the eastern Moslem world, from Istanbul to Bengal.

A breakfast with Shotter provided me with basic information on tribal sexual habits, gleaned from his groom/houseboy. Recently Shotter had asked him what he did about sex, in view of tribal guardianship of the virtue of their women.

"Do you go to whorehouses in town?" he queried.

"Oh, no, Agha, that would be dirty — and shameful!"

"How about a small boy?"

"Allah forfend," cried the Kurd in horror, "that would be *aib*!"

"Then what — you are strong and must have needs?"

"Well, some people use donkeys — but that is not for me. When I can't stand it any longer, I find me a nice, clean little sheep, and tie it to a tree!"

Enlightened by this revelation, I looked on the tribesmen with new eyes as we drove through the passes, climbing ever higher amid mountains clothed with pine and scrub oak to the border town of Penjwin. On the way a cavalcade of Jaf tribesmen flashed by us, magnificently mounted, led by one bearing a green pennant — they were giving someone a send-off on the pilgrimage to Mecca.

The following day, after passing through Suleimania en route back to Kirkuk, we stopped off at the farm of my Baghdad friend Baba Ali, son of Sheikh Mahmoud. There we had lunch in an idyllic valley of tobacco and wheat, framed by mountains covered with fruit trees at their base and topped by scrub oak. After lunch all the Kurds, including the servants, gave us a display of marksmanship, shooting at small coins at short range and at bottles across the valley. Of course, there was political talk, with Baba Ali and his friends saying that all they really wanted was a government that didn't discriminate against Kurds. "We can't accomplish anything anyway," said Baba Ali, "without the backing of a great power." Naturally, Shotter and I were concerned that this backing might, in fact, be at hand. Several Kurds we met on this trip, when asked about the Russians, said that the Kurds would get help where they could find it.

I was thwarted in my attempts to get near the war zone on the northwest border, but on another trip I did get a good look at the area in between, centering on Rowanduz. This journey began in Erbil, a Turkoman town in the midst of Kurdish villages, which was the site of Alexander's defeat of the Persian king Darius at the battle of Arbela. I was impressed by its Kurdish governor, Sa'id Qazzaz, who was frank about his sentiments. "There is a Kurdish proverb that sums up the two things we most dislike: *Na shir-i-shutur na didar-i-Arab* —'Neither the milk of the camel nor the sight of an Arab!' "

Driving up the mountain range from Erbil, we passed from bare hills to green valleys filled with red and yellow flowers, and then to high, snow-covered mountains through deep, tortuous gorges. The fields and orchards, and pastures on higher ground, were full of Kurds, their dark blue costumes ringed with brightly colored cummerbunds. Often they bore shepherd's crooks, and always rifles ready for use — sometimes for more exciting game than the occasional ibex we saw leaping on the crags.

We had lunch by a waterfall in Rowanduz Gorge and then

went via the valley of Desht-i-Dian (Vale of the Christians) to the pleasant little village of Diana — a majority of whose inhabitants were plumed-hatted Assyrians — to spend the night.

The following day we made the expedition to the Iranian frontier, through Berserin Gorge, to the saddle of the pass that forms the boundary. We saw a couple of Kurds riding nonchalantly over the frontier on the opposite crag, their voices carrying across the valley. Then we turned back by a different route to visit the home of Pusho, who had traveled up there from Baghdad. We had dinner with him and an assortment of brothers and relatives who were built like football players. One, Dino, spent much of his time with Mulla Mustafa in Barzan. Another, more slender than the rest, looked just like my friend Lieutenant Dick Walters of Camp Ritchie. Many Kurds are indistinguishable from Europeans, some blond as Scandinavians.

The uneasy truce between Mulla Mustafa and the government became unraveled almost from the beginning. Mulla Mustafa, meanwhile, tried to strengthen his position by marrying the daughter of the rival Zibar tribe, which had been at odds with the Barzanis. Feeling more secure, he became more truculent toward the government. He may have been encouraged in this by the march of events next door in Iran, where his associate, Mir Hajj, had been involved from the beginning. The Soviets' new aggressiveness there, stemming from the end of the war in Europe, was beginning to be of concern to the British in Baghdad.

In late February 1945, Ambassador Cornwallis was replaced by Hugh Stonehewer-Bird. Having served in Saudi Arabia, he saw Iraq more in an Arab-world context than did his predecessor. Not long after he took over, the old Kurdish hands in the advisory staff were replaced, starting at the top with Major C. J. Edmonds, whose post was taken by Major R. H. Ditchburn — an old-time political officer in southern Iraq. The political advisers in the north were also replaced by new officers with neither prior experience nor sympathy for the Kurds. The embassy also put pressure on CICI to remove its similarly qualified area liaison officers. Mulla Mustafa, who had been in regular correspondence with Stonehewer-Bird's predecessor, was undoubtedly shaken by a missive from the new ambassador exhorting him to act like "a good Iraqi."

Mulla Mustafa had increasingly established an administration of his own in the territories of his tribal area, and the Iraqis, by the beginning of August 1945, wished to launch a frontal assault on his mountain stronghold. The chief of the British military mission, General Renton, believed that the Iraqi army was not yet prepared for this action. When his warnings that the army would suffer the same reverses that it had in 1943 went unheeded, he left his forward headquarters at Erbil and withdrew his advisers from the Iraqi troops slated for combat.

Nevertheless, the Iraqis demonstrated their independence of the British by forging ahead with their offensive. On September 4, an army column from Aqra, another from Rowanduz, and a police column from Amadia all converged on the way toward Barzan.

As General Renton had foreseen, all three columns were defeated in the mountain passes by small Kurdish forces, perhaps not more than fifteen hundred men. The Iraqis suffered about a thousand casualties and there was talk of abandoning the campaign for the winter.

However, the British (and probably the Mulla), while correctly assessing the weakness of the Iraqi army, underestimated Iraqi political capabilities. Minister of Interior Mustafa al-Umari went north to negotiate with the tribes. With skillful bribery, persuasion, and threats he detached the most important Kurdish tribal leaders in the area, including even Mulla Mustafa's new father-in-law, chief of the Zibar. During the last two weeks in September, he was joined by other tribal leaders who then acted as assault troops for the Iraqi army, driving Mulla Mustafa and his supporters out of their mountain strongholds.

By October 7, government forces had occupied Barzan; Mulla Mustafa, accompanied by most of his effective fighters and their families, crossed the Iranian border. There he was met by a Soviet general, Lyubov, who directed him to report to Qazi Mohammad in Mahabad and put his tribesmen at Qazi's disposal. The Kurdish revolution in Iraq, such as it was, was halted for the time being, and the focus of its activity shifted to Iran.

When I arrived in Iran in March of 1946, I found that I was, perforce, the Kurdish expert in the military attaché's office, and early in my tour I made the acquaintance of Kurdish personalities in Tehran. The government permitted the publication of a periodical in Persian called *Kuhistan* ("Land of Mountains"), put out by Dr. Ismail Ardelan, a member of the prominent Ardelan family from the Kermanshah area. In it there appeared, by an unknown author, a series of articles entitled "Secrets of Barzan," recounting the background of Mulla Mustafa's rebellion.

There also appeared another series called "The Events of Ararat," by none other than Ihsan Nuri, then living in Tehran. I made his acquaintance there, and he gave me a good firsthand account of his career in the Kurdish insurrection in Turkey. Born in Bitlis, Turkey, he was a regular officer in the Turkish army and was in command of a regiment in 1924 when, unable to accept the Turkish government's brutal suppression of Kurdish nationalism, he led a Kurdish mutiny near the Iraqi border. The mutineers were quickly defeated and fled across the boundary, and over the next few years Nuri led small guerrilla parties on raids into Turkey from Iraq and then Iran. In 1928 he joined the rebel forces that had risen against the Turks in the region of Ararat.

The Soviets did not look with favor on the Kurdish revolt — one reason being Kurdish nationalist contacts with the anti-Soviet Armenian Tashnak organization. Soviet patrols were sent to Ararat in support of the Turks and when, in 1930, Reza Shah reached an accord with the Turks allowing Turkish troops to cross the border at will, the rebellion was doomed. Ihsan Nuri fled to Iran, although some guerrillas continued the resistance until their final suppression in 1931.

I had two other Kurdish contacts in Tehran, on opposite sides of the fence. One was a deputy in the Iranian parliament, Abdol Agha Dehbokri, a leader of the Dehbokri tribe, located south of Lake Rezaieh. Most of the tribe was now loyal to the Mahabad government, of which Abdol Agha strongly disapproved, believing that it was heading toward Soviet-dominated social revolution. My other contact was a young man from Mahabad, Hashim Shirazi, whom I engaged to help me learn the Kurdish language. When I asked him how he came by his name, apparently indicating that his family stemmed from Shiraz (which seemed unlikely, with his blond hair and blue eyes), he said that his father had been given the name because of his love of the Shirazi poets, Sa'adi and Hafiz.

Shirazi was a passionate defender of Qazi Mohammad, kept in touch with Mahabad, and helped pave the way for my visit there. He was also a believer in social revolution and joined the Tudeh party. This eventually brought him a prison term, in the course of which he recanted, but I am sure he never abandoned his Kurdish nationalist beliefs.

On April 12, 1946, less than a month after my arrival in Tehran, I arranged with the Iranian general staff to visit their headquarters in Sanandaj, in southern Kurdistan. The commanding general there was the famous Amanallah Jehanbani, whose mission was to reestablish Iranian rule among the turbulent tribes along the Iraqi border. These were dominated by a bandit chief, Hama Rashid, who had crossed the border of Iran in 1941 when the Iranian army was driven out by the British and Soviet invaders. He settled in the town of Baneh and took control of the neighboring town of Sardasht. He acted unofficially as governor of the area until 1944, when the Iranian army returned and retook both towns. However, he continued to harass the Iranian army up until the arrival of Jehanbani in mid-March 1946. The Iranian troops were still confronting Kurdish rebels in the area at the time of my visit.

My driver, Karapet, an Armenian, was of inestimable value, fluent in Azeri-Turkish (commonly called Turki), the lingua franca of all northwestern Iran, as well as Russian. Also, he was politically alert and frequently found out in conversations with locals more than I was able to discover from official contacts.

It was a full day's journey then from Tehran just to Kermanshah, and as we passed by that city, evening was approaching along with a heavy thunderstorm. Suddenly a military carryall stopped us with flashing red lights and siren. It contained a lieutenant colonel, and a sergeant of the American military mission, who invited me to dinner. When I got to his house, to my surprise the colonel greeted me at the top of the stairs in a dressing gown.

"Step right up, Captain — there is no formality here. I want you to meet the girls."

He and the sergeant then introduced me to two sallow-skinned girls dressed in one-piece sacklike gowns. They were from Soviet Azerbaijan, with the older one attached to the colonel and the teenager clearly belonging to the sergeant.

They proceeded to wait on us, filling glasses all around and getting slippers for my hosts.

I had hoped to obtain some information from the colonel, but he was already quite drunk and asked me suspiciously in a slurring voice, "What do you want to know all that for?"

In the middle of the dinner he retired upstairs, then returned to sit on the floor. After dinner the sergeant went upstairs and the colonel retired to the adjoining room, from which I could hear giggles and scuffling noises. At that point I decided there was no further profit to be gained from the evening and retired.

The following morning after breakfasting with the quartet — all in wrappers — I took my leave and headed up the dirt road to Kurdistan, as the city of Sanandaj is called. It was beautiful country, washed after the storm, with bare, rocky mountains surrounding a broad, green valley. A couple of times, itinerant musicians waved for us to stop and played us a tune or two. While the people of the area were ethnic Kurds, they were, unlike the Kurds to the north, Shi'ites, too assimilated to be interested in Kurdish nationalism.

I arrived in Sanandaj in the afternoon, went to the governor's palace, and sent my card in to the commanding general, Amanallah Jehanbani. He immediately received me, gave me much welcome wine and food, and took me to his headquarters for a briefing on his operations against the rebellious tribes in the mountains along the border. Jehanbani seemed to be having some success, gaining control of the key villages of Baneh and Sardasht, though the Kurds still held the surrounding mountains.

Now approaching sixty, and quite short, Jehanbani had what one might call a civilized face. He wore glasses, and had a full head of white hair. I had read his biography in Tehran. He came from the Qajar family, which had provided the previous dynasty of shahs, and when very young had married a cousin, as is customary. His father had been governor of Tabriz during World War I, when the Russians occupied it and inadvertently executed him.

In compensation for this act, they accepted young Jehanbani at the Imperial Guards Artillery School in Moscow and later at the Russian General Staff College. Because of this background, he was accepted by the Russians as one of them both before and after the revolution — unusual in view of the Russian attitude toward "lesser breeds." On his return to Iran, Jehanbani met a Russian girl, the daughter of the local director of the telegraph company, and after living with her for a year, married her. Known as Elena Khanum, she was a familiar figure in Tehran society and a friend of Mrs. Louis Dreyfus, wife of the American minister, but she was in the Soviet Union during my visit.

Jehanbani returned to Iran at the end of World War I to become captain of an artillery unit in the Persian Cossack brigade commanded by Reza Shah. Reza distrusted him, and when he took over the country in a coup, he kept Jehanbani outside the capital for a couple of days to be sure that he did not play too prominent a role in it. Jehanbani went on to military school in Paris and then returned to take over senior posts in the Iranian army; at various times he held the positions of inspector general, chief of staff, and minister of defense.

But Reza Shah never liked him — possibly because of the social gulf between the cultivated Jehanbani, who spoke unaccented French (which he spoke with me), and the rough-and-ready peasant commander transformed into a shah of Iran. Reza Shah treated Jehanbani like a slave and required servile behavior of him. The Shah nicknamed him Jendeh, meaning whore, and when angry would boot him in the rear.

Finally, in 1939, the Shah became suspicious of him and booted him right out of the army. Now reinstated, Jehanbani had been sent to Sanandaj a month before to keep him away from Tehran and its temptation to would-be plotters.

It was late afternoon when our briefing was over and the general turned me over to one of his staff officers. He walked me through the streets, mostly filled with Kurds in native costume, to the public square, which he told me was called Maidan Che Kunim, meaning the What-Should-We-Do-Now Square, as there is nothing to do in it but walk to the end and choose between turning left or right for another turn.

Early the following morning I joined Jehanbani and his aides on horseback to ride to the garrison west of the town. My horse was a real Arabian — mettlesome and anxious to go — and I had to keep my hands firmly on the reins. All through the morning my steed pranced around, and I was terrified of the humiliation it would have caused had he succeeded in throwing me, especially in front of the troops who met us at the parade ground, running out of the barracks as the alarm was sounded.

They played a war game with the cavalry reconnoitering to the hills to the north of us, followed by the rest of the troops, including ourselves, to confront a supposed tribal assault from Saqqiz. The mountains flashed with old-fashioned signaling by mirrors. Jehanbani reviewed the battle plans with his staff, then we rode around inspecting positions before returning to Sanandaj. My horse fought me until the end and I was most relieved to get off his back. I suspected that Jehanbani would have enjoyed my embarrassment at being dumped in front of his army.

Jehanbani was obviously a Russophile — although no admirer of the Soviet system — and may have had a prejudice against Americans in general. However, he was otherwise most friendly to me; perhaps my French and international background helped. After we had returned to Sanandaj, the general regaled me with stories of how he had defeated Simko in the mid-1920s, with fifteen thousand troops opposing some ten thousand Kurds and Turks.

"Simko just couldn't believe that the army facing him was Persian, as our troops had behaved so poorly in the past, but we were a new army full of enthusiasm," the general said. Now he was doing his best to reinstill that quality in the Iranian army, where it was sadly lacking.

21

The Kurdish Republic of Mahabad

THE STORY of the Soviet-backed Kurdish Republic of Mahabad is a fascinating footnote in history of which I was virtually the sole American observer on the scene. The Soviets, after their 1941 meeting with the Kurdish chiefs in Baku, devoted little attention to the Kurds because of their preoccupation with the war. But they were by no means inactive in the no-man's-land between the Soviet and British occupied zones. The Red Army, then hardly motorized, still depended a great deal on horse transport and Soviet horse traders visited the Kurds throughout this period.

One of them, a man called Abdulayev, appeared to have another assignment — as an undercover political operative. He struck up an acquaintance with a Kurd sitting next to him at an Armenian wine shop. It was no coincidence that this particular Kurd was a founding member of the nationalist organization Komala who in turn introduced the Soviet agent to other leaders of the party. From then on, the Komala moved inevitably into the Soviet orbit, especially after Qazi Mohammad took over the organization at the end of 1944.

In addition to the horse traders, there was a Soviet Kurd wandering among the tribes, Captain Jafarov, a sort of Soviet T. E. Lawrence wearing Kurdish dress, who established contacts with all the northern Kurdish tribal chiefs. He was the only ethnic Kurdish Soviet official of note in the area, the others all being Soviet Azerbaijanis, such as Hashimov, Soviet consul in Rezaieh, and Captain Namaz Aliov, the Soviet political officer in Miandoab. All of these reported to the senior Soviet political officer in Tabriz, General Salim Atakchiov.

Atakchiov wanted to establish a Kurdish leadership to deal with in carrying out Russian designs, and at first made overtures to a number of tribal chiefs without finding his man. By the beginning of 1945 it was apparent that Qazi Mohammad, having now taken over the Komala, was uniquely fitted for the role. In April 1945 the Soviet propaganda organization VOKS founded the Kurdistan-Soviet Cultural Society in Mahabad in a public ceremony in which a Kurdish nationalist play was the main feature. It depicted the Kurdish motherland being abused by three ruffians — Iraq, Iran, and Turkey — finally to be rescued by her sons. The audience, unused to drama, was deeply moved, and lifelong enemies fell weeping on each other's shoulders, swearing to avenge Kurdistan.

Soviet officials were now frequently seen in Mahabad. One day in September, Captain Namaz Aliov showed up in town to invite Qazi and other Kurdish leaders to Tabriz, where they were joined by tribal chiefs and hustled on to a train to Baku. There they were asked to prepare written recommendations for the future of the area, to be transmitted to Soviet Azerbaijan premier Jafar Baghirov, prior to a meeting with him. They duly prepared a proposal for establishing a separate Kurdish state with Soviet assistance.

In the subsequent meeting, Baghirov told the Kurdish leaders that while the Soviets favored separate states for different nationalities, for the time being they should cooperate in establishing a "democratic" autonomous state including all Azerbaijan. He disparaged both the Tudeh party of Iran and the Kurdish Komala. He said that the Soviets supported the new Demokrat party of Azerbaijan, and urged the Kurds to join it, at least for the time being, in the popular struggle.

Qazi Mohammad replied by insisting on the Kurdish claim to autonomy, and Baghirov promised that the Soviet Union would support it. He also responded positively to a request by Qazi for military aid, and an agreement was reached supporting the foundation of a Democrat party of Kurdistan.

Upon his return to Mahabad, Qazi Mohammad was immediately faced with the problem of Mulla Mustafa, who had crossed the Iraqi border into Iran while Qazi was in Baku. In the first meeting between the two men in Mahabad they agreed on the specifics of relocating the Barzanis and positioning their fighting men to cooperate with Qazi's armed forces.

In November 1945 Qazi invited town and tribal leaders to meet at the new Kurdistan-Soviet cultural center and proclaimed the formation of the Democrat party of Kurdistan. The new party then issued a manifesto calling for self-government and autonomy "within the limits of the Iranian State" — a proviso from which Qazi never deviated — and "unity and fraternity with the people of Azerbaijan."

That same month the Demokrat party of Azerbaijan began to take over the province, and on December 12 held its first meeting of a new national assembly, to which Qazi Mohammad sent delegates. These returned, however, after it became apparent in the first sessions of the assembly that the Azerbaijanis were not prepared to grant a separate status to Kurdistan.

Qazi Mohammad then summoned delegates to Mahabad to form an autonomous Kurdish republic, and on January 22, 1946, at a ceremony attended by a large crowd of townsmen and tribesmen, he was proclaimed its president. In consonance with the unusual requirements of his new position, he was wearing a Soviet-style uniform incongruously topped by his habitual white turban.

Qazi was anxious to form a national army, as he was then completely dependent for military support on the chiefs of surrounding tribes of doubtful loyalty. The Soviets in Mahabad sent an officer to help him organize this army, Captain Salahuddin Kazimov, nicknamed Kak Agha. He produced a number of Soviet uniforms, and an instant army was formed with four wearing the uniform of colonel — Kak Agha himself and the three most powerful tribal chiefs: Mulla Mustafa, Hama Rashid, and Amr Khan, chief of the Shikak tribe. Other uniforms were passed out and worn but the army was not really activated, though sixty young Kurds went to Baku for training.

The various tribesmen opposing the Iranian army and attempting to advance north from Saqqiz dwindled until only the Barzanis were left — about twelve hundred men loyal to Mulla Mustafa. After a number of battles, the inspector general of the Iranian army, General Ali Razmara, signed a cease-fire agreement with the Kurdish forces on May 3, according to which the front was established around the little town of Bokan, north of Saqqiz on the road to Mahabad.

While this agreement was never officially ratified by Qazi Mohammad's government, the evacuation of Iran by the Soviets on May 10 undoubtedly influenced the Kurds not to pursue an aggressive policy. The line established by the truce was tacitly accepted from then on by both sides.

The way was now open for me to make my long-planned visit to Saqqiz. On July 12, I set out by jeep from Kermanshah, through wheat and tobacco fields. When I reached the Mahmudabad Pass, we were in military territory and an Iranian army colonel joined us. He pointed out the watch towers on the peaks surrounding the pass, and to the hills beyond held by the rebel tribes who had attacked the pass twice during the past month. Moving on to Saqqiz, we met Major General Fazlullah Homayuni, transferred there about a month previously from Khuzistan, where he had distinguished himself by his ruthless suppression of the Arab tribes there — including the Beni Turuf, whose sheikh I had met in the marshes.

Homayuni was an imposing figure — tall, beak-nosed, with a receding hairline. I was struck by the force of his speech and the sincerity of his smile, not always characteristic of Iranian officers at the time. He was clearly competent and seemed to be working an eighteen-hour day. He took me to his office, where he introduced me to a number of his officers and gave me a detailed briefing. The main force opposing him was about nine hundred Barzanis north of Saqqiz. Hama Rashid had 250 men blocking the pass leading to Baneh, along with Zero Beg, chief of the Herki, and various tribesmen.

Then, accompanied by Lieutenant Colonel Ali Ghaffari — the officer responsible for relations with the tribes — we got into tiny Tiger Moth observer planes. I had never seen anything like them except in World War I movies. Open to the wind, the pilot sat in the front seat and I — separated from him by the fuselage — in the back, wearing goggles and earphones. It was one of the more terrifying experiences of my life.

My pilot was a merry young man who kept saying, "Very good, Johnny," through the speakerphone. I was strapped in by no fewer than eight straps and still didn't feel very secure as we took off. The dashboard looked primitive and the double wings were held together by piano wire. We passed over an Iranian-held stronghold on a mountain crest, surrounded by the tents and trenches of the Kurds. We almost scraped the top of the mountain between Saqqiz and Baneh, and buzzed both Baneh and Sardasht, garrison towns surrounded by the Kurds.

Nevertheless, I felt exalted as an eagle with the wind blowing hard on my face, soaring over pine-wooded mountains and green valleys with the mountains of Iraq still covered with snow to the west. Then we suddenly landed in Baneh and were shown through one of the mud towers defending the garrison. Flying back on our way home to Saqqiz, the pilots amused themselves by doing stunts, and buzzing ground targets. My pilot made a very sharp turn at the end, only just managing to touch down at the airfield at Saqqiz. I think the other Iranian officers were as glad as I was to be on the ground again.

The following day my pilot again took off to start me on my return journey south to Hamadan, which we buzzed twice. In landing, the pilot did a vertical turn, buzzing his friends on the field at a height of a few feet. I was not surprised to learn a week later that one of these pilots had crashed in the pass between Saqqiz and Baneh, and the planes were grounded from then on.

Meanwhile, although the Saqqiz front was quiet, there were riots on the undefined Kurdish border with Azerbaijan to the north. The Kurds and Azerbaijanis were fighting each other, both in Khoi and Rezaieh, as well as Miandoab, and Soviet officials managed to stop them by threatening to bring back the Red Army.

Now that the Soviets had evacuated Iran, they suggested that it might be wise for their surrogates to negotiate a settlement in Tehran with Iranian premier Qavam. The Demokrats reached an agreement whereby Azerbaijan, including the Kurdish area, once more became nominally part of Iran, with the Demokrat leaders "appointed" to positions in the provisional government that they already held. This naturally disturbed the Kurds; whereas the Azerbaijani Demokrats had legalized their position, Qazi Mohammad's government had no legal basis. The Kurds had progressed from the status of a minority in the Iranian state to that of a minority in an Azerbaijani-Turkish state.

Qazi Mohammad then went himself to Tehran and asked Qavam to make him governor of a new Kurdish province consisting of the Kurdish parts of Azerbaijan combined with the much larger area inhabited by Kurds still under Iranian control. The wily Iranian premier agreed to Qazi Mohammad's proposal but with the proviso that Qazi must also obtain the consent of Dr. Javid, the Demokrat governor of Azerbaijan. Dr. Javid indignantly rejected the plan and friction continued between the Kurds and the Azerbaijani Demokrats.

I decided that this was a good time to leave Tehran for a visit to the Kurdish heartland. I had originally planned to make the visit accompanied only by my driver, the ingenious Karapet, but Colonel William Sexton insisted that I take with me a fellow officer in an advanced stage of alcoholism. The colonel thought that the trip might be helpful to the officer's condition and I warned my colleague that alcohol was a no-no in Kurdistan, ruled as it was by a religious judge.

To avoid his starting the trip in an alcoholic condition, I picked him up at his house at four in the morning. Unfortunately, when I arrived at his house, a party was still in progress and my colleague was hardly able to navigate his way into the jeep. I was glad to see that he took along a large can of grapefruit juice to restore his strength but later discovered that most of the juice had been replaced by vodka. Nevertheless, we managed to get through the various checkpoints without incident and drive on up to Tabriz. Although we had to pass the following day there, during which my colleague's condition did not improve much, he appeared to take seriously my warning about the dangers of drink in Kurdistan as we took off from Tabriz on Friday the thirteenth, 1946.

The road between Tabriz and Shahpur was full of shepherds traveling north. The shepherds told us that the flocks were being driven to the border to be handed over to their "brothers"; i.e., the Russians. As we approached Khoi, the white cone of Mount Ararat rose up before us in the northwest. I remembered that it had once been a volcano and was called Ageri by the Kurds, meaning fiery. The battle song of the Kurdish guerrillas of Ararat quoted by Ihsan Nuri passed through my head: *"Ageri, Ageri, tu ager bu . . ."* — "Ageri, Ageri, thou art fire, towering high over the world, the light of Kurdistan, Ageri arise."

Just before entering Shahpur, we saw our first Kurds, all members of the Shikak tribe, their bulbous white felt hats surrounded by the traditional Kurdish turbans. Passing rapidly through the town, thronging with armed *fedayin* and Shikak, we pushed on to visit one of the grand old men of Kurdistan, Amr

Khan, the leader of the Shikak tribe since the murder of Simko. For a time he had been Qazi Mohammad's minister of war, and in May he had even sent some of his tribesmen to the Saqqiz area to fight the Iranian army. Since that time, however, he had pulled away from Qazi and retired to his native village, Zindasht, not far from Shahpur.

We asked the first Shikak tribesman we met after passing through Shahpur where we could find Amr Khan. He looked at us, surprised, and said, "Why should I tell you?"

Then, after scrutinizing us closely, he said, "I will tell you since you are Americans and our chief will be happy to welcome you."

He guided us to a mule track west of the road leading to the hills, and after struggling up the mountainside, we arrived at Zindasht and Amr Khan's house. A fine-looking Kurd — who turned out to be Amr Khan's son — greeted us at the door. He led us to an upper chamber where two rifles lay lengthwise in the center of the room — the significance of which I have never discovered.

It was one o'clock and Amr Khan had already eaten and retired for a siesta, but his son called for chairs; a dozen Kurds came in to take their places and Amr Khan arrived. Tall, clean-shaven, and wearing a *papakh,* or lambskin cap, in contrast to most of his followers with their traditional headgear, he looked far younger than his reputed three score and ten. We sat down, with Amr Khan on our right and next to him a short, stubby, unshaven Iranian in an old European coat. On our left sat a mulla in a white turban and next to him a man in Russian shirt, trousers, and boots, with dark, non-Kurdish features.

While greeting Amr Khan, I gave him a letter of introduction from Abdol Agha Ilkhanizadeh, one of my Kurdish friends in Tehran. He couldn't read it and passed it to his son, who read the text with difficulty and couldn't make out the signature. I chose not to inform them of whose signature it was because of the presence of the man in the Russian shirt. So the letter was clearly not very effective. We were immediately served lunch, which gave me time to ponder what to say next. I was disturbed by the presence of the foreign man, who was never introduced to us, and felt inhibited from engaging Amr Khan in a meaningful discussion. The foreigner could have been one of the Soviet political officers who had been circulating among the tribes.

I asked after lunch if all present belonged to the Shikak. Amr Khan said yes. I started out by explaining that we were military observers for the American government, attempting to learn about the situation in this area, and expressed the hope that he could enlighten us. I asked him what his position was in the present government. He said that he had had enough trouble with politics, having passed some years in Reza Shah's prisons, and had now retired from all political activity, wanting only peace for his tribe and himself. He was obviously reluctant to talk to us and gave only vague answers to our questions.

Although he politely asked us to stay and spend the night, it was clear that our presence was embarrassing to him. I had the distinct impression that we had interrupted some kind of meeting, possibly negotiations with the Demokrats. Our leave-taking was somewhat awkward. As we stepped over the two rifles lying on the floor — with the Kurds looking on disapprovingly — I felt that this was somehow a faux pas.

From Zindasht we drove on to Rezaieh, passing through villages of Assyrians who smiled and waved to us, obviously surprised and delighted to see Americans for the first time in two years. Upon arrival in the town, we went to the residence of the governor, Mohammed Taqi Rafi'i, a short, gentlemanly old man with sparse gray hair. He was the exact opposite of the ordinary Demokrat official. A wealthy landowner, he was formerly a Department of Finance officer in the Iranian government and a member of Parliament under Reza Shah. During the Allied occupation, he became involved with the Soviets, who gave him their support in the election. After the Demokrat "revolution" he became assistant president of the Azerbaijan People's Parliament.

He was extremely nervous and jumpy during our introductory talks. Once when I spoke some pat phrase about efforts of the U.S. government to prevent a third world war, he said this was "in your hands."

I answered, "I don't think this is in our hands anymore — we've made every possible effort and concession and it's now up to certain other powers, who seem only disposed to seize as much territory as possible." I told him that although the American people were eager for peace, they would never tolerate another effort by a great power to gain control of the world by force. Increasingly disturbed, he seemed glad when I broke off the conversation to clean up for dinner.

When we appeared in the governor's parlor, we were presented to a short, vigorous, black-haired man in a general's uniform. He turned out to be Colonel Azar, formerly of the Iranian general staff, who had deserted to Azerbaijan. He had recently arrived in Rezaieh to take command of the military district after spending several months in the Soviet Union. He later told us that he was the son of one of the Azerbaijani revolutionaries of the 1920s and spent his youth with his father in exile in Khorasan. He gave every indication of being a convinced Communist.

Unlike the governor, he spoke perfect French, having attended French military school, and had a broad education, both in European and Iranian culture. He had none of the governor's reserve in speaking to us, and over drinks, dinner, and afterward, we spent a fascinating evening with him. Particularly intriguing to me was his love of Persian literature. He told me that the *Shahnameh* of Ferdawsi was the greatest epic ever produced and that he considered Ferdawsi the greatest of all poets. He showed me a small edition of Sa'adi's *Gulistan,* which he carried in his upper right-hand pocket, and said, "Whenever I get depressed, I take out my *Gulistan* and comfort myself by reading from it."

He said, "We Azerbaijanis consider ourselves Iranian and we are mostly of Iranian origin. But we want the right to speak our own Turki language even though it was imposed on us by the tribes from Central Asia passing through our country."

Up to this point, the evening's discussion was engrossing, especially with the keen-minded Colonel Azar, but then I turned to politics. Colonel Azar proceeded to parrot the Soviet line — the evils of life in the United States and the differences between Western and what they chose to call "Eastern" democracy.

The one subject that visibly embarrassed him and the governor was that of the Kurds. I told them that we had obtained permission from the Tabriz authorities to travel only as far as Rezaieh, as we presumed that the territory from that point on was under Kurdish control. Azar said, "Yes, that is so, for the moment."

I told them that I had heard that the governor of Naghadeh was in Rezaieh and asked if he or one of the other Kurds in town had any authority. He evaded the question, saying simply that there were indeed some Kurds in town, and then spoke with the governor in Turkish, which they knew we couldn't understand. The evening ended inconclusively and before we went to bed, Karapet told us that he heard our hosts calling the Soviet consulate — probably asking for instructions. They had perhaps originally intended to ask the Soviets for dinner, for there were two empty places at the table.

The next day, the governor and the colonel made a sincere effort to induce us to remain in Rezaieh but when we informed them that we intended to proceed on our journey, the colonel accompanied us in his car as far as Balanesh, about fifteen miles to the south of town. We took our leave of him and passed without incident through a Kurdish checkpoint manned by soldiers dressed in shabby uniforms who, we were told, were Zero Beg's Herki tribesmen. Continuing south, passing through another checkpoint at the border of the lake, we turned west toward the Iraqi frontier, intending to visit the Mamesh tribe, then at odds with Qazi Mohammad. Arriving at the crossroads of the town of Naghadeh, we had to stop for gas.

In front of us was parked a truck of the Iranian Soviet Transport Company. Its driver jumped out and confronted us. He was a huge, sinister-looking man — we later found out that he was an Assyrian named George who owned the local garage and who had committed a couple of murders but was protected from vengeance by the Soviets. After glowering at us threateningly and unsuccessfully attempting to open a conversation in Russian with Karapet, he told some Kurdish policemen standing nearby, "Don't let these men pass — take them to the police station."

They led us to a large basement room, evidently the police chief's office; its walls were decorated with a picture of Stalin and one of Molotov, a pair of handcuffs, and a whip. They left us alone and, after waiting awhile, we walked out the door and returned to our jeep. We were immediately surrounded by Kurds and we put on a show of indignation. A big Kurd elbowed his way through the crowd with a companion and said he would like to invite us to lunch with the governor, Seyyid Ahmed (who was Pusho's brother). Seyyid Ahmed was not in town, but the Kurd said he would telephone his house and ask his family to prepare a meal for us. I said we could not accept because we were prisoners.

"Oh, no," said the Kurd, "you are our guests."

"Well," I said, "if we are your guests, we thank you very much and wish to proceed to Mahabad."

"Oh, no, that will not be possible; please come with me to Seyyid Ahmed's house."

I said, "Your customs of hospitality are not those of a civilized people. Until recently I lived in Baghdad, where they showed me great hospitality. The Arabs there told me that the Kurds were savages, without a code of honor [*vahshi u bisharaf*]. I did not believe them at the time but now I see that it is so."

This visibly distressed the Kurds — the big Kurd looked as if he was about to cry. Some discussion followed in which they protested their adherence to the time-honored code of the East; then a swarthy man in a Russian colonel's uniform came up and introduced himself in an ingratiating manner as the chief of police. He said of course we were free to go whenever and wherever we wanted — except to Mahabad — until they could get us clearances to proceed there.

"May we take the western road?" I asked, still hoping to visit one of the tribes there.

He replied, "Certainly, but we are under orders to have you accompanied by police escort because of unsafe conditions."

Since we could now hardly visit the dissident Mamesh, we proposed to go to Ushnuieh. The police chief consented and we showed ourselves to be sufficiently mollified by their profuse apology to accept a cup of tea and an invitation to lunch later at Seyyid Ahmed's house. We were accompanied on our trip by one of Ahmed's servants, who apologized for his people's "savage habits."

On the way to Ushnuieh, we saw several men and boys in the faded gray costumes of the Barzanis. Upon our arrival, we passed through a dark, covered bazaar to an office building where a line of men in khaki turbans and cummerbunds brought their rifles to a sharp salute. They invited us to call on the mayor, Musa Khan, who was the chief of the Zerza tribe.

He was a cheerful old ruffian with a mouthful of gold teeth who hospitably forced us to have a meal at his house. Then we had to go back to Naghadeh and have yet another lunch at

Seyyid Ahmed's, where we were received by his wife and mother.

Bloated by two huge lunches, we were at last permitted to go on to Mahabad. We found it thronging with promenading Kurds all in native dress. We were conducted to the municipal building, and introduced to local officials, who told us Qazi Mohammad would receive us the following day. They invited us to dinner, where we were joined by the director of propaganda, Sadiq Haidari. He was a genial individual and the only member of the cabinet known to take alcohol, and my fellow officer happily joined us in a few vodkas.

Early the next morning, they led us to a building that had apparently been used by the Soviets as a headquarters, perhaps for Mahabad's budding army. Its walls were plastered with Soviet propaganda and pictures of Soviet leaders. Ushered into Qazi Mohammad's office, we found him sitting behind his desk beside a huge map of greater Kurdistan, a short, dignified-looking man in an old army private's Persian coat, with sparse whiskers framing his pale, ascetic face. He later told us that he had a serious stomach complaint and ate little but yogurt.

After I explained who we were and the nature of our mission, he took up a piece of paper and read a prepared speech in Persian in a distinct but subdued voice, occasionally flashing a glance at us with his mystical eyes. The speech outlined the oppression suffered by the Kurds, their national aspirations, and the necessity for freedom-loving people — especially the United States — to help them obtain their liberty and human rights in accordance with the principles on which the war was fought.

I answered, "The United States has always stood for the liberty and free enjoyment of human rights of all peoples. We hope that this ideal will one day be attained throughout the world. We have come to Kurdistan to look into the situation of the Kurds and report to our government, and hope that their situation is improving, that the Kurds are not simply exchanging one tyranny for another."

Qazi Mohammad said, "All people in the parts of the country under my government are free to say and write what they please."

"I have seen myself that this is so," I answered. "While in Demokrat Azerbaijan people are allowed to listen only to

Tabriz and Moscow radio, I heard both London and Ankara broadcasts on the street last night."

Obviously pleased, he said that the situation in Tabriz was entirely different from that in Mahabad. His pleasure diminished when I told him of my problems at his frontier, and then remarked that I had been shocked to find his headquarters plastered with Soviet propaganda.

"The Kurds are compelled to accept help from anyone who will give it but will not accept domination by anyone," he said. "We Kurds presented a petition asking for rectification of our grievances to the Big Three at a European conference" — Potsdam — "but the British and the United States have ignored us." Citing the Atlantic Charter, he said that the Kurds all hoped that the United States — the most advanced nation on earth — would help them overcome their backwardness.

"Instead of sending thirty thousand soldiers to Iran, if only you had sent a hundred teachers. But instead of helping us, you have helped our enemies, like the Turks, by giving them arms and equipment to suppress us."

He then gave us a brief tirade against the British, chronicling various actions over past decades against Kurdish rebels, ending with Mulla Mustafa.

On the other hand, he expressed a positive view of the French, who had "helped the Kurds" in Syria. We later heard that Napoleon Jackel, an Agence France Presse correspondent of leftist views, had recently made a trip to Mahabad, which was followed by pro-Kurdish articles in the French press.

Qazi then went on to talk about Kurdish nationalist activity in neighboring countries and showed us a typewritten communication from Kurdish students in Istanbul universities, on a piece of white cloth evidently hidden in the clothing of a courier. Next he began a detailed discussion of Kurdish nationalism in Iraq.

But he became evasive when I asked him about Mulla Mustafa, who reputedly wished to return home to Iraq. He mumbled something about discussions with the Iraqi government and added that, of course, the Mulla was free to return whenever he wished. He was noncommittal when I expressed a wish to meet the Mulla or at least some of the Iraqi officers accompanying him.

He then spoke about his negotiations with the central government and the proposal to create a greater Kurdish province. He claimed that the initiative for this came from the central government: "It was decided after talks with myself and Dr. Javid to accept this proposal," he said.

He said that the Kurdish Democrat party had not yet decided whether to accept a suggestion by Premier Qavam that he join the new Democrat party of Iran. He also mentioned the problems with dissident tribes and ended the discussion with general statements on Reza Shah's oppression of the Kurds, and how he "cut off our tongues" — in other words, would not allow free use of the Kurdish language.

"The Kurds are not asking for anything extraordinary, merely the same natural rights and freedoms that are the privilege of all mankind," said Qazi. "The UN should consider the Kurdish situation, and if it is not possible to create immediately an independent united Kurdistan, at least it can force the states with Kurdish minorities to set up autonomous districts within their boundaries."

After the interview with Qazi, we explored the town. We had little chance to talk to the general public, as throughout our stay in Mahabad we were accompanied by at least one member of the Central Committee of the Kurdish Democrat party, and were introduced to nobody outside of this small circle.

Our Armenian driver, however, went freely around the town. He said at first the inhabitants had thought we were Russians, and asked why the Russians were returning. On being told we were Americans, they were pleased and wanted Americans to know the Kurds, though some expressed anxiety as to the purpose of a visit by two army officers. In general, the people were happy with Qazi Mohammad and said his government was a great improvement over Reza Shah's. Their only worry was about its permanence.

In my report I summarized the views of the Central Committee members expressed in the course of our brief stay in Mahabad: They were grateful to the Soviet Union for making possible their independence, but emphasized that the Soviets did not interfere with their government and that there were no Soviet officials in town. (Most of them did not seem to be inclined toward Communism, and the old aristocracy seemed still to be in the saddle.) They considered themselves to be in a state of revolution — but a nationalist revolution. They said they wished to expand their state to include all Kurdish-inhabited areas of Iran. This would comprise the Iranian-controlled part of Kurdistan to the south, even including the tribal areas of the Lurs and Bakhtiari, who did not consider themselves Kurds. To the north it would take in the part of Azerbaijan south and east of Lake Rezaieh up to the Soviet border.

The committee members expressed the deepest contempt for the Iranian army, though they seemed quite worried about the presence of the large numbers of Iranian troops to the south. At least one of them mentioned that the central government was intriguing with certain Kurdish tribes.

Early in the morning of September 16, we visited the Mahabad press, which turned out the daily newspaper *Kurdistan* as well as a number of more or less ephemeral magazines in the Kurdish language.

Kurdish, it should be explained, is roughly divided into two dialects: the first, Zaza, is spoken by the Kurds of Syria, Turkey, and the northernmost tip of Iraq, and by the Herki, the Shikak, and all the tribes farther north in Iran. A Roman alphabet was devised for this dialect by the Badr-Khans and is used in Syria. The other dialect, spoken by the majority of Iraqi and Iranian Kurds and differing greatly from the first, is Kurmanji. This is printed in a modified Arabic alphabet, which makes use of vowels, and is the language used in books and publications printed in Mahabad, Baghdad, and Suleimania.

The manager showed us the press, which was rotary and evidently Russian-manufactured, though some of the parts were German or Czech. We obtained copies of all the issues of *Kurdistan* since its inception, as well as a number of magazines and a few collections of poetry, which we forwarded to the director of intelligence.*

Shortly after the Kurds found out that we intended to leave Mahabad early that day, they told us that Qazi Mohammad had invited us to lunch. Thus we had to postpone our departure until the afternoon. Late in the morning we again talked with him in his office, mostly on cultural subjects. "I would be glad to see that you receive copies of our publications, as I want the United States to know all about Kurdistan," he said. "I have nothing to hide."

---

* Some copies of these I have given to the Kurdish Library in New York City.

"In that case," I remarked, "why did the director of propaganda take away from us the most recent issue of *Kurdistan*?"

Qazi pointed to a copy of the issue and showed me where a headline referred to Anjuman-i-Eyalat-i-Kurd, meaning Council of the Kurdish Province.

"This is a mistake that made me very angry," he said. "There is no Kurdish province — we are part of Azerbaijan. I don't want copies containing this error to be released."

This remark apparently reflected his policy. His title was simply *Pishwa*, meaning leader, and the heads of his departments were called *ra'is*, meaning head, not *vazir*, which means minister.

He evidently still considered himself an Iranian official, and his immediate aim seemed autonomy within the boundaries of Iran. He stressed that the Kurds and the Persians were kindred peoples, and gave a dissertation on the origins of the Kurds, who he claimed were descended from the Medes.

Eventually we had lunch with Qazi and his committee and as a special concession, vodka of a particularly powerful and raw variety was provided, though partaken of by only one or two of our hosts.

We were finally able to take our departure around 3:30 P.M., accompanied by a huge Mahabad Kurd to guide us. We went directly over a rough mountain road through Bokan.

It was completely dark by the time we reached the front. Suddenly our guide called "Halt," and we saw three Barzanis running toward us, leveling their weapons. They took us to see Amir-i-Khan, their commander, a fine-looking Barzani, who at first said we could not pass as we had no written permission from the Pishwa. Finally he agreed to make an exception in our case, gave us a warm smile and a handshake, and let us go on.

A few miles farther on we found another barrier across the road. After calling and hooting our horn, we saw two bedraggled little Iranian soldiers running down the hill, one carrying a pen and paper. They took our names, and asked for the serial numbers of our guns. We gave them four improvised numbers. They could not, however, get the number of our Kurdish guide's rifle, since it had been filed off! As we started off, I saw our guide smiling contemptuously and shaking his head. The contrast between these lax and bureaucratic Persians and the alert and determined Barzanis was striking.

At Saqqiz we spent the night with General Homayuni, who was curious to know what the leaders in Mahabad were saying about the dissident tribes, whose resistance to Qazi Mohammad encouraged him. He said that the Mamesh and the Mangur tribes, and a few representatives of the Gurok, had met the previous day and sent a messenger to him asking for arms and help.

By the conclusion of my visit, I was convinced that Qazi Mohammad had managed, with Soviet help, to set up a virtually independent Kurdish republic. Although he looked on the Soviet Union as his best friend, the Soviets were not visibly interfering in the internal affairs of Kurdistan. Qazi Mohammad's movement was nationalist, not Communist, and was accepted by a considerable number of Kurds in other countries. Nevertheless, important tribes in Iranian Kurdistan were opposed to or indifferent toward Qazi Mohammad.

This fact was underscored by action taken by Amr Khan a couple of weeks after my visit, which might have been in preparation when we arrived in Zindasht, obviously at an inopportune moment. On September 27, he sent an ultimatum to the Demokrat governor of Shahpur saying he would occupy the town by force on September 30 unless the Azerbaijan government agreed to settle Kurdish claims. It took intervention by Soviet consul Hashimov, along with threats of a Red Army return, to restrain Amr Khan. The same day Gerry Dooher, the U.S. consul in Tabriz, received from Amr Khan a letter for transmission to Qavam pledging allegiance to the central government.

Apparently what triggered this was a movie shown to Amr Khan by the Soviets during negotiations in Shahpur. It showed peasants revolting against a landlord, pillaging his manor house, and establishing a revolutionary commune. Amr Khan, on his return to Zindasht, held a tribal meeting in which all present swore on the Koran to "drive out the Demokrats."

By this time the tribes, and perhaps others in Azerbaijan as well, sensed which way the wind was blowing, their perceptions sharpened by centuries of struggle for survival in the midst of more powerful societies. The Soviets had written off Azerbaijan, and abandoned their grand plan of controlling Turkey, Greece, and Iran in the face of determined U.S. opposition. The tribes may have sensed it before we were really sure.

By the end of November it was clear that the Iranian government intended to send troops to Azerbaijan "to supervise the elections," and it occupied Zenjan as a first step. On December 5, Qazi Mohammad and his top counselors met and decided on armed resistance, but the next day his brother, Sadr-i-Qazi, failed to convince party and tribal leaders that the Iranian army deserved the contempt with which Mahabad Kurds had viewed it. Clearly, the Kurds would be better advised to see how things went in Azerbaijan.

When the Azerbaijan Demokrat forces and the entire structure of government collapsed quickly, as the Iranian army knifed through the forbidding passes of Qaflan Kuh, Qazi Mohammad and his followers knew the game was up. The Shikak and Herki tribes happily joined the government in attacking the Demokrats west of Lake Rezaieh. The Barzanis abandoned Bokan, and General Homayuni was soon directing operations from Miandoab. Neither fighting nor flight was feasible for the remaining Kurdish loyalists, and the only course open was honorable surrender.

Accordingly, on December 13, Qazi Mohammad, Sadr-i-Qazi, and Saif-i-Qazi presented their submission directly to Homayuni in Miandoab. Although the general asked Qazi a difficult question or two about his loyalty to the government, he treated him with courtesy, even humanity, like the gentleman he was. He agreed with Qazi Mohammad that Mahabad was to be occupied peacefully by the Iranian army, and that the Barzanis — now the only force defending the town — would have to be withdrawn. This Qazi undertook to arrange, and the three Qazis were allowed to return to Mahabad to fulfill this promise.

After his return, Qazi Mohammad managed to persuade Lieutenant Colonel Ghaffari, who was leading bands of hostile tribesmen toward the city, to hold back as the Barzanis withdrew to Naghadeh. The Iranian army was given a good reception as it entered Mahabad, and courtesy visits were exchanged between army commanders and Qazi Mohammad.

A couple of days later, Qazi Mohammad, Saif-i-Qazi, and a number of leaders of his government were arrested. Sadr-i-Qazi, however, had returned to Tehran, evidently hoping that he might be more secure in his status as parliamentary deputy.

Meanwhile, Homayuni invited Mulla Mustafa to Mahabad

and asked him his intentions. The Mulla said that he would return to Barzan in Iraq if his safety was guaranteed, and Homayuni arranged for him to go to Tehran with Lieutenant Colonel Ghaffari to settle his affairs.

On his way to Tehran, the Mulla encountered my friend Abdol Agha Ilkhanizadeh in Qazvin, who asked him, "Aren't you afraid they'll kill you in Tehran?"

"I'm not afraid of death," he replied. "I only care about two things — my honor, and keeping my word."

The same question was asked by Iranian officers of his brother, Sheikh Ahmed. "Supposing we kill your brother in Tehran?"

"His death was certain the minute he came into the world. It will not change my course of action."

On December 28, I met with my friend Dr. Ardelan, editor of *Kuhistan,* who told me both Sadr-i-Qazi and Mulla Mustafa were in Tehran, and arranged for me to see Sadr the following day. I had not met him in Mahabad. His face had traces of his brother's features under his shock of gray hair, but he was much plumper and less distinguished-looking. He gave me the details of the surrender of Mahabad and the arrests, and what had happened to the various Mahabadis I had met. His brother and cousin were still under arrest. Others, including Seyyid Ahmed Taha, had fled to Iraq, where they were also arrested. The printing press had been closed and the teaching of the Kurdish language forbidden. Two Mahabadis, he said, had been arrested in Tehran simply for possession of books in Kurdish. All his news was gloomy, and his obvious apprehension was justified. The following day he was taken by two army officers to see Qavam, then bundled off in a jeep to Mahabad — to face trial with his brother and cousin.

That same day, December 30, Lieutenant Colonel Ghaffari turned up in my office. I had made his acquaintance in Saqqiz, where he was General Homayuni's liaison officer with the Kurdish tribes. I had been struck by his fair and considerate attitude toward the tribesmen, and his faith in the United States as the best friend both of Iran and the Kurds. He invited me to his house to meet with Mulla Mustafa and, along with Colonel Sexton, I went to visit him on New Year's Day, 1947.

Ghaffari met us outside the house and led us up a rickety stairway into a cold room furnished in the usual way —

armchairs around the wall with a small table in the middle. We were introduced to a short man in a black coat — Mulla Mustafa! He had a dark complexion and a rather square head, covered with closely cropped black hair streaked with gray, which came down low over his forehead. His expression was grim, and there was a fierce gleam in his brown eyes. At first I thought of him as a caged wild animal. His general appearance was unimpressive, but he might have been imposing dressed in Kurdish clothes in the midst of his tribesmen. He spoke Persian with a strong Kurdish accent.

"When I was forced out of Iraq," he said, "near the frontier we were met by Soviet General Lyubov and other Soviet officers who told us to proceed to Mahabad to place ourselves under Qazi Mohammad's order. Fifty days afterwards I brought my people to Mahabad. Since then I have had no direct contact with the Soviets, except during a trip to Tabriz where I saw them about an illness in my family, which I wished to have treated in the Soviet hospital. No Soviet officers have advised us in our operations."

Concerning Qazi Mohammad, he said that he was a bad man who was not thinking of the benefit of the Kurds but of lining his own pocket — "He is making *tujarat* ["business"] with Kurdistan!"

The Mulla said that Qazi had been so stingy with him that he had twice been obliged to go to Tabriz for money, wheat, barley, sugar, etcetera. Qazi had, however, supplied him with arms.

He seemed to feel warmly about certain British political officers in Iraq, and to regret their being replaced. He also remembered Doc Hoff.

Then he invited into the room two Iraqi-Kurdish officers, both dressed in fine new European clothes — one had a beautiful Stetson. Izzat Aziz I had seen in Mahabad, without knowing who he was, and had spoken with him there a few words in English and Arabic (my Kurdish escorts had not seemed too pleased about it). He had then worn a magnificent blue costume. He had fine, regular features, and looked rather like Baba Ali, with high coloring showing through his tan. His English was good but rusty — as was that of Mir Hajj, who was a big man with a moustache and a pasty face covered with a light brown stubble. Mir Hajj never smiled, and seemed very nervous; once his hand started shaking seemingly of itself, violently, and then moved in flourishing gestures, as if writing Arabic script in the air.

They tried to explain why they had had to desert from the Iraqi army to join Mulla Mustafa's rebel forces. Izzat said that under Nuri Sa'id's ministry, which was favorable to the Kurds, certain Kurdish officers had been put in charge of districts in the north. He himself had been told by Interior Minister Majid Mustafa to go to the north as military governor. But after the fall of Nuri Sa'id's cabinet, the government began to make trouble for the Kurdish officials.

The British political officers understood the situation — but unfortunately they were replaced and the crisis came while the new political officers were still catching on. Izzat and Mir Hajj were among a dozen Iraqi army officers who joined the Barzanis, along with fifty NCOs and a number of Iraqi soldiers, officials, and teachers, amounting to several hundred.

"What is it you want to do now?" I asked Mulla Mustafa.

"I want to return to Iraq. I have been trying for some time to go home but the Iraqi government will give us no assurances. If negotiations with the Iraqis prove fruitless, we hope to be given a home in Iran. Iran is our country — we are Iranians and this is our people. We would like to return to our homes in Barzan, but if not, we stay here!"

Mulla Mustafa stayed about a month in Tehran. After failing to obtain guarantees through the British embassy for a safe return to Iraq, the Mulla negotiated a settlement with the Iranian government. While the Iranians would not allow the Mulla's followers to remain in Iranian Kurdistan, they offered to resettle them somewhere in the mountainous area between Kashan and Hamadan. Having passed by those barren hills a couple of times, I could not imagine that this offer would be accepted. At the end of the month Mulla Mustafa returned north to "think about it" and discuss it with his people.

But Sheikh Ahmed, among others, strongly opposed the Iranian proposal — perhaps never really acceptable to Mulla Mustafa himself. Then the Barzanis informed Homayuni that all bets were off, that they were staying where they were.

Homayuni lost no time in marching against them from Naghadeh, but by late February they had moved west toward the Iraqi frontier. Blocked from crossing the pass by snow, they remained in Iran, fighting back Iranian army attacks through March. But it was clear that the Barzanis could not hold out much longer, and Sheikh Ahmed in early April took the bulk of the tribe into Iraq and into the welcoming Iraqi army upon receiving a written guarantee of amnesty. While his life was spared, the Kurdish Iraqi army officers accompanying him, including Izzat Aziz, were executed later in June.

Mir Hajj, as it turned out, took a wiser course of action, following Mulla Mustafa, who refused to entrust himself to the Iraqi authorities. He took a different route through the frontier, proceeding to his home mountains around Barzan. Negotiating from there, he saw that he could not trust the Iraqis, but neither Iran, nor of course Turkey, would offer him asylum. Somehow he must have got in touch with the Russians, for on May 27, along with some five hundred followers, he crossed the frontier once more into Iran.

As the Mulla and the Barzanis marched north through the mountains, once briefly crossing into Turkey, the Shah himself gave stern orders to the Iranian army to block their progress. The army did not catch up with them until they had already passed by Khoi and were close to the Soviet frontier. The Barzanis attacked first, and after bloodying the army column, crossed the Aras River into the Soviet Union. They were to return to Iraq in 1958 to resume their traditional role as thorn in the side of the Iraqi government (as detailed in a later chapter).

Qazi Mohammad met an earlier doom. All three Qazis were tried in Mahabad in a military court in camera and, on January 23, were sentenced to death. However, the carrying out of the sentences was delayed by Tehran, where Qavam did not wish to cause ripples in the midst of delicate negotiations with the Soviets.

Shortly before my departure from Tehran in February 1947, General Razmara had gone to Mahabad, and I had reason to believe that he was going to supervise the Qazi brothers' execution. I hurried in to see Ambassador George Allen to see what could be done about it.

"Why are you so concerned about the Qazis?" he asked me. "After all, they did collaborate with the Soviets."

"True, but they were essentially nationalists doing what they could for the betterment of their people, and the Soviets were the only ones interested in helping them. If they are executed, we shall be considered a party to an act viewed with horror by Kurdish nationalists everywhere."

"What do you want me to do about it?"

"I think you should ask the Shah to instruct Razmara to bring the Qazis to Tehran for a fair and open trial."

At the ambassador's request, he was granted an immediate audience with the Shah, in which he expressed hope for the amelioration of tribal problems, including those of the Kurds. Allen then went on to say that while the Qazis had collaborated with the Soviets, they had done a lot for education — and the Shah interrupted him.

"Are you afraid I'm going to have them shot?" he asked with a smile. "If so, you can set your mind at rest. I am not."

On March 31 the Qazis were hanged at dawn, upon orders of His Imperial Majesty, the Shahinshah.

One has to conclude that the Shah may have sent out the order as soon as our ambassador had closed the door behind him.

PART FIVE

Transitions

22

The Lonely Road

"What would ye, ladies? It was ever thus.
Men are unwise and curiously planned."
"They have their dreams, and do not think of us."
"We take the Golden Road to Samarkand!"

ARRIVING IN WASHINGTON at the end of February
1947, I was immediately faced with the dilemma of which road
to take in my career. Never before or since have I had so many
options. The most immediate choice was that of a career in
military intelligence, but after my meeting with the evaluation
board, I eliminated this option. I had also eliminated the
academic choice. I had a contract in hand for a job with
Aramco, where my first assignment would be in the desert
along the pipeline from Dhahran, Saudi Arabia, to Syria. There
was also the possibility of a Cairo assignment for *Reader's Digest.*

But from the beginning, prospects in the Foreign Service
seemed the most promising. When I called on Loy Henderson,
he told me that I would be taking the oral exam within a few
weeks, and in view of the background I had already acquired
and my high grades in the written exam, he anticipated no
difficulties. In fact, he had already decided on my first assignment, as a member of the Soviet-British-American team being
assembled to survey and settle the postwar configuration of the
former Italian colonies of Libya, Ethiopia, Eritrea, and Soma-
liland.

Then fate intervened. My cousin Kermit told me that the
head of the Middle East section of the Central Intelligence
Group (CIG) wished to see me. This was the successor to the
OSS, which lingered on after the war for a while under the
name of Special Services Unit. I went to the temporary building
at the intersection of Twenty-fifth and Q streets and was taken

into the office of a youngish man with dark, aquiline, Middle Eastern features. I recognized him as Lucas Gabriel,* a naval lieutenant I had met in Cairo the year before when I had been picking up my car to take to Tehran. He had told me of his contact with Habib Bourguiba, then in exile from Tunisia, and we found ourselves in agreement on North African affairs. I had been struck by his agile mind and knowledge of Arab affairs. He was the son of a Syrian-born Protestant minister.

We spoke in generalities during this interview, which was obviously a preliminary one in which he was sizing me up. A few days later he called me over to make me a definite job offer.

It turned out that one of his key officers in the Middle East had just been killed in an accident, and he asked me if I would be interested in taking his place. The job was at the GS-13 level, with the then princely salary of $7,700 a year — somewhat more than I would be receiving as a beginning Foreign Service officer. This offer required an immediate decision.

On the other hand, there was an ensured career in the Foreign Service, leading eventually to positions high in the Department of State hierarchy, such as ambassador and assistant secretary. Yet I knew that before attaining these enviable heights, there would be frustrating years of service as vice-consul and junior officer in various embassies, and subordinate roles in Washington. There were minuses also in the CIG job — the future of the organization was still in doubt and there was little certainty in the nature of such a career. But in the end, the attraction of being my own boss in an important Middle East post was irresistible. Also, I thought myself temperamentally and by background better fitted to be an intelligence officer than a member of the Foreign Service, so I accepted the job subject to security clearance.

K.W. did not conceal her distaste for my choice. She had not enjoyed our tour of Tehran and had made no bones about disliking my original intention of joining the Foreign Service. She liked very little about the Middle East or the career I had chosen. However, the decision made, we took off on a much-needed vacation to Key West.

Immediately upon my return, Gabriel called me in and said that there was a security problem. Had I, indeed, been a

* A pseudonym.

member of the "Communist front" American Youth Congress? A close friend of mine, a college professor whose name I had listed as a reference in my application, had told the investigators in answer to the question "Was Mr. Roosevelt ever involved in Communist activities?" that "Yes, he was in that American Youth Congress back before the war and involved in some kind of controversy."

Fortunately, I was able to produce news clippings of the events surrounding my contretemps with the American Youth Congress and soon I was inducted into the CIG. Then I had to inform Loy Henderson. He regretted my choice but put no pressure on me to change it, although he did point out the obvious disadvantages.

Soon after I began at the CIG, Gabriel introduced me to an officer destined for another Middle East post, Miles Copeland, a former OSS officer about my own age who had worked with the British out of London during the war. He was a brilliant, talented extrovert from Montgomery, Alabama, and we soon became fast friends. He was also most helpful in acquainting me with the various personalities of the organization, most of whom were old OSS hands. We were fellow pupils in the training course that began shortly after our meeting, the second course to be conducted by the new organization.

It was pretty rudimentary by present-day standards but included some old OSS courses, such as field problems in surveillance and countersurveillance. However, most of the OSS training — like the military training I received at Camp Ritchie — concerned the Axis powers, which had now disappeared, and there were few individuals qualified to instruct us about the Soviets and the Communist party. In fact, the only expert CIG had was Harry Rositske.

Harry had been an OSS officer in Germany who understood that the Soviets would be our next adversary, and he played a leading role in initiating coverage of the Soviets after the war's end, when most of the intelligence community in Germany was still devoting its attention to rounding up Nazis. He was an inspiring and amusing lecturer as well as a very convincing one. In one of his previous classes, he had given a talk in which he spouted the Communist line on a number of current questions and then gave a written exam to the class asking their own views on these same points. Most of them faithfully parroted the

Communist line. He then demonstrated to them how convincing the Soviet line was to the average uninformed person.

Here I had better digress to explain some basic terms not well understood by the media and the public at large. A staff employee of the CIA is not an agent, nor is he a spy. Unfortunately, confusion arises from the fact that the FBI and other security and police organizations refer to their officers as agents. In the world of intelligence, both American and foreign, the word "agent" refers to an outsider, not a staff employee, whose connection with U.S. intelligence is concealed from his associates. He may be a U.S. citizen or a foreigner normally in touch with Americans, or he may be an employee of a foreign government or a citizen of an unfriendly nation. Only in the last two examples could he correctly be termed a spy and, as one, would be synonymous with a person secretly working for a government or organization other than his own: in brutal terms, a traitor. The original meaning of the word "spy" — as someone dispatched to spy out the land, like the Israelites sent by Moses to the Promised Land — has been lost.

The modus operandi we were taught in 1947 was that an intelligence officer should recruit a "cutout" to serve as an intermediary between the CIG — the "case officer" — and agents, or a principal agent who would recruit and handle a number of subagents. Through these, the case officer would pass directions and payment to the agents and, in turn, receive their intelligence reports. Thus we could preserve our cover and not expose ourselves directly to agents who might reveal our identities to outsiders.

In my division briefing by Luke Gabriel and the desk officers for the particular area of my assignment, I was told that I was fortunate to inherit a first-class principal agent whose reports from a variety of sources, including a Soviet one, were highly regarded. I could expect a good start in my future post, with half of my work already done based on the work of this single agent.

I passed the summer in training and briefings, living in a dingy room in the basement of a rooming house on F Street within walking distance of CIG headquarters. Weekends I would pass at Martha's Vineyard, at the house of that absent-minded professor whose comments had almost cost me my job, where K.W. and Tweed were spending the summer.

Our marriage had been weakened by my long absences during the war and our lack of rapport in our times together since. In the discussions during the course of the summer, it was clear that K.W. was not enthusiastic about accompanying me once more to the Middle East and it was finally agreed that she would remain behind during the first year of my assignment, which would give Tweed a chance to have at least one year of school in New York. I had no option but to accept this situation, while refusing to face the fact that our marriage ties were weakening and might not survive.

On September 10, 1947, full of foreboding, I waved good-bye to K.W. and Tweed at the airport in New York as I left for overseas. I knew that the year ahead might be fatal for our relationship. When I made a brief visit home halfway through the year, K.W. greeted me coldly, without welcome. Although she and Tweed finally joined me, reluctantly, after I had been abroad for a year, she kept her distance from me and participated only minimally in my career. For instance, she would not help me prepare the obligatory dinner parties at home — I chose the menus and arranged the seating of the guests myself. Although her charm attracted friends, these were almost all from the American and European community. She was completely uninterested in the Middle East, and so could not act as a partner in expanding my relationships among the locals. To be fair to her, I was not the man she married, probably destined for the world of academe, where she would have felt at home.

After some unhappy months of nontogetherness, she told me she wanted a divorce. I did not respond, preferring to postpone any discussion until we got home and not feeling ready to face the fact of our incompatibility.

My work was my refuge from this disastrous personal life, and kept me busy enough so that I could avoid thinking about it. Yet what I had found on my arrival at my first station was not encouraging. My office was located in a tiny room in the attic, although I was told we would eventually also take over the office on the floor below when the present occupant left. There I was met by a lively female OSS veteran, my predecessor's assistant. I was sorry to hear that she was about to be transferred without replacement, as she was obviously well qualified and we were clearly compatible. She showed me a letter she had received from the desk officer briefing her on what I was like, which described me as a "human dynamo."

Immediately upon my arrival, I initiated my first exchange of cables with Washington. Miles Copeland had accompanied me on my trip out from Washington, and en route we had stopped over briefly to visit the chief of another station, whom we knew Gabriel intended to replace with a candidate he considered better qualified. Miles and I were so impressed by this colleague's competence that on our arrival at my station, Miles, before proceeding on to his own post, composed with me a joint telegram urging that our colleague be retained where he was. Sometime later I received an "eyes only" reply from Gabriel, which I had to decipher myself. In it, Gabriel strongly objected to our joint telegram, saying, "Such irresponsible free-wheeling will not be tolerated in the future."

And it turned out that in the station I would not have easy sailing, as my predecessor had left me very little of an inheritance after all. The great agent operation I had been briefed on at headquarters soon vanished into thin air. In my first meeting with this much-touted principal agent, he aroused in me a deep distrust. He struck me as a slippery individual who made a living out of guiding naive Americans in the complex ways of the Middle East, to the profit of his official and financial position. I was not impressed by the content of his reports and soon had cause to doubt the very existence of the alleged Soviet source — supposedly a governess of the Soviet minister's children.

After this source had provided a number of bits and pieces about activities in the Soviet legation and visitors from the Soviet Union, I decided to test him.

I wrote down the name Yuri Byelnikov off the top of my head and asked the agent to find out from his source the mission of this newly arrived Soviet.

The written reply came two days later: "Yuri Byelnikov is a Foreign Office Inspector."

I then informed headquarters about this and my views on the worthlessness of the principal agent's other paid sources. Headquarters reluctantly went along with my proposal that we tell our principal agent that the economies imposed upon us forced us to cancel all future payments and close out the operation. I continued to be suspicious of this man, who I thought had probably approached others, such as the Soviets, who might pay for information on his American connections. Later in my tour, I was able to have him followed by a professional, whose reports showed evidence of unusual activity as well as surveillance consciousness unlikely to be shown by an innocent person.

Thus I found myself almost without sources, pioneering on my own. It took me some months to build up a new network of sources, but eventually I was successful enough to get reports flowing in at a pace that led headquarters again to provide an intelligence assistant to handle the volume — who arrived shortly before the end of my tour! I received reports in French, Arabic, and Russian, all of which I translated myself, and was stumped only once, by a source who wrote in Ottoman Turkish. I had begun studying Turkish from a grammar and phrase book, as in those days Turkey was considered part of the Near East and its language, along with Arabic and Persian, I felt I ought to learn to qualify as an area expert. But my knowledge of it had not progressed to the point of translating an intelligence report, especially in the old script abolished by Mustafa Kemal.

My division chief, Luke Gabriel, while duly appreciative of my efforts, was a cautious individual who thought I was too impetuous, took too many chances by exposing myself directly to local sources. One time, during the first winter of my overseas assignment, a friend of mine was visiting Gabriel's office, then located in one of the old temporary buildings on the south side of the reflecting pool below the Lincoln Memorial. He asked Gabriel how Miles Copeland and I were doing.

Gabriel pointed to the ice-covered pool. "Most of my station chiefs test the ice, then move cautiously across the pool. Miles, though, is an architect by nature — he'd build a submarine. And Archie would just rush on across the thin ice to the opposite side, never mind the consequences."

Although Gabriel was an Arab-American, he lacked experience in the Middle East. He idealized the Arabs without really understanding the intricacies of their world and its many divisions, which thwart all attempts to unite them. This got in the way of practical decisions on operational matters I had to deal with in the field, and our cables to each other often read like a dialogue of the deaf. He had inherited the standards of

morality of his reverend father, was insensitive to the complex-
ities of human behavior, and lacked subtlety in relations with
his co-workers.

One example of these failings involved my desk officer,
whom I got to know well. She was an attractive and intelligent
girl and during the breakup of my marriage, I used to take her
out to meals and for walks along the Potomac, and we became
good friends (though it was too soon for me to be thinking
about deeper involvement). She told me that she was Jewish
and found her assignment to Arab affairs difficult, especially
since the outbreak of the war in Palestine, when she had had to
listen to discussions about Jews by colleagues unaware of her
affiliation. She wanted to change jobs, but did not know how to
go about it. Gabriel was not easy to approach.

"Leave it to me," I said grandly. "If you want me to, I'll
handle it."

But when I told Gabriel, suggesting she be shifted to a job in
non-Arab parts of the division, he reacted much more strongly
than expected. At first he denied that she was Jewish, but when
I assured him it was so, he was greatly upset. What I did not
then know was that someone in the State Department had just
been discovered passing classified material to the newly established Israeli embassy.

Gabriel called her in and discussed the situation without
much regard to sensitivities. I found her after the meeting
bathed in tears. "He practically accused me of being a traitor,"
she said. She soon joined another division. Gabriel never
mentioned the matter to me, but I later learned that he had
made such an issue of my friend's small problem that it was
decided to take Israeli affairs away from the Middle East
Division and place it under counterespionage chief James
Angleton, where it remained throughout my career in the
agency!

Gabriel was a decent man, naive in his belief in human
goodness, but he committed an unfair, unprincipled act against
me without even realizing what he had done, for he innocently
told me all about it.

In 1948 it was decided that the United States must find a
mechanism for active measures such as covert subversion and
propaganda to oppose Soviet expansion throughout the world
by "liberation movements." A new mechanism for covert action

and propaganda was formed, under the command of the director of Central Intelligence, with the anodyne title of Office of Policy Coordination, to operate parallel with the Office of Special Operations, the covert intelligence arm of the CIA.

High-level interagency committees were set up, with the State Department playing a dominant role, to choose those who would carry out this effort. Such a committee, formed largely of ambassadors and State Department officials who had held responsible positions in the Middle East, met and proposed me as a suitable candidate to head the OPC Middle Eastern Division.

Gabriel, who was included in the meeting, considered me one of his key field representatives and did not welcome this suggestion. So, as he himself told me, he said, "I think that Kermit Roosevelt, not Archie, would be better fitted for this role." So they gave Kim the job, with incalculable consequences for me — not all of them bad. In fact, as it turned out, this setback was a temporary one and led to a series of events that, in the end, brought me good fortune and happiness. But at the time it seemed like a fatal blow to my hopes for a future as the mastermind of U.S. intelligence in the Middle East, the role I then felt sure I was destined to fulfill.

I was speechless, and had no comment for Gabriel, whose part in this decision I considered despicable. It seemed to close the door to my future career in the CIA. And just then another avenue, almost miraculously, opened before me.

A few months before, in October of 1947, I had encountered George Allen, who was en route home from Iran. He brought me up to date on the many events in Tehran since my departure. The Soviets were trying to bully the Iranians into signing an oil agreement, and Prime Minister Qavam was stringing them along, knowing that the Shah would fire him as soon as these negotiations ended (as indeed he did). Ja'afar Pishevari had been killed and Ghulam Yahya seriously injured in an auto accident in Tabriz. Muzaffar Firuz, dismissed as ambassador to Moscow, appeared secretly in Tehran, and after a few days of mysterious intrigue fled to Paris. And Mulla Mustafa and his tiny band of Barzanis were in a barbed-wire enclosure in Soviet territory just across the Aras River, living on a loaf of bread a day and sneaking across the river to beg from the Jalali Kurdish tribesmen on the Iranian side.

It was a nostalgic reunion and George did not forget me. He was to take over as chief of the United States Information Service (USIS) after his return to Washington. Not long after Gabriel had given me the news of missed opportunity in the CIA, I received a cable from George Allen offering me the job of chief of the Middle East section of the Voice of America in New York at a salary of ten thousand dollars. Without hesitation, I accepted.

I was debating whether to tell Gabriel about it at my next meeting when he asked, "What's this about your accepting a job with George Allen?"

I said it was an offer I could not refuse, but I would find it hard to leave the CIA.

"You may not have that option," he said curtly. "We have an agreement with the State Department, which controls USIS, not to poach each other's personnel."

A compromise was finally arranged whereby I was to go on loan to the Voice of America for a year, and then revert to the CIA.

This turmoil in my career on top of a personal life in shambles put me under great strain in the last months of my assignment. It was a low point in my life, when I felt rebellious against a world no longer friendly, and as outward manifestation of my unhappiness, I grew a beard — then a rare phenomenon among Americans.

In July of 1949, every day at lunchtime, I began to run a high fever, and had to take to my bed for a siesta to sweat it off. I put it down to stress, and ignored it for a while. But the symptoms grew worse — the taste of alcohol, a much-needed solace in my distress, became repugnant to me. A doctor friend became deeply concerned. His resources were not sufficient to enable him to diagnose my illness, and he told me I might be risking my life unless I went at once to the only medical center in the Middle East in which he had confidence. This was the American University Hospital in Beirut.

They put me to bed on arrival and stuck me full of holes for a battery of tests. A couple of days later a Lebanese laboratory assistant came to my bedside to tell me proudly that he had isolated the culprit streptococcus. I had, he said, subacute bacterial endocarditis, a bacterial infection of the heart valve to which only persons with a lesion in the heart valve are susceptible. (I recalled the verdict of my doctor years before.) It is generally caused by a streptococcus routinely found in the mouth, which is passed into the bloodstream by a breaking of the skin, sometimes as a result of dentistry. It had been almost 100 percent fatal before the discovery of penicillin as a medical tool.

But the use of penicillin had been perfected by the end of the war — by luck, or fate, or God's decision, in time to save my life. For six weeks, four times a day, it was shot into my bloodstream. My low spirits lifted as my fever dropped, and I began to appreciate the verve and beauty of the young Lebanese nurses who tended me in the VIP ward of the hospital. How lucky a man would be to marry one of those, I thought enviously, thinking that my life would have been even more worth saving had I something like that to look forward to, rather than the dreariness of a divorce. But all my life I have blessed Dr. Alexander Fleming, the discoverer of penicillin, and AUB Hospital and the people who found and exterminated the source of my disease.

Shortly after my recovery I returned home, with K.W. compelled to share a cabin with me on the long sea voyage. After the mandatory debriefing and administrative procedures in headquarters, and a checkup at a Baltimore hospital, I went on to New York to take up my new duties at the Voice of America.

This was located in the Fisk Building, a dingy structure on Fifty-seventh Street between Sixth and Seventh avenues, and I found myself entering its portals in the late fall of 1949. I was welcomed by Foy Kohler, former ambassador to Moscow, who headed the Voice, and its production chief, Al Puhan. A secretary steered me to the tiny offices where the fledgling Middle East section was located. They were arranged in a square, divided by glass partitions. My office was a cubbyhole in the corner, with just room for my desk, its back to a window, and the desk of a secretary jammed against the right-hand wall. Opposite me was the Arabic program. Next to me, on my left, were the Greeks, divided only by a walkway from the Persian and Turkish programs.

There I was met by Dr. Sidney Glazer, on loan from a university Middle East Studies department, who had been acting chief of the section and was now to organize the Iranian program. He had hired the personnel for the Greek and Turkish sections, which were already on the air. They had competent leadership in the person of an American with long residence in Greece named Griffiths to head the Greek section; Altemur Kiliç, to head the Turkish section, and Dr. Mohammad Reshti, ready to take Dr. Glazer's place when he returned within a few weeks to academe.

Only the Arabic section remained without a chief and a sense of direction, because of problems unique to Arabic and the Arab world. All literature, including newspapers, all public addresses, and all radio broadcasts must be written and delivered in classical Arabic, the language of the Koran, to be understandable everywhere in the Arab world. Yet it has not been spoken for more than a thousand years, and the great differences in the regional dialects are reflected in the pronunciation and intonation of the classical language. The dialect of Arabia is closest to the classical, but the Arabian peninsula in 1949 did not yet have a well-developed radio broadcasting system. The Egyptian pronunciation is unique to that country and, while widely understood because of Egyptian domination of the movie industry, is quite distinct from that of the rest of the Arab world. While most of our listeners would be in the northern Arab states, homeland of numbers of Arab-Americans qualified to serve as broadcasters, the majority of these had the distinctive accent of Lebanon, not the best medium for the message to the Moslem Arab world. The most acceptable accent for all our listeners, at least outside of Egypt, as I already knew from years of hearing comments on the BBC, was that of Palestine.

Glazer had recruited two first-class Egyptians — one a woman — plus a Syrian-American and a Lebanese-American. And he had, some months previously, lined up the top Arabic language producer and announcer from the BBC, Isa Khalil Sabbagh. Brought up in Tulkarm, Palestine, by an exacting father who insisted that he have private tutoring by the best teachers in classical Arabic, Isa had also received a British education at Exeter College. After winning a script-writing contest at the beginning of World War II, he signed on at the BBC and soon his trenchant commentaries and sonorous voice were familiar to all radio listeners in the Arab world.

I strongly seconded Glazer's nomination of Isa, after meeting him in the Middle East, knowing the high regard in which his BBC program was held. He had recently arrived in New York to cover the United Nations for the BBC, and was awaiting U.S. security clearance before coming to work for us.

Shortly after my arrival at the VOA, Isa's clearance came through; he joined me in the office and proceeded to whip the Arabic program into shape. However, Isa's career and my plans for the Arabic program were almost brought to a halt.

Gossip columnist Walter Winchell wrote a mischievous and completely false paragraph in the *New York Daily News* to the effect that a partner of the Mufti Hajj Amin el-Husseini, Hitler's main protagonist in the Middle East, was now heading the Arabic section of the Voice of America. This loosed a surge of letters to the State Department, and Isa got some threatening midnight phone calls. Then I was informed by the State Department that I might have to drop him from the program, especially since his immigration status was in doubt, and Isa was soon summoned to the office of the Immigration Service in New York.

I accompanied him, and we were greeted there in none too friendly a fashion by a huge Irishman.

"Well, Mr. Sabbagh, what are you doing in New York?"

Isa explained that he had been representing the BBC at the United Nations and was now working at the Voice of America.

The immigration officer turned to a huge file of letters and documents on his desk. "It says here that you worked in Germany for Hitler during the war."

"I spent the whole war in London working for the BBC, except for a few weeks as their war correspondent."

"Is there any reason why you can't go back home to join your family?"

"My home has been taken over by the Israelis and my only close family is a sister who is a nun."

The officer was taken aback. "Did you say a nun — are you a Roman Catholic?"

"Yes, I am," said Isa.

"I thought your people all belonged to some funny religion." The immigration officer, apparently surprised by what he had learned, sat for a moment thinking it over.

Then he called for his secretary to serve us coffee, and pointed contemptuously to the dossier at his side. "Mr. Sabbagh, you can relax and forget about all this. As far as I'm concerned, you can stay in the States as long as you like, and here's my card — call me if you have any more trouble."

Isa had no more trouble, and continued as chief of the Arabic section long after my own departure. He became an American citizen and a Foreign Service officer of the U.S. Information Agency, serving for many years in Washington and various posts in the Arab world.

I was less successful in the case of another Palestinian working for the BBC, Yusuf al-Bandak, whom, on Isa's recommendation and after a successful interview, I started to "process." Within a few weeks I got a call from a congressional liaison officer in the State Department.

"Congress-wise," he said pompously, "I'm sorry, you can't hire Mr. al-Bandak."

"But he's son of the mayor of Bethlehem," I protested, "and has a good record with the BBC."

"I don't care who he is, my congressional friends object to him."

Yusuf's father was Greek Orthodox and his mother was Roman Catholic, and during the next week or so a number of priests descended on me to intercede on his behalf. I told them I was powerless, and suggested they direct their efforts toward their congressmen. I heard no more, and Yusuf went back to the Middle East. Disillusioned with the United States, he joined up with Nasser for a while and then became a staff member of the PLO.

I launched the Arabic and Persian programs almost at the same time, in January 1950, addressing our audiences in their own tongue. I had been teaching myself the Turkish language for a year or so, but never having even visited Turkey, I was not yet able to read a script in that language. The Turkish program went extremely well and got the best audience response of any of those under my direction. Turks of all occupations and from all parts of the country seemed to be fascinated with America and sent us many requests for information on American life.

The Persian broadcasts won less of a response, although our talented staff produced what I thought a most interesting program. The Arabic program brought mail from all over the Arab world, with many listeners following the appeal of Isa's voice, which they knew from the BBC. It also brought me a few political troubles.

The Israelis, of course, monitored the program, but only once apparently made any official objection to its content, when Arab League president Azzam Pasha was a guest speaker and voiced some views on what we then called the Palestine problem. The State Department asked me for a recording of his speech, and I informed them that, unfortunately, none could be found. Apparently someone had stepped on and broken the record, in those pretape days.

The other power critically monitoring our program was France. In response to audience requests from North Africa, we hired a part-time Moroccan announcer. He made his recordings outside the building, as he did not wish to be identified. Thus, when the State Department acceded to a request by the French embassy to be invited to visit our premises, we gladly concurred and introduced the officials to our staff of Middle Easterners, with not a North African in sight.

The French objected to the text of one of our editorials, which was a translation of one furnished by the VOA features section entitled "The Policeman in America." It stressed the fact that in America the neighborhood policeman is a friend of the people, not a figure of fear, and the French thought this was meant to denigrate the role of the police in North Africa! I asked that they be informed that the piece was designed to contrast the policeman in the free world with his counterpart in Eastern Europe, and if coincidentally this could be applied to French police in the colonies, this was hardly our fault.

Shortly afterward a member of the French desk of the State Department called on me to warn me of French sensitivities. "We have to be very careful about France's interests in North Africa, where our estimate is that they will be in control for at least the next hundred years." Just four years after this, rebellion erupted throughout North Africa, and in March 1956 both Morocco and Tunisia formally obtained their independence — a privilege denied Algeria until the end of six more years of "the savage war of peace," as Alistair Horne titled his definitive book about the Algerian War.

23

A Companion on the Road

". . . but surely we are brave,
Who take the Golden Road to Samarkand."

WHILE I WAS ENJOYING a new kind of professional life, my personal life was taking many a twist and turn. A little while after my return home, my poor mother made the acquaintance of a new son — one with a beard, at the time a feature sported in America only by a few eccentrics. My mother's feelings about my beard were shared by my father, who used to tell me with pride how, in World War I, he used his ration of hot water for shaving instead of coffee. My mother whispered to my sisters, in Cold Spring Harbor after my first return there, "The children follow him in the village, pointing to him and giggling."

At the Voice of America it was different. Isa Sabbagh sported a fine beard, and one time a visiting Arab came into my office spouting Arabic, thinking me one of his own.

My parents were equally horrified by my impending divorce, the first in history to disgrace my side of the family (in contrast to the shameless progeny of Franklin!). I had found it difficult to accept at first myself. For a month or so in New York I still lived with K.W. in a residential hotel by Gramercy Park, making no move to sever our bonds. It was a suitably dreary fall in 1949, and during one of our infrequent evenings together — for she was often away — she finally said, "When are you going to do something about our divorce?"

I found a lawyer. She already had her father's prestigious firm, Harrison and Tweed. And we separated for good. I went to a bachelor rooming house on Sixth Avenue in the Fifties, a short walk from my office.

We tenants occupied the two top floors, divided between homosexuals on the second floor and heteros on the third, presided over by a delightful French landlady who considered us all her children and asked no questions. I think she fed the residents of the second floor, but we third-floorers had to fend for ourselves, although a maid cleaned and made beds twice a week. The kitchen was usually choked with dirty dishes, and the refrigerator full of food in various stages of decay. My bed almost filled the room, with just space for a dresser, a coat closet, and a ruined armchair, beside which lay a pile of dirty clothes, whose height depended on the day of the week.

And yet I was not unhappy, now that I had faced the fact of the collapse of my marriage, and the realization that it had been a mismatch from the beginning. I pondered it night after night, and concluded that perhaps my nature was too different from that of the New Englanders with whom I had spent my youth. My next wife would not be a Yankee, but perhaps a warm, smiling southerner with a softer nature, or even an Arab girl, a black-eyed houri like many I had seen — but never touched! — over the last few years. I had known a few married to British and Americans in the Middle East and their husbands all appeared to be serenely happy.

Meanwhile, though, I planned to enjoy two or three years of the carefree bachelor life I had never had, having become engaged while still in college. There would be numerous assignations and affairs, but no commitments — a South Sea island type of life — until at last the right girl came along, after a prolonged interval of self-indulgence.

One Friday evening in May I prepared to go home after an exhausting week. We had decided to launch a Hebrew program, and the word got around very fast. I was inundated with candidates, many highly recommended by government officials and congressmen, and tried to give each of them an attentive hearing. All other work had had to be postponed and I was looking forward to a free Saturday at the office to catch up.

As I was rising from my chair, the phone rang and my secretary answered it. "There's a Miss Showker calling from Vassar asking for an appointment tomorrow."

"Put her off — I can't stand one more job interview and need every moment of this Saturday."

"But she has such a nice voice," said my secretary. "Why don't you squeeze her in?"

"Oh, all right — I guess one more won't kill me," I said, going out the door. "I'll see her at eleven."

I was burrowing through a stack of papers the next day when a friendly female "Hi!" caused me to look up. Standing in the doorway was a small, slender girl in a dark red dress and a matching hat with a hint of a black mesh veil. She had a charming Middle Eastern face glowing with a brilliant smile, showing the pearly teeth celebrated by Arab poets. My grumpiness melted in a smile of my own as I invited her to sit down.

"Mr. Edwin Wright suggested I see you about a job on the Arabic program," she said. She had a southern accent. "I have had quite a lot of experience as a newspaper reporter, and here," she said, producing a huge notebook from under her arm, "is my thesis on Communist penetration of the Arab world."

I pretended to read the manuscript while I stole surreptitious glances at this fascinating apparition.

"May I make a phone call, Mr. Roosevelt, while you're looking at my manuscript?"

"Of course," I said grandly, as she dialed what was obviously a boyfriend and finalized the details of a date with him that evening, sprinkling the conversation liberally with *honey*'s.

Then, as she turned back to me, I reluctantly asked the question that would certainly seal her fate, as far as the Arabic program was concerned. "How is your Arabic?"

"My parents spoke it at home, so I can understand a lot of it."

"Do you read and write it?"

"Oh, no, but I've done a lot of research on the Arab world."

There was no chance of a job for her on the Arabic Voice of America without knowledge of the classical language. But I didn't tell her that — I didn't want her to leave.

"Why don't we discuss it over lunch?" I said.

We went to a restaurant a couple of blocks from the Voice where they served passable meals. I ordered an old-fashioned and she joined me in that, and seconds, while telling me about herself. Her name was Selwa Showker — an Americanized form of Choucaire* — "but my friends call me Lucky." Her

* The preferred spelling in Lebanon; the accepted Arabic transliteration is Shuqayr.

parents were Lebanese Druze who lived in Kingsport, Tennessee, which was apparently a very nice town indeed, in the beautiful hills of East Tennessee. She had been a reporter on the *Kingsport Times* and loved newspaper work. Vassar was the most wonderful place for a girl like her to prepare for a life in the media, and especially, with her background, for the Voice of America.

Then she turned her large black eyes on me — framed by a long curve of lashes. "By the way, Mr. Roosevelt, are you married?"

"Well, yes and no."

"Just what does that statement mean?"

"My wife is in Reno right now, getting a divorce."

She stared at me silently a moment, then said slowly, thinking aloud, "She must be a very strange woman."

Of course, after that I was hooked. I couldn't let her go!

"How were you planning to spend the afternoon?" I asked.

"There's a French Impressionist show I want to see at the Metropolitan," she said.

"I'll take you," I said, and she seemed pleased. She did not even seem daunted when, as a matter of course, I led her down the subway steps to the crosstown shuttle, and then up the Lex to Eighty-sixth Street. What with lawyer's fees and K.W.'s bills in Reno, I was too broke to afford taxis, even on a first date. And not until later did I find out that this was Lucky's first subway ride — and her last to date. She hates them!

We saw the exhibition, and parted after arranging for me to take her back to Vassar the next day. That night she told her mother in Tennessee that she had met the man she was going to marry, and the next day, as we walked through the woods near Vassar and I kissed her for the first time, we knew without words that it was meant to be.

She passed the following weekend in Cold Spring Harbor. While my mother was a little taken aback to be greeted by the southern "Hi" — "*How do you do* is the proper greeting," she said later! — Lucky's charm soon won over my family.

Lucky's adorable little mother seemed to take to me right away when we met in Kingsport. She came from a well-known family, and was already educated in Arabic and French literature when she fled Lebanon to escape an arranged marriage to a cousin three times her age. Defying her relatives, she married a Druze immigrant visiting Beirut from Tennessee. She made a mark for herself in Kingsport, despite her foreign background, becoming prominent in the League of Women Voters and other local organizations. Recognizing Lucky's potential, she encouraged her to expand her horizons and win a scholarship to Vassar. Having herself flouted the narrow strictures of Druze society, she would not oppose Lucky's leap into a marriage even further afield than hers was.

Lucky's father, however, was cast in a more conservative mold. Most of his friends were from his own background, and he had hoped that Lucky would follow custom and marry a Druze. A couple of years earlier Lucky had been taken to Lebanon to find a traditional mate, but such arrangements as were made at the time were bound to prove ephemeral for a thoroughly American Vassar girl. At first Lucky's father disapproved of her choice, saying that she was throwing her life away on a New York playboy, with a divorce and a son as baggage, who would soon leave her for another pretty face. But he changed his mind about me, perhaps at the point when I spoke to him in Arabic.

Lucky graduated from Vassar with honors a few weeks after we met, and three months later, September 1, 1950, at my auntie Belle's house at Sutton Place, overlooking the East River, we were married in a small family ceremony by a Methodist minister.

We set up house in a tiny apartment on the west side of Central Park a couple of subway stops from my office. It was the beginning of a marriage that has now lasted thirty-seven years, and we both felt that it was fated, as if "someone up there" had planned it.

In the second chapter of the Koran God tells Moses, *"Anzalna 'aleikum ul-manna wa-s-selwa"* — "We sent down to you manna and *selwa* [quail]" — referring to God's provision to the children of Israel in the Sinai Desert. But these words seem also to have been meant for me. God sent me, wandering in my personal wilderness, manna and Selwa. The word means both quail and consolation, a name sometimes bestowed by an Arab father, expecting a boy, on the precious little girl God has sent him instead. Soon she will indeed not only console but delight him as she darts about the tent, brightening his days with her flashing black eyes, joyful prattle, and tinkling laughter.

Was it not all planned — my losing my incompatible wife, and what I thought was my future through Gabriel's treachery, and ending up at the Voice of America through my relationship with George Allen? And Selwa, come to Vassar all the way from Tennessee, graduating at just the right time, sent to me by a servant of the Lord, Ed Wright, a final act of benevolence toward me of a true Christian gentleman? And she was what I was seeking, an Arab girl from the South, from a background I could understand, and who could understand me, share my interests, and join me in my quest in the East.

And she was brave — as attested by her very act of marrying me and, to continue the metaphor, climbing onto my camel saddle.

As fellow travelers we have complemented each other throughout our lives together. She has a keen, analytic mind, always seeking excellence.

Her abilities and temperament mesh with mine and make up for my deficiencies. I don't believe in astrology, but the fact is that she is a classic Capricorn, well organized, meticulous, striving for perfection, while I am impulsive and erratic, sometimes letting go of a task becoming tedious to follow another road. I'm a messy-desk person, with papers arranged according to improvised systems, if they are arranged at all, while her desk is always neat, with papers stacked in order, and an impeccable filing system. She has a volatile Mediterranean temperament, which includes sudden storms, but is essentially sunny, warm, and glowing, with endless stores of courage and strength in adversity, and an enormous capacity for enjoyment of things going well. She believes that not for nothing is she nicknamed Lucky, and her belief makes it so. On the other hand, I am a bit of a manic-depressive, with unpredictable swings of mood from deep depression to not always justified euphoria. She keeps the mood in balance.

She has the rare ability to handle household responsibilities, as a perfect homemaker, along with an exciting career — successively as newspaper columnist, magazine writer and editor, and now, for almost six years, chief of protocol of the United States.

In short, she's wonderful!

From this point forward, Lucky was my companion on all my assignments to various parts of the world and many of my briefer visits. Her keen sensibilities and newspaper reporter's instincts added immeasurably to my own observations.

I had first visited Lucky's ancestral home some years before I met her, on a trip from Cairo to lovely Beirut in its mountain-studded bay. Over the following years, from time to time, I stayed there for extended periods and became intimately acquainted with the country that had produced my new wife.

24

"From Silken Samarkand to Cedar'd Lebanon"

I HAD FIRST VISITED Lebanon and Syria, then lumped
together in officialese as the Levant States, in 1944, when I
drove with my cousin Kermit from the Sea of Galilee up the
Golan Heights and through the wheat fields of Hawran, strewn
with sad little villages of black basalt, to the green oasis of
Damascus. At first the city disappointed me. I was expecting
something like Fez, a real oriental city with souqs and donkeys
and chanting beggars and all the rest of it. In Damascus, the
souqs were still semi-oriental, but European influence was
gaining and half the population wore Western clothes.

On our first evening in Damascus we had dinner with the
American consul, and the American special representative in
Syria and Lebanon, "an interesting old boy called Wadsworth,"
I noted — an understatement, as it turned out.

From Damascus we went to Beirut, visiting the great temple
of Baalbek on the way. There, we were entertained at a party
given by the Office of War Information for so many editors and
journalists that I thought that there must be more newspapers
than readers in Lebanon. The OWI people asked me to say a
few words to them in Arabic, which I did, thanking them for
their courtesy. and hospitality in my best classical style. It
brought down the house! I was the kingpin of the party, and
everyone rushed up to shake my hand.

The next day I cemented my relationship with Special
Representative George Wadsworth in a most peculiar way.
Being military, I naturally had to have my first official contact

with the military attaché's office. The attaché himself was away, so I talked with his two deputies. One was a typical American small-town boy, bewildered by the Middle East, which held no charm for him. "Before I came to this godforsaken place the only Lebanon I knew was my own hometown in Missouri." I later heard that his assignment to Beirut had been based on the notation in his file that he had been born in Lebanon!

The other assistant military attaché, however, really was of Lebanese origin and clearly well attuned to the local political scene. He told me some forgotten secret, which he said he had not yet reported, and I made the mistake of repeating it to Wadsworth that night at dinner.

"Where did you hear that?" he demanded, somewhat testily.

"I'd rather not say, Mr. Wadsworth," I replied, not wishing to get my colleague in trouble.

"You'd better say. I've had enough of your people being cozy about their sources to me," he snapped angrily. "I'm supposed to be in charge here, and all intelligence comes to me."

"I'm sorry, sir," I said, now caught in my own net, "but I'm not at liberty to discuss this yet."

"In that case, young man, I shall ask tomorrow that you be recalled immediately!" he snorted. Just then someone else came up to speak to him and I made my escape.

The next day I waited for the other shoe to fall, but nothing happened. Furthermore, ever since that time he looked on me with benevolence — fortunately, as our futures were to be bound together for a time. The fact is that Wadsworth, a man of great charm, was also a bully, with contempt for those who let themselves be beaten down to obsequiousness, and respect for those who kept their integrity.

Wadsworth's eccentricities were not yet widely known, but already he was famous for his love of golf and belief that business was best conducted on the golf course. When, as often occurred in the Middle East in his time, there was no golf course in the place of his assignment, he created one.

His last post had been Jerusalem, and there was no site for a golf course in the hills of Judea. So he founded one on the plain by the Dead Sea, and named it the Sodom and Gomorrah Golf Course. There was an annual championship prize awarded, consisting of a naked statue of Lot's wife, executed in salt!

Wadsworth was minister to both Lebanon and Syria and so

was responsible for the consulate in Damascus, where the American consul I had met on my first visit was eventually replaced by an individual reputed to be even more eccentric than Wadsworth. Strange reports about his behavior soon reached Beirut. There was gossip about a movie exhibited by the consul, to which he had invited the consular corps and local officialdom, entitled *The Rape of Ethiopia.* Expecting to see a film about the Italian invasion of that country, the invited guests were horrified to discover that it graphically depicted the seduction of a black girl on the fender of a car. There was a mass exodus.

Wadsworth decided to make an unannounced inspection visit to Damascus. Upon his arrival at the consular residence, Wadsworth was met by a maid and a cook whose head was swathed with bandages. To Wadsworth's polite inquiry about his injury, the cook replied, "The consul got angry while I was cooking and poured the soup over my head! But I like him very much!"

"And I like him, too," the maid assured Wadsworth, "but I don't like his friend." It turned out that his friend was a horse who was brought upstairs to share his bedroom every night. This unconventional consul was soon transferred, but not before causing Wadsworth additional heartburn. On his way home via Beirut he cut his throat in one of the consulate offices, doing more damage to the premises than himself. He went on to a sanatorium in California, a now-forgotten legend of America's first footsteps in the Middle East.

After my first quick trip to Beirut, in the course of time I was to see much more of Lebanon, sometimes staying weeks and months at a time. When I made my first long visit there, my view of the Arab Middle East was mostly from a Baghdad perspective. I was unprepared for the religious factor, which dominates Lebanese society and politics, and it was brought home to me at an official reception shortly after my arrival.

I was introduced to an attractive girl who had some minor function in the office of the president. After exchanging a few words with me, she asked, "What is your religion?" I was dumbfounded. I had never before heard this question asked in the rest of the Arab world, where it would have been considered extremely gauche, but I admitted to being a Protestant. "Shake," she said, extending her hand. Protestants in Lebanon were a tiny minority, somewhat discriminated against. I was soon no longer shocked, as I heard the question asked many times afterward, even by one Lebanese to another when he couldn't guess the religion by the family name.

In this and other ways, my background in the Arab world did not prepare me for Lebanon, a world of its own, not just another Arab nation. It was clearly also a divided country and I would not find — as I had elsewhere in Arab countries — a reliable local friend or group of friends as a basis for understanding this society.

Lebanon as it is today has a very short history, and throughout the millennia, at least as far back as the written records take us, the country recently christened Lebanon formed part of Syria. True, its coastal strip was once occupied by some free cities lumped under the name of Phoenicia, and for a century or so was again detached under the Crusaders, but most of Lebanon remained in Syria, and one can still feel the presence of the larger state in the eastern hinterland as one sits by the sea in Beirut.

Lebanon's religious diversity differentiates it from its more homogeneous neighbor. Long after the Arab conquest in the seventh century A.D., the bulk of its population spoke the Syriac language and practiced Eastern Orthodox Christianity. In the course of time, however, the peasant population of south Lebanon and the Beqa'a Valley adopted the Shi'ite form of Islam. Sunni Moslems from elsewhere in the Arab world settled in the coastal towns. Some of the population of the mountains forming the spine of the country were converted to an offshoot of Shi'ism, the Druze, in the eleventh century. Those clinging to Lebanon's original Christian Orthodox faith were scattered in many communities throughout the lowlands and the coast, and some, the Uniates, shifted their allegiance to the Roman Catholic Church while retaining Eastern Orthodox rites. All of them soon adopted the language of their Arab neighbors.

But the religious group that was to dominate modern Lebanon — the Maronites — was none of these. They are an ethnic blend of people originally inhabiting the northern part of the Lebanese coast. The Maronite sect grew up in the sixth century, when the area still formed part of the Byzantine Empire. After the Arab conquest, these mountaineers maintained their religion and were a thorn in the side of succeeding

Moslem regimes. They were in close contact with the Church of Rome from the time of the Crusaders and, in the seventeenth century, were formally united with the Catholic Church although retaining their Syriac liturgy and married priests. Until the eighteenth century, Syriac was still spoken in the Maronite mountain villages, many of which have Syriac names; although the Maronites speak Arabic today, many do not consider themselves Arabs.

Their increasing numbers and aggressiveness eventually brought them into violent conflict with the original Druze landholders of the central and southern parts of Mount Lebanon, culminating in the bloody massacres of 1860, when European intervention brought about the establishment of a tiny, separate Christian province. This covered only Mount Lebanon, not even including Beirut, until the French took over the area after World War I and created Greater Lebanon. This included Beirut and other coastal towns from Tripoli, in the north, south to the Palestine border, the majority of whose inhabitants were Sunni Moslems, along with the Beqa'a Valley and the southern mountains, mostly inhabited by Shi'ites. Most of the Christians in communities scattered throughout this new addition to Lebanon were not Maronites, but Greek Orthodox or Greek Catholic and affiliated sects (Syrian Orthodox, etcetera).

When Lebanon became independent at the end of 1943, a large part of the Sunni Moslem community opposed the whole concept of an independent Lebanon, for they believed Lebanon should be part of Syria. Many of them, however, became reconciled as a result of the share of power allotted the Sunnis on the basis of the 1942 census. Nevertheless, this census, not repeated since, reflected the Christian insistence that the largely Christian Lebanese emigrant establishment abroad be included, giving the Christians a clear majority.

In July 1942, a power-sharing ratio was established by custom, but never ratified by law, allocating power to the six major sects. Under this agreement, the president of Lebanon would always be a Maronite, representing by far the largest Christian community, with the prime minister a Sunni Moslem, and the speaker of parliament a Shi'ite.

Cabinet positions included the other major sects — Greek Orthodox, Greek Catholic, and Druze — and were distributed according to the various sects' proportion of the population. The Lebanese state assumed an Arab identity and was a founding member of the Arab League when it was established in 1945. While this identity was welcomed by the Moslems and accepted by the Orthodox Christians and some of the Greek Catholics, many Maronites refused to accept it.

Some of them sought a Phoenician identity, while others — citing the fair hair and blue eyes often found in the mountains — claimed a connection with the Crusaders. (In fact, the ancient Phoenicians as well as the Crusaders were confined to the coastal strip now largely inhabited by Sunni Moslems descended from immigrants from elsewhere in the Moslem world; as for the light hair and eyes of the mountaineers, this can be attributed to various non-Semitic ethnic elements, such as the Kurds, who joined the population in the course of history.)

Lebanese society thus formed an intricate maze, and when I arrived in Lebanon three years after my first visit for an extended stay, I decided I really needed an American amanuensis to guide me through it. In every U.S. official mission abroad I have found there is generally one person who is especially clued in to the local scene. It can be someone high up in the hierarchy, even the ambassador himself, or a person buried in a less conspicuous part of the establishment.

In the case of Beirut, it was Alma Kerr of the military attaché's office, whose home was a mecca for Beirut intellectual and political activists. A warm, outgoing personality, she befriended me and invited me to her soirees soon after my arrival.

At her house, I met Lebanese of all persuasions. There were Arab nationalists — mostly Orthodox Christians and Sunni Moslems, who looked on the respected Sunni politician Abd-al-Hamid Karami as their leader. I subsequently met him at Alma's. I had a mental image of him as a fine old Arab sheikh, and was surprised to find him a comparatively young man, clean-shaven, blue-eyed, with a northern European cast to his features. He was mild and moderate in speech and manner, a civilized gentleman-politician.

One evening at Alma's I witnessed the signs of a true Moslem-Christian split in an argument between two members of the Moslem Brothers, a Sunni fundamentalist group, and a young Maronite journalist from the newspaper *El-Amal,* the organ of the Phalange party, who was touting the virtues of his party's leader, Pierre Gemayel. "It's he, and not people like Karami, who represents the real opposition to this government," he claimed.

After his adversaries had departed, the journalist offered to take me to meet Gemayel and led me to the Phalange Club on the water's edge, not far from the St. George Hotel. The club was guarded by Phalange police and its paramilitary nature was manifest in the size of its gym, which was full of sweating, tough young athletes — weight lifters, wrestlers, and boxers. Pictures of traditional Christian leaders and events in the history of the party festooned the walls.

Gemayel turned out to be out of town, but his followers happily provided me with a lecture on the reactionary nature of Islam and the Arabs, generally proclaiming, "We are Lebanese, not Arabs, and we belong to Western civilization. We believe in democracy and a free Lebanon and America is our model — there are already two hundred fifty thousand of us in your country. We do not favor Arab unity, as this means Islamic domination."

A few weeks later they brought me to meet Pierre Gemayel himself — a tall, spare, young-looking man with a dignified but unpretentious manner. He struck me as solid rather than brilliant and by no means a firebrand.

Another political party to which I was introduced at Alma's was the Syrian Socialist Nationalist party, known to the locals by the initials of its French name, PPS — Parti Populaire Syrien (in Arabic, al-Hizb al-Qawmi). A majority of its membership came from the Greek Orthodox and Druze communities and it was an obscure member of the princely Druze Jumblat family who took me to meet its leader, Antoun Sa'adeh.

The party's ideology was based on the concept of a Greater Syria including Libya and Iraq. Like the Phalange, the PPS had Fascist roots, with Sa'adeh referred to as the Leader (in Arabic, *az-Za'im*). Its members greeted each other by raising their right hand and saying, *"Tahya Suriyya,"* "Long live Syria." I met twice with Sa'adeh, once in his headquarters in the mountain town of Dur ash-Shwayr and once in his Beirut home. He was tall with receding black curly hair and strong, rather Spanish features. He started our first conversation by saying that he thought it was in the U.S. interest to support his party.

When I told him that the U.S. government did not support individual parties, he said, "That's because you are new in the area — the French and British know better and you will learn in time. You need to support a strong organized group like our own, and should ignore people like Karami and Gemayel, with their narrow views. We do not believe that the people of this area are Arabs — and I am talking not only of Lebanon but all of national Syria, including Iraq, whose people are really Chaldeans of the same race as our own." He claimed that his party had seventy thousand members, although our own estimates put their numbers at four thousand.

Sa'adeh asked what the attitude of the United States would be in case the PPS had to resort to force. "The people don't always know what is best for them and may sometimes be coerced — just as you Americans had to subdue the South of your country by force in the Civil War. Of course, we really believe in democracy and could eventually win an election, but free elections are now impossible in the Lebanon," he said.

He said that he feared the State Department had a mistaken idea that "our movement is Fascist — far from it!"

I was impressed neither by the man nor his movement and never did understand its strong appeal to some elements of the Lebanese, and even the Syrian population. Yet somehow Sa'adeh attracted a devoted following, well organized and able to maintain itself in the face of government persecution. The party did succeed in gaining some adherents in Syria. Although the Syrian government officially took a pan-Arab position, the idea of a Greater Syria naturally attracted some support, as it did even more in official circles in Iraq. Nuri Sa'id began to envision a role for Iraq as the principal partner in a Greater Syria.

As the PPS grew in strength and won some support from these outside sources, the Lebanese government in 1948 began to feel threatened and banned the party. The following year Sa'adeh and his top associates were arrested for plotting against the security of the state and Sa'adeh was executed. But the party did not die with its leader. When Syria's fragile democracy was overturned, to be succeeded by a series of coups led by increasingly radical Arab nationalists, the PPS continued to oppose Syria. Some of its more active members paid for their opposition with their lives. But strangely, today the PPS in

Lebanon supports the secular Syrian government of Hafiz al-Assad, and is one, albeit minor, element always to be found on his side in the endless Lebanese civil war.

The PPS had one outstanding good feature, which was not shared by any other party in Lebanon except the minuscule Communist party: It was nonsectarian. Virtually all other significant groupings are based either on religion or family clans within religious groups. In the case of the Maronites, political divisions are based on clans, with the Gemayels dominating the scene at present — though other Maronite clans have prevailed since independence. Bishara Khouri and his followers held power in the first days of the republic, giving way in the 1950s to Camille Chamoun's Guardians of the Cedars, and then to Hamid Franjiyeh's adherents in the far north of "Maronistan," near Tripoli. These divisions persist until today, effectively dividing the Maronites in their ultimately hopeless struggle to maintain their domination of the Lebanon.

In the forties, at the time of my early experience of the Lebanon, the Shi'ites were of little political significance. In the 1942 census they still rated only third place, based on population, and so were allotted the third-ranking post of speaker of parliament. Their political power was negligible, as they were almost entirely peasant farmers, represented in the government by large landholders with no ideology except self-interest. They were the "hewers of wood and drawers of water" in Beirut, simple, gentle people of handsome appearance. It is hard for one whose greatest exposure to them took place in those times to conceive of their transformation into the race of religious warriors of today.

Yet, forty years ago, in the southern Shi'ite capital of Nabatiyya, I had a seat of honor in the grandstand overlooking the annual celebrations of Ashura, the date of the martyrdom of Hussein, in which the Shi'ites demonstrated the depth of their faith. I saw the moving performance of the passion play in which Hussein and his outnumbered followers are slaughtered by the army of the Omayyads, accompanied by the tears, groans, and curses of the spectators. And I viewed the procession of flagellant faithful, beating their backs with chains, striking their foreheads with swords, as blood poured down over their white robes.

But the Shi'ites had not yet found a role in Lebanese society.

They were still unaware of their potential political strength, although their proportion of the population, even then, was burgeoning. Members of other sects, educated, mostly small businessmen, fanned out in the world, leaving these farmers behind, to raise their families and unconsciously prepare for their future role.

We have spoken of the Maronites, the Sunnis, and the Shi'ites, with only a mention of the Orthodox and Catholic Uniate sects, who had no politics of their own. They have always blended in well with their neighbors, separated by religion but not feeling of nationhood; they will generally tell you they are Arabs.

I have purposely left the Druze* to the end; while I shall try to maintain my integrity as an intelligence officer in discussing them impartially, they must be allotted more space because of my own affiliation with them — and also, of course, because they are the most interesting people of the area!

I had been fascinated by the Druze before I came to Lebanon, and my first experiences of them predated by many years my marriage into their community. The Druze were originally an offshoot of Shi'ite Islam dating from the eleventh century. Their religion somewhat resembles that of the Baha'is, having evolved into a syncretic religion combining elements of other faiths while clinging to many of the principles of Islam. The Druze religion is a secret one and knowledge of its sacred books is confined to a small priesthood. They follow the principle of certain other Islamic sects, known as *Taqiyya,* which permits them outwardly to conform to the religion of the majority, whatever that may be. Thus, in the Lebanon, the Druze used to say their religion was close to that of the Christians. In Syria and the Moslem countries they claim to be Moslem, and in Israel, they have convinced the Jews that their religion is not far removed from Judaism; they are the only Arabs admitted to the Israeli army and police forces. In the United States, they generally go to Protestant churches; my wife was raised as a Methodist. Yet they have maintained their ethnic identity, even in the United States, and Lucky, a Methodist by faith, will always proudly proclaim her Druze origins.

Druze is the plural, *Darzi* the singular, or, in literary Arabic, *Darazi,* after one of the founders of the sect.

Almost since the beginning of the Druze sect, it has been closed to outsiders. One cannot become a Druze, or, until recently, even marry outside the faith. A swift stroke of the sword was the penalty for a "foreigner" dallying with a Druze girl, or for a Druze girl who gave even a sign that she might bestow her favors elsewhere. My marriage to Lucky was almost a first, though followed by many other mixed marriages in the United States, where opposites appear to attract. Yet shortly after our marriage, a Druze family who were friends and neighbors of Lucky's parents felt compelled to hold the marriage ceremony of their daughter with an "American" in secret!

However, the Druze have never permitted men to practice polygamy and Druze women may, and do, play a prominent role in Druze society and are not infrequently its leaders. Their women do not have to hide behind the heavy black veils of their Moslem sisters — a modest white head covering with a mere flutter of a veil will do.

While the Druze were heavily represented in the PPS, it contained only a tiny minority of the Druze population, most of whom followed their traditional leaders. The two most important noble families were the Arslan and the Jumblat. The official leader of the Arslan clan was Majid, who represented the Druze in the cabinet. However, he was not much admired by the rank and file of his community, who viewed him as corrupted by the Maronite establishment. The hero of the family was his cousin, Shakib, who had participated in armed uprisings against the French and spent most of his life in exile in Geneva.

But at the time of my first visit to Lebanon, in 1944, the leading figure of the Druze was Sitt Nazira, the widow of Fuad Bey Jumblat, killed in a feud in 1922. My cousin Kim and I called on her in her castle in the mountain village of Mukhtara.

We were ushered by a servant through the great stone walls of the castle to a vast hall, almost empty of furniture except for some nondescript sofas and tables against its walls. Sitt Nazira was sitting in a chair in the center of the room, and rose to receive us — to my youthful eyes she seemed like a little old lady. But there was a certain majesty about her, her noble features unconcealed by her carelessly worn, gauzy white head covering. It was cold in the hall, and we were glad to accept her invitation to sit at her side and share the warmth of a brazier of hot coals at her feet.

After we had exchanged a few polite phrases, she said, "I know you want me to tell you about the Druze. It will be easy if you look at this map" — and she reached beside her to unroll a fair-sized map of Syria and Lebanon.

"Here," she pointed, "is Mukhtara, and the Shuf, which is our province. To the north there are our villages in Urqub, and Jurd and Matn, and in Gharb west to the sea. And here, east of us is Wadi at-Taym, home of our race, and past that, into Syria, Jebel ed-Druz, stronghold of the Atrash.

"What we want is to have all of this brought together in one country, the Land of the Druze, and let the others go their own way."

This notion seemed pretty bizarre to Kim and me at the time, although the French probably gave it some encouragement in the days of their mandate in Syria. This coincided with their original plan to break Syria up into more manageable parts, with an Alawite state on its northeast border and a Druze one on its southern border. I never heard another Druze voice an opinion in favor of it.

In fact, not long afterward I met another type of strong-minded Druze woman who had very different ideas, Mai Arslan, the vibrantly attractive daughter of Shakib Arslan. She went out a couple of times with me and my friends bistro-hopping in Beirut. She was a passionate Arab nationalist and lambasted me as the representative of a government supporting Israel. Strangely enough, this firebrand, a liberated woman to say the least, became Sitt Nazira's daughter-in-law, marrying her son and heir, Kamal.

Kamal, a tall, ascetically thin young man, was known for his mysticism when I first came to Lebanon. He was much attracted to the philosophy of Mahatma Gandhi and was reputed to have spent many a night perched in a tree in meditation. He and Mai Arslan were hardly suited by temperament, but at least pro-duced an heir, Walid, who inherited the leadership of the community when Kamal was murdered in the early days of the civil war.

I had only one brief contact with Kamal, in the fifties, by which time his philosophy had developed from Gandhian to Arab nationalist socialism. He formed his own Progressive

Socialist party, allied with the Syrians and the Palestinians, remained generally in opposition to the government, and finally led his forces in armed conflict during the initial stages of the civil war.

With his socialist and Arab nationalist beliefs he was no admirer of the United States and when, in the early fifties, he was brought over on a visit under some U.S. program, Lucky and I undertook to give a small reception for him in the little house we then occupied on Thirty-third Street in Georgetown. We were told by the State Department officer who had escorted him on the drive from New York to Washington that Kamal was not impressed with what he had seen so far of the United States. For instance, when they were driving across Chesapeake Bay and the officer mentioned that this was one of the longest bridges in the world, Kamal remarked, "If you have that wide a body of water, you have to have a long bridge to cross it!"

He was not a gracious guest and hardly spoke to us or those we had invited to meet him — "un-Arab," we thought. He left abruptly, then hurried back to bid us a perfunctory good-bye as an afterthought. He stood apart, an awkward man lost in an idealistic world very different from that of the worldly and cynical politicians of Lebanon.

During Lebanon's halcyon days of the mid-forties and fifties, I came to love the country, its capital, and its people. I had the good fortune to spend a great deal of time there at various intervals during those peaceful years.

For a while I lived in a little house in the Manara quarter, near the lighthouse for which it is named, on a promontory overlooking the rocks of the Corniche. Sometimes I sat on the roof and watched the sunset with the fishing boats heading out to sea. And from my living room, early in the morning, I saw them come in again at sunrise, as the mist rose from the Mediterranean.

It was very much a maritime city and one was always conscious of the sea. The best place to observe the harbor was the great terrace of that now destroyed Beirut landmark, the St. George Hotel. There, one could sit sipping a long drink with genial friends, and watch the swimmers and water-skiers, some of them pretty girls in bikinis. While few seemed to mind going into the water on the very shore of the city, most of us preferred the long beach a few miles south of town, where people in the embassy always rented beach houses. On the way there, we often lunched at one of the seafood restaurants opposite Pigeon Rocks. At night our seafood restaurant was el-Bahri, on stilts overlooking the port.

Beirut boasted many other fine restaurants in those days, with much variety of food — Arab, French, and Eastern European. After eating, we would often go to sample one of several nightclubs. I remember one in particular, the Lido, because the chanteuse there was a conscious imitator of Edith Piaf and gave moving renditions of her poignant songs.

But the best part of Lebanon for me was the mountain range from which the country derives its name, Place of Milk, referring to the white snows of its highest peaks. For a summer season I once rented, with Miles Copeland, a little stone house in the mountain village of Shimlan. It consisted of a couple of rooms off a large open porch facing the sea, with a kitchen down below presided over by an old peasant woman. In the evening, while she plied us with the delights of Lebanese cooking, we could look down on the great amphitheater of the Bay of St. George as it faded into darkness. The lights of Beirut began to twinkle, spreading to a flickering panorama of hundreds of small villages on the hills below.

On weekends we often walked among the olive groves covering the whole mountainside behind us, sometimes passing through the pleasant little stone villages. In these walks we met no foreigners, only local peasants who always greeted us with a friendly smile. They were Druze and Maronites, and seemed to live together in harmony. They appeared to be prosperous, perhaps helped by contributions from the many sons who went down to Beirut to study, then become businessmen, doctors, and lawyers.

This was my first taste of mountain village life, of that idyllic aspect of the Lebanon of those days, and I was to get a more intimate glimpse of it when I first went with Lucky to visit her family's village, Arsoun, a few miles from Broummana. Their home dated from Ottoman days, with a large parlor looking down on the village square. Presiding over it was Lucky's grandmother, her head covered by a light white veil; the quiet majesty of her features reminded me of Sitt Nazira. Lucky's three uncles were there with wives, various relatives, and their children, and they welcomed me to the family with a banquet washed down with milky drafts of arak, followed by aromatic Turkish coffee.

The scent of the surrounding pine forest wafted in through the open windows, and below the house were piled the pine-cones waiting for someone to extract the nuts that enliven the Lebanese diet. It was harvest time and the breeze brought in the humming of the cicadas — *zeez al-hasida,* in Arabic. *Hasida* is the word for harvest, and what better word for cicada than *zeez!*

People from the village popped in and out throughout the afternoon to have a look at their glamorous American cousin and her exotic husband. One of them seemed to be the village character, a genial man in his fifties with long white mustachios, Abu Ali, who exchanged many jokes with the company in a mountain accent, still pronouncing the *q,* which has vanished from city speech.

I visited them once again when I was alone in Beirut for a weekend. I could not reach the house by telephone, so I simply borrowed a car and showed up on a Sunday unannounced — and got the same royal welcome.

It was to be my last visit to Arsoun ever. Next time Lucky and I came to Lebanon it was winter and the family was in Beirut. Then years passed, and I did not visit Lebanon again until it was shattered by civil war.

The seeds of the conflict had been germinating for many years. Yet the problems of the country's many religious sects, the monopoly of power of one of them at the expense of others at a time of demographic change, could conceivably have been solved in time by the Lebanese themselves. But they were not to have that time nor that opportunity because of events in neighboring lands.

Lebanon played only a perfunctory role in the Arab-Israeli War of 1948. Calls for volunteers to fight in the Arab Liberation Army produced only two hundred recruits, mostly from the slums of Beirut's Basta quarter. But as a result of the war, Lebanon was flooded with some two hundred thousand Palestinian refugees.

A few of these were Christians, most of whom obtained Lebanese citizenship and were absorbed into the economy and the Christian-dominated middle class. But the impoverished Moslem majority had no acknowledged place in Lebanese society. They had been mostly farmers, and there was no spare land in Lebanon for them to farm. Crammed into refugee camps, they were an indigestible element upsetting the delicate Christian-Moslem balance of power in Lebanon. The ideologically Arab nationalist opposition, mostly Sunni and Druze, saw in them an asset.

Not so the Shi'ites, in or near whose territory many refugee camps were located, for whom they were an unwelcome intrusion. As Palestinian guerrillas based in the camps began operations against Israel, drawing Israeli reprisals in which Shi'ites were killed and maimed and saw their homes destroyed, resentment of the Palestinians grew apace.

From 1956 to 1958 developments in Egypt and Syria cast another fatal reflection on Lebanon. Gamal Abd-al-Nasser nationalized the Suez Canal, triggering such events as the British-French-Israeli invasion of the Sinai in 1956, culminating in the enfolding of Syria in the United Arab Republic in February 1958, and the Iraqi revolution the following July.

This was echoed in Lebanon with a Moslem revolution that same month, followed by the unopposed landing of U.S. marines and the peaceful resolution of the conflict by compromise, which could, perhaps, have eventually led to a solution of Lebanon's problems.

But Lebanon was not, alas, an island. The Arab-Israeli War of 1967 probably sealed the fate of Lebanon, which became a battleground for a continuation of the war after the Israeli and Syrian armies had settled behind the lines between them established by truce. The Syrians supported their own adherents in the mostly (but not entirely) Moslem and Druze opposition, while the Israelis backed the Phalange and the South Lebanese army. Other Islamic countries, including Libya and Iran, joined in the fray, and Lebanon started to fall apart, finally to disintegrate as a nation during the Israeli invasion of 1982.

Early in the history of that tragedy, a band of Phalangists came to Arsoun. They found Lucky's grandmother alone in the house. As she stood in front of the door, barring the way, they fired shots all around her, until some of the local Christians came to rescue her. The Phalangists blew up the house, and went on to pillage the other Druze houses of the village. They found the village character, the delightful Abu Ali of the white mustachios, and burned him alive in front of his home.

25

Turan

DURING MY TOUR in Iran I had first become aware, both from my contacts with the Soviet military and in my experience in Azerbaijan, that the Soviet Union is, indeed, an Asiatic country. Not only do the Russian people bear the impress of years of domination by the Tatars, but a large proportion of the Soviet Union's inhabitants are unassimilated Asiatics.

I had caught some of the aura of the Caucasus from my early reading in Russian literature, especially Mikhail Lermontov's *Hero of Our Times* and *Hajji Murat*. And my childhood exposure to Kipling had made me aware of the aggressive Russian advance eastward through Turkistan. But in Iran I felt the physical presence of these historic peoples, mostly Turkic, of the southeastern part of the Russian Empire.

At the Voice of America I became actively involved with the Moslem and other minorities of the Soviet Union, and came to a realization of their place in history, and in our world today.

Some months after I had launched the VOA programs to the Middle East, discussions began about the possibility of starting broadcasts to the non-Slavic peoples of the Soviet Union. A few unusual visitors began trickling into my office, immigrants from Russia's Asian borders. I was visited by representatives of the New York–based Caucasian Society, various Georgians, and members of the American Tartar Society — who have their own mosque in Brooklyn. In addition, there were numerous representatives of the large American-Armenian community.

I was also visited by a Turkistani who arranged to have sent to me regularly an emigré publication, *Turkistan,* published in Munich. It was written in the Roman alphabet and I was pleased that, with my burgeoning knowledge of Turkish, I was able to read it without too much difficulty. Once Lucky found me reading it, and asked what I was doing.

"There's an Uzbek coming to see me tomorrow about working at the Voice of America, and I want to be able to exchange a few words with him." She was most impressed, and I have not contradicted her when I've heard her telling dinner partners how I learned Uzbek in one afternoon. But, of course, it was only a form of Turkish, a language I had been studying off and on over the past year. But I had no practice speaking it, and I soon discovered that my best way of communicating with the Uzbek was in Russian after all!

Representatives of all these groups strongly favored VOA programs in their own languages but opposed having them controlled by the Russian director of our VOA Russian program, whom they considered to be a "Russian chauvinist."

By extraordinary coincidence, this person was my estranged brother-in-law, Alexander Grigorievich Barmine, who defected from the Soviet Union in the summer of 1937, when it was not yet fashionable to do so. He had been deputy chief of mission in the Soviet embassy in Athens.

He was about fifty, had fought for the Bolsheviks in the revolution, and afterward pursued oriental studies at the Revolutionary War College. From there he went on to Bukhara as a member of the Soviet embassy. Perfecting his knowledge of the Persian language in a subsequent stint at the Soviet War College, he went on to be their consul general in Gilan, Iran.

His Soviet government career ended in Greece, in the midst of Stalin's purges, which were taking the lives of many of his well-positioned friends in the government. This, and his romance with a bright and attractive Greek girl, led to his flight to Paris, where she joined him in hiding from the Soviets until they could go on to the United States. After a stint in the army, Barmine published an account of his adventures, *One Who Survived.*

Although the American public was not yet ready for a frank exposé of this nature, the book and Barmine won considerable attention from those already aware of Soviet realities, such as Isaac Don Levine. He was a friend of my parents and introduced the Barmines to them; they were at once taken with this exotic pair, and when I arrived home from Iran I got to know them in Cold Spring Harbor.

Sometime in 1948 the Barmines split up, and he eloped with my youngest sister. My parents were most upset by the marriage, especially since Barmine was almost my father's age. Also, he had the personality and adjustment problems common to most Soviet defectors.

The marriage did not last more than a year, at the end of which my sister gave birth to a girl. Barmine sent her a list of acceptable Greek Orthodox female names, beginning with Anastasia and ending with Xenia. My sister instead named her Margot, after her closest friend and old schoolmate who was married to a pediatrician.

Barmine was furious, and in the full spate of his rage telephoned the doctor, who later recounted the conversation to me with some amusement.

"She has to give our child Orthodox name — I am Orthodox, and Orthodox is more than Catholic even!" said Barmine. "And now she wants to name her child Margot after your wife — and I hate your wife!"

"I'm sorry about that," said the good doctor mildly.

"Also, I hate name Margot — is second-class whore's name."

Margot turned out to be a beautiful, brilliant, and altogether adorable little girl, and became a daughter substitute for the one Lucky and I never had. Today she is a successful journalist with *Time* magazine.

My relations with Barmine at the VOA were, understandably, distant from the beginning and soon became worse than that; I decided that if we were to launch programs in the Tatar, Caucasian, and Turkistani languages they should be under my direction, not that of Barmine. I made this recommendation to Production Chief Al Puhan and VOA Chief Foy Kohler, explaining the rationale behind it. I laid out a plan for broadcasts in Georgian, Armenian, Tatar, Azerbaijani, and Uzbek, pointing out that the last three were Turkic and could use some of our Turkish language material.

They were agreeable, though of course Barmine was violently opposed and received some support from Bob Kelley, the grand old man among Soviet experts in the State Department. It was he who had set up the Eastern European Division in the

State Department in the twenties, where Loy Henderson had perched for a time. He believed that the Russian people were the best potential friends the United States had in the Soviet Union, that they were basically nationalist, that Stalin had had to give way to Russian nationalism in touting the "great patriotic war" theme, and that they would be offended by nationalist appeals to the other races of the Soviet Union.

While I was in Washington arguing the case with Kelley, Barmine pulled a trick that I never could have imagined would succeed. He presented Puhan and Kohler with the sentence "Workers of the world unite" in the Slavic languages and Turko-Tatar languages written in Cyrillic script, trying to depict them as belonging to the same family of languages as Russian. Of course, Barmine, experienced in Central Asia, knew better, but incredibly Kohler, ex-ambassador to Moscow, was momentarily taken in. However, in rebuttal, I sent him up the sentence written in Ottoman Turkish and the three Soviet Turkic languages in Roman characters, almost identical!

I finally won, but was admonished by Bob Kelley to be sure the content of the programs was not inflammatory. My first State Department policy directive before launching the programs was that they contain nothing that would offend "Soviet (i.e., Russian) Nationalism."

I strongly believe that the United States has followed a mistaken policy, either from lack of understanding of the facts or, following Bob Kelley's rationale, in not exploiting the issue of Russian colonialism. While one of the principal thrusts of Soviet propaganda since Lenin's time has been the attack on Western imperialists — in which they include the United States — we have never responded with sustained attacks on Russian imperialism in Asia. We have tended to side with the Soviets in forcing our Western allies to give up their colonies, but the subject races of Russia's Asian empire have continued to languish without any encouragement from us.

Much of Russian history concerns the struggle between the Slavs and the Turkic peoples on their borders, which dates back to the foundation of the Russian state more than a thousand years ago. In the Slavs' millennium-long confrontation with their eastern neighbors lies the key to an understanding not only of Russian history, but Russian character. To understand

Russian realities today one has to have a concept of the great Turkic ethnic group that has preoccupied Russians through the centuries.

The Turks are relative newcomers on the Middle Eastern scene. Stemming originally from southern Siberia, a thousand years ago they began pushing south into Central Asia, conquering and often displacing its original Iranian inhabitants.

In the tenth century, under an Iranian dynasty in Bukhara, the Persian poet Ferdawsi, in his semimythical epic history, the *Shahnameh,* depicted the Turks, living in their own northern country, Turan, as the hereditary enemies of Iran.

Turks eventually inundated Central Asia, spreading their language ever south and west and making ruinous attacks on the settled peoples of Iran. Then they overran Iraq and Anatolia, reducing the once-great Byzantine Empire to a shell of its former dominions.

As the Russians, under the princes of Kiev, expanded their territory south into the steppes, they found it occupied by Turkic nomads who had migrated there in previous centuries from Central Asia. The Russians were generally on the march, pushing the nomads south and east — with an occasional reverse, such as the celebrated defeat of Prince Igor — until the Mongol catastrophe.

In the thirteenth century Russia, along with civilized Eastern Europe and the heart of the Islamic world, suffered the devastating invasion of Genghis Khan's Mongols — a people distantly related to the Turks. The Mongols overran all the Turkic peoples of Asia and Eastern Europe, establishing their own rule over all but the Turks of Anatolia, who managed to preserve their identity beneath the Mongol avalanche. They emerged under new leadership — the Osmanli, or Ottoman, dynasty — to found the Ottoman Empire and survive as Turkey, the only independent Turkic state today.

But the rest of the Turkic peoples fell under the rule of Genghis Khan and his successors. Only a minority of his hordes were Mongols, for most had later returned home. The bulk of his armies came from Turkic tribes, who converted to Islam and remained to populate the ruins he left behind him. The Russians lumped the Mongols and their Turkish followers together under the term "Tatar," in Western Europe spelled, incorrectly, Tartar.

The khans of the Golden Horde, the successors of Genghis, held the Russians in subjection for a century and a half. During all this period, called by the Russians the *Tatarstvo,* the Russians were, in effect, living in Asia, and took no part in the intellectual upheaval that drew Europe from the Middle Ages into modern times, the Renaissance. Except for the persistence of the Orthodox Church, an inheritance from the moribund Byzantine Empire, they might well have become part of Islamic civilization. The Muscovite autocratic government, its bureaucracy, its methods of administration and communication, were Tatar, and much of its social underpinnings. Peter the Great pulled the caftans and the beards off the Russian boyars, but he could not really make them part of European civilization. In the eighteenth century the Russians finally had their renaissance, but they lost much of their more Europeanized, educated class in the Bolshevik Revolution. Even today the Russian masses are not really part of our civilization, but to a great extent are still mired in the Third World.

Yet since Ivan the Terrible the Russians have been on the offensive against the Turko-Tatars, taking over the two khanates of the Golden Horde on the Volga. Catherine the Great conquered the last khanate of the horde in Crimea, as Russian armies slowly pushed the Ottoman Turks back first from the southern Ukraine, then from present-day Rumania and Bulgaria.

In the course of the nineteenth century, after a series of wars with Turkey and Iran, the Russians annexed the northern part of Iranian Azerbaijan, as well as Georgia, and after decades of bloody mountain warfare subdued the Moslem tribes of the central Caucasus.

Then they began their conquest of Turkistan. In 1865 they took Tashkent, and twenty years later had annexed all of Turkistan to the Afghan border, allowing the emirs of Bukhara and Khiva to continue to rule puppet states, enclaves in the Russian province.

But the Russians did not attempt to settle this vast territory, already occupied by millions of pastoral tribesmen, oasis farmers, and townsmen. Nor did they interfere with their Islamic religious institutions, nor their culture.

This all changed with the Bolshevik Revolution. As a result of Bolshevik excesses and general anti-Russian sentiment, there was a large-scale uprising against Soviet rule. The rebels, known as the Basmachi, found a natural leader in the former Ottoman general Enver Pasha and at first enjoyed considerable success, but eventually were crushed by the Red Army. The last spark of resistance died when Enver was killed near the Afghan border in August 1922.

The Soviets split up Turkistan. Previously its four Turkic-speaking peoples acknowledged one literary language, Chagatai Turkish, and the Iranian-speaking Tajiks used literary Persian, both of which were written in Arabic characters. These five dialects were now each given separate status as written languages, using the Cyrillic alphabet — quite incompatible with their pronunciation — to cut them off from each other, from their common historical literature and neighboring Moslem peoples. Each of these linguistic units was formed into a separate Soviet republic.

Although in Transcaucasia nationalism was strong enough for all three nations — Azerbaijan, Georgia, and Armenia — to break away from Russia after the revolution, they were overwhelmed by the Red Army in the winter of 1920–21.

Yet nationalism, the greatest of all ideological forces throughout the last two centuries, has not died out in these Russian colonies, even under the suffocating rule of the most complete police state ever known in the world. During World War II, despite the Germans' racist ideology, which had no appeal to these Asian peoples, many of them deserted from the Soviet forces and some were formed into units by the Germans to fight their Russian masters.

When the German troops succeeded in occupying Crimea, the Crimean Tatars joined them en masse, and after the war what remained of the population was deported from its homeland and erased from the map as a people. The same thing happened when the Germans reached the northwestern rim of the Caucasus, and the Chechen and Ingush nations went over to them; they too were deported after the war — though the survivors were later allowed to return.

At the end of the war most Caucasian and Central Asian deserters and prisoners of war in Central and Western Europe were rounded up and forcibly returned to the Soviet Union by French, British, and American forces, but some managed to escape the dragnet and join the vast, miserable hordes of displaced persons.

It was among these that I had to search for announcers for the programs we were planning to introduce in their languages on the VOA. There were very few recent immigrants from either the Caucasus or Central Asia in the United States, and I had to go to Munich and interview displaced persons from the various nationalities. Then we faced the problems of security clearance and immigration. Thus, not surprisingly, my tour was up at the VOA before these programs were ready to go on the air, and after my departure they were all duly incorporated into the Russian section, just as their ancestors were incorporated into the Russian Empire.

26

The Beauties of the Bosphorus

As AGREED, I returned to CIA headquarters at the beginning of 1951, resuming a career that lasted until the end of 1974.

My official statement on my service in the Central Intelligence Agency, signed on the occasion of my departure to join the Chase Manhattan Bank, reads: "My overseas posts were in the Near East and Western Europe, always as Chief of Station. In Headquarters successively as Branch Chief, Chief of Operations, and Deputy Division Chief, and served as Division Chief of two Divisions in succession during the final years of service in the Agency."

Bound as I am by the terms of my service, I cannot give the exact nature of these assignments nor their time frame, nor do I wish to do so, as our relationships with nations with whom we have agreements and individuals whose role is still classified would be compromised. But these constraints will not affect the flow of my story; most readers will not mind the substitution of a pseudonym for a real name not needed for substance; and exact dates of personal experiences, and my title at the time they took place, are irrelevant.

During all these years both with the Agency and the bank I have visited or lived in almost all the countries of the Islamic world. During my military tour in Iran, I reached my nearest point, Meshed, to the physical Samarkand. Still, of course, Samarkand was not a physical goal of my search, but a spiritual one. I wanted to find out for myself — and pass on to policymakers — the truths about the great Islamic world, a civilization on the brink of change, of blending into the global social systems that had their roots in the West. I thought, as a Westerner, I had acquired unique preparation for this search, which has occupied the greater part of my life.

After leaving the VOA, I slowly lost touch with my new Soviet Moslem contacts. I did meet a few Soviet Moslem leaders, mostly dating from post–World War I days, in Istanbul in later years. However, in Turkey they were restricted in their activities. Mustafa Kemal was opposed to political pan-Turanism, since he wanted to establish Turkey as a separate nation, divorced from its Ottoman past, and this remains the national philosophy. Yet Turkic refugees from the Soviets are still welcome in Turkey, where Kazak tribesmen fleeing from Afghanistan have found a home. Also, Turkish language purists over the years have waged a partially successful campaign to replace Persian and Arabic loan words with others drawn from the old Turkic vocabulary.

I did eventually have a chance to improve my knowledge of the Turkish language, as Lucky and I for a time occupied a house in Bebek, a few miles up the Bosphorus from Istanbul. It was a one-storied house, with a large living room and porch looking over the Bosphorus. I have always found it satisfying to live near the water, and the Bosphorus was a continual source of pleasure then. Today, alas, this same view in Bebek is obstructed by ugly new buildings.

In our day it was a comparatively quiet place, in the shadow of the tower and walls of Rumeli Hisar, built by Mohammed the Conqueror in 1452 in preparation for his final assault on Constantinople. Its twin on the Asian side of the Bosphorus was Anadolu Hisar, also the work of Mohammed. Rumeli Hisar sheltered some of the houses of Robert College, a comfortable presence in the background.

Along the Bosphorus passed a continual procession of boats and ships of various sizes, including great tankers, freighters, and warships from the Soviet part of the Black Sea. A ferry constantly crisscrossed the water between the European and the Asian side, where one could still see a few old-fashioned wooden Turkish summer homes, *yalis,* overhanging the banks. In the morning and evening alike from our porch we contemplated the passing scene. At night we watched the lights of the small craft fishing out the delights of the next day's table — especially that most succulent of fish, the *lufer*; swordfish soon to be spitted as kebab; and five- or ten-pound lobsters, as large as a small pet. In fact, someone once put a leash to one in our kitchen! A few miles up the Bosphorus, in the village of Therapia, we often went to a Greek restaurant where they pulled these huge lobsters up from a cage beneath a trap door in the center of the room for us to admire before they went to the chef.

We had many friends living on the Bosphorus, mostly from the American expatriate community. One of the houses we frequented was that of A. V. Walker, a tall, spare Bostonian in his seventies who, with his sharp features and blue eyes, looked like a traditional Puritan Yankee. He had spent much of his life in business in Bulgaria, and his house was a Mecca for Bulgarian exiles. With this interest, it is not surprising that he shared the Bulgarian's traditional dislike of the Turks.

Thus there were few Turkish guests at the Sunday night dinners at his house; most of the guests were fellow expatriates. He served excellent dinners but was opposed to the use of alcohol, which somewhat dampened the atmosphere at the dinner table, where a vapid Turkish nonalcoholic "wine" was passed. Perhaps, though, it was just as well for our performance at the bridge tables to which we invariably repaired after dinner. In any case, I sometimes smuggled a flask in with me to doctor the orange juice served with bridge, and others would remark on the strange hilarity that prevailed at our table.

This transgression otherwise remained unnoticed; had I been caught I might not have been asked back to the house, as there was only one person who dared openly defy A.V.'s ban on alcohol — George Wadsworth, my old friend from earlier days in Syria and Lebanon, now U.S. ambassador to Turkey. He simply could not accept the prospect of a dinner not preceded by martinis, and always brought along a huge shaker of them to A.V.'s house, which he served to us all under our host's disapproving stare.

Other friends lived in Kandilli, on the Asian side, and we would cross in a small boat at night to dine with them. We often banded together for a boating expedition either on the Bosphorus or to one of the islands on the Sea of Marmara.

Among the Turks we met, perhaps the most interesting was a friend of my grandfather's, Rauf Orbay. He had been Turkish naval attaché in Washington during the T.R. era, and he remembered with gratitude how Grandfather took him to visit one of the first submarines of the American fleet. He subsequently distinguished himself commanding the Turkish navy in World War I — and here he was to greet us so many years later. We visited him in the home of his daughter and grandchildren, and sitting in a garden with these charming people descended from a man of the old regime, one had a fleeting sense of being transported back in time to a more genteel, Ottoman Istanbul.

Istanbul itself was a collection of splendid ruins in the middle of what was, then at least, a run-down Third World city, like a bag lady with a raddled face overlying the fine bones of a once-beautiful woman.

I admit I was discouraged by my first sight of Istanbul. Coming from the airport, we passed through crumbling reddish-brick Byzantine walls, into narrow, often unpaved streets, lined with squalid houses and shops. But later, driving toward the Bosphorus, crossing the Golden Horn, with the Sea of Marmara glimmering on our right, we found ourselves in the midst of its many gems — Santa Sophia, Top Kapi Sarai, the great mosques, the huge covered bazaar, the many tiled fountains — and we knew we were in the presence of greatness, vanished only yesterday.

Here and there in my wanderings in the Arab world I had sensed the ghostly presence of the Ottoman Empire, and all Istanbul was pervaded with it. Approached from the sea, at a distance, with its spires and minarets, it is like a vision of fairyland — but as you come nearer, alas, a fairyland forlorn, in a setting unmatched for beauty anywhere I have been.

On our first wedding anniversary, Lucky gave me a lovely book called *Beauties of the Bosphorus,* by Julia Pardoe, written in the midst of the Crimean War. The engravings in the book, by W. H. Bartlett, give one a feel for Istanbul's glories when all those exquisite palaces were filled with the denizens of this lost empire, wearing the splendid costumes their descendants have abandoned for the drab attire of the West.

I'm afraid my reciprocal gesture left something to be desired. Lucky had become a regular customer at Istanbul's Grand

Bazaar, where her Lebanese background stood her in good stead. She was an accomplished bargainer, and invariably returned from these expeditions with a treasure or two; the ones I liked best were relics of Old Russia, sold after the revolution by desperate refugees who had made their way there from Odessa. I was always told to stay silent when I accompanied her to one of these shops, since I couldn't help sympathizing with the shopkeeper as he recounted his family woes to justify a high price. I claimed that the shopkeepers wept when they saw her coming — but of course they enjoyed the exchange as much as she did.

So, on this wedding anniversary, a wet and dreary day, it seemed logical for me to suggest that we shop in the bazaar for her present, and I was surprised when tears started pouring down her face, mingling with the rain. It seems instead that I should have surprised her, and I have tried to remember to do so ever since.

We often drove down from Bebek to Istanbul just to sample the delights of the city, renowned restaurants such as Pandeli's or Abdullah's, and nightclubs featuring belly dancers. Although the leading hotel was the Park, it had seen better days when it was a notorious hangout for the OSS and other intelligence services during World War II. Its orchestra used to strike up the song "Boo Boo Baby I'm a Spy" each time a member of these services dropped by.

Istanbul was still an intelligence center during my stay there. It was the place of asylum for many refugees from Bulgaria and, to a lesser degree, Rumania. While most of these looked on Turkey, once an enemy state, simply as a way station, this was not the case with the Bulgarian Turks, some thousands of whom were allowed to emigrate legally to be resettled in Anatolia by the Turkish government. Turkey has also long been a haven for fugitives from the Caucasus and Central Asia.

Naturally, the Soviets as well as ourselves looked on Istanbul as an important source of intelligence, and their embassy was well staffed. It was there that in August 1945 a top Soviet intelligence officer, Konstantin Volkov, offered to defect to the British with important information on Soviet agents high in their Foreign Office and intelligence establishment in return for a well-rewarded asylum. Kim Philby, handling these negotiations in London, betrayed Volkov, who was whisked back to the Soviet Union on a stretcher. The Soviets had a fine embassy on the Bosphorus — as did many foreign embassies in those days — as a summer retreat from Ankara, and I was a visitor there and at others of these old-style summer embassies, dating from the days when Istanbul was the capital of a mighty empire.

But alas, the United States no longer kept an embassy there, and the ambassador and his staff had only the use of their stark embassy building in unlovely Ankara. Nobody I met, Turks or foreigners, liked Ankara, baked by the sun of the Anatolian plateau in summer, gloomy in the winter rain, and with few trees to enliven the fall and the spring in between. Several Turkish friends repeated to me an ancient joke about Ankara. Question: "What is the best time in Ankara?" Answer: "The moment the train leaves for Istanbul!"

And a fine train it was — and perhaps still is. It was a survivor from the Orient Express, with old-fashioned sleeping cars, porters, and dining room, vanished luxuries of another generation. The most enjoyable parts of the trip itself were the pretty villages, lake, and countryside just before arriving in Uskudar, facing Istanbul, and the ferry trip across the mouth of the Bosphorus, where we would sit in genial companionship on long benches during the short, anticipatory crossing.

Actually, our stays in Ankara were usually very pleasant, with my old friend George Wadsworth as ambassador. He almost always asked Lucky and me to stay at his residence, set in the middle of a large, tree-bordered lawn. There we lived in the lap of luxury, tended by a staff especially solicitous because one of their paragons was a Druze.

It was in Ankara that I was to learn to enjoy the full scope of George Wadsworth's unusual personality. Wadsworth was an ambassador not only of the old school, but of such an old school that nobody but himself remembered it. He believed that the ambassador's place should be in his residence, not an office in the chancery, and he practically never set foot in the embassy offices. He would tell the story of a German ambassador in prewar Washington whose successor paid him a visit to be briefed on his new assignment. Asking about the embassy offices, the newcomer was told by the veteran ambassador, "I don't know anything about them — I've never been inside the place."

Also, Wadsworth's office hours at home did not correspond with those of the embassy. He did all his writing at night, working till early morning, rousing his subordinates from their beds to confer with him when needed. I myself, whenever we went out to dinner, used to tiptoe past his study door on our return, hoping to make it to the guest room. But I never did — he had sharp ears, and would call me in, saying, "Archie, have a look at this cable and see what you think."

Naturally, he did not hold court in the morning, and when sometimes I took the plane from Istanbul to Ankara, I'd arrive at the residence at lunchtime — to have breakfast with him!

In the evening, when not involved in official entertainment, he would invite a few friends in for dinner, and bridge, one of his two great passions. Unfortunately for us, this included those martinis, that most deadly of potions, and before dinner a tray of them was passed around. Lucky did not drink much except wine, and I never touched those things at night, but Wadsworth was insistent. He also appreciated good wine, and after dinner a good brandy. Here Lucky drew the line — but I'm afraid I succumbed. It did not affect his tournament-class bridge game — but it certainly did ours. At least we could crawl off to bed afterward, while he repaired to his study to put in a night's work.

His other passion besides bridge was golf, and it was once more his fate — as it had been in Jerusalem a few years before — to be posted to a country where the game was unknown. Resolved to remedy this state of affairs, he recruited a number of fellow diplomats, dragooned members of his own staff, and shamed his Turkish contacts into starting a local golf club. He explained to dubious Turks that golf was the emblem of a modern nation. As this was something they all very much wanted to belong to, they dutifully, at great expense, imported golf clubs and took up the game.

In no time the club became the social center of Ankara. Our embassy staff and the Ankara diplomatic establishment soon learned that since Wadsworth was unavailable mornings, which were set aside for ambassadorial slumber, even nonplayers had to follow him around the course to have a word with him — and hopefully avoid a midnight call.

The non-golf-playing Soviet embassy soon discovered that social contacts were more difficult for them, with *le tout* Ankara so much at the golf course. So the Soviet ambassador and one of his staff applied to join the club.

"Absolutely not," growled Wadsworth, when the applications reached him. "They don't play golf — they're just joining to follow us around and spy on us."

Despite Soviet enquiries, their applications remained unacknowledged. Then Wadsworth was called home on consultation and the Swiss ambassador, vice-president of the Ankara Golf Club, was left in charge of this prestigious organization. At that moment, he received a telegram from his Foreign Office saying that the Swiss government was asking the Soviets for their agreement to his appointment as ambassador to Moscow. Certainly not by coincidence, the very day the telegram arrived, the Soviet embassy in Ankara again made urgent enquiries about their applications for membership in the club. These were then instantly approved by the club's acting president.

When Wadsworth heard the news on his return, he was furious, but helpless to reverse the decision. "Now they'll be out there every day, with their big ears, spying on us."

Then he saw a silver lining and said to me a few hours later, "Well, anyway, I'm just not going to ask them to the Christmas dance."

This was to be a white-tie affair and Wadsworth was successfully building it up to be the social event of the year. "I wish I could ask you and Lucky," he said, "but it's only for club members."

He had urged us to join even though we were non-golfers, but we fended him off. I expressed scorn for the sycophantic members of his staff who had joined the club despite a complete lack of interest in golf.

One day, at one of our business breakfasts, he handed me some papers. "Here's your invitation to the Christmas ball — and two applications for you and Lucky to join the club. We're having a drive for a hundred-man membership and your applications are number ninety-nine and one hundred."

What could I do? We succumbed and, I must admit, enjoyed the ball. The Soviets, despite many phone calls, never received invitations.

I enjoyed Wadsworth and his eccentricities. In fact, Lucky and I grew to love him. But this was not the case with the embassy staff, who merely endured him and his dreadful office hours. He had a dictatorial manner, and did not suffer fools gladly, nor anyone who showed the slightest sign of what we now term wimpishness. Nevertheless, he was respected and even admired by most of his long-suffering staff.

I was sorry to part from him a few months later, but felt sure our paths would cross again. Turkey was being administratively shifted to Europe by the State Department and the Agency, and Wadsworth and I would be bound to find each other once more in the Arab world.

I was also very glad, however, to have had this opportunity to learn firsthand a bit about Turkey and the Turks. The Turks are a great and courageous people who have proved their friendship with us many times, most notably on the battlefields of Korea. They stand bravely in the front line of Western defense. After years of rejecting their Middle Eastern past — a necessity in order to assert their own Turkish national identity and gain acceptance as a European power — they are now renewing their Asian ties, serving as a bridge between the two continents. I expect them to emerge once more in the future as leaders in a new Middle East, now that they can again take pride in their Ottoman past. And a new Istanbul is coming to life, to encompass in dignity the grandeur of the old.

PART SIX

Lands of the Faith

27

The Holy Land

SEVERAL TIMES in my early career I heard senior military officers justify the selection of an officer with no prior knowledge of or experience in an area by saying, "He will be able to give us the best possible evaluation of the situation there without the biases associated with prior knowledge. He'll be writing on a clean slate."

That pretty well described my own situation on my first trip to what was then Palestine. I had been previously involved only in the western fringe of the Arab world, and had not had time to focus on what was to become its major issue in years to come. I had excellent introductions, both from American official sources and my own private ones, but very little knowledge of the country and its problems.

And yet, of course, I knew the Holy Land. I had been brought up on the Bible and the literature of the Middle Ages, when the Holy Land was the lodestar of Christendom. So it was only natural for me to be touched by the mystique of Palestine, walking in the footsteps of thousands of pilgrims who had gone with cowl and staff before me.

When I arrived in Cairo in the spring of 1944 to join the ranks of the Joint Intelligence Committee, Middle East (JICME), Palestine and the Levant States became my area of responsibility, and early on a May morning I set out with my cousin Kermit Roosevelt for my first trip to Palestine.

Kim had actually arrived in Cairo before I did, on assignment for the OSS. I don't believe his mission came about by an arbitrary decision by his superiors. Rather, it may have resulted from what I had said in Washington about the future importance of the Middle East. In any case, I was glad to see him, for he was, then and later, an excellent traveling companion who shared my interests, tastes, and even sense of humor.

We left Cairo by car, along with a marine captain and his casual girlfriend. I had a bad case of "Gyppy tummy," and as we passed through the Land of Goshen and the wilderness of Sinai I thought I was about to die — until we crossed into the Land of Israel. Then I suddenly perked up and our passage through biblical settings — Beersheba, Hebron, and Bethlehem — seemed like a dream: the stony hills of Judea with their terraced gardens and little stone villages surrounded by olive trees, the Arab men all in kufiyyas, and the women in black robes embellished with brightly colored embroideries.

It was evening when we approached Jerusalem, with the light fading on the hills of Moab across the Dead Sea and the River Jordan. I had expected to feel like Godfrey de Bouillon, viewing the Holy City for the first time at the head of his column of mailed warriors of the Cross. Instead it seemed "a rather nondescript city which is lovely only because it is in those hills," as I first wrote — an opinion soon reversed!

We spent the night at the YMCA and beginning the next morning, it was politics, politics, politics. As I had expected, because of my excellent contacts, I got into the swing right away and we were soon swamped with interviews and invitations.

One of my first interviews was with Eliahu Epstein — the Jewish Agency's Arab expert whom I had met in Cairo. A man of extraordinary breadth of knowledge and understanding, he had spent months living among the Bedouins. Later, under the name of Eliahu Elath, he became Israel's ambassador to the United States and president of Hebrew University in Jerusalem.

I also had a friend on the Arab side. It turned out that my Arabic tutor at Harvard, Awni Dejany, was now a lawyer in the firm of one of the top political leaders, Musa Alami, and I got a royal welcome from him.

We were going on to Damascus from Jerusalem, and Eliahu arranged for us to visit two kibbutzim on our way north. He assigned a young Jewish Agency intelligence officer to accompany us, Teddy Kollek, whom many of us know now as the revered mayor of Jerusalem. Then he was just over thirty, with tousled blond hair, a kibbutznik originally from Vienna. Kim and I took to him at once, and he invited us to spend the night en route to Syria at his home kibbutz of Ein Gev.

Kollek drove us through the Judean hills, the plain of Esdraelon and Nazareth, and to the kibbutz of Degania. There we took an old launch down the shore of the Sea of Galilee, where fishermen were spreading and drawing in their nets. "One of the charms of this place," I wrote in my diary, "is the association with all you have read ever since you were a child — Christ meeting the two brothers mending their nets and saying you shall be fishers of men, Christ walking on the water, stilling the winds. . . ."

Arriving at Ein Gev, we found that Teddy had arranged for us to ride up the hills to the Syrian village of Fiq, on the Golan Heights, for dinner with the local mayor. So in the late afternoon we set out, riding without a bridle — only a halter, surprisingly easy because of the wonderful horses. The party included Teddy, a political officer from Ein Gev, and the sheikh of the adjoining Arab settlement: a classic type, in a kufiyya and brown aba, or cloak, with gold bordering.

I seized an opportunity to question the sheikh privately about his political opinions, or rather, lack of them: "We are simple folk and leave all these things to our leader, Jamal Husseini." Asked about his relations with the Jews, he said that his fellow villagers got on well with their Jewish neighbors, who gave them help with irrigation and farm equipment. My Jewish friends told me that these Arab villagers conducted raids against distant villages, not their neighbors. (In Arab mores, one has a special duty to one's neighbor.)

We climbed up the steep and rocky mountains overlooking the sea to the ruined Greek city of Hippos, completely destroyed by the Romans in A.D. 70 after a long siege during the revolt of the Jews. Only the walls were left standing — the pillars had fallen and the houses were nearly all razed.

"It used to be a mighty city of the Roum [the Greeks] with two huge iron gates, one on the west and one on the east," the sheikh told us. "Finally the armies of the Moslems came, under Khalid ibn al-Walid, the Sword of Islam, and they laid siege to the city, but could not take it. Khalid prayed to Allah and was changed into the shape of a little boy, and was admitted to the gate. Then he resumed his manly form, and opened the gates to his warriors."

After looking over the city we went on to Fiq and rode through the village under the fascinated stares of its inhabitants.

The mayor turned out to be a very intelligent, modern, French- and American-educated Christian. Conversations in five languages — including Turkish and Russian — took place at dinner. However, a mild contretemps developed about Kim's field jacket, which had disappeared from his horse's back, where he had trustingly left it. Mounted policemen searched the entire district while we were at dinner, and the Arabs were concerned that we would think all Arabs were thieves. I suggested that maybe the horse had eaten it, and instead of laughing, they seriously protested that this was absolutely impossible!

Later the elders of the village came in, sat down, and stared at us — a row of solemn white-bearded figures. Finally, at about eleven, we left. There was no moon, and how the horses picked their way down those precipices is beyond me. Sometimes we got off and walked, but stumbled so much we had to get on again. The sheikh sang Arab songs and regaled us with stories. It was a lovely trip — in fact, the high point of our travels.

A few weeks later Kim and I returned to Jerusalem and were able to take enough time off from politics to see the holy places of the three religions. I was much more impressed by the shrine common to the Moslem and Jewish faiths, the site of the Temple and the Dome of the Rock, than by any of the Christian holy places, with one exception. This was the Garden of Gethsemane, where amid the silence, under centuries-old olive trees, one can feel the spirit of Jesus in the night of his spiritual agony.

The Church of the Holy Sepulchre, whose site is of dubious authenticity, I thought almost squalid, a travesty of the faith, distorted by the priestly hierarchies who have transformed religions based on love and compassion into instruments of intolerance and hatred. Every inch of the shrine is the property of one sect or another, with the powerless Ethiopian Copts relegated to the roof and the Protestant latecomers to the courtyard. A few months before, priests of one Orthodox sect had cut off the corner of a rug belonging to another, which they claimed infringed on their territory.

These battles between the Christian sects became so violent that beginning in the fifteenth century the Ottoman authorities had to install a Moslem official to keep the peace. By chance his traditional divan covered one of the tombs of the Crusaders set in the pavement, preserving it from the footsteps of pilgrims, which have obliterated the inscriptions on all the others. It is now protected by a grate, through which I could read the name of Philippe Daubigny, almost certainly a direct or collateral ancestor of mine. My mother's grandmother was a Dabney, descended from the well-known Huguenot Breton family of Daubigny (also spelled Daubigné), which produced a famous poet as well as Madame de Maintenon.

Except for these holy excursions, we spent two days visiting groups of Arabs and Jews. On the Arab side our most interesting new friend was Katie Antonius, whose late husband had written *The Arab Awakening*, the classic account of the rise of Arab nationalism — "clever, witty, charming, and fiery as hell" was my first impression of her.

The third day we went down to the Dead Sea with one of my favorite new friends, Eliahu Epstein. We looked over the potash factory where salts were extracted from water pumped up from the sea, got covered with bitter salt from head to foot, then explored the most interesting of the Jewish agricultural settlements we saw in Palestine.

The Dead Sea Valley is impregnated with salt, like the country around Salt Lake — the deadest-looking place I have ever seen. To make the land productive, the settlers covered stretches of land with fresh water for a year or two, which drove the salt down and washed the soil. Then screens had to be set up to block the hot winds from killing the crops. Another peril was the notorious Jericho boil, spread by the sand flea, and very painful, which often left an unsightly scar on the face. Jewish physicians had just developed an inoculation against it.

We went swimming in the Dead Sea. With prior experience in Salt Lake I knew I had to be careful not to get salt in my eyes. I wanted to make a tour of the sea and view the sites of Sodom and Gomorrah, but there was no time. At least I got a look at the nearby Sodom and Gomorrah Golf Course, created by George Wadsworth.

The following day Nelson Glueck, the renowned archaeologist of the Nabataeans, took us over to Transjordan. He was a rabbi who loved the Nabataeans, an Arab people whose capital, Petra, was the famous "Rose Red City half as old as Time." But he had no use for the Arabs of today, whom he considered to be their unworthy barbarian successors.

We passed through the wilderness of Judea (absolutely barren hills, where Christ fasted forty days), down to the Jordan Valley, to Jericho, then across the Jordan. Talk about one wide river — it's about the width of a New York side street! While just leaving the Jordan Valley, the road passed through a mound, which Glueck told us was a Stone Age site. We stopped and Glueck picked up some pottery lying on the side of the road. Then we went on through a deep valley, with ruins of terraced agriculture all around, up the mountains to Es-Salt, and finally to Amman, ancient capital of the Ammonites and then the capital of Transjordan.

I was astonished by the green, rolling country, full of wheat and growing vineyards. I had supposed it was all desert. Glueck told us that all this strip across the Jordan and the Dead Sea — ancient Moab, Edom, and Ammon — used to be full of forests, fields, and vineyards, but finally the Bedouins broke through, laying waste the land, which became ruined by erosion. The Turks cut down much of the remaining forest to feed the railroad to Mecca. Only since World War I was the land beginning to show signs of life again and the Bedouins were settling down. Almost every hill was covered by a ruin.

South of Amman we met many armed Bedouins, with their goats, sheep, camels, and horses. These all belonged to the Beni Sakhr, who before the last war were nearly 100 percent nomad or seminomad.

We did not visit any Jordanians during our tour; it would not have been politic. Dr. Glueck was not persona grata with the authorities.

Returning to Jerusalem, the next day we lunched at Musa Alami's country home — a delightful spot in a village not far from Jerusalem. And in accordance with our "evenhanded" policy, that evening we had dinner with Eliahu, who waxed mystical about the three cities where one could feel the living presence of the people of the ancient world. It was true that the streets of Jerusalem, like those of Rome and Athens, seemed haunted.

The next day we went to have drinks and sandwiches with

David Ben-Gurion in Tel Aviv. "A real prophet of Israel," I wrote. He had a mane of white hair floating on each side of his head and talked to us in a prophetic vein for two hours straight. What I liked most about him was a twinkle in his eye. We all refused whiskey, knowing how rare it was and not wanting to use his last, but he said, "I know you want it, why don't you take it." We liked him from that moment.

We were accompanied by Captain Nicolas Andronovich, attached to the U.S. consulate in Jerusalem. Nick still had (and has) his Russian accent, and motherly Mrs. Ben-Gurion took a great shine to him. After ascertaining that he was not yet married, she spoke of an absent daughter and expressed the hope that he would return sometime soon to meet her. Then she suddenly asked, "Are you Orthodox?" and when Nick replied in the negative there was no further mention of the daughter.

"But, Nick," I protested on the drive back, "you are Russian Orthodox, aren't you?"

"Yes, but that's not what she meant," he said, wiser than I in the ways of Israel.

I returned many times to Jerusalem in the course of the next few years. On one visit, I crossed the desert from Baghdad in the company of Colonel Paul Converse. I lunched again with Musa Alami. Musa expressed great distress at the stepped-up immigration of Jews, for which he blamed the Americans. Then I had tea with Teddy Kollek, who told me that most of his people thought the new quota, fifteen hundred a month, unacceptably low! Teddy introduced me to Abba Eban, then a major in the British army. A top orientalist about to take a chair at London University, he was then deputy commander of the British Arabic School for budding political officers in Jerusalem. He later served as Israeli ambassador to Washington and the United Nations and then as foreign minister. I was also fascinated to meet the chief of the British Arabic School, the famous Bertram Thomas, former British political officer renowned for his crossing of the Empty Quarter of Arabia.

The main purpose of this trip was to visit Transjordan and meet the legendary Amir Abdullah, brother of King Feisal of Iraq and grandfather of King Hussein of Jordan, in his palace on the highest hill of Amman. He was wearing his customary large white turban, and stroked his beard as he spoke, over

coffee and pomegranate juice, of the "mess in Europe," with
the Allies "all quarreling in Germany" — his view of the beginnings of the Cold War there. We were interrupted as he heeded
a call to prayer, but saw him again at the opening of parliament
the following day.

At this ceremony, as supposedly distinguished guests, Colonel Converse and I sat on the dais to the left of the speaker,
with ministers and foreign consuls. To our right was the Amir,
with the British resident and the heir to the throne, Talal, a
sour-looking man with a moustache, known to be at odds with
his father. Facing us were some thirty deputies, mostly wearing
tarbushes, with a few Circassians in lambskin caps and a couple
of Bedouin sheikhs.

Then in came Glubb Pasha, British commander of the Arab
Legion, a spare, small man with a large scar running down his
chin and neck, his chest blazing with medals and stars. He
looked at us with his sharp gray eyes, obviously annoyed to see
us sitting there, and I thought we had perhaps taken his seat.
When the resident's secretary urged him to sit down, he waved
impatiently and stood huffily against the wall throughout the
session.

All rose as the Amir entered. "As my speech is a little long,"
he said, "please be seated." Then the speaker read the speech
from the throne. For the first time the Amir requested that
Transjordan be granted her independence. He expressed the
hope that Britain would stand by her white paper on Palestine
and the United States by its statement that the Arabs would be
consulted on the future of the mandate.

After the speech, the Amir left and we all filed out to a
military parade in front of the building. Later we called on
Glubb. He was not pleased to see us but at least favored us with
some comments: "It is a mistake for this country to have an
army separate from the police force. It is of no use against
foreign foes, and serves only for internal control. It will run the
country as soon as we get out. We cannot expect the Arabs in
just a few years to adopt the institutions and concepts we have
taken hundreds of years to develop. All we need is a strong
police force capable of taking care of tribal disturbances."

Yet this was the man who organized the Arab Legion, the
only Arab force that later gave a good account of itself in the
1948 war with the Israelis. Glubb was too much an old-line

British political officer to last in King Hussein's independent Jordan. And after his departure, an army chief of staff did indeed try to take over the country. But his coup attempt failed, and the Jordanian army, descendant of the Arab Legion, today loyally supports King Hussein.

During my trips to the Holy Land I met virtually all the Jewish and Arab political leaders. The points of view that separated Arab and Jew in Palestine at that time, before the creation of Israel, can be summarized much more simply than they could be today.

The Jews, in general, believed Palestine was their original homeland, and that the Jews of the world should be allowed to "return" there. The Arabs wanted to limit further Jewish immigration, which they saw as a threat to an Arab Palestine state for which they hoped to gain independence. The land occupied by the Jews had been bought by them from Arab owners, and their lodging for the most part they had built themselves. There had been no forced seizure of Arab lands, no evictions of Arab homeowners, and no Arab refugees — and, of course, no nation of Israel.

The Mufti Hajj Amin el-Husseini, who headed the Arab Higher Committee, had established himself in Germany during the war and thrown in his lot with Hitler. He was not popular with other Arab Palestinian politicians, most of whom looked to the leadership of Jamal Husseini, who came from another branch of the same family and did not share the pro-German position of the Mufti.

In his absence the most respected Palestinian leader was his brother-in-law, Musa Alami. Scion of an ancient Jerusalem family, a Cambridge law graduate, he was to play a key role, with Prime Minister Nuri Sa'id of Iraq, in forming the Arab League.

Musa was not by nature a politician. It seemed to me that this role had almost been forced on him. He loved his farm, off the road to Bethlehem, which he was to lose during the creation of Israel. He was fundamentally a humanitarian, and loved all mankind. It was not in his heart to hate the Jews, and alas, this doomed him as a politician in the violence of the events of 1948 and afterward. He then bent his efforts to improving the lot of those dispossessed by the war, especially their children. He set up the Arab Development Society to create a farm on the salt flats near the Dead Sea, surrounding a village and school for orphaned children. Despite tragedy, both personal and professional — his wife left him, and his farm was twice destroyed, once by an Arab mob and once by the Israeli army — he persisted in his project. He died in 1984, but his farm for refugee orphans, under the Arab Development Society, lives on.

On the Jewish side there were also men of goodwill toward the Arabs, but not in the top leadership. They were too close to the war of extermination waged against them in Europe to contemplate the brotherhood of man. In fact, the numerous young Jewish intellectuals we met in Palestine we found to be remarkably unconcerned about the Arabs. They discussed the future as if the Arabs did not exist.

There was one notable exception — Dr. Judah Magnes, president of Hebrew University, to whom I had an introduction from David de Sola Pool. He invited me, sight unseen, for a Sabbath evening with his family. It was the only time I was to meet with this remarkable man but I vividly remember sitting down at table with him, as he placed a yarmulke on my head. "The Jews and the Arabs are too close to each other to be drawn apart by political passions," he said. "After a generation or two they will get along, as the Arab standard of living rises to bring them up to the same level as the European Jews, to make it easier for them to understand each other."

He and his small group of followers believed that the only way for the two peoples to live together in peace was to form a binational state, with each people under its own leaders, joined in an administrative whole.

But the fate of Palestine was not to be in the hands of men like Judah Magnes and Musa Alami. If it had, the olive-clad hills of Judea would not, once more, have been drenched in the blood of peoples slaughtered and slaughtering in the name of God.

During the next couple of years, men of goodwill both in Palestine and the outside world in the United Nations sought a formula for peaceful coexistence for the forces of Zionism and Arab nationalism. But the search was in vain, and it became apparent that armed conflict was inevitable.

The question of Jewish immigration, the big issue in Palestine during my visits in 1944–46, gave way to the larger question of the future of the British mandate in Palestine, and what would replace it. As both British foreign minister Ernest Bevin and President Truman supported stepped-up Jewish immigration, protests in the Arab world were coupled with a demand for an independent Palestinian state, countered by Zionist insistence on a Jewish state. At the end of July 1946, Jews and Arabs alike rejected an Anglo-American Conference proposal for a federal state uniting both peoples.

When a London conference failed to reach agreement in January 1947, Bevin turned the problem over on February 18 to the United Nations, which formed the Special Committee on Palestine (UNSCOP). This committee, after several months of meetings in the Lake Success UN headquarters, as well as in Jerusalem, Beirut, and Geneva, voted on November 29, 1947, for a plan to partition Palestine. The vote was strongly favored by Zionists, backed by the United States. The few supporters of Judah Magnes and others advocating a binational state were overwhelmed.

The Arabs unanimously opposed partition, but for different reasons than those of Dr. Magnes. Under the terms of partition, the Jews formed only half the population of the 56 percent of Palestine allotted to them, and had previously owned only a tenth of the land, while the area allotted to the Arabs was almost entirely Arab in population and ownership.

Yet the Arabs, we know by hindsight, would have been wise to accept partition, especially since it provided for the internationalization of Jerusalem. Their principal reason for rejecting it was not its unequal distribution of territory, but their Arab nationalist belief that Palestine was, and must be forever, an Arab state. Thus they institutionalized the conflict between two nations claiming the same land, which has endured until today.

Before the final vote on the UN plan, the Arab League met in September in the Lebanese hill town of Sofar — where I visited them in the company of my cousin Kim. We didn't learn much from the delegates while the meeting was in session, but their decision to oppose the UNSCOP plan and set up a military committee to prepare for armed confrontation was announced at the closing session. Military preparations were already under way when, the following month, I sat in on a press briefing held by my old acquaintance, Arab League president Azzam Pasha.

The military committee had established an Arab Liberation

Army, and Azzam said elements of it were already moving to the Palestine frontier. I had a chance to talk to him after the briefing, and he told me that he expected the Palestinian Arabs to rise in revolt as soon as an attempt was made to implement the UNSCOP plan. Outside Arab forces would then move in.

The announcement of the UN decision to implement the UNSCOP partition plan on November 29 set in march the fatal chain of events that continues today. The following day the Haganah — the principal Jewish defense force — called on all Jews in Palestine to register. The Arabs called a general strike. The sound of gunfire began to be heard once more in Palestine, silent since the end of the Arab revolt in 1939. A mob in Damascus attacked our embassy there, tore down and burned the flag along with three cars. A student demonstration in Beirut the following day aroused little response, as Lebanon at that time was not much concerned with events next door.

At this point I found myself in Beirut. In its inscrutable wisdom, Washington decided I was just the man to go have a firsthand look at Palestine.

I didn't want to go at all. In the first place, my driver couldn't come because he didn't have the necessary papers. He was a Moslem and it would have been nice to have him along. Next, the car, an old one I had never driven before, seemed to have plenty of things wrong with it. But I was ordered to go and so I did. There were no candidates to accompany me, and conditions on the road were precarious. I started at 6:00 A.M. and by 8:00 I had reached the frontier. At first the Lebanese customs officer was inclined to make trouble over letting my car through — it had no papers whatsoever. Fortunately, foreseeing this possibility, I had asked Don Bergus, who happened to have possession of the consular seal, to fabricate an impressive paper for me. Before letting me pass, the customs man had to rouse his superior officer, but the paper did it. It was a pretty one.

On the Palestine side — at Ras Naqqura — the British policeman advised me to ask for a police escort at Haifa, and even asked if I wanted one from there. "They don't like you chaps very much, you know." I was damned if I'd ask for anything and give our British cousins that much satisfaction.

Two Arabs, a peasant and a customs official, asked for a lift to Akka; I gave them one, nothing loath to have a conspicuous kufiyya and *agal* (headband) in the car with me. I knew that any car without a British army plate, or not filled with Arabs, would be considered Jewish and treated accordingly.

As we drove off, I happened to look in the rearview mirror, and had the pleasure of seeing one of the Arabs at the frontier post walk up to my tire tracks and spit after me.

Meanwhile I was running out of gas, and had to stop to get some at an Arab gas station. They were, or I imagined them to be, cold and hostile, and I was glad to drive off.

Believing as I do in getting right to the point, I engaged my two passengers in conversation on the Palestine situation. It didn't take much to get them started. They were very *"muta'assabin"* — a word that means something between nervous, angry, and fanatical — and when the Arabs are in that mood, almost anything is likely to happen. They said, "We will fight, and we don't care if we have to fight the whole world until we die, but partition will not take place!"

Later I asked them if they thought it would be safe for me to take the Nablus road, running through Arab hill country, where they had been putting stones in the road, stopping cars, and asking passengers to prove they were not Jewish. Sometimes they would inspect non-Arabs, thinking all Christians were uncircumcised, and assuming those circumcised were Jewish. Fortunately, I was not subjected to this examination, which I would have failed.

The customs man assured me that I would be OK, that they were killing Jews, and not Americans, *yet.* "It's between us and the Jews. What have you got to do with it?" However, I decided that I would take the coast road, thus staying as much as possible in Jewish territory.

I let my passengers off at Akka, and took on a rather simple-looking peasant, with whom I didn't talk at all. A bad cold, the depressing atmosphere, and the rain, which fell from time to time, left me little desire to talk to anyone. The Arab tapped me on the shoulder and said he wanted to get out. He kept the door open and reached around in his pockets. Finally he came up with some change, which he offered me in return for the ride. I was flabbergasted, this being the first time this had ever happened. I pondered the rest of the way to Haifa, trying to decide if it was a sign of honesty and simplicity or a delicate oriental insult.

Then I picked up a Jew, who told me he could direct me through Haifa and tell me how to get on the Jerusalem road. He was from a collective farm in the plain of Esdraelon: a pleasant-looking youngish fellow with prominent features and a head of curly reddish brown hair. He originally came from Germany, so his English was weak, but he was a genial type and we got on very well. He said he was an actor, and liked music — he gave an excellent imitation of a trombone — but now he was a farmer. He liked his work and seemed very happy. I asked him how they got along with their Arab neighbors. "No trouble," he answered. "Friendship." "But aren't you worried about trouble now?" "No," he said, "we're prepared."

The main street of Haifa was split in two by high barbed wire, and heavily patrolled by soldiers and policemen. Just as we were passing through the Arab section, swarming with people, every one wearing the kufiyya, and apparently feeling *muta'as-sabin*, giving us dirty looks, the car started to stall! I managed to keep it going, but this was the first of a number of attempts on its part to interrupt our trip. Next day I read that a bomb had exploded that morning in the main street.

I was rather relieved to drop my Jewish friend at a village halfway between Haifa and Tel Aviv, and I picked up a couple of Arab peasants as I turned up toward Lydda. They were polite and pleasant, and helped me find the way before getting off at a very dilapidated Arab village on the plain. They were the only ones who did not seem worried about the future.

"How can you partition a little country like this?" they said. "It's absolutely impossible. Let's all be in one state, and we'll have our ministers, and they'll have theirs. But *taqsim* [partition] — impossible." Shortly after passing the Lydda airport I let them go with many salaams. As I approached the Judean hills, a whole raft of Arabs waved at me from a crossroad. I let only four of them into the car: two Arab auxiliaries and two peasants.

Shortly afterward, I was stopped by a police patrol — Arabs in tall astrakhan hats — who said, "You've got to turn back — they are shooting Jews on this road." I explained that I was an American, and the Arabs in the car urged the police to let me go, so they did. As we proceeded, the Arabs in the car kept talking very excitedly. I gathered that a band of Arabs had ambushed some Jews from the forest that covered the hills on this part of the Lydda-Jerusalem road, and a Jewish girl had been killed. The Arabs were indignant at a Jewish attack on a cinema, and they also must have done something in or near a mosque, as one old man kept insisting that mosques, churches, and synagogues were sacred and it wasn't right to shoot them up.

Every time I dropped off an Arab, I picked one up — they all seemed to know each other — and so I came into Jerusalem with four Arabs still in the car. The shops were all closed and people were milling about on the streets, which were tangled up with barbed wire. I dropped off my Arabs as I came to the heavily guarded zone in the area of the King David Hotel and our consulate. British Tommies patrolled everywhere.

At the consulate, they were amazed to see me. "How did you ever get into the area without a pass?" Blissfully ignorant of the pass system, I had driven with such assurance that none of the Tommies had stopped me. The people in the consulate felt cut off from the outside world and seemed to think of themselves as being in enemy territory. They were astonished that I had taken Arabs in my car, and were full of horror stories of mobs and looting in Transjordan, where Americans had to flee the country. But I found that once I established rapport with an Arab, I could relax. I remembered what Major Berkeley, the British officer in the Lower Euphrates tribal area, once told me: "If you establish a personal bond there's no excuse for getting killed by the Arabs." However, one can get knocked off by snipers — which is one reason I kept my car full of Arabs.

After a night at the YMCA, punctuated by occasional rifle and machine-gun fire, and the tramp of heavy Tommy boots in unison, I got off the next day. There was nobody on the road, and so I took no passengers. Once a Bedouin waved at me, but when I stopped, and he saw my non-Arab face, he turned away in shyness and said, "Go," waving his arm. The orange groves of the plains, full of "toiling peasants" of both races, seemed peaceful — though there had been pitched battles in Jaffa and Tel Aviv that night, and the firing had kept everyone awake. But when I got to Haifa, something was going on. We were routed up side roads, away from the main streets. Policemen were everywhere, pointing their guns uncertainly in all directions. There was shooting in town and I wasn't sorry to get out of it. In fact, I wasn't sorry to get to the border and find myself back in Lebanon, and heading for Beirut along the Mediterranean at sixty miles an hour.

I remained in Beirut, off and on, throughout what was to be the first in a series of Arab-Israeli wars, a witness from next door, if not directly on the scene.

Beirut was the ideal spot from which to watch the northern front and, indeed, much of the Arab side of the war. Thus a large number of newspaper correspondents flocked to the city, making the St. George Hotel bar their headquarters. With the exception of Sam Souki of the United Press, who knew the language, they had to rely on local stringers to keep them abreast of developments, and in the coming and going the bar almost resembled a railroad station.

I became close friends of *New York Times* correspondent Samuel Pope Brewer and his wife Eleanor, and spent many hours with them as Sam picked up and digested the news as it came from the front. Then, many drinks later, around midnight when most of the bar's denizens had left, Sam managed to tap out a masterly dispatch on the war.

Eleanor was a devoted wife. Like a medieval lady at her tapestry board in a castle tower, she sat at the Ritz knitting hour after hour as Sam pursued the news. I was astonished to learn some ten years later, after Sam returned to Beirut to cover the latest Middle East crisis, that Eleanor had left him. Not only that, but she had left him to marry a renegade Englishman she met at that very bar, which was also his favorite hangout. He was Kim Philby, visiting this traditional news headquarters in his capacity as Middle East correspondent for the *Observer* and the *Economist* of London, and also, unbeknownst to Eleanor, as a thirty-year veteran agent of the KGB.

Four years later, in January 1963, alerted that the game was up, Philby left Beirut suddenly for Moscow, to be joined in September by Eleanor. The following year, while she was in America passing a holiday with her daughter by Sam Brewer, Philby became entangled in a liaison with the wife of Donald Maclean, another British traitor in residence in Moscow. Though she did not for months really accept the truth of Philby's relationship, spring brought confrontation and separation, and in May Eleanor left Moscow for London.

I happened to be in London about the time she arrived there. I was sitting with Lucky looking out the window of our house when I saw her approaching the door — my first sight of her in fifteen years! I had only time to explain to Lucky who she was when she walked in. As I kissed her I noted a strong whiff of alcohol, and she immediately asked for a martini. Then, incoherently, she poured out bits and pieces of her story, her miserable life in Moscow, her alienation from Kim as a result of his affair with Melinda Maclean. After an hour or so she left us, tottering, and we made vague plans for another meeting. I think she just needed to find a friendly face in a moment of desperation. I never saw her again. Some time later she retired to Sidi Bou Said, in Tunisia, and not long after, cancer brought an end to her unhappiness.

The Israel I visited in later years is much changed from what I saw in those early times at the end of the pioneering period, and many of my old friends were gone. At least I could visit Eliahu Elath in his retirement, and also was several times the guest of Teddy Kollek, the great mayor of Jerusalem. Even as a patriotic Israeli, he is as well liked by the Arabs as is possible for one in his position — he is a man of understanding and humanity who deals with the whole community fairly and justly.

The change in Jordan is even more striking, but there I had few old friends to lose. In fact, my close association with that country did not really begin until 1956, when I first met King Hussein. He was only twenty-one years old at the time. Most of his contemporaries were just graduating from college, but that year and the one following marked his own passage from youth to maturity as crisis followed crisis in the Arab world.

In the early part of 1956 Hussein had to deal with the problem of Glubb Pasha, a symbol of Britain's imperial past who was now an anachronism in the Middle East. It was painful for Hussein, with his British training and close relationship with the Arab Legion, to dismiss this long-time friend of his family, but it had to be done.

Nineteen fifty-six was also the year of Nasser in the Middle East, of the Suez crises followed by Egypt's war with Israel, and the opening round of Nasser's campaign to lead the Arab world and eliminate its rival leaders, especially its kings. Hussein was the target of many attempts on his throne and his life, as first Syria, then Iraq, fell to the new extreme nationalist forces. With

a display of great personal courage, Hussein put down a coup
attempt by his army commander Ali Abu Nuwar. (Typical of
Hussein's greatness of spirit is the fact that Abu Nuwar,
pardoned, now lives quietly in Amman.) In 1958 his cousin
King Feisal of Iraq was overthrown and murdered by revolutionaries, and later in the year the Syrians tried to shoot down
Hussein's plane.

From the time I met him he impressed me as the finest, most
truly motivated leader of the Arab world. He speaks softly, but
with a voice that resonates and conveys his utter sincerity. He
knows that the Arab world needs the West and the United
States, despite our frequent signs of indifference to him, and
has handled the precarious situation of his country like the
master ruler he is.

Later, in England, Lucky and I made the acquaintance of his
younger brother, Prince Hassan, while he was a student at
Oxford in the mid-sixties. After I joined Chase Manhattan
Bank, I visited him and his growing family in Amman many
times, and consider Jordan's people fortunate to have such a
crown prince, in addition to their king.

King Hussein, and many men of goodwill — Arabs, Israelis,
and others — have sought in vain to bring about peace between
the Arabs and Israel. I cannot count myself among these, being
an intelligence officer, not a diplomat. Intelligence officers
have an obligation to provide an understanding of the constantly changing nature of the problem. The diplomats must
take it from there.

28

"Arabia, Where the Princes Ride at Noon"

I CAN REMEMBER the very moment my fascination with Arabia began. It was when, as a fourth-former at Groton, I read the news item about Ibn Saud's defeat of Imam Yahya of Yemen. After that I read avidly everything I could find about Arabia, and was delighted to discover that masterpiece by Charles Doughty, *Travels in Arabia Deserta,* in my father's own library. I acquired for my coin collection some silver pieces from the Himyarite kingdom of Yemen dating from the time of Christ.

From that moment dated my resolve to see Arabia for myself someday. And exactly eleven years later I paid my first visit there, in the company of Armin Meyer, my old friend the OWI chief in Baghdad. The general manager of the Bahrain Petroleum Company arranged for us to go to Dhahran, Saudi Arabia, as guests of the Arabian American Oil Company, so I embarked on one of their launches, filled with American oil workers. I had only a small bag with me, and one of the company told me to make sure I was not bringing any dolls for Aramco children, as they were forbidden entry, being considered idols. My informant told me that one time an oil party got into trouble for gathering the bones of fossils in the desert; a local government official reported that they were collecting them to set up idols. Then I told him that I was carrying a bottle of whiskey in my bag. He was horrified!

Armin Meyer solved the problem, good public relations man that he is. He had heard that one of the few Aramco wives in

Dhahran had introduced the art of waffle cooking to Arabia. Seeing an attractive girl sitting nearby, he walked up to her and said, "Aren't you Mrs. Barger — the one who makes waffles?" She laughingly acknowledged it and we introduced ourselves. Her husband, Tom, a government relations man, joined the conversation and we talked about the Arabian desert. It turned out that he had spent two years in the Empty Quarter. He promised to fix up the problems of my bottle and customs.

When we arrived, a rather agreeable customs officer began to search the bags, and Tom introduced me as a relative of President Roosevelt who spoke Arabic. The customs man gave my flight bag a short poke and motioned me through the line. We were met by Gerry Owens, head government relations man, who invited us to spend the night. It was a house straight out of Berkeley, California, complete with lawn, shrubs, and swimming pool, with American bathrooms and kitchens, a great luxury for us Baghdadis.

Tom and Kathleen asked us to dinner to try her famous waffles, and helped us dispose of the bottle of whiskey in the course of it. After dinner Tom was summoned to the telephone, and then motioned to me. It was Bill Sands, the American consul in Dhahran: "The acting foreign minister Yusuf Yasin and the finance minister Abdullah Suleiman are in Dhahran on an official visit. They have just heard you are in town and wonder who you are and why they have not been informed of your visit." I promised to call at the consulate in the morning so we could straighten the matter out, and passed a rather miserable night worrying about what might happen next.

It seemed as if I had just fallen asleep when a siren shrieked at six o'clock, summoning Aramco employees to work. After breakfast we hurried off to see Bill Sands at the tiny lean-to that served as a consulate, next to Aramco's imposing headquarters. He arranged for us to see the Saudi ministers later in the day, and we went on to visit our new friends in Aramco.

Tom Barger showed us around their installations, beginning with the compound next to the headquarters where company officers were meeting with Arabs of all stripes discussing pay and terms of employment. About ten thousand of them were employed by the company at that time — many of them Bedouins fresh from the desert — and I saw some of them in the compound, with their hair hanging down in twin braids, framing their kufiyyas. Tom said, "It's astonishing how fast these simple tribesmen learn how to handle machinery."

He also showed us the relatively clean quarters of the Arab workers, the large hospital Aramco was building to bring American medicine to the area, and the sewage plant. This last was important, since its purified water — a precious commodity — was used to irrigate the vegetable gardens there. He also explained how Aramco favored local business enterprise, encouraging local contractors to handle as independently as possible the nontechnical business of Aramco, cutting down the need for imported labor and materials. Some of these small businessmen — such as Suleyman Olayan, to give just one example — became the business giants of the burgeoning nation.

This was in marked contrast to the situation I had observed in Bahrain, where the British-owned Bahrain Petroleum Company relied heavily on its own expatriates for almost everything. This was one reason why, for many years, Americans were much more popular in Arabia and the Gulf than the British. Both the Arabs and the United States owe much to Aramco.

British officialdom in the Gulf, with some reason, looked with suspicion on Aramco, especially as it extended its explorations more widely in the peninsula. Company explorers had recently discovered an oil deposit in Abqaiq, to the southwest of Dhahran, which they told us was second only to Kuwait, the world's largest. "We're sitting on a liquid gold mine," said Tom Barger. An Aramco scout sent to the nearby Gulf sheikhdom of Qatar was discovered and clapped into prison by the British, who were anxious to hold on to their monopoly there. The Arabian oil boom was ready for its postwar takeoff.

After inspecting the Aramco installations, Armin and I went on to tea to meet the ministers. Abdullah Suleiman was a quiet, dignified, venerable person, a Nejdi from the interior of Arabia, while Yusuf Yasin, an inquisitive and quick-minded Syrian, was a somewhat comic-looking tubby figure with a beard dyed jet black.

Meanwhile Aramco had hired a boat to take us on an afternoon fishing trip, and after tea Armin and I embarked with the ministers to cruise around the Gulf. Abdullah seemed almost a professional fisherman as he knelt on the carpets spread over the deck and cast his line into the warm sea.

Although even he could find no fish, the expedition was a good icebreaker; after the formalities of tea, we chatted about affairs of Arabia and the world as the sun sank lower over the quiet waters. Sheikh Yusuf spoke of the recent meeting of President Roosevelt and King Ibn Saud on the battleship on the Red Sea.

As the sun touched the horizon, Sheikh Yusuf cleared the decks and announced the time for prayer. Armin and I discreetly retired to the stern, and the ministers and two or three of the ship's company rose up and knelt down with the cadence of their prayers, facing west to Mecca away from the Iranian coast. It was a timeless vignette of the peace of Islam that still lingers in my memory.

While in Baghdad and Tehran I had several occasions to visit Dhahran, and saw the rapid growth of Aramco. For a while, as I have mentioned, I seriously considered going to work for the company in Arabia. The colony and its facilities had grown and the hills at night were bright with fires flaring off the gas from the oil wells.

On one of these occasions, by chance, I was witness to a visit to Dhahran of the great Abd-ul-Aziz, King Ibn Saud himself, whose face I had first seen in the *New York Times* in 1934. I was brought to him as he stood in the opening of a vast tent set up by the American settlement, surrounded by his ministers — including Abdullah Suleiman and Yusuf Yasin — his guards, and his black slaves. He was truly a majestic figure, towering over us all, with a red-checked kufiyya, his strong features expressing a smile of welcome. I was given a seat of honor opposite him as he sat down to host the long table set under the center of the tent.

Tom Barger and the ministers had informed him of my kinship to the late president Franklin Roosevelt, and looking at me closely, he said, "*Wallahi,* how I enjoyed meeting and speaking with your cousin, the late president, on the ship just before his death."

But in the custom of old Arabia, mealtimes are for eating, not for social conversation — or any other kind. We devoured the roast lamb, rice, and various viands on the great platter before us almost in silence. Immediately after dinner, one rises and takes one's leave, and Abd-ul-Aziz's handshake was our final parting.

I have visited Dhahran many times since then, and have seen

the American settlement grow into a sizable town, with a company store modeled on the large military post exchanges found in European capitals after the war. The war's end also brought an influx of middle-level workers from job-hungry Italy, who occupied a village of their own below the American town.

In the years immediately following my first visit, when I brought that precious bottle of whiskey, Saudi authorities began taking a more relaxed view of the importation of alcohol. This was especially welcomed by Aramco, since its American work force needed something to brighten its evening hours after long days in the desert sun. Then came a crackdown, as the Saudis suddenly imposed and strictly enforced a ban on bringing in even a flask of the forbidden liquid.

At first consternation reigned in Dhahran, with Aramco envisioning mass resignations of its liquor-guzzling American workers. But it happily failed to take into account the regional origins of many of these folk: Oklahoma and surrounding states, the home of moonshine and home brew. The first days after the fearsome liquor ban, consumption of frozen orange juice rose several hundred percent, as workers toted crates of it home from the company store. Soon bottles of white lightning graced the bars of these suburban homes, sometimes altered by the addition of a few tea leaves to a whiskeylike brown.

Aramco even issued a booklet of instructions for the installation of home distilleries, with warnings not to serve the product to Saudi nationals or sally forth onto the streets under the influence. Some ingenious entrepreneur in the United States designed a packet containing small bottles of alcoholic drinks disguised as skin and hair lotions known as an Aramco Kit. The Italian community manufactured from raisins a wine that was quite acceptable, except for a residue at the bottom of the glass.

The local moonshine, eventually manufactured wherever foreign private enterprise flourished in Arabia, became known as *sadiqi* — "my friend," in Arabic. It was best drunk with its crude taste disguised by tonic. Next to the bottle of sadiqi on the bar usually sat — and still sits — a bottle of scotch, smuggled in at some risk by small boats to coastal towns on the Gulf and the Red Sea, costing about a hundred dollars a bottle. Foreign-educated Saudis have a taste for it. As you come in to dine at an

American home in Saudi Arabia, your host asks you, "Whiskey or sadiqi?" If you opt for whiskey, reserved for Saudi guests, you are unlikely to be invited again.

For some years after the ban on liquor imports, there was one sector of the foreign community from which a person with discriminating thirst could get relief — the diplomats in Jidda, who could still import it under the immunity they were granted for their personal supplies. But an unfortunate incident put an end to this escape hatch.

King Ibn Saud, the standard-bearer of the strict Wahhabi sect of Islam, could not tolerate tobacco — not to mention alcohol, but some of his sons took to the forbidden drink. After one of them, in 1947, tried out his own home-distilled brand at a dinner party, six of his guests died. When the king found out about it, he personally beat the offending prince with his cane. Perhaps this led to the ban in Dhahran. But, in November 1951, there was another fatal mishap. A nineteen-year-old son of Ibn Saud, overimbibing at a party given by a British vice-consul, had a row with his host, and was shown the door. He returned with a gun and killed the vice-consul.

The young prince hid for a while, but finally had to give himself up to his father, and the furious king summoned the vice-consul's widow to his palace. In the presence of the cringing prince, he said, "According to our custom, you may now shoot my son as he shot your husband," and allegedly offered her a pistol. But she refused it, saying, "Shooting your son will not bring my husband back."

The king was angry, not only with his son, but with the foreigners who had exposed his son to these noxious liquors. He decided to extend the ban on imports to diplomats, though, possibly deterred by their protests against this breach of their immunity, it was not officially decreed until November 1952.

It was just two months after the imposition of this ban that I took Lucky to Jidda on her first visit to Saudi Arabia. Fortunately, the American embassy had a large stock of stored liquor, with which Ambassador Ray Hare entertained us and our fellow travelers, Armin Meyer and his wife.

One evening, after preparing ourselves for dinner at the ambassador's residence, we stood vainly by the side of the road trying to find a taxi. When a car finally stopped, heeding our frantic cries of "Taxi," its driver, after going along with the game for a time, finally revealed himself as a pilot for Saudi Arabian Airways, giving us a lift to the embassy. Arabia was full of good-hearted people in those days.

The embassy residence lay in the middle of a compound enclosing California-type houses like those of Dhahran. These seemed out of place in the old Jidda we had toured that afternoon, now vanished forever, with brightly painted adobe houses topped by latticed wooden balconies jutting out over the narrow streets. Here and there the rows of houses were broken by open coffee shops on high matted stands. The streets were full of costumed figures, strolling, squatting, and lying down on doorsteps. There were Sudanis, Somalis, and Ethiopians from across the Red Sea, Yemenis with long matted hair, heavily bearded Hadramis from South Arabia, and Bedouins from the desert with their twin braids and gleaming eyes.

We were lodged in a villa in the old Jidda Gardens at the edge of town, having decided to share a cottage with the Meyers after we found out the cost. The only currency in general circulation was the silver riyal, dozens of which one carried in an old sock. They were actually sold from sockfuls of 3,500 riyals ($1,000) by money changers (we used up most of a sockful paying our hotel bill the following day).

During this stay we passed through still another Jidda, bidonvilles of battered tins, grass, and mud huts, and next to the compound itself, a Sudanese village of mats wrapped around poles. In the midst of these wretched settlements we saw three great palaces — those of two of Ibn Saud's sons, Saud and Abdullah, and the other belonging to our old friend Abdullah Suleiman, with great limousines gliding to and fro in their midst.

I was not to visit Saudi Arabia again for more than three years, during which momentous events changed the face of Arabia and the whole Arab world. Gamal Abd-al-Nasser had become the leading figure of pan-Arabism, and in 1956, by nationalizing the Suez Canal, had thrown down the gauntlet to the West. King Abd-ul-Aziz ibn Saud had gone to his maker, leaving his throne to his incompetent heir. Saud ibn Abd-ul-Aziz was weak — physically, mentally, and morally — and the new oil riches of the kingdom were squandered in the vulgar luxury of his court and courtiers. Fearing the populist appeal of the fiery Egyptian, he had taken the easy road of collaboration with Nasser in his attacks on the West and the pro-Western elements in the Arab world.

It was to examine, and perhaps to rein in, this collaboration that I went once more to Jidda, in 1956, to find my old friend George Wadsworth in residence there.

In Saudi Arabia, of course, he had found the same deplorable situation as in his previous posts, a complete ignorance of golf. Unable to find land or to gain permission for the establishment of a golf course, he had created his own individual course around the tiny yard of the embassy, which had to be circled three times to cover all nine holes. There he was to be found in the heat of the day, doggedly knocking the balls around this dusty circle.

He took me to Riyadh to have lunch with King Saud in his gaudy new Nasriyyah Palace. Before lunch we sat in the huge audience hall, surrounded by the same entourage that had accompanied King Abd-ul-Aziz on his visit to Dhahran a few years back. But this time our meals were served European-style, at a table covered by a white tablecloth in the adjoining dining room. There was no Arab flavor to our food, which had been prepared by the king's American chef. At each place sat a crystal wineglass, periodically filled with fruit juice.

Riyadh was in the first stages of its conversion from a desert port to a formless, semi-European city of nondescript architecture. Like Jidda, it was being stripped of its picturesque old buildings.

In the ambassadorial compound of Jidda — presided over by a haughty Levantine majordomo — George Wadsworth managed to maintain the high standards of his residence in Ankara, with one exception: the embassy stores of liquor had run out, and he lacked the wherewithal for his regular rounds of martinis. He tried to keep up our spirits with some beer he had brewed himself, guided by an instruction book, of which he seemed undeservedly proud. Even in the thirsty air of Jidda I couldn't swallow much of it.

I was due to visit Jidda every weekend on a regular military flight that left Beirut on Friday night and arrived at Jidda at six-thirty in the morning. I promised to bring Wadsworth a few bottles on my next trip if he could somehow get me through customs, and the ambassador promised to see to this problem personally.

He was as good as his word. On my next trip, when I arrived in Jidda as dawn broke over the Red Sea, there was Wadsworth waiting to meet me. He took from my hand my only piece of luggage, a flight bag full of bottles prevented from clinking by my pajamas, and hurried me to his waiting limousine. This was, of course, about six hours earlier than his usual time for starting the affairs of the day.

My freight consisted mostly of gin, with an occasional bottle of scotch or brandy, and we passed a number of good weekends together. After my second such expedition the majordomo rebuked me for not including vermouth — "You know the ambassador likes his martinis three to one," he said reprovingly.

One night Yusuf Yasin came around after dinner, perhaps divining what I might be bringing to Jidda, because he had no clear business reason for calling. When shortly after his arrival he said he was thirsty, I knew what he was after and so did Wadsworth, who took unholy joy in offering him a Coca-Cola.

But Saudi officialdom found no ready explanation for the mystery of why our ambassador, famous for never viewing the morning light, should get up at dawn to receive this apparently junior officer arriving regularly from Beirut, and concluded that I must, despite appearances, be someone of considerable importance. So the last time I arrived, a palace official was sent to greet me along with Wadsworth. As I stepped off the plane, he addressed me: "His Majesty the king would like to invite you, Mr. Roosevelt, to spend your weekend as his guest in the royal palace."

He reached for my bag, but Wadsworth snatched it away, saying, "I'm afraid that's impossible. Mr. Roosevelt and I have important matters to discuss, I cannot spare him for a minute."

The palace official was upset but Wadsworth was adamant, since he knew I was carrying an especially heavy load of liquid gold. The climax that would end my visits was approaching — an audience with the king in which I was to outline the extent of Saudi support for Nasser's propaganda campaign in the northern Arab states.

The audience turned out to be an unpleasant affair. The king received me and the ambassador with Yusuf Yasin at his side. Sheikh Yusuf's wily features looked sour in anticipation of my message, which I accompanied with a written list of particulars. Saud reacted with some anger, reading a few of the items

with a sarcastic comment, while Wadsworth, anxious to preserve his good relationships, remained on the sidelines as I
struggled to keep up a dialogue. After a brief exchange there
was nothing else to do but take my leave, apparently without
accomplishing anything except arousing royal rage.

Yet I was to see the king again less than six months later
under very different circumstances, at the Saudi embassy in
Washington. The Saudi ambassador, as it happened, was a
fellow Druze and by then a friend of Lucky's and mine. At a
couple of dreary receptions at this residence, replete with
anemic iced fruit juice, he had given his blessing for surreptitious visits to the pantry with its hidden bottle of accursed
spirits.

Saud had had time in the intervening months to gain a
different appreciation of Nasser's role in the Middle East, as he
found himself increasingly a target of populist Nasserism.
Meanwhile, U.S. prestige had risen dramatically in the Arab
world when, in November 1956, President Eisenhower forced
British, French, and Israeli forces to withdraw from Suez and
the Sinai peninsula.

By the end of January 1957, Saud paid a state visit to
Washington and was received by the president himself at
Andrews Air Force Base — an unprecedented gesture, with
honor guards, bands, and crowds lining the streets all the way
to Blair House. One of his coffee boys was quoted by the
Manchester Guardian as saying that the president must be
poverty-stricken, with such an old guesthouse that could not
compare to the Disneyland magnificence of Saudi palaces.[*]

But the Washington visit went well, the press being enchanted
with the infant prince Saud had brought along for medical
treatment. I was apprehensive as I waited in the receiving line
at the embassy to shake his hand, and was overwhelmed with
embarrassment when he unexpectedly beamed at me and
clasped me to his bosom in front of a set of curious newsmen
and cameramen.

Since then I have met each of the kings of Saudi Arabia. I
had my first and only interview with Feisal on the occasion of a
quick visit he made to Washington for one of those never-

---

[*] Perhaps he might have been less critical of Blair House today. My wife, as chief of
protocol, has just supervised its redecoration with private funds donated by patriotic
citizens from all parts of the nation.

conclusive discussions about an Arab-Israeli settlement. He summoned me for a private talk at the Saudi ambassador's residence. I was struck by the deep sadness of his face, which never changed throughout our interview.

He invited me to sit by him and, sighing deeply, delivered in short disparaging sentences the litany I have heard so often about Palestine. I could make no comment, as at the time I was not involved at all with this problem, but none seemed to be called for. Apparently he thought that perhaps I was another channel through which to express his views, and after delivering them, he bade me a mournful farewell.

My talk with Feisal was my last contact with Saudi Arabia for some years, and before that there was my final reunion with George Wadsworth. He had just ended his tour in Jidda and returned to Washington with a medical problem requiring an abdominal operation. He came to our house in Georgetown for a festive lunch before going to the hospital. There were the usual martinis, followed by a good meal with wine, and wide-ranging, merry conversation of Middle East old-timers. He took his leave to go to the hospital, and died on the operating table. He was erratic, irascible, sometimes difficult, stimulating, amusing, wonderful company, a good friend and a great ambassador. His like will not be seen again.

29

"The Spicy Shore
of Araby the Blest"

ABOUT THE TIME of George Wadsworth's death I parted from the Middle East, which I was not to see again until the fall of 1974, during my last months in the Agency.

When I joined the Chase Manhattan Bank the following January, my supervisor was Chuck Fiero, executive vice president in charge of examining banking opportunities in the explosively rich oil states bordering the Persian (or Arabian) Gulf. Soon thereafter I found myself back in Iraq, which I last knew as a Hashemite kingdom.

The whole face of Baghdad had changed since the revolution of 1958. Not much was left of the city I lived in during the war except Rashid Street, now cowering in the midst of a modern city of wide avenues often choked with cars — the arabanas had vanished from the scene. The ramshackle buildings lining Rashid Street no longer overhung the Tigris, now cut off by a grand new avenue called Abu Nuwas, after Haroun al-Rashid's poet and boon companion. Between the avenue and the river now lay a park full of trees and greenery, where Baghdad families walked and picnicked in the cooler air along the riverfront. At least I saw from time to time a fire, surrounded by a little ring of simmering fish, the *samach masgouf* I used to wash down with beer with Baghdad friends on the islands south of town.

All these friends were gone, scattered by the revolution, and I saw them only in exile. But I visited Kerbela, Nejef, and Samarra and found these cities much the same. The tribal areas were closed to foreigners, and the sheikhs had lost their power — and their lands. Only in Kurdistan did history appear to have reversed itself. After the revolution, the new government had allowed Mulla Mustafa — now fifty-five years old — and his followers to return to Barzan, and within a couple of years, predictably, he was again in revolt, joined once more by Kurdish officers from the Iraqi army.

The rebellion went on, interrupted by periods of truce, with a flare-up in 1968, when the Mulla and his men began to receive major weapons assistance from the Shah. As a result of subsequent Kurdish successes, they were able to win an agreement providing for local autonomy from the Iraqi government. Then in 1974 war broke out again after relations with the central government deteriorated. Once more the Shah came to their aid, only to pull the rug out from under them, after reaching an overall agreement with Iraq in the Algiers accords of March 1975.*

The Kurdish rebellion rapidly collapsed; and the government razed villages and deported many Kurds to the south. Mulla Mustafa fled to the United States, where he died a few years later. But his sons held on, and with the outbreak of the Iraq-Iran War in 1980, they found new support from Ayatollah Khomeini. Today, with his help, the Barzanis continue their ancient rebellion from their mountain home, still fighting the war Mulla Mustafa's brother, Sheikh Ahmed, had started sixty years before.

Thus today, more than forty years after the fall of the Republic of Mahabad, there is still a free Kurdistan! However, the Barzanis are no longer allies of the Kurds across the border in Iran. There Khomeini's Shi'ite fanatics are the natural enemies of the Sunni Kurds. So the Iranian Kurds side with Iraq!

The Iran I visited soon after joining the Chase was still ruled by the Shah, and I made several trips there while he was still in power and our bank still welcome. Tehran was much the same in form as when I had lived there. The old quarters in the center and south were almost unchanged except, as in Baghdad, the droshkies had been replaced by cars, and the often-

---

* Contrary to statements made in a couple of published accounts, I played no part in these events. My responsibilities lay elsewhere.

accompanying gridlock. As a consequence the lovely mountains to the north were hidden by smog, with the remaining skyline cut by dozens of high rises, piled-up boxes. At least Isfahan and Shiraz remained unspoiled, and I took Lucky there while the bazaars were still friendly to infidels.

In Baghdad and Tehran the charms of the old Islamic cities were losing the battle to the banalities of secondhand Western modernity, but it was Saudi Arabia that was altered the most. I did not pay my first return visit there until I had been with the Chase a couple of years and had the title of director of international relations for the Middle East and Africa. In that capacity I visited many Arab countries with David Rockefeller, our chairman, and accompanied him on visits with presidents and kings — among them King Khalid and later King Fahd ibn Saud. Their courts in Riyadh, except for the modernity of the new palace setting, were not much different from that of Abd-ul-Aziz.

But the cities and countryside had changed radically. The camels and donkeys had left the streets, no longer friendly with their hordes of automobiles, squeezed together by rush-hour jams and traffic lights. Even more numerous than high rises were derricks and cranes, swarming with foreign workers from many lands. While manual labor is scorned by the haughty Bedouins, they had mostly forsaken their camels and the life of the desert for acceptable employment as guards, taxi drivers, and members of the lower scales of the bureaucracy. The country was and still is in the throes of change — a traditional theocratic society evolving into one where professionals and technocrats will steer their country into the twenty-first century. It has passed through the larval stage to that of the less attractive pupa, and one can hope that something fine and beautiful will emerge in time.

Kuwait and Bahrain, at the end of 1975, had mostly completed the metamorphosis, one a prosperous city-state and the other a modern island kingdom. Even though their rulers maintain the trappings of an Arabian sheikhly court, their societies have peacefully evolved into a blend of Arab and Western styles, without losing their individuality.

But the United Arab Emirates, when I first set foot in them, still bore the imprint of old Arabia, despite the increasingly visible effects of the oil boom. Bedouins and their camels were still seen in the towns, and camel herds were a menace to night drivers on the Abu Dhabi–Dubai road. While Abu Dhabi was essentially a building lot set in the desert, the old town of Dubai still had its ancient charm, divided by a creek filled with dhows and fast smuggling boats for carrying contraband to Iran and India.

I paid a visit to the northernmost sheikhdom of the union, Ras al-Khaimah, a spring-fed oasis on the border of Oman's Musandam province on the Strait of Hormuz. The sheikh who received me, Sheikh Saqr — his name means falcon — met me in his stucco palace. His retainers and scribe and his gahwachi, making the rounds with his brass beak-nosed kettle and clinking cups, reminded me vividly of counterparts in southern Iraq.

Saqr's ancestor and namesake had ruled Ras al-Khaimah at the turn of the eighteenth century, when it was the capital of the Qawasim tribe, which dominated the coast. Their fleets of pirate dhows were a plague on the British plying the routes to India, who retaliated by twice capturing and razing Ras al-Khaimah before agreeing on a "permanent truce" that gained the area the name of Trucial States. The last Sheikh Saqr, proud of his lordly heritage, was at first reluctant to join the United Arab Emirates as a junior partner to Abu Dhabi and Dubai on its formation in late 1971, but joined up early the following year. Unlike the leaders of Qatar, the other holdout, the sheikh realized he lacked the political and economic muscle to stand alone.

During these early days Iraqi exiles played a prominent role in Abu Dhabi, especially in its finances, and I passed a couple of nostalgic evenings in the seaside home of my old friend Adnan Pachachi. I had known him as a recent college graduate at the soirees of Badi'a Afnan, and his attractive wife, Salwa, was the daughter of Ali Jawdat Pasha. All the guests were Iraqis of the old school, except for one Abu Dhabian and his wife.

"Foreigners think we are primitive Bedouins," this man said to me. "But see, here is my wife, going out socially," he added proudly.

An Iraqi wife said to me later, "Isn't it wonderful how that girl, straight out of a Bedouin tent, can now sit and talk in a group like this? She was so shy at first, but caught on fast. It shows how bright Arab women are."

"Are there many like her, going out to mixed dinner parties?"

"No, she is the only one."

Today there are many. Dubai, like Abu Dhabi, has also turned into a building lot, and throughout the emirates the peace of Islam has been replaced by the turmoil of our civilization.

One unspoiled country I visited in my most recent wanderings in Arabia was Yemen; even though it, too, has at last found oil, it intends to preserve its ancient style — at least externally. The government decreed that all new buildings should be traditional Yemeni stone buildings, and Sana'a, the capital, remains a charming city; its buildings are about five stories high, with the living room on top, lit by stained-glass windows. I stayed in one a couple of times when it was our embassy residence. The American ambassador, Tom Scotes, with his attractive wife and young daughters, all spoke their ancestral Greek among themselves to keep up the language. He is also a first-rate Arabist and Farsi-speaker who had been around various Middle East posts. He loved Yemen and I caught some of his feelings for it during my brief stays.

To begin with, it is a charming country, dubbed by the Romans *Arabia Felix* — "Happy Arabia" — as opposed to Stony Arabia to the north. Its mountains, at least in the seasons during and after the monsoon, are green, terraced by thousands of tiny farms and orchards of its industrious inhabitants. The Yemenis, unlike their Bedouin cousins, have a work ethic, and a million of them now provide the rich Saudis with the bulk of their working class. They are a picturesque people, with their own style of dress: They wear a distinctive turban and always carry a curved silver dagger, hooked at the base, with a rhinoceros-horn handle, tucked into their waistbands. These are a necessary symbol of manhood, and have contributed to the near-extermination of the African rhino.

Imam Yahya, the tyrannical old ruler of Yemen whose defeat by Ibn Saud I'd read about that morning in Groton forty years before, was long gone, and the government was now nominally a republic.[*] In fact, it was a modified military dictatorship, a military command council headed by whoever was the most powerful man in the army. At the time of my visits this was

---

[*] Officially the Yemen Arab Republic (YAR) but often referred to as North Yemen, as opposed to Marxist South Yemen, the People's Democratic Republic of Yemen (PDRY).

Ahmed al-Ghashmi, who had come to power after a mysterious murder of his popular predecessor, Ibrahim al-Hamdi, in October 1978.

Al-Hamdi had forgotten to attend the regular monthly luncheon meeting with other members of the council, and when they called to remind him, he set off for the meeting place with his brother. They never made it. Their car was ambushed and their bodies were found in it. Later a story was circulated by the government that the bodies of two French prostitutes were found with them, but the postmortem physician said that the prostitutes had been killed later. Al-Hamdi's funeral was attended by a large, silent crowd, but as the car of the new president, al-Ghashmi, left the ceremony, they started to howl in mourning, throwing their shoes at his car, crying "Murderer." But he was strong enough to hold on to his position, backed by his tribe, the Hamdan, which held many villages north of the capital.

One day al-Ghashmi invited David Rockefeller and his party, who had joined me in Sana'a, to a lunch at tribal headquarters. On our way to the village we passed through orchards of *qat* trees, the leaves of which are chewed by most Yemenis daily, providing a mild narcotic. On the road in the afternoon one passes Yemenis with bulges in their cheeks, green juice staining their mouths, as they while away the rest of the day. Not only is time wasted in qat chewing that could better be spent in the useful labor in which they excel, but Yemen's once-rich coffee orchards, which produced berries famous throughout the world, have given way to plantations of more lucrative qat.

Thus we were hardly surprised when, after lunch, our hosts placed green branches in front of each of us. Beside our plates were individual brass jugs, the purpose of which soon became clear. After munching the grainy, tasteless leaves as long as you could stand it, you spat them out into these convenient spittoons.

Tom Scotes informed me that he had tried this exercise several times and noticed absolutely no physical effect, stimulant or otherwise; it is supposed to produce mental energy combined with spiritual euphoria. None of us experienced any feeling except the discomfort of leaf particles stuck between tooth and gum.

However, it clearly had some effect on the locals. Our hosts had asked some of their fellow tribesmen to amuse us with a sword dance, and after a creditable performance with traditional weapons they did another number with Kalashnikov submachine guns, now the tribesman's favorite. One dancer became overexcited and lurched toward David Rockefeller, waving the gun in his face. Others rushed over to subdue him and the show went on. We left shortly thereafter, with feelings of relief rather than euphoria.

Soon after our visit, al-Ghashmi in turn was murdered, under even stranger circumstances than his predecessor. He was receiving an emissary from the Marxist People's Democratic Republic of Yemen who carried a briefcase that exploded, killing them both. One theory among several is that the bomb was planted by the PDRY's hard-liners to destabilize the country while launching a guerrilla operation.

Al-Ghashmi was succeeded, however, by another military tribesman, Ali Abdallah Saleh, who still remains in power, after successfully dealing with the guerrillas in a civil war lasting several years.

Under all three of these military rulers, however, the business of government was carried on by an American-educated cabinet, headed by Abd-ul-Aziz Abd-al-Ghani. The cabinet invited the Chase Manhattan party to dinner during David Rockefeller's visit, and we were all greatly impressed by the high caliber of this outstanding handful of officials. They appeared well fitted to deal with the many problems of this beleaguered country, afflicted with pressures both from Marxist South Yemen and from big brother Saudi Arabia to the north.

Our visit took place in the midst of a crisis involving the South Yemenis; their Marxist ally, the Mengistu government of Ethiopia; Sudan; and Egypt. On the eve of our departure the North Yemeni foreign minister flew to Cairo to confer with the Egyptian government, returning early the next morning to bid us good-bye.

Just before David's arrival in Sana'a, Ambassador Tom Scotes took me along to the Soviet embassy, where they were celebrating Red Army Day. The Soviets have a large embassy, plus a military mission instructing the Yemenis in the use of Soviet weapons, which form the bulk of their arsenal. Shortly after my arrival I was joined by a Soviet counselor named Ivanov, who stuck with me like a limpet as I circulated around the embassy. I realized at once that he must be the KGB resident and had been informed of my past service with the CIA. He naturally assumed that I was still with it (though I no longer had any ties with my former employer). He clearly thought my presence had something to do with the area crisis, and would never have believed that I was there to join up with the Chase group.

Oman, another country I had never visited until the late seventies, is also managing to make a graceful transition from traditional Islamic civilization to modernity. Perhaps this is because, like Yemen, it is a nation with a long history; it is not seeking an identity, like the new Arab nations of the north — it had one when Westerners first appeared. These were the Portuguese, who seized Muscat in 1508 and held it for a hundred and forty years. Two Portuguese castles, Jalali and Mirani, perched on the heights on either side of Muscat's tiny bay, still watch over this picturesque little capital hemmed in by mountains.

Omanis view the world very differently from their brother Arabs to the north, separated by vast stretches of mountain and desert, and share few of their concerns. The Iraq-Iran War interests them as guardians of one side of the Strait of Hormuz, but generally their attention is directed south and east; until recently they held small enclaves on the coasts of Iran and Pakistan. Many of them have some eastern ancestry and there are even tribes of Baluch in Oman's northeastern mountains. With this varied ancestry, a style of dress more like that of the Yemenis, and the bearing of a people who know who they are and are proud of it, they differ in appearance and manner from their brother Arabs — though their dialect is much the same as that of the rest of the Arabian peninsula.

The latest of my trips to this uniquely fascinating part of Arabia was in November 1985, when I accompanied former president and Mrs. Gerald Ford as part of the official American delegation to the fifteenth anniversary of the enthronement of Sultan Qabus.

The new coastal highway from the airport to Muscat was lined with lights, and arches overhead inscribed with graceful Arabic greetings and slogans. The large buildings near the road, some of them government offices newly built in traditional style, were illuminated with imaginative displays of orange, green, and yellow lights along their windows and rooftops.

The two-day celebration was climaxed by a midnight feast on the lawn of the sultan's new palace, occupying the whole of Muscat's waterfront between the two castles. As a band on the shore below the diners blasted us with stirring music, in which bagpipes played a major role, we were treated to displays of images electrically projected to appear to float on the water, depicting the major themes of Omani life — a dhow passing by palm trees; a fish; a *khanjar,* or dagger; the Omani coat of arms; a camel — and the laser beams sketched a camel and an oryx on the walls of the cliff lining the western side of the harbor. The battlements of Jalali and Mirani sprang to life, red lights shining from their windows and crenellated towers hung with banners. Then laser beams shot between the castles, which exploded in fireworks, simulating an ancient battle — the sky seemed on fire. It was a tasteful blend of modern technology and ancient splendor.

PART SEVEN

Fringes of Islam

30

Dar as-Sudan

GRANDFATHER BROUGHT AFRICA to Sagamore Hill, filling the house with the heads and skins of animals he carried back from his famous expedition to East Africa in 1910. But I viscerally rejected the pursuit of game, and when I first became involved in Africa, I had never even read Grandfather's *African Game Trails*!

However, I began to take an interest in Africa after seeing the movies at Cousin Frannie's house, and hearing his tales of the *people*, as opposed to the animals, of Africa. In the course of my Arabic studies I naturally perused the accounts left by Ibn Battuta and al-Bekri of Dar as-Sudan — the "Home of the Blacks," as the Arabs called sub-Saharan Africa. I first approached it in Marrakesh, one of the "desert ports" of the Sahara, the home of many blacks from across the desert. There I saw the Blue Men, camel nomads whose brown complexions turn blue from the indigo dye of their robes. They wind their turbans across their faces, following an ancient tradition; they are called by the Arabs "the veiled ones."

In 1944, en route to Cairo, I was briefly stranded in the Khartoum airport, in Sudan, and received there my initiation into one of the many problems of Africa. Suffering from a slight fever, lolling in a chair alone in the airport snack bar, I found myself in the midst of a crowd of airport workers speaking Arabic.

I struck up a conversation with them, in the course of which I asked them, "Of what people are you?"

"We are Arabs," they replied proudly, and indeed their black faces showed traces of Bedouin ancestry.

"All of you are Arabs?"

"All," they said.

"I have heard that there are also blacks in this country," I said boldly.

"Oh, yes," said one, "in fact that man over there is one."

They pointed to the person cleaning up the corner of the room, who looked up apologetically. To my untutored eye he did not appear very different from the others, but I kept this thought to myself. Today, a number of visits later, I think I would recognize him as a member of one of the Nilotic tribes of southern Sudan, many of them at this moment involved in a revolt triggered by the Arab-dominated central government's attempt to impose Islamic law. Sudan is typical of modern African nations, its boundaries drawn by European powers without regard to ethnic divisions.

At the time of this first stopover, I was not completely ignorant about Sudan. One of the movies I saw on the lead screen in Cousin Frannie's basement was about his visit with the Hadendoa Arabs. They are not Arabs at all, speaking a Hamitic language and belonging to the race in the Horn of Africa called Cushitic by some anthropologists, after the Egyptian name for the area. With great masses of bushy hair, these Fuzzy-Wuzzies are the men whose courage Kipling praises, recounting how "they broke the British square" in the battles for Sudan in the nineteenth century.

After that first brief visit, I was not to see black Africa again for more than twenty years, and indeed did not give it much thought. But in late 1957 a series of developments in Africa finally brought it to the attention of U.S. policymakers — and the intelligence community. Independence movements throughout the continent had grown so strong in the wake of World War II, and the fatal weakening of the British and French empires, that they began to prevail.

Beginning with Ghana, in 1957, the British and French colonies in Africa became independent in rapid succession. By 1960 Belgium, which had up till that point hoped to hold on in Africa, was forced to pull out of the Congo by a violent revolution. Independence for the countries of East Africa followed.

The Soviets had always been influential in the African nationalist movements; it was the basis of their propaganda offensive against Western colonialism beginning with Grigori Zinoviev's Congress of the Peoples of the East in Baku in 1920. Marxism — and by extension the Soviets — naturally attracted revolutionaries from the Western European colonies, and many of the leaders coming to power in the new African states leaned heavily in this direction, notably Kwame Nkrumah of Ghana, Sékou Touré of Guinea, and Patrice Lumumba of Congo, followed by his lieutenant Antoine Gizenga. The Congo — later Zaire — became the battleground between forces backed by the West and the Soviets, culminating in the bloody confrontation in Stanleyville (Kisangani) in 1964.

Except for the revolution in Zanzibar in 1963, further bloodshed was avoided. However, a battle of ideas raged between Marxists backed by the Soviets (and sometimes the Chinese) and moderates supported by the West. While Kenyan president Jomo Kenyatta was firmly in the Western camp, his vice president, Oginga Odinga, was pro-Soviet, and Julius Nyerere turned Tanzania into a Marxist state.

All this was of geopolitical importance to the United States and its intelligence services, and I now had good reason to extend my interests to Africa. I made the first of a number of trips there in 1965, and Africa gradually became a major preoccupation. I was fascinated by its intricate puzzle of peoples and found I had a natural sympathy for Africans — though it is hard to generalize about them. I still look forward to every trip there (I have a responsibility for Africa at the Chase Manhattan Bank) and find that the Romans were right in saying that there is always something new in Africa.

The Semitic races have been expanding from Arabia into Africa since prehistoric times, and Ethiopia ethnically is largely an extension of Arabia. Its ruling establishment and many of its peoples resisted the Arab explosion of Islam, fiercely maintaining their Christian religion against Moslem invaders. Yet their language and alphabet spring from Arabia. Invaders from Yemen, beginning some three thousand years ago, absorbed peoples of the East African Cushitic type.

From this mixture a new race evolved, coffee-colored, tall like the original Cushites, but with Yemeni eyes and features. The Ethiopians are a strikingly beautiful people, with a natural pride of bearing, an aristocratic look. The loveliness and grace of their women are prized far beyond the boundaries of Ethiopia. In the old days one of their number would often be the chosen for an Islamic harem.[*]

I was fortunate enough to meet on two occasions with the last representative of a great Ethiopian dynasty, the emperor Haile Selassie. Both times I passed through the palace gates guarded by lions to the great hall where the Lion of Judah himself greeted me, sitting on a throne raised on a dais against one of the walls. Two small dogs were disporting themselves at his feet.

He was short and slender in build like his Yemeni ancestors, and his face and features, known throughout the world since he defended his nation before the League of Nations thirty years before, were completely Arabian. One could easily believe him to be the descendant of Solomon and the Queen of Sheba, who, according to a time-honored Ethiopian legend, founded the royal dynasty.

Haile Selassie was a man of great dignity, of majesty. He spoke in a low, melodious voice of the problems of Africa and the world, with a royal tone of quiet authority. I am sure he had no forebodings of the terrible revolution to come, and his sad fate as a lonely prisoner a decade later.

In those days Ethiopia was friendly to Americans — indeed, I am told it still is, even under Communist rule, though I have not returned there since the revolution. I was received in a number of homes, and sat in a semicircle sipping *tej*, mead made with honey by the lady of the household. This was followed by a meal rich in spices of the cuisine unique to Ethiopia, the basis of which is *injera*, a flat bread made of an Ethiopian grain called *teff*, and *wat*, a peppery stew. It is the only true cuisine of non-Arab Africa — the rest of Africa eats what is at hand, which has varied with the ebb and flow of influences from outside the continent, and lacks a true culinary tradition.

Leaving Ethiopia, I made my first acquaintance with Kenya. The lingua franca of the area is a Bantu language with a largely Arabic vocabulary called Swahili, which in Arabic means language of the coast people. It developed in the Arab coastal

---

[*] For instance, the mother of the famous Glaoui of Morocco was an Ethiopian.

settlements, many of which became centers of the slave trade, as a patois in which the Arab masters communicated with their African slaves. American blacks using Swahili names and words to avoid the English "slave language" are simply substituting the Arabic slave words such as Ujamaa and Uhuru, and personal names like Juma.

Swahili is the official language of Tanzania, and the purest form of the language is spoken in Zanzibar, once an Arab island. The name of Dar es Salaam — "Abode of Peace" — Tanzania's capital and principal city, is identical to the official designation of Baghdad under the Abbasid caliphs. The populations of Mombasa and Malindi on Kenya's coast still have traces of Arab blood. Swahili is not only the common language of Kenya and Tanzania, and used in newspapers, radio, television, and political speeches, but also extends into Uganda and eastern Zaire.

Naturally, in Kenya and Tanzania I was drawn to the game parks, to view or photograph the animals admired by my grandfather. In the course of many trips I visited most of the larger ones, and enjoyed the feeling of being transported into the age of mammals, like primitive man passing through the great herds of zebra, giraffes, wildebeests, and antelope on the dusty plains, seeing a lion at his kill in early morning, or the rhinos coming to the water hole at night — and best of all, those magnificent elephants tearing down treetops with their trunks. If I had to pick just one game park for a visitor who had time for no more, it would be the vast crater of Ngorongoro — with Masai tribesmen clustered near the ragged cliffs of its edge.

The most fun trip, though, was the automobile ride I took in 1969 with my colleague John Waller from Nairobi to Entebbe. We spent the first days driving through the Kenyan plain, its monotony broken by thorn trees, and occasional herds of game. Over us lay the vast African sky, clear except for tiny clouds scattered here and there.

We passed the night at a little village recommended for its good hotel, and noted for its English pub. And indeed we found it worthy of its reputation, with a completely British clientele of expatriates looking slightly exotic in their bush jackets and desert boots. When they heard we were driving to Uganda, they gave us dire warnings.

"The frontier's a dangerous place," they said. "The frontier guards are an undisciplined lot — they beat up Europeans and take their money and valuables. Perhaps you'd better reconsider."

As we drove along the next morning, somewhat daunted by these warnings, I took out my Swahili book and memorized a phrase, something like, "We are very important people, *wa-Amrika,* and close friends of the ambassador."

We approached the frontier during the heat of noon and a sleepy Kenyan frontier guard waved us past. But at the Ugandan post, a man in a nondescript uniform slouched against a tin shack motioned to us. He took our passports, saying "You wait," and disappeared in the direction of a larger building off the road. On the wall by the door of the shack I saw a piece of paper tacked up, consisting of short sentences under the heading Rules of Conduct. These read a bit like the Ten Commandments, mostly prohibitionist:

There will be no further drinking on duty.
Uniforms should be worn neatly at all times.
Obscene language will not be used.
There will be no more roughing up of foreigners.
Visitors will not be asked for money or valuables, etc.

As I was finishing the list the guard sidled back with our passports and bid us a polite good-bye. In view of the commandments, we felt lucky to be passing through the frontier at this moment, as apparently the hazards cited by our companions of the previous evening were not imaginary.

All went well as we drove through the bush until we reached the shores of Lake Victoria, when we had a flat tire. Opening the trunk of our rented car, we found it contained a spare tire, a lug wrench, but no jack. What to do? I thought of a similar experience on a road deep in the Iranian desert, where a passing truck driver had gradually mounted the wheelbase on a pile of rocks, a common practice in that country always short of spare parts. But neither John Waller nor I knew how to do this, and anyway, there seemed to be a shortage of rocks on the clay surface of the land.

As we waited helplessly, leaning against our crippled vehicle, we were surrounded by a group of primitive-looking villagers, naked except for an occasional loincloth. (This was more than they wore in Grandfather's time. He described the area as "the

Kavirondo country, where the natives . . . go absolutely naked, although they are peaceable and industrious.")

I fetched my Swahili book and tried a few phrases on them, but they shook their heads in bewilderment. John and I exclaimed simultaneously, "What do we do now?"

As we were discussing the matter further, one of the villagers tapped me on the shoulder, then said something to the others. They crowded up to the car, took it by the fender, and lifted it up. A couple of them pulled off the old tire and put the new one in place. We thanked them fervently, pressed some currency notes in their hands, and after a few turns of the lug wrench, were once more on the road. We remarked to each other how these primitive villagers had not, like ourselves, lost their common sense when faced with a failure of our technological gadgets.

Then we passed through a countryside far richer than the arid plains of Kenya. In the green meadows scattered through its tropical forests we saw several of the crested cranes that are the national symbol. Grandfather in his *African Game Trails* spoke of them as Kavirondo cranes, describing one as "a most beautiful bird, black, white and chestnut, with an erect golden crest, and long, lanceolate grey feathers on the throat and chest." He was by avocation an ornithologist, among other things.

On the way to Kampala we stopped at Jinja to look at the falls where the White Nile begins its tortuous course through Uganda and Sudan, joined in Khartoum by the Blue Nile — which springs from the highlands of Ethiopia — then passing through Egypt to the Mediterranean. As I stood there I thought of the extraordinary explorers who had sought, and sometimes found, this tumbling stretch of water, as recounted in Alan Moorehead's riveting book *The White Nile*.

Kampala at the time of our visit was an enchanting town, still, as Grandfather had remarked, "bowered in flowers, on tree, bush, and vine, of every hue — masses of lilac, purple, yellow, blue and fiery crimson." It is enfolded in green hills, and on the crest of one lay the residence of the American ambassador.

From his porch we admired the panorama of the capital of the country Winston Churchill called the Pearl of Africa. In the late afternoon we wandered in the town square, along with throngs of Indians and their ladies in bright saris. Neither we, nor they, nor the thousands of peaceful blacks we had seen along the way, their huts bordered by yams and banana trees, could anticipate the horrors that would engulf this tranquil paradise.

From Uganda I flew to Zaire, previously the Republic of the Congo. Its capital, Kinshasa — formerly Léopoldville — lies on the mighty river Congo, which flows slowly by, with a green leafy covering of water hyacinth. Crocodiles occasionally gobble up an unwary victim from its banks, or an unlucky capsized canoeman, but the river also produces a succulent fish, a type of Nile perch, the *capitaine*.

I was met at the Kinshasa airport by a rather dull-witted Belgian employee of the American embassy. Passing through squalid slums on the city's outskirts, we drove down the broad central avenues crowned with arches of crimson blossoms of the giant plane trees lining the sidewalks. We passed a couple of first-class hotels and stopped at a hostel bearing a sign proclaiming it La Résidence.

It looked run-down. It had no doorman, and the ragged porter who took my bags upstairs — there was no elevator — dumped them in a dank little room with no windows. A large, unmade double bed filled most of the room; cockroaches scuttled across the floor. I opened my suit bag, thinking I might change my clothes, limp with the sweat of Africa, and go call on our American ambassador, McMurtrie "Mac" Godley. To my horror, the bag disgorged someone else's dirty clothes, and some open correspondence bearing the letterhead of a safari company.

This was surely life's darkest moment, and things could only get better. They did. The phone rang. It was Mac Godley.

"Where are you, Archie — I've been waiting for you — and they told me to call this number."

"I'm at some fleabag where your man dropped me, La Résidence!"

"That bonehead! He was meant to bring you right here — the best residence in town."

A half hour later I was glorying in the ambassador's shower — even though I had to get back into that same tired suit.

I had a once-in-a-lifetime chance to explore the eastern

reaches of the country, as President Mobutu graciously lent me his plane for a week. A trio of colleagues and I set off in the morning, heading east over the rain forest. We spent the first part of the day flying over the seemingly endless closely packed treetops, setting down at last in Kisangani, known until 1966 as Stanleyville, after the great explorer.

Henry Stanley's visit preceded ours by more than ninety years. He was accompanied by the acknowledged lord of the district, the half-Arab slave trader Tippu Tib from Zanzibar. With the collaboration of the great warrior tribe of the area, the Batatela, Tippu Tib had dragged a large part of the population to the slave markets of Zanzibar.

When the Belgians took over the Congo, they enlisted many Batatela, hated by their neighbors, in the Force Publique, their native army. It was a mutiny of the Force Publique that triggered the 1960 revolution against the Belgians, following the political leadership of Patrice Lumumba, himself a Mutalela.[*] After Lumumba's murder by Moise Tshombe's followers in 1961, his deputy and ally, Antoine Gizenga, was able to set up a virtually independent government in Stanleyville for a while. But in 1962 Gizenga was imprisoned while Stanleyville was reoccupied by the central government.

However, the Lumumbists, mainly Batatela and related tribes, started a rebellion in Albertville in June 1964, under the leadership of a Force Publique Mutatela, Nicolas Olenga. His followers, known as Simbas — the Swahili word for lion — were for a time an irresistible force, under the control of their witch doctors. These had convinced the Simbas that after an initiation ceremony they would be immune to bullets because of a special *dawa* (Arabic and Swahili for medicine, in African use extended to also mean charm). Provided the Simbas followed the proper ritual and observed certain taboos — most notably to abstain from sex — all enemy bullets would turn to water.

In accordance with this ritual, they would march along the roads, led by a witch doctor looking straight ahead, waving palm fronds, and chanting *"Mai, mai"* — Arabic and Swahili for water. Central government soldiers, after firing a few shots with their notoriously bad aim, fled in superstitious terror. The few

[*] Singular of Batatela.

Simba casualties were easily attributed to infractions of the taboo, and no witch doctor was ever wounded, as the government soldiers were afraid to fire at one.

When the Simbas captured Stanleyville on August 5, some sixteen hundred whites, including a few American missionaries and the five-man staff of the American consulate, were subjected to a reign of terror. A friend of mine, David Grinwis, the American vice-consul, managed to keep a diary on scraps of paper, and it makes horrifying reading.

Grinwis tells how the Simbas invaded the consulate on August 11, beat its staff with rifle butts and bayonets, and forced them to chew the small American flags they found on the premises. The head of the Simbas threatened to take them to the Lumumba monument for execution.

The Simbas had virtually deified Patrice Lumumba, and had erected a shrine to him in a square in the middle of town, a life-size color portrait on a pedestal. From time to time during the Simbas' occupation of Stanleyville, Congolese and European captives were led to be executed by the Simbas, cheered on by a mob of their followers. The Simbas routinely killed "intellectuals," meaning almost anyone with a high school education. Many of them were government employees.

Fortunately for Grinwis and his associates, the Simbas' chief, after cramming them into a truck, decided to take them to the headquarters of "General" Olenga instead, who permitted them to return to the consulate under house arrest.

Ten days later they were taken to the airport and, after suffering a night of beatings by drunken Simbas, spent the next three months either at the airport or the central prison under constant threats of violence or death.

Once they were actually taken to the monument and tormented by a mob for the better part of an hour while awaiting execution, only to be reprieved by the last-minute appearance of Olenga.

Finally, on November 20, they were jammed into the Residence Victoria Hotel along with some 250 Europeans, amid rumors of approaching government forces from the capital.

In the next couple of days, word reached the terrified captives that a Belgian rescue team was planning to land at the airport, and in the early morning of November 24, they heard the sound of planes overhead. Almost immediately thereafter the Simbas went from room to room hauling out the Europeans, then formed them in triple files on the street outside and began to march them in the direction of the airport, where they could hear the sound of firing. Then a truckload of Simbas appeared, announcing that the Belgian paratroopers had landed. The Simbas ordered the Europeans to sit on the street. As the sound of shooting came closer, the Simbas apparently panicked and started shooting into the crowd of Europeans. Most of them escaped death, jumping to the side of the road and hiding behind the walls bordering it. As the paratroopers appeared around the corner, they found Grinwis and his four associates among the survivors.

Certain actions had contributed to the failure of the Simba rebellion. One was the defection of Mama Onema, the leading witch of the Simbas, a hideous hag who was favored by Olenga. She had been an effective speaker on the rebel radio, her words terrorizing government soldiers listening to the program from the other side of the front. After she was bribed by the government to defect, Mama Onema announced to the rebels on Radio Léopoldville that she had canceled the power of their charms against enemy bullets, which would no longer turn to water. As these were now being fired mostly by European mercenaries — the so-called wild geese led by "Mad Mike" Hoare, who were mowing down Simba ranks — this propaganda contributed to the collapse of the Simbas.

Another coup was executed in Khartoum by a friend of mine. He had advance notice that a Simba courier carrying more than $300,000 in notes — then not an inconsiderable sum — would be stopping at the airport. He spotted the man sitting in the transit lounge with his briefcase, and had him paged, summoning him to the main terminal. My friend correctly assumed that the courier would not wish to bring his briefcase through customs. After a moment of hesitation the courier hurried off through the barrier, leaving the briefcase on his seat. My friend beckoned an associate, who picked it up and made off with it, while he himself waited to see the outcome.

The Simba, returning and searching wildly for his briefcase, went into hysterics, hitting his head with his fists, shouting *"Pauvre Pierre!* What shall I do now?" This money was badly needed by the rebels in Stanleyville, as they had exhausted the funds they had expropriated from the banks and the Europeans. We never found out what happened to *"pauvre"* Pierre.

When my colleagues and I arrived at the Kisangani airport five years later, we followed the identical route of the paratroopers as they entered the town on their rescue mission. The road was lined with fine houses the Belgians had built for themselves years before, now in ruins and filled with African squatters.

Already somewhat spooked by our ride into town, we stopped at the site of the Lumumba monument, now marked only by the remains of its pedestal. At the turn of the road some blocks farther on we saw where the Simbas had shot their hostages. In the quiet of the streets, bare of traffic, we could almost hear the shouts of the Simbas and the screams of their victims.

After spending the night in Kisangani's only first-class hotel — now a shadow of what it was, with no electricity and hence no working elevators, and rooms reminiscent of La Résidence — we happily set out for Goma, on Zaire's eastern border, the following morning. Our captain piloted us on a long detour, over the craggy Ruwenzori range, down to the valleys of Lake Albert and Lake Edward on Zaire's border with Uganda. The lake and riverbeds were dotted with herds of animals, especially hippopotamus, and there was no sign of human habitation until we got to Goma.

This is the capital of a high-altitude province called the Switzerland of Zaire, full of pastures, vegetable gardens, orchards, and vineyards, owned by the last of the European farmers. The town had a Swiss-style hotel, a welcome experience after the rigors of Kisangani, and was full of Europeans, buying produce to take back to their homes in the "heart of darkness," as Joseph Conrad termed the Congo.

The following day we took a short flight south to Bujumbura, capital of Burundi. As we landed, I was greeted by a colleague who quickly briefed me on the situation at the embassy.

"The ambassador and his wife have asked you to drop by for drinks tonight. Don't pay too much attention to him — he was a big contributor to the party in power and they put him here because they didn't think much of importance is likely to happen here anytime soon. But please be nice to his wife — she runs him and the embassy. All she really cares about is a horrible little dog called Twinkie. Just pat it on the head and you'll be off to a good start."

Arriving at the residence and settling in with the harmless ambassador and his formidable wife, I followed instructions and patted her tiny spoiled pet. I suppose since I was raised with dogs in my youth and probably have a friendly smell, dogs generally take to me at once, and this one jumped onto my lap. Shortly thereafter, just as conversation began to unfreeze, he proceeded to deposit a St. Bernard–size turd on the lap of my only suit.

Mrs. Ambassador apologized profusely, and servants with wet cloths did their best to eradicate the traces of Twinkie, which nonetheless lingered. During the rest of my swing through Africa, I thought I noticed dinner partners turning away from me to sniff the purer air.

Yet if this was another low point of my trip, from then on everything got better. My friend in Bujumbura took our Zaire group to a restaurant in this obscure Central African town that would have rated at least two stars had it been located in France or Belgium. The menu was the size of a large coffee-table book, starting with appetizers such as Belon oysters and snails, and continuing with all the variety Sabena could carry straight from Brussels.

And the ambassador's wife tried to atone for Twinkie by taking me on a guided tour of Bujumbura the next morning. Its African population was still a picturesque one, mostly tall Watutsis — all their women seemed to be stately beauties whose carriage proclaimed their nobility. She took me to a shop for local artifacts, mostly from the forests of Zaire's Uvira province across Lake Kivu, now haunted by the remnants of Stanley-ville's Marxist guerrillas. A number of wooden ritual masks were displayed on the walls, and she drew my attention to one of them, which had some wisps of feathers hanging on it. She did not need to tell me this was the pick of the lot, but I could not buy it. Looking at its grim ebony features, I felt "spooked," and knew I could not bring this threatening, bewitched presence into my home in Washington.

Many Westerners who live a long time in Africa, especially West Africa, come to gain a certain respect for, and even fear of, witchcraft. Among them was one of my colleagues, Tom Giles,[*] a tough veteran of the FBI who later joined the Agency. He was the last person one would ever suspect of involvement with witchcraft. Yet, once catapulted into Africa on his first tour abroad, he became a true believer.

Tom had caught his African houseboy, Kwame, stealing, and had summarily dismissed him. Shortly thereafter Tom became ill with a fever that his doctor was unable to diagnose. As the days and then weeks passed, he got no better. Blood tests provided no clues and medication proved useless, and his body's resistance began to fail.

One morning his cook knocked timidly at the door of his sickroom, and after entering and asking after Tom's health, he said, "Sir, you know who is make you sick?"

"Who?" asked Tom.

"It is Kwame."

"Kwame?" exclaimed Tom in astonishment.

"Yes, Kwame. After you send him away, he call his friend — that man across the street."

He pointed through the window, where Tom saw an old black man sitting on the side of the road, a tattered bag at his side.

"He witch doctor," said the cook.

Tom at first dismissed the cook's statement as nonsense, but he couldn't help glancing at the figure across the road from time to time during the day. The man did seem to be staring back at his window with a malevolent expression.

"I felt a chill," Tom told me later, "sort of a premonition of death. And I really began to feel afraid."

He sent for the cook in the evening.

"If it's true, about Kwame and that man across the street," said Tom, "what can I do about it? Send for Kwame, try to reason with him?"

"Oh, no," said the cook. "He pay witch doctor and now too late."

"What can I do, then?" said Tom — the hardheaded, down-to-earth FBI veteran.

---

[*] A pseudonym.

"I send for my cousin, good witch doctor, very strong. He stand next to that one, make good medicine against bad, you get well."

The next morning the cook's cousin took his place next to Kwame's witch doctor, who disappeared that evening. A few days later Tom Giles was out of his bed, fully recovered.

31

The Road to Timbuktu

I HAVE WANDERED AWAY from Islamic and Swahili-speaking Africa into "pagan" Africa, but without this digression I couldn't explain Nigeria, my next stop, where the two kinds of Africans live side by side.

I found Nigeria fascinating, and always enjoyed my visits there. This may surprise those whose acquaintance with that country has been limited to Lagos, an overpopulated sinkhole, full of poverty and squalor and in some places reminiscent of Calcutta. The steaming, fetid atmosphere rising from the cesspool of its lagoon, like the stench of Calcutta's river Hooghly, is enough to discourage even the hardiest traveler.

But I was fortunate in my friendship with our long-term ambassador there, Elbert Mathews, whom I'd previously known as consul-general in Istanbul, and Naomi, his wife. They were everything an ambassadorial couple should be. Their residence was located on Ikoye Island, with a wide lawn dotted with flowering tropical trees leading down to a quiet lagoon, disturbed only by an occasional fisherman's canoe. Their house was a Mecca for Nigerians of all types and persuasions, and the Mathewses' enthusiasm for the country, its peoples, and its many-faceted culture was contagious. For me it was an oasis in the turmoil of Africa, with the self-contained tranquillity of an island, despite the constant stream of visitors.

But this island stood at the edge of a country that was far from tranquil. Nigeria is a troubled marriage between a Christian and animist south and an Islamic north. Islam exacerbates ethnic divisions because it profoundly affects the personality, character, outlook, and life-style of its devotees. The animist African originally wore little clothing and his was the image first projected to the West as a free-living, sexually uninhibited, dance- and music-loving African, with a ready smile and lively sense of humor. On the dark side was witchcraft and the sometimes-bloody manifestations of animist cults, including cannibalism.

When the fourteenth-century Arab traveler Ibn Battuta toured the Moslem African kingdoms on the southern borders of the Sahara, he was shocked by their surviving pagan habits of sexual license and the nudity of the women — even the sultan of Mali's daughters. But such practices have long ago been eradicated; today's Moslems are robed and turbaned, dignified and austere. They resemble other Africans in little except physical traits — and sometimes not even in these.

The largest ethnic group in northern Nigeria is the Hausa-Fulani. This is a merger of two tribal and linguistic groupings, both of them with some ancient admixture of Caucasian blood, as evidenced in their lighter complexions and sometimes almost aquiline features. The northerners have dominated Nigeria politically since independence. Because of their military tradition they dominate the army, and their emirs still wield a degree of secular and spiritual authority.

While the southerners have a far higher standard of education and are generally more sophisticated in both the private and the public sector, they are deeply divided. The majority ethnic group, the Yoruba, in the west, vies with the self-sufficient, modernizing Ibos, the dominant tribe of the east.

Southern military men, chafing under northern rule, launched a coup in January 1966, in the course of which a number of leading northerners were assassinated. The following year the northerners mounted a coup of their own, which was followed by a massacre of many of the large colonies of Ibo traders in the north. This led to the flight of the surviving Ibos, and the establishment of the separatist Ibo state of Biafra. The central government, under General Yakubu Gowon, set out to suppress the rebellion, and the civil war with Biafra was just breaking out when I became increasingly involved with Africa.

In the course of my visits I had several occasions to call on General Gowon in his Spartan office in the Dodon Barracks. He was a handsome figure in his uniform, with the sharper facial features of a northerner, though in fact he was a Christian from the middle belt of Nigeria. His military bearing reflected his Sandhurst training, but he was always at ease when we talked — outgoing and frank in his conversation. He was also a man of compassion who had the rare quality of being able to forgive his enemies.

A colleague of mine presented Gowon with a set of Carl Sandburg's multivolume biography of Lincoln. I saw it lying close by on his bookcase, and realized he not only read it but consulted it. I feel certain that this — along with his native humanitarianism — influenced his treatment of the Biafrans after their surrender. There were no reprisals, no punishment for the rebel leadership. Both civilians and military were gradually accepted back in the establishment — treated like "dissatisfied fellow-countrymen," as Lincoln said in his first inaugural address.

While Gowon represented the official government of Nigeria, a parallel authority exists in all parts of the country that predates the formation of Nigeria, when its colonial boundaries were established by the British without regard to the traditional ethnic and religious networks of power. These networks still remain in place.

I have visited two of the traditional chiefs in their homelands in the course of my trips to Nigeria, one in Yorubaland and another in Hausa-Fulani territory. The contrast was striking.

When I came to Oshogbo, in southwest Nigeria, I was taken to see a chieftain in his palace, the Oni of Ife. All his Yoruba subjects were dressed in traditional tie-dye Yoruba robes — *agbaras* — of blue and green; some were sitting by their drums, and they began to make them "speak." These were "talking drums," sending a message about us to other villages. Few Europeans really understand how drumbeats are translated by faraway listeners into human speech — and no one has given me a satisfactory explanation.

We went on from the Oni's palace to a sacred grove, a sort of cemetery whose shrines were adorned with offerings of fruit and other produce. An eerie silence blanketed the clumps of trees, and bibs of cloth were hanging on branches here and there. I had the same creepy feeling as when I had seen the mask in the shop in Bujumbura — a spirit presence haunted that forest.

The people change completely when you go north to Moslem country. They have too much dignity to indulge themselves in singing, dancing, and laughter — the Prophet disapproved of laughter. They have also, at least in part, shed the darker elements of African animism: witchcraft, fetishes, and the sometimes bloody rites of African cults. They follow the code of conduct common to all the great revealed religions under the eye of a merciful but demanding god. They are no longer simply Africans, but members of the world community of Islam.

In the north, the various local Emirs, while having no place in the government structure, have even more of a hold on the people's allegiance than their southern counterparts. In addition to their royal courts and retainers, they generally have an acknowledged position in the Islamic hierarchy. On my very first trip to Kano I saw one of the most important of these traditional rulers, the Emir of Kano, in the full exercise of his power.

Kano lies in the middle of large, semi-arid fields of peanuts, and at the time of my first visit there — 1967 — I could see pyramids of these "ground nuts" near the road not far from the city. It is rather like Marrakesh, a desert port to the south of the Sahara, and one can see great blocks of salt being transported on camels into the city from the salt mines of the desert. The city's buildings are dazzlingly white under the tropic sun, and many of its inhabitants wear white cotton robes. Thus the colors of the market stand out, especially the dyes of indigo blue, which color the clothes and the complexions of the nomads of the great desert.

I was fortunate enough to be in Kano at the time of a Moslem feast, and the embassy arranged for me to attend its celebration. I shared the platform as an honored guest with the Emir and the governor, and witnessed the ceremony called the *Salah.* Here various dignitaries pay allegiance to their ruler, attended by several hundred horsemen, wearing scarlet and green robes, scarlet turbans, and traditional swords. Leading the group was an official in a much more ornate version of the uniform. His vest of ostrich feathers was decorated with hammered metal plates, and his helmet of scarlet padding was topped with a brass plate and an ostrich plume. He was the *Dan Lepide,* the champion of the Emir, who traditionally challenges any foe of his lord who dares raise his voice.

Then the Emir's special bodyguard rode up, the *Sulke,* in white turbans and robes bound with a red sash, covered by ancient coats of chain mail. This mail is said to date from the time of the Crusades, but was actually in general use among nomad tribesmen before firearms replaced the traditional swords and lances of the desert in the nineteenth century.

What followed was essentially the same as a Moroccan Berber fantasia, with the horsemen executing mock charges across the square toward the Emir's platform. But instead of the sober browns and grays of the Berbers, robes of many colors floated behind the charging Hausa warriors.

Afterward we were received by the Emir, Alhaji Ado Bayero, in his adobe palace, wearing a white robe, with the traditional red turban, and gilded slippers trimmed with ostrich plumes. We greeted him with due respect, and he replied in perfect Oxford English — not surprising, since he holds a degree from that institution.

I had occasion to make another visit to the Emir about fifteen years later with David Rockefeller. This time men in the same red and green robes as the fantasia riders were lined up on either side of the path to the entrance to the palace, shouting *"Garak"* — "Take care" — in chorus as we approached. The Emir was dressed in the same costume as before, speaking about the situation in Nigeria in his Oxford English. It was good to find something traditional unchanged in all too rapidly changing Africa.

The Arab influence is palpable in all this: the walls of the Emir's chamber are inscribed with quotations from the Koran, and of course, as his title indicates, he had made the pilgrimage to Mecca. I don't know if he speaks Arabic, but many pious folk do in these regions.

My journey to Timbuktu began in Ouagadougou (in what was then known as Upper Volta and today is Burkina Faso) in the last week of January 1970. I brought along the best traveling companion I have known, my son, Tweed, then nearly twenty-eight years old. Although our personalities and interests are quite different, we have much in common, including that trait so useful for people living in close contact, a sense of humor. He had just caught the Africa bug, which had by then been in my bloodstream almost a decade.

We were seen off by the number-three man of our three-man embassy, Theodore Roosevelt IV, known in the family as T-4. He had become a well-known figure in "Ouaga," as he dashed around town in his motorbike doing gofer errands for the embassy. His life was not a hard one, however — a handsome youth, he was much sought after by the girls. In vain, as it turned out; his fiancée visited him there, and a few years later I rediscovered him on Wall Street, a member of the financial community and proud father of T-5.

Tweed and I set out by four-wheeled vehicle on what could hardly be called a road — more like a trail — and headed toward the Niger River across the plain of Upper Volta. The country was monotonous: dry pasture broken by clumps of thorn trees and an occasional baobab.

The baobab trees have a certain mystery about them. I never saw a small one, and it seemed as if they had sprung, fully grown, from the dusty plain. Local legend has it that they are hurled upside down into the earth by an angry god, with roots pointed toward the sky. They never grow tall; their growth goes mostly into a wide spreading tangle of limbs, completely without symmetry, borne by a very thick gray trunk. The inside of the trunk is hollow and used by the Africans as a final resting place for a distinguished corpse.

The monotony of the scenery was broken by an occasional straw-hut village lying away from the road, along with some dispirited-looking cattlemen and their womenfolk. I pondered what it must be like to live the whole of one's life in such isolated desolation, and how dreadful it would be if in my next incarnation I awoke in such a place.

We also rode through a couple of sizable towns surrounding mosques built of adobe. Finally, after struggling along over this endless bumpy pasture all day, we crossed the frontier into Mali and spent the night at a place called Sangha. We passed the morning visiting the mountains of the Dogon people, famous for their religion based on the movements of the stars and planets, then drove on to the little port of Mopti on the Niger to board the river steamer that was to be our home for the next few days.

It was hardly a luxury liner. We walked through the main

body of the ship at evening, crammed with masses of African voyagers, to climb a worn iron staircase to the upper deck. We occupied one of a half-dozen cabins reserved for first-class passengers, mostly French. The engine of this venerable craft had perished long ago, but a small tugboat pulled it up and down the stream.

We spent a leisurely two days on the upper decks, passing through an immense plain, stopping from time to time at a small settlement. All its inhabitants thronged to the riverbank to see the most interesting sight of the week. They wore colorful Islamic garments, with a few men in turbans. They were black but their features sometimes reflected a Berber or Arab mixture. Canoelike boats crammed with market women approached our gunwales. They carried baskets of local fruits and vegetables to sell to hungry passengers on the lower deck. We superior beings on the deck above were also rather hungry, as we were allowed nothing besides tasteless canned foods.

Early the third morning, we arrived at the port of the magic city of Timbuktu. It was not clearly visible from the steamer, since it lay a little way north of the river, and when it finally came into view I found fully justified the disappointment expressed by the French explorer René Caillié in 1828: "I had formed a totally different idea of the grandeur and wealth of Timbuktu, but the city presented, at first view, nothing but a mess of ill-looking houses built of earth."

Timbuktu owes its reputation simply to the fact that it was for centuries the southernmost limit of Islamic culture in Central Africa. It had been the capital of the Islamic empire of Mali in the fourteenth century, and in 1591 it was conquered by a Moroccan army largely composed of Andalusians. The Moroccans actually ruled it for only a short time, and their descendants, much mixed with local blacks, still vaunt their Moroccan ties.

But of Andalusian civilization there is no visible trace. The Great Mosque and the lesser ones are mud-built, completely African, and the Arabic language is spoken no more. Timbuktu was never the metropolis and center of learning it was reputed to be, located as it was in the middle of tribal Africa. With the gradual suppression during the century preceding World War I of the slave trade, which was its principal source of revenue, it shrank to an even smaller size than the city of perhaps forty thousand it once was. Our inn was as unimpressive as the city and to the disgust of all the former inhabitants of the upper deck, we ran out of beer the second day of our stay.

We were happy to catch the Mali Airways plane, driven by a steel-toothed Soviet pilot, and head for Bamako, Mali's capital, where a friendly American ambassador and his staff were planning a hospitable welcome. A couple of days later we flew homeward across the great Sahara, from whose immense wastes the veiled ones once emerged to conquer northwest Africa and Andalusia, and cut to pieces a whole army of the chivalry of Christian Spain.

32

Jazirat al-Andalus

THE ARABS KNEW Spain as Jazirat al-Andalus, "The Island of the Vandals," so called after the people who briefly occupied it in the fourth century. Lucky and I fell in love with Spain on our first visit in 1953. It became our favorite foreign country and we were destined to spend three of our happiest years there and visit countless times afterward.

Spain is special, with a magic in the very air you breathe, an atmosphere hard to define. The spell is everywhere, in the high plain of Castile, surrounded on all sides by mountains, in the green uplands of the Basque country, the lowlands of Galicia and Catalonia, the sad pastures of Estremadura, and the vast groves of olives and live oak of Andalusia.

As a preparation for living there, we read H. V. Morton's *A Stranger in Spain,* and when we arrived we realized that we were not strangers at all. We had, in a sense, been there before — in the Arab world. Asked once to describe the Spanish character, I replied, "Catholic, Romance-speaking Arabs."

Of course, this is an oversimplification, but with much truth in it. The traditional machismo of the Spaniard, his willingness to die for his faith, his clan, and his honor, are undeniably Arab traits. The Spanish *pundonor* — "point of honor" — for which so many Spaniards have died through the centuries is the Arab *sharaf.* The Spaniard's individualism, his unwillingness to compromise with those outside his clan (whatever he conceives that to be), have hindered attempts at political unity within a larger frame — Arab traits that have destroyed every Arab state, sooner more often than later.

Not only are many Spanish words of Arab origin but even certain everyday expressions. A Spaniard often follows a statement about future plans or events with the caveat *Si Dios quiere* — a direct translation of *Inshallah,* "If God wills." The Spanish expletive *ole!* derives from *wallah* ("by God!"). When he invites you into his home, an old-fashioned Spaniard says, *"Es su casa,"* which in Arabic is *Beitak,* both of which mean "It is your house."

Of course, many Arab place names dot the country, and indeed, the southern two thirds of Spain is still haunted by the unseen presence of *los Moros,* the Moors, evoking mystery and even a little fear. Actually, the Moors of Spain consisted of an Arab elite, Berber tribesmen, and a majority descended from Spanish converts. The memory of the Moors is still alive in the public consciousness — you see representations of them in festivals — and their name is preserved in expressions like *"Hay Moros en la costa,"* which translates loosely as "The coast is not clear." After all, they are much closer in history to modern Spain than the Mongols to the Russians. The last Moorish kingdom fell in 1492, and the remaining Moorish population was expelled early in the seventeenth century.

However, a few Moors managed to avoid deportation; thus Moorish blood — whatever that was — runs in the veins of many Spaniards, especially in the south. Even the Spanish nobility, including the royal families, sometimes intermarried with the Moors. The term *sangre azul,* blue blood, refers to the visibility of veins in the arms, plainly discernible in fair skin, implying *limpieza de sangre,* i.e., pureness of blood untainted by the dark Moorish stain. But in fact few Moors were of black African origin or noticeably darker than their Christian neighbors. Many of Berber blood were fair like the Rif tribes across the Strait of Gibraltar, who have the highest proportion of redheads in the world, not excluding the Scots and Irish. The Berber who led the Moorish invasion of Spain, in A.D. 711, Tariq ibn Ziyad, was a redhead!

There are many legends in both Arabic and Castilian song and story about the events leading to the Moorish invasion. They revolve around the romantic tale of Roderic, last king of the Visigoths, who from the walls of his castle in Toledo saw a beautiful girl bathing in the river. He recognized her as

Florinda, daughter of the governor of Ceuta, the last Visigothic foothold in North Africa.

Although eighty-two years old at the time, King Roderic sent for Florinda and deflowered her, either by force or persuasion. Her father, incensed, sought an alliance with the Arabs, who had already conquered the rest of North Africa. Thus a beautiful face, a seduction, and a betrayal led to an Arab occupation that was to last almost eight hundred years.

Tariq the Berber brought his troops across the Strait, defeated and killed Roderic in a decisive battle, and soon was in possession of Roderic's capital, Toledo, which remained in Moorish hands until the eleventh century. Toledo was never again the capital of Spain — so it is still unspoiled, a spectacular walled city on a hill circled by the Tajo, or Tagus, River.

Lucky and I have visited Toledo often through the years, occasionally approaching that dark stone city under a stormy sky, as it appeared to El Greco in his wondrous painting. We often sat in the old souq — Zocodover — and imagined it full of turbaned Moors hawking their wares. While exploring the narrow cobbled streets winding through the city, with the balconies of the houses projecting overhead, I was constantly reminded of Fez.

On our first visit to Toledo, in 1953, we entered the city by the Puerta del Cambron, not far from the banks of the Tajo, and came upon the great Convent of San Juan de los Reyes, built by Ferdinand and Isabella to celebrate the victory of Toro, cementing the unity of Spain. On its walls still hang the manacles of Christian captives freed from their dungeons during their conquest of the Moorish kingdom of Granada.

We were often the guests of Dr. Gregorio Marañon and his family, at his *cigarral,* or country home, in the hills south of the city. Toledo country houses are called *cigarrales* after the *cigarras,* locusts, whose whispering song throughout the long summer pervades the olive groves covering the slopes.

Dr. Marañon was a true sage — a great medical doctor, historian, philosopher, and a wonderful human being. When he learned of my interest in the Moors, he told me there were still peasants in the area with Moorish antecedents, and that as a doctor he had seen patients from the villages with Moorish-type tattoos on their wrists. His cigarral, he told me, rested on

Moorish foundations, and set in the walls on each side of the door were Moorish memorial stones, inscribed in Arabic.

Although Toledo's illustrious past might have tempted the Moors to make it their capital, perhaps it was too alien to them, too far north, too gloomy, so unlike their sunny Arab homelands.

Andalusia was more congenial, and at first the Arab ruling clans consigned northern Spain to the Berbers, while they themselves settled in the south. Within a few years Cordova was acknowledged as the capital of the Moorish domain in Europe. Alas, most of Cordova was built of adobe, and here, as in other cities of Andalusia, little remains to remind one of what was, under the Omayyad caliphs, by far the greatest city of all Europe after Constantinople.

Unlike the dark mud lanes of the squalid cities of Christian Europe, Cordova's streets were paved and lit at night by lamps. Cordova's rulers lived in a palace as splendid as Versailles at a time when their northern counterparts huddled inside stark, primitive castles. And Cordova had three thousand mosques, now mostly reduced to dust, with one glorious exception: the Great Mosque, built in the eighth century, and still one of the architectural wonders of the world.

Along with the Alhambra, the Great Mosque is one of the most evocative monuments of Moorish Spain — yet, like so much in the Arab world, there is nothing in its bare external walls to hint of the majesty within. When we entered its gate, we found ourselves in a forest of columns of many kinds of stone, their variegated tints illuminated dimly by light from windows high in the walls. The lower parts of the columns are polished by the touch of thousands of worshippers passing by during the centuries of Moorish rule. They are crowned by a double row of arches, the lower ones broad stripes of white and red, the upper ones monochromatic, dark in the ceiling's gloom.

As we walked amid the silent columns we felt the presence of those thousands of vanished worshippers and shared their religious awe. And we were shocked by the intrusion of a Christian chapel in the middle of the serried ranks of columns. It was built in the early sixteenth century at the insistence of the church hierarchy and against the wishes of the Cordovans. Even the emperor Charles V, viewing for the first time this desecration wrought by his own subjects, exclaimed, "You have built what could be built anywhere, and have destroyed what could be found nowhere else on earth."

The grandeur of the mosque endures despite this excrescence; after all, only sixty-three of its twelve hundred columns were knocked down to make way for it. However, it serves as a symbol of the evil of religious intolerance, in the midst of a monument to religious faith.

Strangely enough, the builder of this chapel, Hernan Ruiz, actually improved on another Moslem monument — the Giralda, now the tower of the cathedral of Seville, once the minaret of a mosque. It was built in the twelfth century by the same architect who conceived the Tour Hassan of Rabat and the Koutoubia of Marrakesh. Ruiz added five stories to convert it to a belfry, giving it the height to dominate the city. A century later, a tall bronze figure representing the Christian faith was placed on its top, turning with the wind, giving the tower its name — *giralda* means weathercock.

Seville, an ancient Iberian town on the Guadalquivir River, became one of the capitals of Moorish Spain after the breakup of the Omayyad caliphate in the beginning of the eleventh century. Its first rulers were the home-grown Abbasids, of whom the last was the poet Mutamid, whose romantic and tragic history is reflected in his poems. He fell in love with and married a slave girl who capped a verse he had improvised as he walked along the bank of the river where she was washing her master's clothes. One day the new princess, looking out of her palace window at the dreary countryside, muddy with the winter rains, told Mutamid how she missed the snows of the northern mountains where she had spent her youth before her capture by the Moors. Mutamid planted an orchard of almond trees so that when she looked out the window the following winter the plain was white with blossoms.

Unfortunately, his realm was threatened by Christian knights advancing from the north, and he called on his Berber coreligionists in Africa to help him. These were the Almoravids, a religious brotherhood formed by veiled nomads from the Sahara, who had conquered northwestern Africa and founded Marrakesh as their capital. These fanatical barbarians overcame the Christian northerners in a battle in 1086 that set back the Christian recovery of Spain by more than a century. Then they took over Seville and most of Moorish Spain, sending Mutamid and his family in chains into a long, impoverished exile in a remote Moroccan town. His poems lamenting his fate survive.

The Almoravids and their Berber successors, the Almohads, made Seville their capital, until it was conquered by the Castilians in 1236. Most of the Moors took refuge in North Africa or in the Moorish kingdom of Granada, the surviving remnant of a once-great domain. But at heart Seville remains very much a Moorish town, in the appearance of the people, their voices, their manner of life.

Lucky and I got a strong sense of this in April 1960, when we went to the annual *feria*, or fair, of Seville. The songs and dances of the Sevillanos are much influenced by the gypsies, who themselves arrived in Spain from North Africa at the end of the *Reconquista*, as the reconquest of the peninsula by the Christians is known.

All during the feria we were surrounded by gypsy singers and dancers, and also witnessed those enchanting duets by little girls with flashing black eyes, whirling in the traditional dance called the *sevillana*.

Like many of the ladies visiting from Madrid, Lucky wore a gypsy costume, but on her it looked not exotic, but as if it belonged. As she rode *al grupo* — the traditional style, on the croup of a horse ridden by a caballero — she drew many admiring looks, and I have a picture of her being photographed by a tourist happy to have found a genuine Sevillana!

Before the feria we observed the *Semana Santa*, or Holy Week, in Malaga, another historic Moorish town. Although Holy Week is not Moorish, in some ways the procession is as much pagan as Christian. Sometimes, in the course of the procession, we heard a woman's voice from a balcony singing a *saeta* — a couplet of praise to the Virgin, the melody straight from the Moors.

There is little of the old Moorish town left in Malaga, except for the fortress frowning down on the city from the heights, the Alcazaba — the Casbah. Below it lies the bullring where Lucky and I in the summer of 1959 saw a renowned series of bullfights. The stands were packed in the furnace heat of those August afternoons. An overflow crowd lined the battlements of the Alcazaba on the day of the *mano a mano* of Antonio Ordonez and Luis Miguel Dominguin, described by Ernest Hemingway in his *Life* magazine article "The Dangerous Summer" as "one of the very greatest bullfights I have ever seen."

Hemingway had a ringside seat directly below us. He was a well-known figure in various Spanish bullrings that summer, and whenever he appeared he was cheered by the audience. Often a man who was Hemingway's look-alike, and deliberately copied his beard and dress, would appear. This double, known as *El Falso Hemingway,* would cheerfully collect the plaudits intended for the real McCoy.

Once we witnessed a confrontation between the two at the small provincial bullring of Escorial. There had been a rumor that Hemingway had died or been killed — eerie, in retrospect, as he might well have been already contemplating his suicide — and the stands were buzzing with comments about it. Suddenly we thought we saw him entering the ring and joined in the spontaneous cheers to greet him. But it was only El Falso, happily bowing to our applause.

The crowd fell silent at once as we realized our mistake. While El Falso was still looking for his place, the great Hemingway himself finally appeared. Pandemonium broke out. Hemingway walked slowly by El Falso and, just as he passed him, shot him a look of utter contempt.

Yet he was already clearly on his last legs. I don't know how he ever wrote "The Dangerous Summer," as he appeared to be drunk all the time. Lucky and I met him on a few social occasions, surrounded by admirers listening to his drunken ramblings. He seemed to focus on Lucky — he generally did so with attractive women — and in their brief conversations he called her "daughter."

After we saw him in the first of the daily series of bullfights in Malaga, Lucky said she was going to bring her copy of *Death in the Afternoon* for him to autograph at the next bullfight.

"Please don't do it," I begged Lucky. "Lately there have been several cases of people handing him books to autograph, and he's written horrible obscenities. You won't be able to show the book to anyone."

But Lucky is never easily discouraged, and at the bullfight she handed the book to a small boy to take to Hemingway's seat at ringside. Just as his hero, the matador Antonio Ordonez, was executing a graceful *capada,* testing the bull with his cape, the boy tapped Hemingway on the shoulder.

In what looked to me more like fury than annoyance, Hemingway turned his head, grabbed the book, wrote a few lines, and handed it back to the boy.

I was almost looking forward to reading what he had to say. Next time Lucky would listen to me! But all it said was "To Lucky Roosevelt — best always from her friend — Ernest Hemingway"! The book is one of Lucky's cherished possessions.

Hemingway's *For Whom the Bell Tolls* was one of the books I read in preparation for Spain, and it helped me understand the depth of feeling about the civil war still palpable in the Spain of the 1950s. Just as Spain is haunted by the Moors, it was, and still is, living in the shadow of the civil war.

The years of the civil war, 1936–39, corresponded with my own years at Harvard, just as I was developing a political philosophy. Thus Spain's agony was imprinted on my memory as it was on that of all my age group. Places like Teruel, Brunete, University City, and the Alcazar of Toledo evoked grim images in the intervening years before I first saw Spain.

The intellectual establishment of Harvard strongly favored the republic, but its most active advocates were the Young Communist League and the Student Union. The only supporters of Franco's rebel government were to be found among Catholics. I could not really empathize with either side. The Spanish republic was certainly nothing like our own, and Franco's people hardly presented the menace of Nazi Germany. It was a quarrel between strangers.

In Spain, most of the people we knew, while generally not enthusiastic about Franco, gave him credit for "saving Spain from the Communists." Many had family horror stories of atrocities and massacres perpetrated by *los rojos* — the Reds.

Some had lost their parents and most of their relatives, and showed us sites of massacres, such as the little square in Santander on the edge of the cliff from which the rojos had pushed their victims into the sea. In front of many village churches we saw monuments listing the names of martyred clergy. Those who had been on the Republican side simply did not talk about it.

What became obvious to me was the connection all this had with the legacy of the Moors — which goes far beyond the participation of Moorish troops in Franco's army. Of course, these troops did arouse historical memories and the atrocities they committed reinforced the evil image the very name "Moor" provokes in Spain.

It is similar to the image of the Tatar in Russia. In fact, while the Russians and the Spaniards are in temperament far apart, they share one characteristic, their "otherness" from the rest of Europe, because of the oriental part of their heritage.

While Western Europe was rediscovering classical antiquity, building on ancient wisdom, examining new vistas, breaking the bonds of the Middle Ages, Spain was in the midst of the crusade to oust the Moors. Like Russia, Spain never really experienced the Renaissance, and certainly not the Reformation. Strangely enough, the Spanish civil war brought about the first real contact between Spaniards and Russians, the two peoples on the fringes of Europe.

The role of the Russians in the civil war left bitter memories not only on the Franco side, but among Republicans as well. It was the Russians who took over political direction of both the army and the police, and following the Soviet example, the Chekas of the Communist party carried out their executions. In the final days of the civil war Communist troops temporarily took control of Madrid in a battle with their fellow Republicans. The memory of all this lingered, and is one of the reasons why, with the restoration of the republic, the Communists were unable to win much popular support in free elections.

While I was in Spain I witnessed one legacy of Russian involvement in the civil war. As it became apparent that the Republicans were losing the conflict, many sent their children to France for safety. When the parents tried to recover their children after the war, they found that the Communist party had arranged to ship thousands of them to the Soviet Union. The parents' protests went unheeded as World War II broke out, cutting them off completely from their children.

The Spaniards did not realize it, but the spiriting away of their children was deliberate Soviet policy, perhaps based on a belief that if you can direct the training of children in their earliest years, they are converts for life. For instance, in 1948, as the Communists were losing the civil war in Greece, they sent thousands of children over the border behind the Iron Curtain; some of them were seized from their parents by force. The Greeks called this program the *pedomasoma* — literally, the "chewing up" of children, many of whom were never seen by their parents again, as author Nicholas Gage has portrayed in his wrenching account, *Eleni*.

Now, in the eighties, the Soviets are carrying out the same policy in Afghanistan, shipping Afghan children off to schools in the Soviet Union.

After World War II the Spanish government tried in vain to negotiate the return of Spanish children. In the absence of diplomatic relations between the two governments, negotiations had to be conducted through the Red Cross in Geneva, and for more than a decade there were no results. However, in 1957 a dynamic military surgeon, Dr. Luis de la Serna, coaxed the Soviets into permitting at least some of them to come home.

I knew Luis — a humane man, with liberal views; in fact, he was a victim of the alliance between Franco and the Catholic Church. Unable to obtain a divorce after an unhappy marriage, he could not marry the wonderful woman with whom he had shared his life for years, the mother of his children. She could not accompany him to mixed parties with his friends, and was shunned by society. I could not help comparing his lot with mine — he the victim of religious hierarchy, I the beneficiary of separation of church and state, a theme I shall revert to later.

As a result of Luis's efforts, during the last years of the fifties about three thousand children of Spanish Republicans, dubbed *los niños,* trickled back to Spain. Their parents, meeting them at the gangplanks of Soviet vessels, were often unpleasantly surprised to see them followed by Russian spouses and their children. On the other hand, they were pleased to see them bringing along household appliances and even sometimes automobiles, purchased with their accumulated social security contributions, returned to them by the Soviet government.

The Soviets clearly hoped to reap a propaganda benefit by this display of riches from Russia. Unfortunately for the niños and their families, however, these appliances were difficult or impossible to use in Spain because of differences in current and sockets. Also, when they inevitably broke down, spare parts were unavailable.

The Soviets are not in the habit of acting from purely humanitarian motives, and would not have returned the niños unless they thought there would be a net advantage to them. The very act of returning the children was a propaganda plus, as was the matter of the appliances. Soon another one would become apparent.

While the niños themselves had managed to hold on to shreds of their Spanish identity, including the language, their Russian wives and children who could not communicate found it difficult to adapt to a closed Spanish society built on lifelong family relationships. The niños often felt like aliens in their motherland, and many had problems finding work to match their technical training. About three hundred of them finally gave up trying to adjust and returned to the Soviet Union. There, interviewed on Soviet television, they drew comparisons between the "idyllic" life in the Soviet Union and the lack of social amenities in Spain.

Also, some niños had been co-opted by Soviet intelligence, with a mission either of finding employment in a field where they might be productive sources for their spy masters, or as sleepers to be activated when the Communists could once again operate in Spain, or in a wartime situation. Spanish security authorities soon became aware of this, which cast suspicion on many innocent niños, compounding their adjustment difficulties.

On the other hand, having been given job opportunities in technical fields in the Soviet Union, they provided valuable intelligence to the West. Because many of them could communicate only in Russian — a language spoken by few Spaniards at the time — the Spaniards sought help from U.S. sources with Russian language capability. When this was fully realized by Soviet authorities, they abruptly halted the return of the niños remaining in the Soviet Union.

With the return of democracy to Spain in 1977, and the restoration of diplomatic relations with Moscow, the Spanish government again sought the return of the niños. By then, however, few remained who were young enough to reorient their lives, and only a couple of hundred have since come back to Spain.

The otherness of Russia and of Spain are about all the two peoples have in common. The Spaniards are the heirs of a great civilization, that of the very Moors they expelled from Spain, and this led them to far horizons even without the full benefit of Western Europe's Renaissance.

The pervasiveness of Moorish influence in Spain and especially in Andalusia, where they lived for almost eight hundred years, is greater than that of the Tatars in Russia, who were never actually settled in the heartland. The Moors held on to the kingdom of Granada in the southeast corner of the peninsula for two and a half centuries after the rest of Spain had been reconquered by the Christians. There they reigned from the palace of the Alhambra, leaving behind to this day one of the most storied and evocative monuments of Moorish history.

When I first saw the Alhambra, I realized that I had already sensed something of its essence in the palaces of Fez and Marrakesh. Lucky and I wandered in the sunny courtyards surrounded by chambers cool in the middle of the day, their cedar ceilings and walls carved with arabesques, with the rubric spelled out over and over, *"La ghaliba illa 'llah"* — "There is no victor but God." These were the words with which Ibn al-Ahmar, the founder of Granada's last dynasty, replied to crowds cheering his victory over his enemies.

The silent courts of the palace for me were full of echoes. I had just read Washington Irving's *The Alhambra* and *The Conquest of Granada*. Irving had wangled an appointment to the U.S. embassy in Madrid in 1826, and visited Granada, arriving on muleback from Seville as part of his preparation for writing his biography of Columbus. He was enchanted by the Alhambra, and camped in its ruins for several weeks. His books later influenced the Spanish government to restore the Alhambra to its former glory.

He must have often thought, looking up to the snowy Sierra Nevada, which forms a backdrop to the scene, of the sad procession of the defeated Moorish king Boabdil, disappearing over the pass. As he gazed for the last time at this beloved city, crowned by the crenellated walls of his abandoned palace, the king burst into tears. His stern mother, the legendary Ayesha, turned to rebuke him: "Weep like a woman for the lost kingdom you could not defend like a man!"

The pass is still known as *"El Ultimo Sospiro del Moro"* — "The Last Sigh of the Moor."

And Irving also must often have stood gazing, as we did, through the delicately carved arches of the castle window at Granada and the Vega, its plain stretching toward a horizon of other mountains, contemplating the scene of the beginning of one of history's great epics. For there, during the final siege of

Granada, in 1491, Columbus won the support of Queen Isabella for his expedition to the Indies. In January 1492 Granada surrendered, ending 780 years of Moorish rule in Spain, and in October of that same year Columbus discovered America. The conjuncture of the two events marks a point in history of momentous consequence, as what then developed in America sprang directly from the centuries-old process of the Christian Reconquista of Spain. The Spanish empire was born in the ashes of the last kingdom of the Moors.

The modern history of Spain, its society, its religious outlook, the special characteristics of its people, spring from the Reconquista. For much of the Middle Ages, the Moors were the most civilized people in the Western world. Cordova was the most important center of learning in Europe, and Arab culture was absorbed in the West, some of it in matters we think of as basic elements in the Christian Middle Ages. For instance, the songs of the troubadours are thought to have derived from Moslem Spain; the Arab ideal of sharaf translated into the medieval code of chivalry.

For almost four hundred years Moslem, Christian, and Jew practiced their respective religions in relative freedom throughout the Iberian peninsula.

Large numbers of Christians called Mozarabes, who had never accepted the religion of their Moslem overlords, continued to live peacefully in Moorish Spain. Christian rulers were equally tolerant of the Mudejars, the Moslems living in the northern kingdoms.

All this came to an end with the invasion of the fanatical Almoravids. The Mozarabes fled or were forcibly converted to Islam, although the Jews were allowed to stay. In Christian Spain, while the Moslems were still tolerated, increasing numbers of them immigrated to Granada or Africa.

The struggle between Moors and Christians, culminating in the conquest of Granada, was now a full-fledged religious war. The Catholic Kings, Ferdinand and Isabella, planned to continue the war against the Moors in North Africa, when fate intervened in the form of Christopher Columbus. The crusading zeal of the Spanish people, the drive and energy fueled by the Reconquista, found their outlet in the New World instead of spilling over into North Africa. The unfortunate inhabitants of the West Indies, the Aztecs, the Incas, and countless others were the principal victims of the "Spanish fury"* instead of the Moors of North Africa.

At the same time Ferdinand and Isabella introduced forced conversion of the Moslems in Granada as government policy. The Jews were expelled from Spain in 1492 if they refused to convert, and soon even Jewish and Moslem converts became victims of the Inquisition.

This religious zeal, carried by crusading armies into the New World, molded the Hispanic nations that arose there. These societies have a heritage of Spanish aristocratic, military, and religious hierarchies, a middle class without power, and an oppressed peasantry largely of Indian blood. The social turmoil we see in Latin America today derives from the Reconquista, and ultimately from the Moorish domination of Spain.

Thus the influence of Moslem civilization, which extends from the Atlantic to the Pacific in the Old World, has also left its many traces in the New World.

---

* A term used by other Europeans in the sixteenth century to describe the courage — and brutality — of Spanish troops.

PART EIGHT

The Truth Shall
Make You Free

33

The Truth Shall Make You Free

WHILE THE MAIN ROAD of my journey has been through the world of Islam, I have taken many side trips, and some of my assignments in the Agency have been "global." In the process I have come to certain conclusions about intelligence, the search for truth, and its practical applications in our society.

The motto of the Central Intelligence Agency, marked in gold lettering in the giant vestibule at its headquarters in Langley, Virginia, is a quote from the Gospel of Saint John: "And ye shall know the truth, and the truth shall make you free."

It was to seek the truth that I embarked on my long journey to Samarkand. It is normal for every developing human being to wish to know the truth about the phenomena unfolding before his or her eyes. But for most the search for universal truths fades as their vision narrows to focus on their individual needs. The vast majority of humankind relies on some kind of outside authority — religious or political leaders or the media — for their views on the universal, while they concentrate on the individual truths that bear on their own lives. But some, professionals and specialists in various disciplines, continue throughout their lives to search for truth in the world beyond their horizons.

The intelligence officer is one of these. His natural curiosity to seek out the ways of the many tribes of mankind is tailored to the needs not of himself, but of his government.

A basic quality required of an intelligence officer is objectivity, an ability to analyze the truth without regard to accepted beliefs, which might distort his findings.

There can be only one limit to his objectivity — he must believe in his own society, his country, and its form of government. He should not imitate the cynical protagonists of John Le Carré's novels, essentially craftsmen who find their side no less amoral than the other. The intelligence officer, to be effective, must not only know whose side he is on, but have a deep conviction that it is the right one.

I have, since adolescence, admired the great Russian people, and studied their language and their culture. But I think that the Soviet Union represents a threat to the civilization of which we are the heirs, the greatest danger faced by mankind today. Therefore, the belief that we must understand all the forces of the world we are contesting has guided my steps on the Road to Samarkand ever since I became an intelligence officer.

That said, I must return to the theme that the enemy of truth is ideology. It was the doctrine of the church in the Middle Ages that was the greatest obstacle to man's search for truth, for scientific progress. By breaking the bonds of theology in the Renaissance and the Reformation we escaped from the Middle Ages into the Enlightenment — that is, some of us escaped. Many of us to this day are bound by the chains of theologians in the prison of the past.

I find religious fanaticism one of the worst scourges of mankind and by this I do not mean the religious beliefs that guide the lives of most of us. Tolerance of the beliefs of others is essential for the civility under which our society ideally must operate. Tolerance is preached from many pulpits — though some organized religions have shown a higher regard for it than others. The Unitarian Church, to which my mother belonged, has always fostered it, as have the Quakers. The Buddhists, for instance, seem not to have any zeal for requiring those holding other beliefs to conform.

But the record of many organized religions, past and present, is not a shining one. Proselytism by example and persuasion cannot be faulted, but unfortunately many hold that unbelievers should be forced to conform to their own faiths, and hate them as their enemies. The Khomeinists instantly come to mind today as a glaring example, but we see fanaticism and hatred of others in most religions: Hindus, Moslems, and Sikhs in the Indian subcontinent; Jewish Orthodox extremists in Israel; certain Protestant fundamentalists here at home — the list is long. The senseless horror of Lebanon provides a daily reminder of the curse of fanaticism. And among these fanatics we must count the Marxist orthodox under the command of the Soviet Union.

All of these are the enemies of truth, their perceptions clouded by their narrow beliefs, both religious and ideological. While the intelligence officer may privately hold any number of personal beliefs in addition to his basic loyalty to his society, he must not let them affect his judgment. He must also be able to empathize with true believers of every stripe in order to understand and analyze them.

He must study the language, the culture, the society of other peoples, so that he can learn to think like them, and see the world in their terms. He must, like Chairman Mao's guerrillas, be able to swim in foreign seas. But then he must be able to pull himself to shore, and look back calmly, objectively, on the waters that immersed him.

When I speak of an intelligence officer, it is in the old-fashioned sense, perhaps best exemplified in fiction by Kipling's British political officers in India. I do not mean the analysts toiling in headquarters to make sense of reports from all over the world, but the man "in the field," as they say in the CIA.

The backbone of our foreign intelligence apparatus is composed of case officers, whose job it is to spot, assess, recruit, and direct agents to report on our principal targets, the major one of which is the Soviet Union. This requires him to be in contact with individuals in many walks of life in the country to which he is assigned, although in friendly nations his main task may be working with the intelligence service of the host government.

The Agency's team in each country is headed by the station chief. In a small capital he may be the only case officer, fulfilling all the Agency's functions there himself. In a larger place his task may involve him less personally in operations, and more in directing and coordinating the activities of others.

Theoretically, he is only a producer of "raw intelligence" to be processed by the analysts in Washington, distilled and distributed to others of the intelligence community and to the policymakers in the State Department and the White House. In fact, the station chief has to be not only the eyes and ears of the U.S. government, but also a part of its brain, which interprets the messages it receives to form a complete picture.

To perform this function the station chief must have an intimate understanding of the country where he is posted and the various social elements that compose it. He must understand and empathize with all of them, while maintaining the hard core of his own identity as an American intelligence officer, like a gemstone unaffected by outside forces of nature.

Our country is blessed with a fine, professional Foreign Service, many of whose members are also intelligence officers in the general sense of the word. Those who reach the pinnacle of their career as ambassadors are most often the best of the breed.

While the ambassador heads the country team and is responsible for all functions of an embassy, his principal task is carrying out the policies of the U.S. government. If an ambassador does not empathize with the people of the country to which he has been assigned, or fails to understand them, he is generally a poor ambassador. A good ambassador, like a good intelligence officer, becomes immersed in his host country.

But sometimes in the process he catches a special kind of malady, known in the Foreign Service as "clientitis." His dispatches no longer refer to "the king of Graustark," but to "our king." He becomes one of them. Such an ambassador may provide an important leavening to judgments being made by a Washington "which does not understand" — a favorite phrase of clientitis-stricken ambassadors.

But an effective intelligence officer cannot fall into this trap. He must never forget that his service is the front line in a precarious world, facing an enemy who, despite periods of detente, has been seeking to subvert our society for half a century. So he cannot let himself believe that peace initiatives are anything but tactical. The Soviets have not abandoned their goal of replacing our social and economic system, the basis of our civilization, with their own, the basis of their repressive society. We can reply to "the smile on the face of the bear" by a grin of our own, but keep an eye on his ready claws. That bear has not changed since Kipling's time — indeed, we now see him in Afghanistan on the northern rim of the Khyber

Pass. You have only to go there, the true front line, to feel the chill winds of the Cold War blowing over those forbidding mountains. Everything is khaki brown: the treeless rocky slopes of the pass, the villages, the costumes of the grim-faced tribesmen. You are approaching the trenches.

But most of the world is not so grim — it is varicolored, and the intelligence officer must make out these different hues, assimilate them, interpret them. He should become an area expert, and on him and his diplomatic co-workers depends the success of our policies abroad. Our failures often, in fact nearly always, result either from the failure of our policymakers to take his views into account, or from the deficiencies of our field representatives because they lack the background necessary for understanding the terrain they are working.

I have seen, even participated in, both kinds of failures.

In the early days of my career with the Agency, I was involved in "political action" in the Arab world. During the period of 1956–58 we tried, mostly unsuccessfully, to stem the course of nationalism in the Arab world. This ideology was fueled by the pan-Arab passions aroused by Gamal Abd-al-Nasser, from his uncertain base in Egypt. During the forties, the days of my ephemeral passages in Egypt, Egyptians never spoke of themselves as Arabs. Civilized Egyptians looked down on Arabs as people of the desert, much as their ancient forebears viewed the Semites of the East as "sand eaters." But Nasser changed all that, setting fire to the East with the flames of Arab nationalism.

Our policymakers constantly confused the sources of this conflagration with Communism, with the machinations of the Soviets, who were indeed trying to exploit the forces unleashed by Nasser. But they never gained control of them.

The distinction between Communists and the nationalist extremists has not always been understood by the "wise men" of Washington.

I recall vividly being asked by CIA deputy director General Pearre Cabell to attend a meeting of these wise men in the State Department, presided over by Secretary of State John Foster Dulles, in 1957.

A decision was being made about countering the forces of Arab nationalism, specifically their radical form in the United Arab Republic of Egypt and Syria, using the instrument of the

Baghdad pact. I looked around the table and saw only one other person, Loy Henderson, who had a firsthand understanding of the Middle East and really knew what we were talking about. The subject under discussion was a mission on which Henderson would be sent to the presumably friendly capitals of the periphery to line up opposition to the UAR. Secretary Dulles was canvasing us for our views.

I slipped a note to "Pree" Cabell saying, "I wish to voice my strong dissent from the opinions expressed here." He scribbled a comment and passed it back to me: "It is not for us to give our views on matters of policy." He was a soldier who saluted when a commander gave him his orders.

So when Dulles said, "I presume we are all in agreement with the decision we have reached here" and looked around the room, I kept my eyes on the table and remained silent. But the question nagged at me after the meeting broke up and I could not sleep that night. The next morning — it was a weekend — I could bear it no longer, and frantically tried to locate Henderson, but it was too late. He was already on his way to the airport and unreachable.

Afterward he told me, "I heard you were trying to get hold of me, and I knew why. The decision was a mistaken one." The Henderson Mission, as it was then called, to the capitals on the periphery of the Arab explosion then taking place died aborning. The Baghdad revolution of July 1958 put an end to this policy of containment.

Yet we did not learn. We are repeating the same errors today, as we continue confusing the separate streams of Marxism and nationalism. And not only in the Middle East.

In Africa we see so-called African Marxist governments whose elites were trained by theoreticians at the London School of Economics, the Sorbonne, and the like. They were encouraged in their struggles with their colonial masters by the Communist party and the emissaries of the Soviet bloc. But they remained Africans, with their own firm core of tribal tradition. Marxism is only a European coating, and the African socialist states today bear little resemblance to the slavish satellites of Eastern Europe. The Africanists of our State Department and our intelligence community understand this, but sometimes our generalists do not.

Our country needs the brilliant insights of global thinkers like Henry Kissinger — if indeed there is anybody like him! But we also must heed our area experts, whom we ignore at our peril. To cite an example of the results of the "valor of ignorance,"* we have only to look at Iran.

For many years in that tragic battlefield, "our side" enjoyed considerable success. But this success derived from our support of dominant nationalist forces in the country. George Allen supported the Shah in defeating the Demokrats in Azerbaijan, and he was successful because the army and most people — including the Azerbaijanis — were behind the Shah.

At the beginning of the fifties, the erratic Iranian prime minister, Mohammad Mosaddegh, nationalized the Anglo-Iranian Oil Company. This led to a political confrontation between Mosaddegh's government and Britain and a virtual British blockage of the export of Iranian oil. Mosaddegh, in defiance of the Shah, gradually directed his country away from the Western allies and toward the Soviet Union. In June 1953, Secretary of State Dulles, alarmed by this trend and in accord with the British, authorized my cousin Kermit to launch Operation Ajax to oust Mosaddegh and restore the power of the Shah. (I played no role in this, being occupied in another part of the world at the time.)

Kim was able to accomplish this with a minimal use of American personnel and funds, because Mosaddegh's support was shallow, mostly stemming from leftist intellectuals. The dominant forces of the country stood behind the Shah, including the bulk of the army officer corps and the *bazaris,* who poured out of their little shops to demonstrate their support.

In the traditional Middle East, one sees these bazaris, owners of small businesses, squatting in their cubicles along the streets of the souq. Unimpressive individually, collectively they are an important part of the power structure of the country. Of humble origin initially, they came to form a caste of their own, passing their businesses from father to son.

They are sober, hardworking, conservative people who cling to their own culture and religion; it is they in Iran who are the

---

* The title of a book written by Homer Lea at the turn of the century warning a heedless America about the rise of Japanese militarism.

strongest supporters of the religious establishment and the maintenance of the religious education system of which they themselves are the product. And they are the organizers of the religious processions on holy days.

The bazaris have nothing in common with the Western-educated elite that has grown up in the Middle East, who speak English, wear Western dress, and whose women do not wear the veil. In Iran a social gulf divides the new elite and the mass of people — villagers, manual laborers, the "lower classes" in general. And the mullas, who have been their spiritual guides, have now become their political leaders as well.

In recent years I have often had cause to remember the warnings of Ali Loqmani, my Persian teacher in Baghdad, about the iniquitous power of the mullas. When I was transferred to Iran in 1946 I found them ubiquitous — bobbing along the side streets, their turbans and abas setting them off from the rest of the people in Western dress — but hardly iniquitous. The threat then came from the Communist party, the Tudeh, and in the struggle with "godless Communism" the religious establishment, backed by the pious majority, had to stand on the side of the Shah.

The participation of those masses in demonstrations led by the Tudeh gave a false picture of the power of the Marxists, deceiving both those who feared them, like ourselves, and their supporters the Soviets. We were both surprised by the speedy collapse of the Demokrats in Azerbaijan, who clearly lacked any popular base.

Similarly, we were surprised by the Shah's lack of support by the masses when Khomeini was making his bid for power. Had they not supported him in 1946, when the Soviets were trying to take over Iran? Had they not marched in the streets to cheer him, both then and in 1953, when he overthrew Mosaddegh?

The fact was that the Shah then stood for the defense of the nation and its Islamic religion. But in the late seventies the Islamic majority saw their religion threatened by their own more fortunate countrymen. They saw the streets of the city filled with affluent, Westernized people, whose women flaunted their bare faces, arms, and legs to tempt the faithful, who flocked to bars and discos to drink forbidden liquor, and who danced shamelessly in public view. And it was the Shah himself and his family who gave the example for this immoral behavior.

Was it not his father, Reza Shah, who tore the veils off the faces of the women, who broke the mullas, and even invaded the holy shrines? Was it not he himself who drove the great Ayatollah Khomeini into exile?

Westerners in Iran had few contacts outside the European-ized educated class and hence had a distorted view of Iranian society. American business and government representatives did not count bazaris and mullas among their friends, not to speak of working-class and peasant Iranians.

These people had little in common with their Western-oriented fellow countrymen, whom they viewed as *taghuti* — "idol worshippers" — and *kafirin* — "unbelievers." Neither did the bulk of the Iranian people share the sentiments of intel-lectual opponents of the Shah and the ruling establishment. These English-speaking, foreign-educated lawyers and profes-sors aroused little sympathy among the masses in their appeals for democracy.

There has never been anything like democracy in Iran. From earliest times it was ruled by an autocratic shah. Genghis Khan and his Turkic successors carried on the tradition — as did the Turkic tribes who overran the country. Turkic tribal society is dominated by an all-powerful khan and has none of the Arab tradition of the majlis, the tribal deliberative body.

The Iranians were despised by the Arabs at the time of their conquest of Iran as a slavish people. It was the Iranians who handed down the traditions of oriental court life to the Arabs, particularly under the Abbasids. The Arab rulers exchanged the more democratic traditions of Bedouin tribal chiefs for the despotic splendor of the East. It was the Iranian custom to prostrate oneself before an all-powerful shah. The eunuch did not exist in Arabia — and neither did women's veils, another import from Iran. Contrary to general belief, the veil is not mentioned in the Koran.

The Iranians respected the power of their rulers and could only be seduced from their loyalty to the khan by the appear-ance of someone more powerful. The shah ruled only as long as he held not only the reins of power, but the whip. And his whip lay with his army.

Mohammed Reza Shah, despite the trappings of royalty, always had the soul of the timid, diffident young man I met in 1946. He did not inherit his father's will of iron. Indeed, he had been broken by that will. When the young Shah's throne was threatened by Mosaddegh in 1953, he abandoned it and fled to Italy, while the army and the bazaris — prodded by Cousin Kim — won it back. Unnoticed, he ran away once again in the sixties when his power was threatened. And in 1979 again he cut and ran. If, in the beginning, the Shah had shown the ruthlessness of his predecessors — Darius the Great, Genghis Khan, Reza Shah — the Iranian masses would have bared their necks, and prostrated themselves before the Great Khan. Instead, they turned to worship at the feet of the Grand Ayatollah.

In the West, especially in the United States, we excoriated the Shah for failing to follow the dictates of democracy. We praised the intellectuals trying to establish a political party system in Iran, with free elections to a free parliament. We pressured the Shah for democratic reform, and told him to throw away his whip. He did so, and threw away his throne.

We worried about the Tudeh, the Communists, the Soviets working behind the scenes. Dire predictions were made by pundits in the media. The mullas were simply being used by the Soviets and the Marxists. The Tudeh would take over the country. Or the country would split; the Azerbaijanis would rise again. If you said to an American audience — as I did — that the Soviets had nothing to do with events in Iran at the end of the seventies, that it was a purely Iranian phenomenon, you were told — as I was — that you were being duped, that like traditional Western liberals, you were accepting the Soviet line.

Most U.S. policymakers, both conservative and liberal, consistently see the Soviet hand in extremist movements in the Middle East; however, the Soviets generally are not the prime movers. They may play an auxiliary role to disrupt societies and governments allied to the West, but exert no control. And they often view these movements with dismay, because of their uncontrolled character, as in the case of Khomeini.

How did we ever let ourselves be led so far astray in Iran? How did we fail to read the signs? How could we permit ourselves to become the victims of these fanatics, and undergo the humiliation of the seizure of our embassy and the ordeal of the hostages?

Where were our cadres of those who understood because they had passed years of their lives among these people? They were not to be found in our embassy in Iran. There were not many of them in Washington. Some of the old-timers had been dismissed by a director of Central Intelligence with no feeling for his own operations men. Others, of more recent vintage, had been scattered to the far winds in a period when area experts were denigrated. These "satrapies" of inbred area specialists should be broken up, and one should be a generalist, a jack-of-all-trades — such was the current thinking in Washington. Those were the people who mostly staffed our embassy in Tehran, few of whom knew the language or had experience among those who spoke it. And they received their direction often from a hierarchy that knew even less than they did about Iran.

When the fanatics seized our embassy and held its staff and its acting chief of mission captive, I'll wager not a single participant in the higher councils of the Carter administration knew the history of the rights of embassy. These predated by millennia the Vienna Convention of 1961 codifying the rules of modern diplomacy, especially diplomatic immunity. When most of mankind lived in tribal societies, ambassadors passed from one tribe to another, protected by sacred tradition, to settle their continuous quarrels and wars.

Virtually every literate Iranian knows what happened when a thirteenth-century shah executed the ambassador of Genghis Khan. The Mongol chieftain, in righteous vengeance, herded all his tribesmen westward. They reduced the cities of Iran to smoking ruins and their inhabitants to heaps of rotting corpses. The scars are still there today.

Nobody in our government in 1979 thought to remind the Iranians of this, the most terrible catastrophe of their tragic history. Nor did anyone seem to know of the hallowed tradition of embassy, and think to remind all the powers of their obligations. While suggesting that they recall their ambassadors from Iran, we could then have proceeded, in accordance with the Law of Nations, to give the Iranians a time frame within which to vacate our embassy and free its officials; meanwhile, we would be positioning our fleet for a blockade, the first of a series of internationally justified steps to force the Iranians to return to acceptable diplomatic norms.

At that point the Iranians might have recalled the vengeance wrought by the Great Khan on that shah for his acts against an embassy seven hundred years earlier. Instead they saw their

new shah, the Ayatollah, humiliate the embassy of the foreigner, the infidel, without retribution. The mullas and their
followers knew nothing about the "human rights" that so
preoccupied our government at the time of the Shah's downfall.
They applauded their new absolute ruler, Khomeini, as they
filled the dungeons and torture chambers vacated by the Shah's
prisoners with "heretics" and "idolaters."

This religious underclass did not include the Westernized
business contacts, friends, and acquaintances of American
embassy officials. They did not go to dinner parties and attend
learned international conferences. Their cohorts are the sons
of the people we saw marching in the main square of Tehran in
1946 crying "Down with the Reactionaries!" and who, when we
asked who the Reactionaries were, answered that it was the
brother of a certain Sayyid Zia!

Having criticized in detail the Carter administration's handling of the embassy hostage crisis, it would be unfair not to
refer to the Reagan administration's Iran fiasco. There is little
I can add to the voluminous factual material and commentary
about it except to emphasize a single point.

One think piece by a CIA officer suggesting consideration be
given to a change of U.S. policy on Iran, in view of the
possibility that the Soviets might be able to exploit instability
there in the post-Khomeini era, was developed by the National
Security Council as a basis for its new approach. Subsequent
reports submitted by Agency and other area specialists gave no
support to it; on the contrary, all were agreed on the continued
strength of the mullas' regime and the lack of any threat, from
the Soviet Union or anyone else, to its stability.

Israeli intelligence, filtered through Israeli policymakers
whose interests differed from those of our own government,
should not have been considered a substitute for the views of
the American intelligence community. But it was used as the
basis on which this unfortunate affair was pursued by NSC
military officers, nobly motivated but unschooled in the wiles of
the wheelers and dealers of the Middle East.

We have a fine intelligence system coordinated by the Central
Intelligence Agency. Those who act without consulting it in
reaching policy decisions do so at their peril, and the peril of all
of us.

34

The Truth and the Arabs

THE UNITED STATES is an extremely ethnocentric country. Most of us believe that we have a superior social and governmental system, the best in the world; the lucky ones from
outside have joined us here, leaving behind their rigid old societies. We know little about these societies and understand them
less. We devote minimum attention to them — just look in any
newspaper in our heartland, and search for the foreign news in
the back pages. In 1940, when I worked as a reporter in Spokane,
the Capital of the Inland Empire, the front page of the newspaper featured only what was going on in "our empire." Some
little war in Europe might rate an item low on page 3.

With this background, it is no wonder that the decision
makers of our government lack understanding of an outside
world so alien to them. They turn to the intelligence community
to explain it all. And those in the intelligence community who
do the explaining are analysts whose principal qualification for
the job is academic training leading to a higher degree. Few of
them have any firsthand experience in the country they are
analyzing; their analyses are often founded on wrong assumptions pieced together from the works of their colleagues.

In the Agency there are two principal organizations involved
in intelligence production, named after their deputy directors:
the Deputy Director for Plans (DDP) — which was given a cover
name hiding its true function until 1974, when it became the
Deputy Director for Operations (DDO) — and the Deputy
Director for Intelligence (DDI).

The DDP-DDO is responsible for all overseas stations conducting intelligence operations, producing raw intelligence. Its personnel spend most of their lives in foreign countries, acquiring by practice the knowledge of foreign cultures necessary to understand and reach their targets. During intervals of service in Washington, they oversee and coordinate overseas operations, passing on the raw intelligence they produce to the DDI.

The DDI academics receive this intelligence as well as that from many other sources, both overt and covert, such as the embassies, the military attachés, and the media, foreign and domestic. They then edit and screen it, passing it on to the various government "consumers."

To distill and refine this mass of information, there used to be an Office of National Estimates (ONE), which met with other members of the intelligence community and produced estimates for the guidance of policymakers, the cabinet, the president.

DDP-DDO officers returning from the field were formally debriefed in meetings with the DDI and ONE. I, like others in my category, was amazed at the lack of knowledge of local realities displayed by these academics even though they had been reading all our reports.

Given this, one can understand how our government can make serious policy errors based on intelligence estimates distilled by theoreticians. Such estimates often tend to reinforce the world view of our leaders, of white hats and black hats, with enemy Marxists on one side lined up with the Soviet Union, and our friends and allies of the free world on the other.

Khomeini and the other strains of Moslem fundamentalists do not fit into this mold. Neither do the self-proclaimed Marxist states of Africa. Marxism was useful to them when they needed Soviet assistance in fighting for their independence, but it is only skin-deep, easily sloughed off when reality brings them to turn to the Western democracies. The Soviets offer only weapons, military and security training, and an inefficient, outworn economic system; the West offers the means of survival.

Today, of all the African Marxist states, only Ethiopia remains firmly tied to the Soviet system — and one man alone, Haile Mariam Mengistu, is responsible for keeping it there.

When he leaves the scene, the unforgotten traditions of an ancient people will eventually prevail over this aberration.

In the Arab world, despite the best efforts of the Soviets and their Communist supporters, only the "People's Republic" of South Yemen is a Marxist state. And the Soviets can hardly be said to control that country, since in 1985 their embassy was partly demolished in a brief civil war that took them by surprise. We should also note that the Ethiopian Marxist Mengistu backed the leader opposed by the Soviets!

It is perhaps in dealing with the Arab world that our policymakers have most often confused nationalism and fundamentalism with Marxism, attributing them almost entirely to the machinations of our Soviet enemy.

John Foster Dulles, in other ways a respected secretary of state, failed to understand this. He was at least in part responsible for the chain of events leading to the various crises in the Arab world at the end of the fifties and to our confrontation with the new wave of Arab nationalism led by Gamal Abd-al-Nasser.

I myself had one personal meeting with Nasser, in 1953. He received me in the diminutive dining room of an obscure cottage in a Cairo suburb. Wearing a plain khaki uniform with open collar and no insignia, he was a tall, broad-shouldered man with a vigorous handshake. His handsome features were typically Egyptian sharpened by a touch of classic Arabian aquilinity, topped by a close-cropped head of curly black hair interspersed with strands of gray. He had an open face and a ready smile as he spoke in a baritone voice, chain-smoking all the while. His words were less remarkable than his personality, expressing the views of mainstream Arab nationalism. But he radiated charm, energy, youthful enthusiasm, expressing these thoughts as if they were his own, just burst out of his brain.

I felt that here was a man we could work with, or at least coexist with, as in time his ambitions were bound to clash against the older, more stable forces in the Arab world. We would have our differences, but at least, I thought, this man had a vision surpassing that of most Arab politicians. This might be the leader who could unite the Arab world in seeking accommodations and solutions for the area's problems.

But it was we, not he, who nipped in the bud any hope for working together to accomplish this — if, indeed, such hope was justified in those bright beginnings of Nasser's rule in Egypt. In time, even without our intervention, his course was probably doomed to follow that of many Third World charismatic leaders, from early idealism to arrogant dictatorship.

On December 15, 1955, the United States in coordination with Britain offered to lend the Egyptian government funds necessary to launch Nasser's pet project, the Aswan Dam. Nasser delayed acceptance, hoping to balance U.S. assistance and consequent dependence on us with Soviet aid. But he found out, as have so many Third World leaders since, that the Soviets are tight-fisted with all except military aid.

The Egyptian ambassador to the United States, on instruction from his government, publicly accepted on July 17, 1956, the offer of U.S. aid for construction of the Aswan Dam. Two days later, wanting to "cut Nasser down to size," and particularly angered by Egyptian recognition of Communist China, Secretary of State Dulles announced the withdrawal of our offer of aid.

Faced with this humiliation and loss of face, Nasser reacted predictably, giving a riposte to drown out the noise of the slap he had received from Foster Dulles. On July 26 he nationalized the Suez Canal.

While this primarily affected the British and the French, it was an action of defiance against the whole Western world. The United States, in partnership with the British, undertook to stem the tide of Arab nationalism, now overtly hostile to the West, by counteraction. A focal point of Nasserist effort was Syria, where Nasser was in the process of orchestrating a replacement of the old conservative leadership with nationalists holding views similar to his own.

In this Nasser was supported by a small contingent of true Marxists including the minuscule Communist party, abetted by the Soviets. Marxists and nationalists could work together under the vaguely defined umbrella of "Arab Socialism," though the aims of Communists and nationalists were diametrically opposed. And Foster Dulles and the U.S. foreign policy establishment could lump them all together as a leftist coalition of forces supported by the Soviets, and thus a target legally authorized by statute for CIA political action.

I can still vividly recall going to Foster Dulles's home in answer to a summons one Sunday morning in late July 1956, after having been informed by my superiors that I was now the point man on Syria. Dulles was sitting behind a desk in his study loaded with papers and greeted me in his usual, somewhat diffident, scholarly manner.

"As you know, Archie, we're much concerned about what's going on in Syria — especially the way the Communists and nationalists appear to be ganging up for some kind of action there. The army seems to be the key to the problem. I'd like you to fly out to Damascus right away, talk to our ambassador, and see what you can find out about goings-on in the army and what can be done about it."

Our ambassador was my old friend from Baghdad days, Jimmy Moose, and when on a steamy day in August I called on him in his office in the Damascus embassy, he was even gloomier than his normally not very cheerful self.

"This place is really deteriorating, and Foster's quite right — we're likely to have a leftist-nationalist coup at any time."

"What is the attitude of the chief of staff, Shawqat Shuqayr?" I asked.

"I'm afraid he's going along with whatever the Nasserists are cooking up. He's a strong nationalist, and anyway, as a Druze he knows he must trim his views to those of the majority."

"Perhaps you're not aware of it, Jimmy, but Shawqat is Lucky's mother's first cousin, and I'm sure he'd meet with me on a family basis, and perhaps be willing to talk a little more frankly to me."

Moose approved the idea, and arranged an appointment for me through the military attaché, who updated me on the state of the Syrian army. Shawqat was a product of the French mandate government's policy of recruiting much of the Syrian army and its officer corps from among members of Syria's two heretic Islamic sects, the Druze and the Alawites. The Druze have a warrior tradition and had spearheaded the 1925 rebellion against the French, so were temperamentally suited for the military. The far larger Alawite sect, located in the mountains on Lebanon's northern boundary, was composed of poor, oppressed peasants who welcomed the opportunities offered by a military career, and dominate Syria today. The French had originally hoped to detach the Druze and the Alawites from Sunni Syria and form their home provinces into autonomous states, but the project was never implemented. Most of the

Alawites and the Druze joined the mainstream of Arab nationalism and Shawqat Shuqayr was a fervent supporter of Gamal
Abd-al-Nasser.

He was considered the *za'im** of the Shuqayr family, and I
entered his office expecting to confront a mustachioed Arab
warrior. But the man who rose from behind his desk to greet
me was a clean-shaven little man of undistinguished appearance. He was friendly and courteous, but after a few polite
family exchanges embarked on an unvarnished exposition of
the standard Nasserist Arab nationalist position. I wrote him
off as a contact of any significance. I correctly concluded that he
would play no part in the military power struggle, and he was
soon retired from the Syrian army, but I underestimated him as
an individual. He later played a significant role in Lebanon as
Druze leader Kamal Jumblat's chief of staff.

For a few months we all wrestled inconclusively with the
problem of the progressive takeover of Syria by radical nationalist army officers, to be thwarted in all countermeasures we
were considering by the unexpected invasion of the Sinai by the
Israelis on October 29, 1956, followed by the British and
French intervention.

This put an end to any hope of slowing down the progressive
assumption of power in Syria by radical army officers. In fact,
there was little we could have done to change the course of
events, perhaps inevitable, once the military threat to Nasser
had been blunted by President Eisenhower. Nasser now no
longer had to depend solely on the Russians for support, and
viewed the extension of their influence in Syria with alarm.

In February 1958, when Communist officers and politicians
there were clearly moving to take power, the Nasserite faction
in Syria forestalled them by announcing a federal union with
Egypt.

Eventually this group in turn was overthrown by right-wing
officers and in September 1961 they dissolved the union with
Egypt. During the next year or so of government by conservative politicians, the Ba'ath Socialist party, banned under Nasser,
reorganized itself, and took power in another coup in March
1963. Ba'ath party leaders and army officers struggled for

---

* A word conveying a meaning of both hero and leader, used in Lebanon to designate
the chiefs of the country's warring factions.

power in a series of coups during the following years, until Hafiz al-Assad finally settled the Ba'ath leadership question in his takeover in November 1970. He is still with us today.

What all this should show us is that the ability of the United States to influence events in Middle Eastern countries — and in most of the Third World as well — is limited. Local forces essentially govern these nations' own political systems, and we can influence the course of events only when we give our support to a force strong enough to prevail.

This we did in Iran in 1953. In Syria we swam against the tide of Nasserism, and were swept aside by events beyond our control. In Iraq in 1958 our friends were overwhelmed, while in Saudi Arabia and Jordan they were strong enough to prevail, as they did for the time being in Lebanon.

And what about Lebanon?

Lebanon is a prime example of what I am talking about, the powerlessness of the United States when we swim against the stream, when we ignore the voices among us of those who know, who empathize, who understand the undercurrents of a foreign society.

To understand the debacle of 1983–84 in Lebanon, we have to start with Israel. One of the myths widely current in the United States is that of the efficacy of Israeli intelligence; it is simply not very reliable in coverage of its primary target, the Arab world surrounding Israel's narrow boundaries. The Jewish communities that used to inhabit the Arab countries today are gathered in Israel, viewed by most Arabs with abhorrence. Thus Israeli intelligence can rarely count on ideological volunteers inside the Arab target. Furthermore, except for their now-established embassy in Egypt, they have no embassies in the Arab countries from which to conduct operations. So they must try to find recruits without a local base, from afar, a very difficult task.

Of course, they can occasionally locate an Arab who will work against his government for venal motives, or because of a personal grudge against his regime, but such are hard to find. There are, however, a few religious and ethnic communities in the Arab world, such as the Maronites in Lebanon, whose members find it ideologically acceptable to work with the Israelis. The mostly Maronite Phalangists in Lebanon provide valuable intelligence assistance to the Israelis in their operations in Lebanon, such as raids against Palestinian targets.

However, the Israelis cannot easily find recruits in the mainstream of Arabs, particularly those groups involved in active measures against Israel. This accounts for Israeli mistakes in pinpointing the perpetrators of terrorist attacks abroad. Most notorious of these was the murder by Israeli agents in Oslo of a Moroccan cook, mistaken for the Palestinian who masterminded the killings of Israeli athletes at the 1972 Munich Olympics, which resulted in damaging repercussions in Norway.

In the broader field of intelligence judgments about their Arab enemy, the Israeli government and intelligence establishment are mainly composed of people who cannot empathize with the Arabs. There are old-timers, for years divorced from intelligence, who really know the Arabs, like Eliahu Elath and Teddy Kollek. Though I have never worked with Israeli intelligence, I suspect that my friend Ari Chill, the Haganah representative in Baghdad, is more typical of them. They are basically European in outlook, like the French *colons* in North Africa, viewing the Arabs as alien, threatening, hateful, and inferior, and as a people with whom they have nothing in common. Hence their own intelligence failures.

In 1973, although my responsibilities did not involve the Middle East, we were very much of one family in the operations side of the Agency. I was in daily contact with colleagues patrolling my old stamping ground. They knew very well that the Egyptians and the Syrians were preparing to avenge the humiliation of 1967, that they were certain to go to war; all the signs were pointing in that direction. But the academics of the DDI did not believe the signals and a reassuring estimate was sent to the intelligence community and the White House — later cited as another example of a CIA intelligence failure.

Israeli intelligence, like the DDI, thought that the Arabs were as usual indulging in empty bombast and impotent threatening gestures. The Israelis turned their backs to participate in a long weekend observing Yom Kippur — and it required all their courage and ingenuity, with considerable military aid rushed from the United States, to turn back an Arab attack that was almost fatal to the Israeli state.

In Lebanon a decade later, the same lack of understanding both on the part of the Israelis and our policymakers (though not our intelligence) led to catastrophe, not so much for the

Israelis, but for ourselves and of course the Lebanese, already racked by civil war. Encouraged by our government, the Israelis launched their invasion, convinced that it would end in a Lebanon free of the PLO and controlled by their allies the Phalange.

But Prime Minister Menachem Begin and Ariel Sharon had overestimated the extent of their support from the United States. Even though our government had sympathized with Israeli objectives, it could not stomach the slaughter of thousands of civilians and the reduction to rubble of what was left of Beirut after years of civil war. The massacre of Palestinians in the refugee camps of Sabra and Shatila in 1982 by Phalangists under Israeli protection was the last straw, in America, in Israel itself, and in the world.

Yet our policymakers still shared the view of Lebanon held by their Israeli counterparts. We committed our fleet and marines to the defense of the Phalange-dominated regime, and reaped the whirlwind. Our embassy was wrecked in an explosion that killed many fine officials.

Then another explosion destroyed our marine headquarters, killing and maiming hundreds of marines. We had to retreat ignominiously in the face of forces our policymakers failed to understand.

The strongest element in Lebanon today, which must sooner or later play a dominant role in its government, lies in the Shi'ite community. The Shi'ites generally welcomed the Israelis on their arrival, expecting them to rid their communities of the hated PLO and be done with it. Now, after years of occupation by the Israelis and their Christian Lebanese allies, they look on the Israelis as the enemy. But, unlike the PLO gazing across the boundary on old Palestinian homelands, the Lebanese Shi'ites will no longer threaten Israel if and when the Israeli army and its surrogates leave Lebanon.

The Shi'ites of Lebanon could once have been harnessed by the extremist protagonists of Arab nationalism. But in 1978 Muammar Qaddafi had the Lebanese Shi'ite Imam Sadr murdered in the course of a visit to Libya. Qaddafi is now one of the Shi'ites' most hated enemies. Most Lebanese Shi'ites follow a moderate leadership under the banner of the organization named Amal, the word for hope, and in them and others like them lies the hope of Lebanon. Yet to most Americans the very word "Shi'ite" connotes extremism, since we associate the mass of that community in Lebanon with the Khomeinist minority party, Hizbollah, responsible for the hijacking of the TWA plane in 1985 and the kidnappings and murders of Americans and Europeans.

We have devoted an inordinate amount of effort in the Middle East to combating terrorists, a category in which, following Begin and Sharon, we lump all the more "leftist" of the Arab nationalists. Our policymakers have failed in their objectives in the Middle East because they are ignoring the advice of those who have gained an intimate knowledge of the area through years of firsthand experiences. Instead they listen to academics and ideologues whose views correspond with their preconceived notions.

There are no easy solutions to Middle Eastern problems in general and to those of Lebanon, or of the Arabs and Israelis in particular, and no absolute solutions, acceptable to all parties, are now attainable. But progress toward solutions, truces under temporary arrangements, peace, and civility in the intervening years before the lion may lie down with the lamb — all are possible. But only if both Arab and Israeli leaders can listen to voices other than their own.

35

The Great White Case Officer

$\mathbf{M}$Y FIRST FEW YEARS in the Agency were spent overseas or on detail to the Voice of America in New York, so I never got to know my earliest director, Rear Admiral Roscoe Hillenkoetter. His successor, General Walter Bedell "Beetle" Smith, was a less shadowy figure to me. I met briefly a few times with this dynamic director, respected by all and feared by some, but the first director with whom I became closely associated was Allen Dulles.

I had known him and his family since childhood. He was then a handsome young man with a fair moustache, and devastating to the ladies, though always a devoted husband to his wife, Clover. The Dulleses were good friends of my parents, and their two daughters went to a school my mother established primarily for my sisters in our house in Cold Spring Harbor.

I had not seen him for more than a decade when, returning from the field in the spring of 1953, I met him again as director. Though he greeted me warmly, recalling the days in Cold Spring Harbor, I was to see little of him during the next three years. Two or three echelons of superiors stood between myself, then a comparatively lowly branch and division staff chief, and the office of the exalted director.

All that changed in 1956, because of the tendency of Allen Dulles to involve himself personally in operations, which caused him to be known by his troops as the Great White Case Officer. By then his hair and moustache had turned white.

I was working on various operations in the always crisis-ridden Arab world and Allen Dulles jumped into the fray. He was often on the phone to me, so often that whenever he called, my secretary would sing out, "It's your friend, the director." He frequently summoned me to his office in Central Building, where he sat behind his desk, often resting a gouty foot on a stool beside him. He would push his glasses up on his wide forehead to the fringe of his receding white hair. He was never without his pipe. When he was not actually smoking it, he seemed always to be either tamping in more tobacco, knocking out the dottle on an ashtray, or reigniting it. This also gave him time for deliberation. He would peruse a cable before him, going through it with care, writing corrections between the lines in his somewhat oversized handwriting. These corrections and additions always improved on the original, based on acute and detailed attention to the case at hand.

From time to time he would pick up a phone on his desk, sometimes in answer to a call, and holding his hand on the receiver, he would whisper to me confidentially, "My brother" — John Foster Dulles. He would then discuss a sensitive operation over the phone with circumlocution so transparent that even the stupidest eavesdropper could have understood the subject — to the helpless despair of our security people.

More rarely the red telephone would ring. He would pick it up, cover its mouthpiece, and tell me in an awestruck whisper I found charmingly naive, "The White House."

We established a sort of uncle-nephew relationship, and he and Clover sometimes invited Lucky and me to their house on Q Street *en famille*. He was universally loved by all of us who worked with him in the Agency, and I was not the only one who found in him "a kindly uncle." Only a couple of years ago I read a memoir by a colleague, David Atlee Phillips, entitled "The Great White Case Officer,"* in which he uses this phrase to describe Dulles's avuncular image. He also mentions his "Santa Claus laugh — ho, ho, ho!" which still rings in my ears.

Of course he was not always jovial; he was a humane, truly Christian man — the Dulles brothers were sons of a Presbyterian minister — and deeply affected and saddened by occasional misfortunes and tragedies in both his official and

---

* The article appeared in the first issue of *International Journal of Intelligence and Counterintelligence,* in early 1986.

personal life. He also had a temper, and once lost it with me, castigating me in fury when I sent a cable not to his liking. Yet he apologized afterward for his moment of rage, soon forgotten.

For eight years Allen Dulles reigned as director, crucial years for the Agency, in the course of which we enjoyed some success in penetrating our major target, the Soviet Union. Not only were there important defectors such as Yuri Rastvorov and Peter Deryabin, but invaluable agents inside the Soviet system such as Pyotr Popov and Oleg Penkovski. Then we built the great tunnel under the Berlin wall, which enabled us to listen to the Soviets conducting business from their East Berlin headquarters.

In some of this I was involved directly or indirectly, but as all of these cases have been covered exhaustively in the writings of various colleagues and others, I shall confine my comments to a few personal observations on Soviet defectors, espionage, and counterespionage.

Before becoming directly involved in Soviet affairs in the Agency, I had had my own experience with a Soviet defector, in the person of Alexander Barmine, who became my adversary at the VOA. His was a tortured soul, and I think he was typical of Soviet defectors.

The force of Russian, as opposed to Soviet, patriotism lies deeply buried in the Russian psyche — the feeling for that vast sad land of beech forests, endless steppes, and long, snowy winters, of mournful music echoing the tragic story of a great, long-suffering people. No Russian can ever, in his innermost being, forget Mother Russia, which is why Stalin had to temporarily abandon Marxist for purely Russian slogans in the desperate days of the "Great Patriotic War."

So the man who finally takes that final step from the darkness of Soviet life into the blinding daylight of the democratic West blinks and shakes his head, trying to find his way. Usually he adapts himself to the freedom of the West, finally pushing away that other world, which has been compared to the dark side of the moon, but sometimes the magnet of the past is too strong.

While the Soviet defector is in the throes of transition, he must be able to reach out to others who can share the anguish of his struggle, who can suffer with him, helping him pass over the bridge to our society in his own language. In the days of

Allen Dulles there were people in the Agency of Russian background who could shepherd the defector through the time of his passion.

Today these people are gone, and we can hardly blame a Yurchenko* for leaving us, tugged back by "the sacred chords of memory," after facing for weeks on end a barrage of questions by stony-faced interrogators from another world.

As for those Soviets who dared to change their allegiance and remain "in place" to help our cause, I am amazed by their incredible courage. They realized, as we did not — at least in the early days of the Cold War — the extent of Soviet penetration of Western governments and intelligence services. Most of them paid with their lives for their daring. For instance, the British service was particularly vulnerable because of their traditional respect for individual rights, and a pride that made it difficult for them to believe that one of their own could betray them. Thus a Burgess, a Maclean, a Philby could, despite a past history of Communist association at university, be accepted into the heart of their foreign policy and intelligence apparatus. Much of the British effort against the hard targets of the Soviet Union and its satellites came to naught because of the Britons' unwillingness to face up to security problems and take appropriate steps to solve them.

Of course we ourselves had — and are still having — our own espionage cases, but instances of ideological penetration of our foreign service and intelligence organizations have been few since the initiation of President Truman's security measures in 1947.

These resulted from serious revelations of espionage in the two previous years, many of them documented by Igor Gouzenko, the Soviet code clerk who defected in Ottawa in 1945. There followed the exposure of various Soviet agents, most notorious of whom were Alger Hiss and the Rosenbergs and their associates.

Revisionist "liberal" commentators have attempted to cast doubt on these various cases, lumping them with the frequently irresponsible accusations of Senator Joseph McCarthy, and depicting them as manifestations of an exaggerated reign of

* KGB Colonel Vitali Yurchenko, after defecting to the CIA in July 1985, redefected to the Soviet embassy in Washington three months later, to the great embarrassment of the Agency.

terror. The fact is that our government and indeed significant sectors of our intellectual establishment *were* penetrated by Soviet agents, either for the purpose of espionage or to gain political influence. As for the guilt of spies such as Hiss and the Rosenbergs, it is established beyond a doubt, especially with the additional evidence provided by the KGB 1945 code traffic, now largely made public.

This traffic consisted of a series of messages deciphered by the use of coding material captured by the Finns from the Soviets, which the Swedes sold to the OSS. Franklin Roosevelt angrily forced the OSS to return it to the Soviets, our ally at the time, who immediately changed their cipher systems. But at least we were able to decipher past messages, revealing the identity of many Soviet agents.

The security clearance system inaugurated by President Truman, predictably criticized by the liberal establishment, deserves at least some of the credit for the comparatively good security record of our government during the period when I was in the agency. I say "comparative" meaning compared with other governments and their security services, of which many were successfully penetrated by the Soviets. The KGB used to consider the Americans the most difficult people to recruit because of their patriotism.

There were, of course, unpatriotic Americans aplenty who would have been willing to cooperate with the KGB — but most of them were eliminated through security checks. It was the British, our teachers in the last world war, who showed us the way with their "positive vetting," as they called their system. Yet the British system was faulty. I was told by British friends that formerly a security check consisted of looking at a man's boots* and asking who his father was! There is some truth to this. You were considered a good risk if you came from a good family and went to a good university, such as Cambridge, mother of Burgess, Maclean, Philby, Anthony Blunt, and countless others. If a young man was a Communist in college, no matter, he would grow out of it.

We Americans took a very different view. Despite the efforts of the authorities at some universities to prevent it, a careful check is made on political activities in college, the recruiting

---

* I.e., to see if they were made by a good shoemaker.

ground of the KGB. A college Communist who later drops out
of the party often does so upon instruction, as was the case with
virtually all the British spies.

The success of Soviet intelligence in the past was due to the
ideological support it could count on in every country in the
world. Some of this support was "witting," to use intelligence
parlance, given by convinced Marxists, Communist party members working for world revolution. Other support came from
the "useful fools" mentioned by Lenin, idealists who composed
a large section of the intelligentsia. With their idealistic view of
"progressive" Soviet policy, these people gave "unwitting" aid
to Soviet objectives. Soviet intelligence could entrap them.

Today the hard-core Marxists have faded away. Few thinking
individuals in the eighties consider the Soviets to have that ideal
society. And the greatest symbol of the Iron Curtain is the ugly
physical reality of the wall that divides Berlin and all Germany.
Anyone who sees it will never forget this abominable monument
to oppression. The Chinese Wall — like the almost vanished
ones the Romans erected along their boundaries in Western
Europe — was erected to keep the barbarians out, to protect
civilized society. The Berlin Wall was built to prevent people
under barbarian rule from escaping to civilization.

This was vividly brought home to me on a visit to the wall just
after its erection in 1961. It was in a time of crisis when we were
perhaps as close as we ever have been to World War III. I stood
by a pile of rubble on Friedrichstrasse, almost leaning against
the wall. People were then able to look down on us from
windows in apartments on the other side, since boarded up. To
one side of us were little shrines by the wall, pathetically
adorned by a bunch or two of flowers, commemorating the
place of sacrifice of those who had failed in attempts to escape.
On the other side was the ominous but comforting presence of
American tanks, their guns pointing east, reassuring and at the
same time terrifying in their implications.

Later I was taken by helicopter around the circumference of
the wall. The crew had thrown open the doors on one side, and
we clung to the fixtures on the opposite side as the helicopter
tilted, flying low over the ugly gray stones. There were knots of
Soviet soldiers at fortified points along the wall. As they turned
their faces up to us, I was reminded of our flights over

Azerbaijan many years before — here I was again. The locale was different, but the enemy and his intentions were one and the same.

With all this, no wonder that Soviet intelligence no longer attracts new agents, self-recruited, following ideological conviction. Useful fools may be willing unwittingly to subscribe to Soviet policies, but generally recoil if approached to work with the KGB, even in their eyes an instrument of oppression. Soviet intelligence, unable to find suitable agents among the dwindling number of the ideologically committed, now has to rely mainly on monetary inducement to the corrupt or the desperate.

For this reason, in the course of determining a candidate's fitness for a sensitive assignment in the U.S. government, security officials must ascertain if he has personal problems that could subject him to pressure, and make him a poor security risk. These could stem from simple inability to handle his finances, or an addiction to gambling, which could provide the Soviets with an opening to offer him money in exchange for information. They could be personality or psychological problems, or physical addiction to drugs or alcohol — or an abnormal sex life, which of necessity includes homosexuality, now a cause of controversy.

Anyone who has long been involved with intelligence has probably experienced the security risk inherent in homosexual officers. He may — as I myself have — worked with a colleague he knows or suspects has homosexual tendencies without dreaming of reporting it to security. But the fact remains that homosexuals have problems which make them prime targets for Soviet recruitment, as, for instance, in the case of William Martin and Bernon Mitchell, who defected from the National Security Agency in 1960. We in the Agency knew about many other cases, mostly near misses, where those approached by the Soviets with compromising evidence of homosexuality conscientiously reported the approach to their superiors. We all know of cases where they did not. And there must be successful recruitments in this category known only to the Soviets.

In conjunction with the normal background positive vetting, the polygraph, or "lie detector," is an effective tool in establishing reliability or indicating unreliability in prospective candidates for sensitive positions. It is also used for periodic checks on those already in the service to ensure no vulnerabilities have arisen in the course of time. It has naturally aroused controversy as an invasion of privacy, and many even outside the liberal establishment have opposed its use.

I do not propose to present a detailed defense of its merits. The polygraph is not an infallible instrument, only a valuable tool through which many potential security problems have been uncovered. Its efficacy depends to a large degree on the abilities of the operator and the interpretation of the indications it produces.

There are instances of its fallibility. One time, as a division chief, I wanted to send out an extremely well qualified officer as chief to a sensitive station. For certain doctrinaire reasons he had been considered by an element of our service a possible security risk and had failed the polygraph test. I checked with the officer ultimately responsible for such judgments, the director of security, who said that the man in question was an "overreactor" whose natural nervousness caused the indicators on the machine to jump. He gave me his personal and official guarantee of the officer's reliability, and he turned out to be an excellent chief of station.

There are those who have "beaten the machine" — and indeed, I did so myself.

In an early polygraph test, as returning chief of an important station, I was hooked up to a machine operated by the chief of the polygraph unit, an urbane, sophisticated individual. When we came to the question of drugs, I turned the tables on him and asked him a question myself.

"In a country where hashish is a part of their culture, what would you think of a station chief who never tried it?" I asked. "Certainly I tried hashish, and an extraordinary experience it was. I shall never be touching the stuff again, but I learned something from the experience."

"OK, Archie," he said, "let's rephrase the question. Other than the time you tried hashish in the pursuit of essential knowledge of your intelligence objectives, have you ever or do you currently use drugs?"

The machine duly confirmed my negative reply.

However, in my next polygraph examination, after my return from another key assignment, I faced an operator of a different mold, whose features reminded me of the Neanderthal man in the American Museum of Natural History. He looked at me with hostility, and I felt I represented to him a type for which he felt a natural dislike — a "pointy-headed intellectual," "probably pinko," an "Eastern establishment type." When he came to the drug question, I firmly answered no.

The machine registered nothing and he went on to the next question.

A few days later I ran into the civilized unit chief and crowed to him about my defeat of his beloved machine.

"Ah," he said, "you have simply proved its efficacy. You felt no guilt about your use of hashish in the line of business, and the machine duly confirmed this fact."

He was right. Of course, spies as well as hardened drug users can "beat the machine" if they feel no guilt — but most of them do fear the results of exposure. This fear causes many of those who have something to hide to refuse the polygraph, thus disqualifying themselves for employment, and others who undergo the test to expose themselves during the examination. It is only a soulless instrument, not an infallible judge, but an extremely useful one we should abandon only when something better is discovered.

One should not overemphasize these negative security checks, essential for the reduction of security risks. The other side of the coin is the patriotism of Americans that the Soviets find so great an obstacle to their operations. We have emerged from the revolution of the sixties — whose participants constituted only a small and unrepresentative sector of our society — a strong society, which has traditionally found unity in its diversity.

Patriotism was and is characteristic of our corps of intelligence officers, though we would be embarrassed to talk about it. We in the CIA were always conscious of having a special mission, of being the reconnaissance patrols of our government. We had an esprit de corps which I can only compare with that of the U.S. marines, intensified by the loyalty we felt for our quintessential intelligence chief, Allen Dulles. Though the CIA has had directors since who in some ways surpassed him, there will never be another one quite like him.

He might have continued as our leader for some years longer but for the disaster of the Bay of Pigs.

I was on an overseas assignment during the preparation and

execution of this unfortunate operation, and shared the doubts of others, including Richard Helms, about the advisability of the Agency's involvement in such ventures.

The importance of the CIA lies in its function as the only intelligence arm of our government capable of producing analyses of situations without regard to parochial considerations. The military intelligence services are responsible to authorities whose primary concerns are physical defense against the enemy; thus military intelligence estimates can be bent to conform with the views of these authorities, including those involving the military budget. State Department intelligence is subject to policy considerations.

Only the CIA can and must "tell it like it is."

The covert operations sector of the Agency is the only arm of our government with the resources and ability to carry out nonintelligence, truly covert functions like secret support to foreign leaders, political parties, or guerrilla forces in "denied areas" such as Afghanistan. But giant paramilitary operations in disputed parts of the Third World are not in the Agency's field of expertise. The Agency must co-opt military personnel to participate in them. Huge programs such as those in Vietnam and Nicaragua become matters of public concern, with nothing covert about them. The Agency is called upon to defend them in the councils of government and even in the public arena, in Congress, and thus loses its objectivity, its purity, its rationale for existence as an intelligence agency unaffected by policy considerations.

These massive undertakings should be the responsibility of the military, utilizing such units as the "Special Forces."

The Cuban operation was a borderline case. In those days our media, unlike today, considered that they had a responsibility to their government not to reveal intelligence that came to their attention when to do so would hurt the national interest. So, although the operation being mounted against Cuba became known to elements of the media, they remained silent.

Like any covert action undertaken by the Agency not falling under the heading of intelligence collection, the Cuban operation was under the supervision of the committee meeting in the Situation Room in the basement of the West Wing of the White House. This was chaired by the equivalent of today's White House chief of staff, and its small membership included undersecretaries from State and Defense and the director of CIA, plus other department representatives as appropriate. At the time of the committee's formal creation in 1955 — though informally it dated from the birth of the Office of Policy Coordination in 1948 — it was called the 5412 Committee after the number of the document authorizing it. Throughout its various rechristenings it was referred to as the Special Group.

Later the Agency was to be criticized for rampaging out of control — a complete misrepresentation, as controls on the Agency were very strict indeed. The Agency is not an initiator of action, but only the instrument through which action is carried out by order of the government, as represented in the Special Group. And in the case of the Bay of Pigs the Agency may indeed have yielded too easily to controls so strict that failure of the operation was certain.

In the original plan, the invading force was to land in Trinidad, a small town below the Escombrey Mountains, to join up with anti-Castro guerrilla forces. After State Department objections to a landing point near population centers, a new beach was selected a hundred miles farther east, on the edge of an uninhabited swamp — the Bay of Pigs. Perhaps this substitution alone doomed the operation to failure.

But any chance it had to succeed was killed by a decision taken after the operation had already begun.

Allen Dulles had the notion that it was better for him to be away from Washington at the time of the launching of a major operation, so that he could "plausibly deny" — the accepted jargon — involvement in it. (At the time of Operation Ajax, Kim's foray to restore the Shah of Iran to the throne, Allen betook himself to Rome. Plausible denial, unnecessary, as it proved, would also have been difficult in this case, since by purest coincidence the Shah himself was staying in the same Rome hotel.)

So Allen Dulles chose to absent himself from town on the eve of the operation scheduled for April 17, 1961 — a decision fatal both to his career and possibly the operation itself. His deputy, General Pearre Cabell, was in charge on April 16, and had to face pressure from horrified liberals, notably Adlai Stevenson, the U.S. ambassador to the United Nations, who had not been previously informed. Stevenson, told that it was too late to cancel the operation with the landing already in progress, demanded that the vital air strike planned to support the invading force be called off. Asked for his views, Cabell, the disciplined military officer, said he would abide by whatever decision was reached. Accordingly, President John Kennedy canceled the scheduled air strike, which was the last hope for success.

Dulles, with Cabell, endured the humiliation of failure, and bore the brunt of the subsequent opprobrium heaped on the Agency from all sides. It is said that success has many fathers but failure is an orphan. Yet a foster parent is always found for failure — the fingers point to each in turn around the council table, until by common agreement they all point to a chosen scapegoat. In this case it was Allen Dulles. The timing of his official demise could hardly have been worse for him, as he was about to move into a new office in the New Building, the realization of a cherished concept on which he had been working for years.

Up until that time, the director, his immediate staff, and some technical and administrative units were housed in three respectable buildings on the corner of Independence Avenue and Twenty-third Street. The bulk of us occupied a line of temporary two-story World War II structures unimpressively named I, J, K, and L buildings, on the south side of the reflecting pool below the Lincoln Memorial. They were dilapidated, impractical, hard to heat or cool, yet we developed a certain affection for them. We were all within reach of each other in well-defined territories along the corridor connecting all the buildings. We walked together at noon by the pool in warm weather, and those sufficiently high in the hierarchy to enjoy offices with windows facing the pool and the Lincoln Memorial could gaze out at the skaters in winter. Others in the back wings could at least contemplate their colleagues at work in the buildings next door, giving us a comfortable sense of camaraderie and intimacy.

Sometimes this propinquity led to security problems, and windows had to be screened off to prevent other elements of the Agency from seeing papers or maps they had no need to know about. At least in one case I know of it led also to personal embarrassment. One of my friends, working in his second-floor office on a weekend, happened to look down and see a colleague in an office below in the process of undressing a pretty secretary, with the obvious intention of committing a bit of unauthorized covert action.

Surrendering to an irresistible impulse, my friend picked up the phone, dialed his colleague, and watched him draw away from the lady to answer it.

"This is God speaking," said a deep, commanding voice. "I see what you are doing. It is a grievous sin."

He hung up and saw the parties separating, hurriedly dressing to leave the building. His colleague reproached him at their next meeting for bringing an operation he had been working on for months to an ignominious conclusion.

Now we faced the prospect of leaving these familiar ramshackle offices for a huge cement structure in the country, far away in Langley, Virginia, eight miles from the White House and the State Department. We did not like the idea at all and criticized our misguided uncle Allen for moving us to a sort of academic campus far from the corridors of power. We read with derision the bulletins on distinctively tinted paper describing the progress being made on the New Building and laying out general directives for the use of our new quarters. The stilted language, resembling that of military bulletins, was a subject of many gibes.

One day a bulletin on regulation paper was distributed to all of us. It was entitled "Toilet Arrangements for the New Building," and read something like this:

> During the transition period there will be insufficient toilet facilities to accommodate all personnel, both male and female.
>
> Therefore, in case of necessity, personnel are authorized to make use of the shrubbery surrounding the building to satisfy urgent personal requirements.
>
> Unfortunately, this shrubbery includes a considerable proportion of poison ivy, which can cause painful itching and swelling in sensitive areas of the anatomy.
>
> In order to enable personnel to identify this weed and avoid contamination, a picture of poison ivy leaf is attached herewith.

General Cabell, a straight-arrow officer not renowned for his sense of humor, ordered security to locate the perpetrator of the bogus memo. According to legend, he was discovered and discharged at once by special order of the deputy director of the CIA.

I'd like to throw in a gloss here — I don't think I've given a very positive picture of Pearre Cabell. He was not only a fine officer but universally liked and respected for his human qualities. It was not easy being a deputy to Allen Dulles. Indeed, a deputy's job is a hard and comparatively unrewarding one, especially in a sensitive position where a wrong decision brings disasters and a right one little acclaim.

The Agency during my tenure was served by a series of exceptionally fine deputies, all of them, with the exception of Dick Helms, military men: Lieutenant General Marshall Carter, Vice Admiral Rufus Taylor, Major General Robert Cushman, and Major General Vernon A. Walters. This last, of course, was my old friend from Camp Ritchie days, and I was fortunate to travel with him a few times during my last two years in the Agency. A more delightful companion I cannot imagine, and his hosts in many countries enjoyed him as much as I did. His other qualities are public knowledge, now that he is our ambassador to the United Nations, possibly the man best qualified to be so in the country.

The Bay of Pigs debacle was fatal to Pearre Cabell, as well as to Allen Dulles, and we bid them a sad farewell on a gloomy November day in 1961. Allen Dulles's departure was the end of an era, and the move to the New Building symbolized it. Our exchange of the informal atmosphere of those rattletrap "tempos" for the featureless tin boxes of the New Building coincided with a change in character for the Agency. Despite the blow to its prestige suffered in the Bay of Pigs, its existence was no longer in dispute and the CIA was now an established part of the U.S. government. Its esprit de corps remained intact, and it never became a slave to a suffocating bureaucratic straitjacket like other government agencies; the CIA was no longer a little band of pioneers, but an organization.

36

The Caravan Moves On

It ürür Kervan yürür.
("The dog barks but the caravan moves on.")
— *Turkish proverb*

IN AN ATMOSPHERE OF TREPIDATION, John A.
McCone was sworn in on November 29, 1961, as Allen Dulles's
replacement. Educated as an engineer, McCone was a shipping
tycoon from California, most recently director of the Atomic
Energy Commission. From there terrible stories filtered over to
us, giving a picture of a stern, tyrannical boss. I was thus rather
surprised to meet a small, neat, gray man, impeccably groomed
and dressed, speaking in a low, unobtrusive voice. But it was the
voice of authority, and at first he was feared as stories of his
toughness spread through the New Building.

One was that he had called in an officer for a briefing and
told him, "I can spare you just ten minutes to state your case."

The officer, ignoring this stricture, went on to give a long
exegesis of a complicated case, droning on despite a couple of
interruptions from McCone pointing out that he had exceeded
his time limit.

McCone finally rose from his seat. "Your ten minutes were
up some time ago, Mr. Jones. Please make arrangements with
my secretary to pick up your final paycheck as you leave this
office."

The story may have been apocryphal, but John McCone was
just the director the Agency needed at this critical point in its
history. He was almost an opposite to Allen Dulles in everything. He had little interest in the glamor of covert intelligence
operations, which he entrusted with confidence to the management of Richard Helms. Helms had replaced Richard Bissell as

Deputy Director of Plans when Bissell also had to resign as a result of the Bay of Pigs, an operation in which Helms had played no part and which he had viewed with dismay.

With Helms in charge of operations, McCone, an engineer by background, concentrated on the analytical and technical collection areas of the Agency. In the aftermath of the Bay of Pigs, he was immediately faced with the problem of Cuba, which engrossed the Kennedy administration.

Shortly after the Bay of Pigs, I found myself back at headquarters in a senior position with overall responsibilities. Thus I was kept generally informed of our activities in Cuba and, as I spoke Spanish, was directly involved with anti-Castro Cubans on a few occasions.

In the wake of the disaster, President Kennedy, having lost confidence in the Agency's direction, entrusted to his brother Attorney General Robert Kennedy the task of overseeing future operations against Fidel Castro. For his staff chief in this function, Bobby Kennedy picked former air force brigadier general Edward G. Lansdale, whose legendary operation in the Philippines, under Agency direction, helped Defense Minister Ramón Magsaysay defeat the Communist guerrillas, and was memorialized in the novel *The Ugly American.*

In the Agency itself Cuban affairs, under the sobriquet Operation Mongoose, were conducted by a separate unit dubbed Task Force W, headed by Bill Harvey. A more unlikely candidate for such a task would have been hard to find. He was a huge, froglike man with bulging eyes, his face swollen from heavy drinking. Even his voice, rumbling from deep in his chest, was froglike. He came originally from the FBI, and unlike any other Agency officer, he wore a pistol; his image was that of an old-fashioned chief of police, and he completely lacked the sensitivity of an intelligence officer.

Thus, General Lansdale easily assumed the more complex political aspects of the operation. He felt that the Cuban counterrevolutionary forces lacked a "rationale," as he called it, an ideological underpinning under which its disparate forces could rally. I was called upon to meet with groups of Cuban intellectuals in various safe houses — one as far away as Malibu — to discuss the terms of this rationale. The fact that I remember nothing about our discussions perhaps illustrates the futility of the exercise.

But in the course of this brief involvement I heard quite a bit about Operation Mongoose and attended several meetings where Bobby Kennedy was present. His was a restless, impatient presence, and I heard that he was dissatisfied with the ineffectiveness of Agency attempts to "eliminate" Castro, as he was constantly, through Lansdale, spurring us to do. I still suspect that there is at least a possibility that his brother's assassination was an act of retaliation by Castro. I also consider it unlikely that the Soviets had no motive in allowing Lee Harvey Oswald to take his Russian wife home with him after his stay as a defector in the Soviet Union — an act for which there is hardly a precedent. Two months before the assassination Oswald visited both the Soviet and Cuban embassies in Mexico City.

During this critical period, in the closing days of 1961 and only a month after his appointment as director of Central Intelligence (DCI), John McCone suffered a personal tragedy in the loss of his wife of many years. He called President Kennedy in a state of shock, saying, "I am no longer the man you appointed to this job — I think perhaps I should resign." The president talked him into staying on, fortunately for the United States, as he was to play a crucial role in the upcoming Cuban crisis.

Covert operations in Cuba had not hitherto been of primary interest to McCone. His direct, personal involvement came when the photographs brought back by U-2 reconnaissance planes and agent reports combined to give a picture of Soviet ship landings and construction of sites guarded by Soviet troops, leading McCone to report to the president that "something new and different" was being prepared in Cuba. Contrary to the belief expressed by the Office of National Estimates, McCone felt certain that the Soviets were about to install intermediate-range missiles threatening most of the U.S. mainland.

At this very moment there was another, happier event in John McCone's life that might have impeded his participation in the course of events, had he not been the man he was. In the devastation of the loss of his wife, he had shared his grief with the wife of a close friend who had just lost her husband, and in September 1962 they were married.

In the midst of the brewing Cuban crisis, John and his bride Tylene left for a honeymoon in the south of France. He ordered a special communications unit established in their cottage so he could keep in constant contact with headquarters. From there he directed his troops to continue their search for the evidence he was sure would point to the installation of ICBMs. To his frustration, U-2 flights had been interrupted by bad weather, but on October 14 they brought back definite photographic evidence, with the ICBMs clearly in place. Mc-Cone never let the Office of National Estimates forget its error and his correct assessment.

I was in London at the time, and on the weekend of October 21–22 Ambassador David Bruce and I each received orders to report to a remote military airport. We rode out there together, ignorant of these latest developments, speculating about the reason for this strange summons.

At the airport we were met by an equally unenlightened officer and led to a map room under the airport control tower and told that a plane from Washington was expected momentarily.

Soon an orderly rushed in accompanying the familiar figure of Sherman Kent, venerable chairman of the Office of National Estimates. With him were two associates, one of whom I recognized as Chester Cooper.

They were carrying several satchels and briefcases, and from them Sherm selected a number of slides, which he projected on a screen; they were U-2 photographs of missile sites in Cuba, bristling with ICBMs in place.

"We have come to show our European allies the evidence and seek their backing for whatever action we decide to take," he said. "I am going myself to Germany, dropping my two colleagues off here and in Paris. We'd like you, Mr. Ambassador, to arrange for Chet Cooper here to give a special briefing to the prime minister. Then you, Archie, are to arrange for Chet to give a demonstration to the British intelligence community."

Despite the lateness of the hour, David Bruce and I had a lively ride back to London, hearing the details of the latest Cuban developments from Cooper.

After the ambassador and I arranged and sat in on our respective briefings the following Monday, I told Chet Cooper, "It's all very well for you to have briefed the prime minister and the British government, who are certainly sympathetic to our position. But we haven't taken care of the sectors from which we can expect severe criticism, unless we have fully explained the problem to them — the opposition and the press."

The opposition was no problem. The deputy leader of the Labor Party, George Brown, was a friend and I arranged a briefing for him and the party leader, Hugh Gaitskill, in the house Lucky and I were living in. But the press was another matter.

We had received immediate clearance from headquarters for briefing Gaitskill and Brown, but their reaction to our suggestion about the media was strongly negative. Chet said he would straighten this out. He got on the phone to Washington, and after a lengthy conversation told me he had received the green light. The British press corps crowded into a U.S. embassy projection room, was duly impressed by the slides shown on the screen, and was allowed to take copies. The next day the front pages of all the British newspapers were filled with these photographs, and they appeared on a continuing series of television programs.

Washington reacted with consternation — the U.S. press corps, scooped by its British colleagues, was up in arms. Chet Cooper, summoned by several angry phone calls from headquarters in which he was castigated for these disclosures that they insisted had never been authorized, returned to Washington, crestfallen after his initially triumphant appearance in London. He was certain he was about to be fired in disgrace, as he had apparently already been told on the phone. He left London still insisting headquarters had given its approval, and must have somehow made his case on his return, as he was still with us when I made my own way back.

While in London I was also tasked by the director in another matter, the Profumo scandal. This involved a relationship between the British defense secretary, John Profumo, and two British call girls, Christine Keeler, a dark-haired classic beauty, and Marilyn Rice-Davies, a clever little blond cockney. The press made much of the fact that the girls were also friendly with a Soviet military attaché, Yevgeni Ivanov. The girls' patron was a well-known osteopath, Dr. Stephen Ward, also an amateur portraitist.

For a reason then unclear to me, the director took an inordinate interest in this case, and I got frequent cabled inquiries about it, especially with regard to the association the girls might have had with U.S. officials. Soon I was required to cable the director a daily report on developments in the case. I termed it "the director's daily pornography bulletin." John McCone was a man who took his Catholic religion very seriously indeed, and I am sure he must have been shocked by some of the spicy items I served him.

One morning I was greeted by a cable asking me to investigate a report that our revered ambassador to the Court of St. James was himself involved with the notorious Dr. Ward. I took the bull by the horns, went directly to David Bruce, and cabled home his indignant denial.

No sooner had I got the cable off than I was summoned to the ambassador's office. He received me with some embarrassment.

"My secretary has informed me that I did indeed meet Dr. Ward. Some months ago he came to the residence to make a sketch of me!" Bruce admitted.

The only other U.S. "officials" ever found to be involved with any of the principals of the case were three U.S. airmen who had briefly enjoyed the girls' favors. They were flown home for what I am sure was a fruitful interrogation.

At the time I never realized the reason for the director's interest in the case and in possible American involvement. I later found out that it was based on an allegation that President Kennedy had also enjoyed a brief fling with the lovely Keeler in the course of a short visit she made to New York in July 1962.

During this London interlude John and Tylene McCone made a number of visits, during which Lucky and I became their friends, and we have enjoyed their company at all too rare intervals ever since. He was a great director of the CIA, as well as one of the keenest analysts the Agency has ever had.

McCone, on whom President Kennedy relied almost as a father figure, never got on the same wavelength with Lyndon Johnson after Kennedy's assassination. He resigned in April of 1965, to be replaced by the totally miscast Admiral William F. Raborn. All of us breathed a sigh of relief when he was replaced a year later by the deputy director who had kept us on the track, Richard Helms.

Dick Helms was the last first-class director of the Agency during my time, with his tour sandwiched between two unfortunate appointments. He was a classic professional intelligence officer who successfully kept the Agency from involvement in further disaster during his tenure as Deputy Director for Plans, next as deputy director, and finally as DCI from June 1966 until February 1973. He kept his eyes and those of the Agency on our principal mission, the collection of intelligence and counterintelligence, and when his steadying hand was removed, the Agency lurched into a decline that almost led to its demise.

We had six and a half good years with Dick Helms during the remaining years of the Johnson administration and Richard Nixon's first term. His reputation for honesty, as a straight shooter, won respect from a Congress often not too fond of the Agency, but perhaps eventually did him in with the Nixon White House. He refused to participate as a team player in the administration when this team became embroiled in the "dirty tricks" of Watergate.

Also, Richard Nixon was not happy about the Agency in general, whose estimates did not always conform with his views, and he focused on the numbers of its personnel as a target for his concern. When he flew back and forth from Camp David, he is said to have remarked on the size of our building and the number of cars parked around it, and appointed James R. Schlesinger director to clean it up and clean it out.

Schlesinger proceeded to do this with a vengeance almost immediately upon taking over at the Agency in February 1973. He is supposed at that time to have made the statement, "This is a gentleman's club and I'm no gentleman!" We all agreed with the second half of this analysis, but not the first. The Agency was composed of people from all segments of American society. In fact, one of its strengths lay in its large proportion of officers with foreign antecedents. There were a few in high positions, holdovers from the OSS who came from the Eastern establishment, and Schlesinger lost no time in getting rid of most of them.

I think he really hated the whole of the Clandestine Service operations corps (as the DDP was known), and we hated him in return.

He came to the Agency with a few retainers he kept around him, and found at least one supporter in William Colby. Except for wartime service in the OSS, during which time he was parachuted into occupied Norway, and a stint in Italy, Colby had passed his whole career in the Far East. The last part of his tour was in Vietnam, where he was the only officer of the Agency ever to attain the rank of ambassador. On his return to headquarters he had wanted to be Deputy Director of Plans, but Dick Helms apparently thought him better fitted for administrative rather than global operational responsibility and made him executive director. This was theoretically the third-ranking job in the Agency, but in fact was really that of an administrative overseer.

Colby managed to ingratiate himself with Schlesinger, and told him that he would have his greatest difficulty with the DDP. Colby convinced Schlesinger that he himself would be the best man to handle the problem of the DDP, a position to which Colby was immediately appointed.

Schlesinger, with Colby's help, proceeded to put into effect a 7 percent cut in DDP personnel, which clearly was only the prelude to further cuts. On the basis of fitness reports, this proportion of personnel was presented with an impersonal two-paragraph notice informing them that they were surplus. Supervisors were ordered to hand out these notices without comment.

The Agency, with its high standards of excellence, did not have much fat; the few unqualified people who made it through the recruitment and training were soon dropped, and at best shunted off to staff jobs. There were not enough of this last category to complete the 7 percent, and so the number was filled by pushing out the door old-time officers, mostly female, who though not qualified for operational work performed valuable support functions. They were hardworking people, devoted to the Agency, and the worst thing I ever had to do as division chief was hand them these notices, helpless to give any explanation or soften the blow. All their years of work, from which they gained their self-respect, were denigrated as "surplus to the needs of the Agency."

Fortunately for the Agency, especially the Clandestine Service, Schlesinger's plans for its further decimation were interrupted after only five months by his appointment as secretary of defense. The surprise announcement of the appointment came in the middle of my weekly staff meeting, and my secretary passed it to me in a note. When I made the announcement, all those gathered around the table broke out in spontaneous applause. I told a fellow division chief about this at lunch, and he said he had had an identical experience. His office was located close to that of the director, who he had feared might hear the noise, correctly interpret it, and fire my friend on the spot, making him Schlesinger's last casualty.

A legacy of Schlesinger's mercifully brief tenure provided a lighter touch to these desperate times. Portraits of all past directors hang along the hallway giving onto the patio of the Agency's main building. Now it would be necessary to place Schlesinger's likeness beside those of his illustrious predecessors. It was rightly feared that angry employees might deface his portrait. A number of meetings were held to discuss this weighty problem. The obvious solution of covering it with a protective unbreakable coating was rejected. This would have been unseemly unless all the other portraits were similarly covered — considered too expensive and conspicuous a solution. It was finally decided to establish a twenty-four-hour watch on the portrait through a television monitoring station, manned by a security officer.

During the weeks that followed the monitor saw countless employees pass by Schlesinger's portrait without bothering to look at it. After all, the man was better forgotten, like a bad dream. But one day the monitor was alerted as a girl stopped in front of it, and appeared to be considering some kind of action. The security officer was about to leap on her from his place of concealment when she put her hands up to her face, thumbed her nose, and passed on.

Bill Colby had placed himself in the position of chosen heir, and was officially sworn in as DCI in September 1973. He then staffed the top echelons of the Clandestine Service with his old associates from the Far East. Agency morale, shattered under Schlesinger, did not improve under Colby, though not all the problems were of his making.

Perhaps his biggest problem was Jim Angleton and counter-intelligence/counterespionage. Jim was an eccentric genius whose monopoly in the field of his unquestioned expertise — chief of the counterintelligence staff — had gone on too long. He had been in the position virtually since the beginning of the Agency, and had built his staff into an effective machine, independent of the rest of the organization and responsible only to the director.

A major part of his responsibility was to follow Soviet operations against the DDP and DDP intelligence operations, especially those directed at the Soviet Union. This brought him into conflict both with the director of security, with regard to Soviet efforts to penetrate the Agency, and the chief of the Soviet Division.

While the division chief was generally responsible for handling Soviet defectors, Jim Angleton managed to get control of one, Anatoli Golytsin, who alleged that the Agency's Soviet operations were compromised and that the Agency itself had been penetrated by Soviet recruitment of two or more of its officers. The resulting conflict has been aired in the media and a number of books, with varying degrees of accuracy.

It did affect all of us in further poisoning the atmosphere of a demoralized Agency. By this time I myself had decided it was time for me to leave the CIA, no longer a happy place to work. There were also practical considerations: I had worked long enough in responsible jobs in headquarters, but did not want another overseas assignment. I was also, at fifty-six, only four years from the age of mandatory retirement. I began casting about for outside employment, and by the latter part of 1974 was completing arrangements to join the staff of the Chase Manhattan Bank, located opposite my father's old office on 40 Wall Street, the very street I had fled from at the beginning of my career!

I had already announced my departure from the Agency and was in the process of "phasing out" at the time of the first of a chain of events that almost destroyed the Agency.

Dick Helms understood counterespionage, worked closely with Jim Angleton, and was able to keep him and the rest of the Agency in balance. Bill Colby, involved for years only in Far East operations, without much contact with counterespionage and Soviet affairs in general, had little comprehension of what the problems increasingly plaguing the Agency were all about. Jim Angleton had contempt for him and went his own way unchecked. Colby saw that the situation was out of control, that he would have to face up to a direct confrontation with Angleton.

Then along came a God-given opportunity to bring Angleton down. On December 22, just before leaving the Agency for good, I opened my Sunday *New York Times* to find these headlines: "HUGE CIA OPERATION REPORTED IN U.S. AGAINST ANTI-WAR FORCES, OTHER DISSIDENTS IN NIXON YEARS." The story, by Seymour Hersh, started with the statement that the CIA "conducted a massive domestic intelligence operation against the anti-war movement and other dissidents in the United States." It then went on to describe various operations in sensational and distorted terms designed to appeal to an audience conditioned by the trauma of the Vietnam War.

The operations described by Hersh were completely within the Agency's charter to work against foreign targets, but were made to appear as if they violated the prohibition against involvement in domestic espionage, the province of the FBI. To give just one example: The Agency would recruit American students involved with radical groups on campuses to be sent abroad to infiltrate similar groups in foreign countries. Any reports such students submitted on their activities while still in the United States were simply sent on to the FBI, and not further distributed by the Agency. Only after the students' arrival overseas would their reports be processed by the CIA.

I was horrified. Fired with indignation, I tried all that Sunday morning to contact Colby or someone else in authority to urge them to refute the allegations immediately before they could do further damage. I later found out that Colby had been shown the article by Hersh in advance, and did not challenge its assumptions. Either he did not understand the falsity of its basic thrust, or simply saw in it a chance to get rid of Angleton — and in the process the remaining members of the Eastern establishment in the Agency whose wider world experience made him uneasy.

From then on the process of demolition of the Agency was irreversible. Colby accomplished his objective of eliminating Angleton, but went on to "spill his guts," as a former colleague put it to me, to the media and Congress. Senator Frank Church seized on the subject to further his presidential ambitions; he treated the public to a series of "revelations," which implanted in its consciousness the notion that the CIA was not only a sinister Big Brother organization looking into U.S. citizens' private affairs, but also a "rogue elephant" free of any government controls. Universities closed their doors to the Agency, depriving it of a major source of support. People no longer looked on it as their own intelligence service, but as an almost foreign, hostile organization. The Congress was given a hunting license to delve into its files, and expose secrets to the media as it suited individual congressmen and their staffs. Foreign intelligence services and individuals likely to cooperate with the Agency refused further collaboration in the absence of confidentiality.

All this no longer concerned me as an intelligence officer, since I had, when I resigned, cut all ties with the Agency. I was naturally concerned, but there was nothing I could do about it until Colby resigned in June 1976, to be replaced by George Bush.

Based on an acquaintance of some years, I went to see the new director, taking advantage of my retired status to give him my own views on rehabilitating the agency. One of my suggestions involved the prevalence of academics among the analysts and producers of intelligence estimates. I proposed that these no longer be recruited from the ranks of Ph.D.'s fresh from universities, but from among operations officers with a history of field experience.

I'm afraid those who have gained their knowledge of foreign countries from academic studies will resent some of the remarks I have made in these pages. I have the greatest respect for those who have spent many years studying other nations and cultures and would have joined their ranks myself had it not been for my experiences in the course of World War II. They make an enormous contribution to our knowledge, indispensable for understanding other parts of the world.

But that does not qualify them as intelligence officers in the CIA. They are not sufficiently in touch with the realities one can comprehend only by intimate contact with foreign nationals. When one considers, for instance, that well-informed citizens of the United States are often mistaken about developments in their own country — I remember when it was confidently predicted that Thomas Dewey would replace Harry Truman as president! — one realizes the difficulty of interpreting events abroad.

Actually, I think that the best preparation for an intelligence officer is the sort provided by the Peace Corps. Because of the anti-CIA hysteria whipped up in the media and Congress, with its repercussions abroad, causing the Peace Corps to be looked on with suspicion, the Agency is forbidden by statute from recruiting personnel leaving the Peace Corps for five years after the date of their separation. This effectively deprives the Agency of a prime source of potential intelligence officers — as was perhaps the purpose of some of those framing this bit of legislation.

I don't know what action, if any, George Bush took on my suggestion, but today, at least, National Intelligence Officers — who replaced the Office of National Estimates as the final Agency producers of intelligence estimates for our government — are now largely drawn from the ranks of those with field experience in the area of their responsibility.

The Agency was beginning to recover under the capable direction of George Bush, intellectually acute and with a warm, outgoing personality, when after only a year he was removed by the newly elected Carter administration in the beginning of 1977. Replacing him was Admiral Stansfield Turner, who shared Schlesinger's distrust of the Clandestine Service but not his undeniable capability. He completed the process begun by Schlesinger, instituting a drastic purge, ordering mass firings to which most of the remaining old hands fell victim.

It was a decimated, demoralized agency that William Casey inherited at the beginning of the first Reagan administration in 1981. He then began the long process of reconstruction, winning the loyalty of his troops with whom, by virtue of his experience and personality, and the advantage of wartime service with the OSS, he enjoyed warm rapport. Despite attacks by those elements of the press and Congress that can be counted on to oppose all efforts to maintain a strong U.S. intelligence service, Casey succeeded in rebuilding the Agency into an organization in which I would be proud to serve, if I were starting over again.

I think that he was just the man to accomplish this at the time, and the service he performed was essential to the survival of the Agency. However, he was a close associate of the president's, completely committed to his policies, and even tried to install briefly a politician as DDO, violating all the rules that should govern the intelligence system.

Thus, I believe that William H. Webster was an excellent choice as a replacement for Casey, especially since he was originally appointed director of the FBI by the Carter administration and can be considered apolitical. Under an apolitical director, the Agency is more likely to distance itself from overt paramilitary operations, such as the contras and political action derring-do, and reemphasize its primary functions, the collection, dissemination, and evaluation of intelligence, uncontaminated by political pressures and biases.

Our government will then be able to make policy decisions based on the facts of the case rather than wishful thinking. Someone has to serve up the truth, unpalatable as it may be, to our policymakers. One can then hope that, armed with the facts, they will be shielded against the consequences of mistakes such as those that have caused us such pain and loss in the past fifty years of turmoil — to cite a few major ones, the Pearl Harbor disaster, certain decisions reached at the Tehran Conference, the decision to take on China in the Korean War, the Vietnam tragedy, and all the disasters of our dealings with Iran.

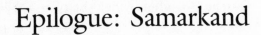

Epilogue: Samarkand

If that unkind Shirazi Turk
Would take my heart within her hand,
I'd give Bukhara for the mole
Upon her face or Samarkand.
　　　　　　— Third Ode of Hafiz

THERE IS A STORY that the conqueror Tamerlane was furious when he first heard these lines and summoned the poet Hafiz to his presence.

"With the blows of my lustrous sword have I subjugated the globe and laid waste thousands of countries to embellish my capitals Samarkand and Bukhara, and you, wretch, would sell them for the mole of a Turkish girl from Shiraz!"

Hafiz, bowing deeply, said, "My lord, it is through such prodigality that I have fallen on evil days."

Of course he got a generous present instead of a punishment.

Samarkand had already become a symbol rather than just a place on the map. And so it is for me. I doubt if ever I shall visit the real Samarkand, especially in view of the opinions I have expressed about the Soviet Union. By the time Samarkand becomes the capital of a free Turkistan, I shall be gone.

But perhaps I would be disappointed by the reality — a mosque and a square that might not bear comparison with the Meidan-i-Shah of Isfahan, in the middle of a drab city of decaying apartment blocks. So I may be better off with an illusion of a medieval walled city of towering minarets, turbaned merchants crowding its narrow streets and bazaars, disturbed on occasion by a galloping band of fur-hatted warriors.

And my caravan has become a thing of the mind, not a procession from one far country to another. I still enjoy traveling to these distant lands and hope someday to pass over the silk route followed by Marco Polo into Kashgar, in Chinese

Turkestan (Xinjiang), and also revisit the land of the great Moguls, in India. But I will always return to my home in Washington, where I continue my spiritual journey to the golden spires of the Samarkand of my youthful dreams.

And with me will be my companion on the Road to whom this book is dedicated, who has found out many truths in our journey together, which she plans to relate in her own time. She has no mole on her cheek like the Shirazi Turk of Hafiz, but she has Arabian eyes and a smile that lights up the world. For their sake, there was no need to exchange Samarkand, because long ago she took my heart within her hand and joined me on the caravan. Now it is

> *Sweet to ride forth at evening from the wells*
> *When shadows pass gigantic on the sand,*
> *And softly through the silence beat the bells*
> *Along the Golden Road to Samarkand.*

Index

In subentries, AR refers to the author; his grandfather appears as TR, his father as AR Sr., his cousin Franklin as FDR, and his younger cousin Kermit as KR.